Culture Smart!

Ready-to-Use Slides & Activities for Teaching Multicultural Appreciation Through Art

SUSAN RODRIGUEZ

Photographs by Paul Blumenthal

Illustrations by Krissy Krygiel

With thanks to Paul Gourhan and Eileen Ciavarello

PRENTICE HALL
Paramus, New Jersey 07652

Dedication

This book is dedicated to: **My husband, Costa**
my son, Rennie
my daughter, Nicole
my mother, Toby

Special dedication to my cherished and devoted friend, **Joanne Harris,**
whose steadfast belief and *Angel de la Guarda* spirit
moved CULTURE SMART! to be written.

ISBN 0-13-145863-9

ATTENTION: CORPORATIONS AND SCHOOLS

The Center for Applied Research in Education books are available at quantity
discounts with bulk purchase for educational, business, or sales promotional use.
For information, please write to: Prentice Hall Direct, Special Sales, 240 Frisch
Court, Paramus, NJ 07652. Please supply: title of book, ISBN number, quantity,
how the book will be used, date needed.

 PRENTICE HALL
Paramus, NJ 07652

A Simon & Schuster Company

On the World Wide Web at http://www.phdirect.com

Prentice Hall International (UK) Limited, *London*
Prentice Hall of Australia Pty. Limited, *Sydney*
Prentice Hall Canada, Inc., *Toronto*
Prentice Hall Hispanoamericana, S.A., *Mexico*
Prentice Hall of India Private Limited, *New Delhi*
Prentice Hall of Japan, Inc., *Tokyo*
Simon & Schuster Asia Pte. Ltd., *Singapore*
Editora Prentice Hall do Brasil, Ltda., *Rio de Janeiro*

Cover Art for CULTURE SMART! was created by talented students from the
Philadelphia School District's Belmont School, under the guidance of art teacher
Patricia Jordan. Ganesha, our elephant mascot, was drawn by an Overbrook
Educational Student, Joanne Gaswieski.

About the Author

Susan Rodriguez is an educator, artist, and author who teaches in the Philadelphia School District's Overbrook Educational Center. Her students are culturally diverse and possess a wide range of ability levels.

Susan is also an Adjunct Professor at The University of the Arts in Philadelphia, where she specializes in teacher education with an emphasis on diversity and special needs. An advocate of teacher renewal through the arts, she conducts courses and programs in Professional Development that endorse cultural learning, museum appreciation, and the creative process.

She has been awarded numerous grants and commendations for her work in the visual arts, and is the recipient of *The Pennsylvania Teacher of the Year* (1996), *The Disney American Teacher Award in Visual Arts* (1993–94), and the prestigious *Milken Family Foundation Outstanding Educator Award* (1994–95). Susan is the author of several other practical resources for teachers, including ART SMART! Ready-to-Use Slides and Activities for Teaching Art History and Appreciation (Prentice Hall, 1988).

With Thanks to the Contributors . . .

For their immeasurable contibutions, I would like to especially thank: Joanne Harris ("one thousand-warriors"), Carol Guinn, who was instrumental in lifting *Culture Smart!* into flight! Schuyler McClain, Lyn Jankowski, Madeline Ullom, Julie Choi-Kenney, Trudy Kraft, Connie Kirker, Ron DiCecco, Joseph Deissroth, Amy Jared and The Philadelphia Museum of Art, Barbara Bassett, Thora Jacobson and Chamroeun Yin of Fleissher Art Memorial, Marlene Adler, Karen Floreen, Chris Houston, Katy Devine, Christine Lee, Joyce Mathers, Parvis Yathrebi of Woven Treasures, Arlene Gostin of the University of the Arts, Janis Norman and Elaine Evans, Dan Hazel, Aimee Volpe, Johnny Irrizary and Taller Puertorriqueno, Frank Chance of the Japanese House and Garden, Betty Ann Lawrence, Lisa Diviny, Margaret Alcala, Mishov and Tony Sawan of Fez Restaurant, Carolann Melora, Jermiah Nabawi, Queen Aishatu, the parents of Ayako Wakamatsu, Mohinder Gill, Janet Cusack, Usha Balamore, and Ishaq Deis of Episcopal Academy.

To all the students who contributed their wonderful art and to the Philadelphia School District and it Art Education Division under the leadership of Tessie Varthas. Further thanks to Overbrook Educational Center: William Hanscom, Rose Skolnick, faculty, students and parents. For initial encouragement to the author and her work, I thank Marilyn A. Moller and Evelyn Fazio. The staff at Prentice Hall, Susan Kolwicz, Win Huppuch, Mariann Hutlak, and Dee Coroneos are thanked for their remarkable wisdom and patience. Additionally, I'd like to recognize with credit Pam Carunchio and Linda Lipson at the Foundation for Architecture in Philadelphia, the Pierpont Morgan Library, Running Press, and Rubber Stampede.

ADDITIONAL THANKS TO:

Bonnie Kane, Carol Heppenstal, Ruth Wagner, Ayako Wakamatso, Ruth McGee, Betsy Heeney, Joe Baker, Dan Bare, Dr. Whitney, Crystal Durant, John Serpentelli, Pamela Hart, Wendy Worrell, Melissa Tolbert, Valerie Zimany, Sharon Prior, Tahtianna Friend, Ed Schultz, Wendell Jeffrey, Susan Duncan, Claudia Luongo, Cornelia Maxiom, Patty Gregory, Patricia McBride, Jen Sipple, Alyson Pouls, Alison Emery, Romy Burkus, Cheryl Gearhart, Marianne

Lai, Patricia Bilotta, Cheryl Hendershot, Marge Horner, Carrie Nunnaman, Robin Reiss, Maureen Baquero, Gregory Kelly, Aina Roman, Laurie Smith, Jessica Horniak, Heather Evans, Lisa Neary, Wendy Leuchter, Paul Adorno, Doug and Kim Cerzesimo, Dan Deslourier, Christine Maurer, Eleanor McDaniel, James Dupree, Gwen Gatto, Ann Marie Ridley, Alicia Rihacek, Dan Deslaurier, and Dr. Cheryl Grant-Stevens.

My dear friends Bette Simons and family and Helene Silverstein are loved and thanked—along with Paul Blumenthal, Leora Ruth Chwalow and daughters Dena C. Blumenthal and Ilana C. Blumenthal, for creating art, modeling—and putting up with this author; Krissy Krygiel and parents, and the family of Joanne Harris for their support. My sister Kathy Rosen and brother David Rosen are loved and appreciated. For insight and inspiration: Jamake Highwater and the "Mythos," Lobsang Samten at the Tibetian Center, Habiba, Pang Xiong Sirirathasuk. Mary Martin at the Middle Eastern Studies Center at The University of Pennsylvania, and the late Marge Sieger. For their friendship, mentoring and caring—Harry and Jane Bonelli. For all who have cheered this project on—thank you—friends, university students, fellow teachers and our children everywhere. Please know that every effort was made to remember all contributors—any errors of omission are unintended.

A special note of remembrance to dear friend Jeffrey Johnson, who lives in our hearts and in every page he helped to create.

"The World and Everything in It . . ."

On my own journey through education—yes, teaching *is* a journey—I was surprised to find that I would write books. My first book, *The Special Artist Handbook,* was inspired by my students, who are blind and visually impaired. As an art teacher who is also a painter (in the third generation of a family of visual artists), I found it somewhat intimidating to be asked to teach students with vision loss. It was 1973 and Public Law 94-142 was stirring with a Special Education mandate. This early teaching assignment, which I met with trepidation, turned out to be the greatest lesson of my life. The students who I initially believed would need a restricted artroom diet of clay and papier mâché, showed this teacher a thing or two! Not only did I learn that blind children paint and draw, I discovered that the way I viewed the creative process itself was through a narrow curtain that was soon to be pulled wide open. Watching special-needs students paint alongside their sighted peers with all the confidence in the world changed me forever. It became pretty difficult to focus on limitations when action is so convincing. Blind children painting became a metaphor for teaching and creativity, a message of artistic faith. It was a basic belief in art and in education that led me on to write *Art Smart!*

Art Smart! was intended to bring art history and great artists to life in the art classroom. As it turned out, *Art Smart!* has reached countless art classrooms, art programs in communities and international museums, for which this teacher author is extremely grateful. There is hardly greater personal and professional satisfaction than to help fellow teachers through one's own labors of love. *Art Smart!* also had an effect on me that the Japanese call *satori*—literally meaning "awaking" or "kick in the eye." As I was checking references in various art history texts at the time, I realized how little attention was given to world art beyond the West. The lack of information in books and even course offerings was startling. For this reason, I included a healthy multicultural section in *Art Smart!* Yet, in my heart I knew that an entire other book was needed to gap a mighty missing link: the knowledge of multicultural art. It was to be that *Culture Smart!* would be written—a complete guide to multicultural art appreciation and understanding. The job proved to be slightly monumental. If anyone asked me what *Culture Smart!* would address, I'd usually say, *"The world and everything that's in it!"* The truth is in the art. As a teacher who appreciates a clear, approachable treatment of a complex subject, *Culture Smart!* is intended to tell an expansive tale with simplicity. After all is said and done, the book *Art Smart!* is now the *yin,* and the book *Culture Smart!* the *yang,* in a full circle of art history and tradition. Both books, complete in themselves, will together tell the whole story of art. It's a big story, one that should feel as simple to the reader as its companion book *Art Smart!* . . . as natural as bamboo . . . and as affirming to the creative spirit as blind children painting.

Susan Rodriquez

How to Use Culture Smart!

Culture Smart! is designed for all grade and skill levels. Activities provide teachers with choices—a direct lesson presentation or an extended lesson unit may be derived from just about any of the *Culture Smart!* projects. Many cultures are represented by a variety of lessons created to offer the essential nature of the culture through its art. All lessons are genuine—straight from the art classroom, based on authentic cultural traditions. The thematic approach is practical for multicultural presentation in the art classroom. Most often, the plan of cultural study follows a sequence that matches curricular cycles and other educationally-driven rotations. The book is set up in a format that begins with ASIA and AFRICA . . . on to THE MIDDLE EAST . . . then to EUROPE . . . and THE AMERICAS.

Schools often plan curriculum with a time-honored agrarian calendar! The use of holidays, seasons, festivals, and harvest cycles provides markers for program planning. In multicultural education, the assignment of specific cultures to a day or month exclusively, is currently being debated—yet there is nothing wrong with a "spotlight" on a culture, a tradition, an individual or an achievement! Multicultural learning is a National Educational Standard practiced nationwide. In whatever manner a teacher or school district plans the introduction and study of art and culture, they will be served by the format offered in *Culture Smart!* This resource is fully programmatic in content:

- *Slides*—40 distinctive cultural icons in painting, sculpture, architecture, and design

- *Cultural art lessons*—Over 120 fully explained thematic activity units

- *Maps*—For convenient use in the art classroom by teachers and students

- *Reproducible pattern and design pages for art reference*—Additional practical worksheets with step-by-step illustrations of methods and techniques

- *Section introductions for teacher information*—Background essentials on the art, history, and culture of all ten segments of the book

Culture Smart! respects all cultures and values the richness of cultural diversity. Art allows for cultural exchange, interdisciplinary curricular planning, cooperative learning, teaming, community involvement and outreach. The art program leader will find that elements and principles of art education are readily taught through multicultural themes and activities. It is strongly suggested that *Culture Smart!* be used collaterally with *Art Smart!* which chiefly addresses Western artists and art history. Cross-cultural connections are not difficult to match. In fact, multiculturalism is the basis for 19th and 20th century modern Western art. Artistic and cultural exchange has itself been in place ever since the first camel set hoof upon the very first trade route. There are many opportunities to combine the two resource programs—as balanced as *yin* and *yang*!

Culture Smart! provides a complete world of art and art history when used with *Art Smart!* Traditions rather than individual artists are the focus of *Culture Smart!* In many cultures, the group rather than the individual is of greatest importance. Nevertheless, there are many named as well as anonymous masters throughout the ages of world art. Please also realize that *Culture Smart!* centers on long cultural traditions that inform teachers with past and present practices. It should be remembered that cultural arts are very much alive today, practiced by groups and individuals with ever-evolving and vibrant spirit.

The question of how to qualify an image or object for its artistic value is answered throughout the world in similar ways. An artist in the Arctic would, for example, be valued through demonstrated mastery of craft, originality of idea within the tradition as well as the achievement of spiritual power within artistic representation. Ceremonial art may have specific purposes while containing artistic merit as well. In various world traditions, art may not be made for permanence nor necessarily require conservation efforts. Ephemeral art is not intended to last beyond its immediate use. The Tibetan Sand Mandala is a physical example of the Buddhist belief in impermanence. The intricate Mandala is wholly dismantled after its completion: That is its artistic and spiritual intent.

The fear of offending cultures by misrepresenting sacred ideas is another concern in multicultural art education. Generally speaking, common sense goes a long way. Of course, one would not consider the replication of a sacred religious text. Other matters may not be so clear. *Culture Smart!* activities have been discussed with friends and colleagues in the cultural communities represented. We do our best to be respectful—our goal is one of education. Actually, the author put this very question to the Venerable Lobsang Samten, a Tibetan monk who is also a dancer and an artist. His answer: ". . . if the intent is right-minded and sincere, the teaching is justified . . ."

Culture Smart! anticipates greater appreciation with the accumulation of experience and knowledge. Although the art of diverse cultures can be highly codified, there are universal artistic values that are powerfully conveyed through the great works of many nations. The joy of multicultural art appreciation is also in the discovery!

It is also important to remember that in many cultures there is no specific word for art. Unlike the Western notion of placing art in museums, many world peoples do not sequester art from daily life and religious practice. Art is often part of dance, music, and ceremony. To remove a dance mask from a dancer and place it in a glass museum case would have made no sense to many world societies. Today, international communication and travel along with world economy provide less likelihood for "culture shock" when a ceremonial object is acquired solely for its aesthetic merit. Artistic exchange has opened up possibilities for cultural fusion in the visual and performing arts. The results are fresh, exciting, and powerful! Still, traditional and contextual meanings are deeply respected. Efforts to keep heritage strong is a task to which many communities worldwide are giving great dedication.

To teach multicultural art is to teach mythology and belief. Teacher will want to take note: Mythology is not religion and vice-versa, although there is sometimes overlap. The language of *Culture Smart!* is constructed with these concerns in mind. Consider when you use the term mythology to describe a religious belief that it can be misleading and even offensive. As a kind of reflective exercise, teachers can think about beliefs they personally hold and whether or not the referral to these beliefs as mythologies would be acceptable. A myth is a story of origin—by this definition, *Noah's Ark* is a myth . . . yet many would prefer *Noah's Ark* described as a Bible story. Sensitivity is an asset in the multicultural realms of mythology, belief, and religion. All are important human concepts and integral to cultures throughout the world. There is no need to avoid these vital subjects—just be aware of the possible implications and handle accordingly.

On the subject of religion: it is not wrong to give straightforward information about belief. Religion is part of human history. How much or how little the teacher chooses to convey within the context of multicultural learning is within the domain of one's good educational judgment. You know your students, community, and school district. If you teach in a religious educational setting or in a private school, certainly the way in which belief is taught would have been discussed and communicated to the staff. In American public education, religion is subject-worthy and lawful when objectively presented. Teachers are *not* to render subjective personal opinions about belief and, certainly, not to proselytize in school settings—all are highly inappropriate, for obvious reasons. Respect is always given to customary practices upheld by teachers and students of diverse faiths—the wearing of a head covering, for example. Even-handed and fair treatment should always prevail.

Culture Smart! activities enable teachers to enhance upon or minimize religious and spiritual emphasis. Again, mythology is central to worldwide art appreciation, from Romulus and Remus . . . to Raven the Trickster. How can this important position be further reinforced in the art classroom? Storytelling . . . books, tapes, and volunteer readers from the community all contribute. Professional storytellers are available through contact with state arts organizations who are ready to provide names. As African–Caribbean storyteller Jeremiah Nabawi says, ". . . *the untold story has no meaning.*"

Language itself is important. The teacher who refers to world cultures as "them" and to self and the immediate community as "us"—would do well to try to break the habit. The "us" and "them" thinking may sound innocent, but it undermines multicultural unity—in art and in life. In the bigger picture, it is "we" . . . we as a people, we as a human family, we as . . . equal. Efforts to adjust this language "message" are well worth it. Who, after all, is meant by "them?" Watch out for pejorative terms. "Primitive" is often a misused word, with connotations that the art is made by people who are "uncivilized." A good substitute for primitive is primal or indigenous. Names and words do hurt deeply—they endorse negative perceptions and stereotypes. We have higher goals!

What's the good word? *Respect . . .* the foundation for tolerance and understanding. What does respect *not* include? The answer is that respect does not suggest the suppression of individual creativity—nor does it support conduct in which others are disregarded. Respect is simply respect. In Japan, humility—particularly present in the traditional Teahouse Ceremony—is a principal virtue. The multicultural art classroom respects all cultures, world views, teachers, students, each other, the environment, and our expressive work. A healthy atmosphere is a respectful one—not one of chaos and distraction—at least most of the time! The art classroom is a safe, comfortable place; it is one of creativity and honor.

Placing hands together and bowing heads slightly, let's welcome multicultural arts with a greeting from India . . . *Namaste* . . . which means . . . *"I respect the spirit within you."* With the greeting *Namaste,* please begin with joy your auspicious multicultural journey.

About Multiculturalism

> . . . *The world is so full of a number of things, I'm sure we should all be as happy as kings . . .*

> Robert Louis Stevenson,
> a Scottish writer and world traveler.
> *A Child's Garden of Verses*

Multiculturalism has arrived at the gateway of education and entered into the main framework. Why is multiculturalism proliferating at this point in time? The shift in demographics may be principally responsible for bringing attention to the important issue of "an equitable education for all." Now and into the future, large numbers of groups once called minorities will become part of the mainstream. In the United States, the rise of Latin American and Asian populations is so dramatic that the responsibility to adjust our educational scope is clearly justified. Furthermore, for groups of Americans who have been under-recognized for too long there is, at last, widespread inclusion. It's about time. We are in a period of growth and change. In this age of information and technology, an urban Chicago classroom may be electronically linked to a tented yurt in remote West China. The concept of a global community is possible. We have the technology. Do we have the understanding?

Nowhere is tradition and custom more intrinsic that in the art of world cultures. A Japanese teabowl, if its context is conveyed, can teach Japanese art, architecture and history; social practice, aesthetic values, and spiritual belief. What a wonderful way to learn—through art and multiculturalism! Art eloquently expresses humanity. In *Culture Smart!* the intent is to let the object reveal itself in contextual terms. Students who experience the shaping of a Zen teabowl will learn schematically through an authentic creative process.

. . . Walk a mile in my moccasins and know my road . . .

Native American wisdom

Authenticity is offered by art production when practiced with a sense of cultural meaning. It is important to understand that objects expand beyond their physical appearance. A Pueblo pot, a Peruvian textile, a Celtic illumination . . . each represents centuries of culture and civilization. *Culture Smart!* provides text that will help connect objects with the cultures that conceived them. Works of art are valued for their artistic contribution, originality, purpose, collective identity, and universal appeal.

. . . The journey of a thousand miles begins with a single step . . .

Chinese proverb

Multiculturalism is so much more than curriculum—it is a worldview. It is also a process that takes place over many various stages. Art is an ideal means of conveyance of multiculturalism and offers room to grow. If all students can learn, then all teachers can learn too! The principles for multicultural learning are simple—keep an open heart and an open mind. Withhold judgment when faced with the unfamiliar . . . and be patient with yourself. There's quite a bit to learn, which is both exhilarating and sometimes overwhelming. There's no hurry to learn everything at once. Take your time to savor new ideas. This is as true for teachers as it is for students. The essential identity of the object will reveal itself to you . . . given the chance.

When the student is ready, the teacher will appear . . .

Arabic saying

Many teachers have admirably embraced the richness of world cultures. Current interest suggests we are living at a time of abundance. Yet there are still concerns about the nature of multiculturalism. Does the acceptance of new ideas require the disposal of treasured existing beliefs? Of course it does not—as in the case of art, a French Impressionist oil painting is every bit as valued as a Japanese *tokonoma* scroll. Likewise, learning about spirituality and belief is in no way a threat to personal faith. It's important to note that all art—from the East to the West, the North to the South—contains images and objects of devotion. Teachers, as professionals, are able to decide how much emphasis to give spiritual content by measure of their own assessments.

*. . . Flowers are never identical. It would seem that beauty derives
from this very diversity . . .*

Pierre-August Renoir,
French Impressionist

The United States is a multicultural nation. We are Asian, African-American, European, Native American . . . we are Buddhists, Christians, Jews, Hindus, and Muslims . . . or we may not follow conventional religious belief. This is our right and our freedom. Be mindful that general assumptions about any of us can be misleading, for cultural identity is often complex. Multiculturalism itself honors heritage, community and tradition, recognizing the "one and the many", as Hindu belief states. Art encapsulates broad and specific attributes. Above all else, multiculturalism in all its forms is about *people*. It is the people who make multicultural education necessary—all people! To the credit and worth of American education, multicultural learning is a National Standard. State education frameworks uphold the Federal guidelines. Yet most significant to the commitment to multicultural education is one simple belief: It is the right thing to do.

. . . We may be different on the outside, but inside, we are all the same . . .

Mason, Age 9

Teaching in the Multicultural Classroom

THE NEW ROLL BOOK

It's a different world today . . . is an observation often noted in American communities. It is different now, in many ways, than it was for decades before this time and sometimes we may feel a bit nostalgic. There is also a great deal *not* to miss—human rights violations, internment camps, open and covert prejudice, discrimination and segregation, gender inequality and war. Who misses racial, religious, and ethnic hatred? No one who is teaching our future generations, it is hoped. We still have our work to do in healing and rebuilding from dreadful realities that do not make us proud. Yet it's critical not to ignore the past. Consider the Holocaust—atrocious history must never repeat itself. Now is just the point in time to elevate ourselves with the light that knowledge can bring. Although these topics are difficult, they are of strong rationale for multicultural education. The more we know—the more human we become to each other. Every effort made in the classroom to inform, enlighten, and to create a more peaceful environment is not wasted. What we teach and how we teach it become a pebble dropped into a pond. The ripples go on beyond us . . . what we do and say as teachers does count.

Should we teach a spectrum of topics to our students as part of the multicultural curriculum? Yes, we as teachers collectively will address the peace making process at a significant level when we teach from a broad multicultural point of view. The grade, age, student population, and school culture help to determine the shaping of a school-wide multicultural commitment. History and social studies materials are becoming more truthful today. Resources, local and worldwide, are plentiful as well. More than anything else, how we treat our own students in our classrooms on a daily basis is our most immediate and powerful tool. Roll sheets that once listed Billy, Betty, Jack, and Sue are now joined by Jamar, Okezie, Shanta, Esperanza, and Thuy (pronounced Twee)—a common Vietnamese name. Every one of the names on the roll sheet brings tradition along with hopes, fears, and dreams. Each student brings the gift of self and of culture. We are sure to welcome all our students through word and action. What a thrill to see a big smile grow on the face of a shy student who is new to America when the art activity is a familiar reminder of family and home! We all want to feel valued and recognized. Pride in cultural heritage helps students learn. Art is a reaffirmation of who we are. The benefits of a multicultural arts program are manifold:

- Increased awareness of one's own culture as well as the cultures we collectively share.

- Expansion of knowledge base in art, as well as social studies, language arts, history, geography, environmental science, mathematics, and electronic visual media.

- Opportunities for cross-curricular thematic studies, including the performing arts—dance, drama, and music.

- Increased multisensory and tactile methods to better serve multiple learning styles and special needs.

- Endorsement of inclusionary educational practice: *"All means all."*

- Multicultural learning standards engaged through experiential activities.

- Increased global awareness through international thematic planning and study.

YOU ARE HERE!

Art and classroom teachers, think about the black dot on the map that marks: *"You are here."* Wherever you are, whether your student population is currently monocultural or multicultural, students will appreciate a chance to know as much as possible. Multicultural education assumes the best in us. Your own community is filled with stories, events, traditions, artisans, and history, This is known as folklife education. Make it real! Invite community artists and members—young and old, new and long- standing—into your classroom. Art projects may readily incorporate human resources. Are you planning a lesson on festival arts? Perhaps a retired veteran's association member is available to talk about parades, past and present, with photographs, costumes, uniforms, and memories. This is known as *first voice* learning.

Authenticity and human connections are dynamic components of multicultural arts and education. Every one has a culture, a story. Understand that multicultural education is inclusionary . . . Asian, European, African, Latino, Middle Eastern . . . all heritage is cherished equally. This is the basis for the multicultural world view. How you think is how you teach . . . *remember to open your heart!*

BRING OUT THE MAP

Teaching multicultural art requires a map—whether it is on the wall, folded into a work apron pocket, or taped to the front of an "art cart"! The use of a map at the start of a lesson helps students learn geography as it provides an orientation point for cultural origins. The map is the first step to setting up a multicultural environment. Here are other items and ideas for the multicultural art classroom:

- *Posters with art images from around the world on display.* Remember photocopy shops can enlarge page-size images (and even postcards) to poster size. Lamination or clear plastic does lend appeal. Include diverse faces and places! It is good for students to become familiar with cultural arts through displayed visual material. Do be sure that your students also see images that reflect themselves. "Culture Smart" poster sets are highly recommended!

- *Picture Books.* Children's books today are beautifully illustrated with accompanying multicultural stories and folk tales. **Note:** Many reading series match the *Culture Smart!* activities quite well! Read stories aloud to students! Tell an original "make-believe" story! Storytelling may be used as lesson introduction or to enhance the art activity while students are busy at work—imagining, creating, and learning.

- *Travel Magazines and Guidebooks.* Along with the time-honored copies of *National Geographic,* please note that there are many specialty travel magazines available. Topics such as island living and nature travel are the subjects of magazines sold in well-stocked bookstores. Series of travel guidebooks offer great photos and useful information.

- *Party Goods and "Prom" Props!* Authenticity is important, but so is imagination! If you think of the space in which you teach as a kind of educational stage set, an installation seems completely reasonable. Display houses, party good stores, and prom and music catalogues can help you, inexpensively and easily, to create a theme. It doesn't have to be a big production—your students will enjoy the spirit, even if your installation is only a paper palm tree or two under a big paper tropical moon— with a woven strawbasket filled with fruit nearby!

- *Display Boards With Cultural Themes.* Teacher- or student-made trifold panel boards, available through teacher educational suppliers, can convey information quickly and effectively. Themes may vary from a focus on a country, such as Cuba, to a topic, like World Dance Masks. Board displays make great references and handy teaching and exhibition tools.

- *Musical Tapes or Compact Discs.* Start a collection of diverse musical tapes—music from around the world, from Broadway plays to international children's songs. Storytelling tapes from various cultures, such as Navajo stories or Russian fairy tales, are a tremendous classroom asset. Playing appropriate music during art presentations enlivens the senses and adds to the experience. For many teachers, art and music, together, are a must! Note of caution: Be sure to select music or stories that are age-appropriate and *not* overly stimulating. Music also assists with classroom management . . . it really affects atmosphere and mood.

- *Educational Media, Technology, and the VCR.* The VCR has an unseemly reputation as a boxed babysitter for rainy indoor recess periods. In fact, many fine cultural videos are available through sales and rental. Suggested use for video in the art classroom: children's' short stories, pre-selected "clips" from films related to thematic cultural units, and travel videos. Electronic technology offers possibilities for multicultural learning through informational access and human linkages. Worldwide web sites and the Internet provide infinite possibilities. Computer technology is a vehicle for autobiographical, oral history documentation and creative image composition. Experimentation that joins computer arts to works of hand is strongly encouraged.

- *A Multicultural Treasure Chest.* A recycled steamer trunk, an old toy chest, or a roomy closet storage box can easily be transformed into a multicultural treasure chest. It is recommended that teachers begin a diverse collection of masks, sculptural crafts, dolls, fabric, banners, hats, and other objects to be incorporated into *Culture Smart!* lessons. These do not have to be expensive—flea markets, craft stands, and souvenirs are good sources. Students will appreciate examining and learning from the various world objects. Remember "Show & Tell"! Let students bring in their own treasures and tell their stories. It's good to coordinate specific multicultural items with lesson units. Objects speak volumes.

Contents

Contents

Africa
To Know the Art of Africa 45

The Middle East, Turkey, and Greece

To Know the Art of the Middle East, Turkey, and Greece *81*

India and Tibet
To Know the Art of India and Tibet 117

☒ *The Pacific Cultures: Oceania*

To Know the Art of the Pacific Cultures 151

The Caribbean Cultures

Mexico, Central and South America

Contents

✤ Native America

To Know the Art of Native America 271

Russia, Europe, Ireland, and the British Isles

To Know the Art of Russia, Europe, Ireland, and the British Isles 311

Contents

The United States of America

Slide Identification Script

1. **"CHINESE SCULPTURE OF A DANCER." FREER GALLERY OF ART.** The female ceramic dancer sways gracefully to a silent rhythm as indicated by the direction of the folds in her garment. The custom of royal Chinese burial included clay objects to represent houses, camels, horses, musical instruments, and entertainers—all the pleasures and comforts of earthly life. The tri-color glaze of amber, green, and yellow emerged during the Tang period, a time of worldly expansion and renaissance of Chinese art and trade.

2. **"BAMBOO IN WIND AND RAIN." TAO-CHI, 1642–1707. CHINESE HANGING SCROLL, INK ON PAPER.** The artist Tao-Chi (also Shih T´ao) was a monk, a painter, and scholar during a period of individualism and eccentricity in China. He did not like to be categorized; Tao-Chi was inventive and became an inspiration to many other painters. Bamboo is shown here in several stages of life—from tender shoot to mature growth. Each calligraphic brushstroke reveals the character of bamboo in the gusty rain; its endurance is demonstrated by the essential nature of its flexibility.

3. **CHINESE EMPEROR PORTRAIT. FREER GALLERY OF ART.** Chinese commemorative portraits portray individuals of rank who held significant roles in the history of their times. A nobleman and his wife, a court lady, or an Imperial prince were suitable portrait subjects. Realism was employed to depict specific individual features as well as age and countenance. This portrait denotes great power as shown on the Dragon throne. The lavish robe reinforces the dragon status of an Emperor who appears worldly and wise. Imperial portraits may also display the accouterments of the scholar's study—desk, writing instruments, letter box—to indicate extensive knowledge.

4. **"STANDING CRANE" TYPE HAG WARE GLAZED STONEWARE.** Simplicity is a deeply honored Japanese virtue as the lovely and understated tea bowl indicates. The presence of the crane is reduced to only the most minimal calligraphic marks. Note the foot or base of pot which appears broken—this is known as a "split-foot." In Zen, perfection is in imperfection. The cup is at the heart of the tea ceremony (or *chanoyu* in Japanese). Tea bowls such as this one are appreciated for a sense of elegance within humility.

5. **JAPANESE WEDDING KIMONO. 20TH CENTURY. THE TEXTILE MUSEUM.** Much like the Japanese colored woodblock print, the kimono is designed with strong narrative content. This wedding kimono appears with flying cranes which, according to Japanese legend, promise "one thousand years of happiness." The uplifted design of this kimono suggests a heavenly or "bird's eye" view; elements of nature, a beloved Japanese value, provide motif. The kimono is, traditionally, the national garment of Japan and has many meanings in a full range of styles, weaving techniques, and colors. There is a kimono for every occasion and every season in Japan.

6. **QUEEN MOTHER HEAD. AFRICA: BENIN BRONZE.** The lost wax casting method achieved in the Kingdom of Benin was in its early period in the fifteenth century; courtly production reached its height in the sixteenth and seventeenth centuries. Stately, commemorative heads were cast to honor kings, or *Oba*, and queens, such as this magnificent *Queen Mother Oba* head. Often identified as the most naturalistic period in African art, the Benin heads remain consistent with artistic ideals. In African art, the head is of great importance and often of prominent scale. Queen Mother heads exemplify values of reason, composure, beauty, nobility of character, womanhood—and honor for the ancestors. Trade with Europeans, particularly the Portuguese, was incorporated into bronze plaque motifs: Portuguese figures may be identified as decorative details in Benin Sculpture.

7. **APPLIQUÉ CLOTHMAKERS, DAHOMEY (ABMONEY). FON PEOPLES OF THE REPUBLIC OF BENIN. SMITHSONIAN INSTITUTE.** The graphic arts of the Dahomey peoples, with roots in the earlier culture of the Fon, include the painting of sacred and important walls, incising calabashes, and the art of fabric appliqué. Family guilds of men, as suggested by this slide, held the rights to sew banners. The Fon banner appearance is recognized by bright-colored shapes of animals, figures, and objects, commonly offset by a black background. Banners tell legends, histories, and cautionary tales and are both symbolic and decorative. Fon banners also serve as funerary shrine cover memorial cloths. The Fon appliqué banner tradition traveled from Africa to the American South where African–American women incorporated appliqué ideas and techniques in the art of the quilt.

8. **PARAMOUNT CHIEF NANA AKYANFUO AKOWVAH DATEH II AND HIS COURT KUMASI, GHANA. ASANTE PEOPLES, GHANA. SMITHSONIAN INSTITUTE.** The Ashanti ruler wears the moon and stars as his golden crown while he proudly sits beneath a state umbrella with royal attendants by his side. The picture is filled with emblems of status, from bells to batons, from cloth to gold. The Asante Kente cloth is worn as a prized garment, customarily wrapped around the body and draped over the left shoulder. Note the fly whisk held by the chiefly leader, an official extension of authority, carried by African heads of state. The fabric umbrella reinforces the importance of the Paramount Chief; twenty-three are owned by the Ashanti king!

9. **GABON, KOTA RELIQUARY SCULPTURE.** Village Guardian figures are attached to bundles or bark boxes that contain relics of ancestors with the purpose of honor and protection. Copper- or brass-covered guardian figures, made of wood, typify the stylistic features favored in African sculptures: dynamic interplay of surface patterns, geometric abstraction, and rhythmic spatial placement of elements. The Kota (or Bakota) form can be specifically identified in the Cubist paintings of Picasso; African sculpture led the way for Western Modern Art.

10. **THE NIGHTMARE OF ZAHHAK: THE SHAH-NAMEH PERSIAN ILLUMINATED MANUSCRIPT FROM THE COURT OF SHAH TAHMASP.** The Shah-nameh is an extensive Persian book that chronicles the legends, history, and culture of a multi-faceted civilization. The manuscript pages are exquisitely illuminated by artists in the employ of a certain *Shah* or King. Many stories are illustrated that feature recognizable heroes and villains, along with royal personalities. In this illuminated folio, a wicked ruler, who did evil deeds as a prince, is visited by a horrible dream. The scene depicts a magnificent palace that shook with Zahhak's scream of terror! Activity of graceful women, palace guards, and attendants is in response to the nocturnal awakening. The book artist approaches this chilling dream with composure and telling details: women along the central bridge, as well as the man above, hold fingers to their lips in a characteristic gesture of astonishment, while a woman engages the palace bell. Each spatial compartment tells a story within a story. Of least visual interest is Zahhak himself, who is tucked away in his palace bed chamber. The reaction to the royal shriek is the basis for the painting—a palace gentleman in the lower corner almost loses his turban!

11. **THE MOSQUE SHARJAH, U.A.E.** The Islamic house of worship, meeting, and learning is the mosque, an Arabic structure found around the world. Important architectural achievements include The Blue Mosque at Istanbul, Turkey; The Great Mosque in Cordoba, Spain; the mosques in Morocco and in Cairo, Egypt; the Alhambra at Granada, Spain; the great mosques of Isfahan, Iran; and, of course, mosques at Medina in Saudi Arabia, which is mecca (makkah) the epicenter of Moslem belief. Much like European cathedrals, mosques employ a classic architectural plan, yet vary according to regional style and expressive interpretation. Mosques generally incorporate basic features, such as domes and minarets (towers of "Call to Prayer"), as seen in this slide. The use of calligraphic ceramic mosaic and tile inlay may be seen throughout walls and niches. The Mosque Sharjah, presiding by the quiet water, demonstrates the use of an Arabic invention, the *"pointed arch"*—which extends to the *"horseshoe arch"* and the *"ogee,"* that appears as a *"wishbone"* shape. Mosques are intended for human participation. Can you find a *"muezzin"* (caller) on a minaret?

12. JEWISH SPICE BOXES. THE JEWISH MUSEUM, NYC. Beautiful ornamental objects follow tradition and belief. The weekly Jewish observation of *Sabbath,* called *Sha-bat,* brings with it spice containers along with other cherished delights. The *havdalah* or "separation" marks the close of Sabbath, which begins at sundown on Friday evening and ends on Saturday night. Spice containers come forward for havdalah. Scents emanate from spices placed into the small compartment "doors" seen in the two "castle tower" boxes; the taller object is a candle holder for a special Sabbath candle. Medieval European architecture is a strong source of spice box forms, which denote the strong Jewish presence throughout and beyond Europe. The Jewish homeland is considered Israel, yet influences are universal. Aromatic spice boxes may take many delightful shapes!

13. *THE CARPET MERCHANT* BY FRENCH PAINTER JEAN-LEON GEROME IN 1887. This oil painting is a prime example of a style of Academic painting that dominated artistic tastes into the nineteenth century, until it was profoundly challenged by the Impressionist movement. A lesser-known school of French Academic painting was Orientalism, which focused upon the intrigues and exoticism of the Near and Middle East. Eugene Delacroix was an earlier master of Romanticism, featuring scenes of Arab markets, Algerian women, and equestrian events with a vibrant intensity. *The Carpet Merchant,* on the other hand, provides with startling accuracy and photographic realism a glimpse into the world of the Oriental rug dealer. A moment, frozen in time, catches a typical debate over the purchase of large-scale medallion carpet, fully displayed for sale from the balcony. The artist's pictorial arrangement of strewn rugs in the foreground may indicate other rugs rejected by the prospective buyer. In countries throughout the Near and Middle East—and well into the Western world— rug-buying dramas like this one are still enjoyed in a variety of settings everyday!

14. BULL-LEAPING (TOREADOR) FRESCO FROM THE PALACE AT KNOSSOS, MINOAN, CA. 1450–1400 B.C. Ancient Greek civilizations flourished along the Mediterranean and Aegean seas; the earliest of the historical periods is that of the Minoans on Crete. Named for King Minos, the Minoans developed an impressive society, complete with agricultural abundance and artistic production—metalworks and pottery—along with commerce and impressive architecture. Through archeological discovery, a grand palace at Knossos was uncovered. The walls of the palace were decorated with scenes of courtly entertainment—in this case, the sport of bull-leaping. In this highly dangerous activity, one young athlete would leap by the horns of the charging bull, tumble over the bull's back, with the hope, to be caught by another team gymnast. It was both by skill and the favor of the gods that the bull leaper would survive to win! In spite of the lurid possibilities, the fresco at Knossos appears to have the grace of ballet movement, enhanced by its light linear treatment. The bull and the minotaur are at the core of Minoan mythology and belief. The elegant depiction of action that evokes the Minoan tradition also anticipates the later Greek line work found on classic pottery forms—an art to become known as classic Greek line drawing.

15. *IMAGE OF GANESHA DANCING,* 10TH CENTURY. MADHYTRADESH OR UTTAR PRADESH, INDIA. THE PHILADELPHIA MUSEUM OF ART. Ganesha is potbellied and auspicious, a beloved elephant-headed figure seen all over India, especially in doorways. Ganesha is, "The Remover of Obstacles" and, as an elephant is, certainly powerful! He is mischievous enough, placing obstacles in the way—yet, he will remove them when evoked. His appearance varies in painting and sculpture; he is often seen as joyful and wise. In *Ganesha Dancing,* the portly figure swings with ease to the drummers' rhythm, shown with drum at the lower left base. Ganesha takes after his own father, Shiva, "Lord of Dance." In India, dance represents the cycle of life. Ganesha cradles in his four arms the objects known as attributes that identify him. His upper left hand holds an ice-cream-cone-shaped radish, considered a delicacy for elephants! The radish symbolizes unity, a strong value upheld by Hindu belief.

16. **"THE MONKEY KING SUGRIVA SENDS EMISSARIES LED BY HANUMAN TO FIND SITA, CA. 1820. NATAGARH (HUDUR) SCHOOL, INDIA. OPAQUE WATERCOLOR WITH GOLD ON PAPER.** A hero of the Indian epic tale, *The Ramayana*, is none other than a monkey named Hanuman. In this miniature painting, monkey Chief Hanuman receives his mission from the monkey King Sugriva. General Hanuman is shown twice in the picture: first in counsel with King Sugriva and then exiting the cave below with staunch determination. He will lead a rescue army that must form a monkey bridge from India to Lanka, where Princess Sita is held captive by the wicked King Ravanna—to the heartbreak and dismay of Prince Rama. The clever and cunning of Sugriva combined with the valor of Hanuman will destroy the monstrous Ravanna, save Sita, and restore Rama's kingdom. The painting illustrates with charm and precision the preview episode to the military action by visually drawing back the layered caves at the top corner as if they were stage curtains; the departure appears below almost as a backstage exit. In the lush landscape of northern India, with its caves and sharply edged rocks create a dramatic presence. Consistent with Indian painting tradition, the scene is multi-layered and atmospheric—with architecture to further enrich and support compositional design.

17. **THE TAJ MAHAL AT SUNSET, POND WITH REFLECTION IN FOREGROUND. 1632–64.** The Taj Mahal was built near Agra in northern India by the Moghal Emperor Shah Jahn as a mausoleum for his beloved wife, Empress Mumtz Muhai. A clarity and scope of vision must have possessed the imagination of Shah Jahan whose Taj Mahal was to become a masterpiece of world architecture. The building material itself, a shimmering white marble, allowed the monumental structure to gleam in its formal garden. With the Jumna River flowing at its back, the mirror pond reflects its grand beauty. The surface interacted with time of day, weather, and season. For scale alone, the Taj Mahal must be physically experienced to be fully understood; its demeanor creates a world of perfection devoid of life's harsh realities. Along with Taj Mahal grandeur, each detail was lovingly attended by master craft workers who knew Italian inlaying techniques. Precious and semiprecious stones were set like jewels in arabesque and abstract floral patterns, charging with sparkle the architectural paradise known as the Taj Mahal.

18. **EMPEROR SHAH JAHAN. MUGHUI DYNASTY, 1630. 22.2 × 13.4 CM GOUACHE ON PAPER.** In refined profile stands the man who built the Taj Mahal—the Moghal Emperor Shah Jahan. His hands are lightly placed together in a respectful gesture, with his head turned in profile to reveal his comely features, accented and framed by turban and beard. Around his head appears a glowing, elliptical circle of power and enlightenment. It is a portrait of both a specific emperor and a style of painting that infused Hindu expression with Islamic ideals. Just as he accomplished with the Taj Mahal, the Shah Jahan remains within an enchanted garden in this painting, where the everyday world is held far away. The Shah Jahan himself seemed quite pleased with his portrayal, to which the painting bore the inscription, *"a good portrait of me in my fortieth year, by Bichitr."*

19. **THE PARADISE OF GREEN TARA. TIBETAN THANKA. 19TH CENTURY.** The Thanka scroll is the place where one is most likely to encounter Princess Tara, the Benevolent Goddess of Tibet. She is considered a Celestial Being in either of her two forms: White Tara or Green Tara. There are many stories to explain the two Taras. In on one tale, the green and white forms of Tara were the two wives of the first Buddhist King of Tibet. In either color, her nature is "all-seeing" since Tara has a third eye of enlightenment on her forehead, and an eye on each palm of her hands and on the soles of her feet. Tara seems to qualify as a celestial teacher, given her ever-present eyes and enduring compassion. In this thanka, Tara is surrounded by

specific deities and is, as always, centrally placed. Thanka painting, whether in the figurative or geometric mandala format, follows specific compositional guidelines. The curtain draped above the painting may be released to cover the image when it is not being viewed; the square below represents a "cosmic door" for visual entry. Thankas, which are contained in brocade cloth frames, came into use as portable teaching aids for nomadic monks who traveled from temple to tent. Tara also appears in brass or bronze as a sculptural figure and is sometimes offset by small jewels, always with a kindly smile on her peaceful face.

20. **BALINESE PAINTING: HINDU FESTIVAL.** The island of Bali in Indonesia is known worldwide for its lush natural beauty, terraced landscape, splendid temples, and performance arts. The fabric arts of *batik* and *ikat*, often seen as *sarongs,* were developed through Indonesian artistry. Bali is Hindu, influenced by both belief and mythology of nearby India. Festivals, such as the one pictured in this Balinese painting, are held in villages, temples, and courtly settings. The theatrical hero, pictured in the center, wears a dance mask and displays Indonesian fabric finery; a larger and more arresting mask appears from behind. Commonly, this mask form may represent the Indonesian version of Hanuman the Monkey General from India's epic tale *The Ramayana,* or the mask of the *Barong* character who offers protection by chasing evil. The layered compression of picture space at the festival scene heightens the decorative effect, emphasizing patterns of foliage and vegetation. The use of white and pink contour lines defines outer edges of shapes: it is a technique reminiscent of batik resist. At the very core of the composition is a structure that would also be "at home" in the center of an Indonesian tree-of-life puppet, also called *gunangan,* where the house-temple containing "The Most Powerful Spirit of All Things" dwells! Balinese painting may also be referred to as story cloth, for there are indeed many dramas and intrigues in this Indonesian art.

21. **THE FORK-TONGUED LIZARD AND KANGAROOS. OCHRE AND NATURAL PIGMENTS. ABORIGINAL BARK PAINTING, AUSTRALIA.** In an action-packed encounter between a fork-tongued lizard and two "see-through" kangaroos is a story that qualifies as *"more than meets the eye."* Aboriginal Australian bark painting has an invested thematic interest in keeping the creation beings of the Dreamtime alive. The Dreamtime is the source of the Aboriginal universe. Everything was dreamed into existence on the earth—plants, animals, rocks, sky, moon, and sun. Painting on bark and stone has retold the mystic origin belief for over 35,000 years! Techniques such as x-ray painting enable an "inside" view of the animal's internal anatomy, readily recognized by the people of the land. Other painting methods include dot fields, symbol systems, contrasting pattern bands, and cross-hatching—apparent in this animated bark painting. If you were to invent your own "Dreaming" or Dreamtime myth about the clan animal icons in the slide, how would the story go? Start with "Long ago in the Dreamtime . . ." A *Didgeridoo,* made from a large hollow tree branch and played in accompaniment with the storytelling, is completely optional!

22. **GATEWAY OF PUKEROA, PA (DETAIL). NEW ZEALAND NATIONAL ARCHIVES.** The Maori (mow-ry) were the first people to inhabit New Zealand. In its early days, the island group was named *Aotearoa* (Oh-teh-ah-roh-ah) or "the land of the long white cloud." In the 18th century with Captain Cook's arrival, *Aotearoa* was soon to be renamed New Zealand by the Europeans. The gateway head figure shown in the slide captures the intensity of a people who are fiercely proud of an ancient Pacific heritage. Carving is a time-honored and powerful art in Maori tradition, where objects were carved from bone, wood, and stone. The incised figurative gateway head appears here with a traditional facia *moko* or tattoo design showing tribal associations. A *tiki* (or hei-tiki) adorns his neck, a symbol of *Mana* or great spiritual power. The gateway face itself represents Pukaki, an 18th century chief who once appeared with his wife and their two children on this architectural structure. The vestigial chief protects the Pa, a fortified village that usually sits atop a hillside overlooking the land once called *Aotearoa,* with his iridescent shellfish eyes.

23. **CARIBBEAN MARKET. "BANANAS AND BLUEBIRDS" BY CATHERINE GALLIAN SAINT-CLAIR. ANDRE EXBRYAT.** The art of the Caribbean is as diverse and multifaceted as the people who inhabit the more than twenty countries of the Greater and Lesser Antilles. The ethnic and national expanse of the Caribbean encompasses a heritage of almost every major cultural source and religious belief on earth. The Caribbean is African, Asian, Middle Eastern, Amerindian, and European (Spanish, British, Dutch, German, and French). Impressionist painter and teacher Camille Pissarro, a Caribbean Jew, was born in St. Thomas. Paul Gauguin visited Martinique, where his interests in island culture flourished. The past and present artists of Caribbean origin are both known and unknown in history from ancient petroglyphs to the exuberant festival arts. Caribbean painting and sculpture is presently bursting with a variety of styles and subjects. For "each and every bit of difference" the art of the Caribbean cultures still has a personality that conveys its island identity. Where else other than the Caribbean would this exact market day take place? The vivacious colors, lively market-goers, industrious shopkeepers, a coconut cutter, chickens, dogs, bananas, and bluebirds brightly sing, "Caribbean!" Open-air shelves are stocked here with the tropical fruits of the Caribbean, while the local men, women, and children fill the everyday scene with the buoyancy of island life.

24. **PITCHY PATCHY COSTUME. THE JONKONNU FESTIVAL, JAMAICA. THE ST. LOUIS ART MUSEUM.** Pitchy Patchy is a Jonkonnu dancer who flies into action during the annual festival in Jamaica held primarily during the Christmas season. Pitchy Patchy is above all a **Roots** festival character, which is one that is profoundly linked to African ceremony and dance. The strips of colorful cloth are designed to accentuate body movement to a point where dancer most effectively dissolves into the dance. As it occurs in African sculpture, costume art is conceived to reveal an essential aspect while dynamically manipulating visual space. Pitchy Patchy fabric arts has sources in many African societies: the Yoruba people, for one, employ textiles that cover the face and body. Camouflage is inherent to African masking traditions overall. African-Caribbean carnival elements are represented by Roots characters; European traditions are shown in fancy dress, as historically seen in masquerade balls. Pitchy Patchy may be relied upon to dazzle onlookers with spins, jumps, and unexpected moves—showcased during the "breakout" when the Jonkonnu parade allows skillful performers to be spotlighted. Along with the spellbinding action, Pitchy Patchy is a testimony to the spirit of creativity through transformation—strips of rags turned magically into a dancing rainbow that stretches form Jamaica to the African village ceremonial arts.

25. **CARIBBEAN ARCHITECTURE. GINGERBREAD HOUSES AND PALMS. MUSTIQUE ISLAND, GRENADINES.** The architectural styles of the Caribbean are expressive of its rich cultural heritage, while their inspirations draw upon the beauty of the natural surroundings. Environment and habitat are in complete harmony in this image of two Gingerbread houses, accented by decorative trim as sweet as icing on a birthday cake! Lattice and cut-out trim function artistically and practically—the decorative open work allows for air circulation and shade. Nestled inside the tall palms, the airy houses display their affinity for Victorian fretwork popular at the turn of the 19th century. Just as the umbrellas shield the patio, the pitched roofs shelter the structures from the blazing tropical sun. An imaginative and lively assemblage of architectural elements—along with the joyful use of pastel colors— proclaims a distinct Caribbean architectural personality that uplifts the heart!

26. **"DAY OF THE DEAD—CITY FIESTA" (DIA DE MUERTOS, LA FIESTA EN LA CALLE). DIEGO RIVERA (1866–1957). DETAIL OF MURAL. MINISTRY OF EDUCATION, MEXICO CITY.** *"Where in the world is Diego Rivera?"* The artist has tucked himself into the busy crowd that attends a street celebration of the Day of the Dead. To find Diego, you must first identify a round face, with a bit of a cagey grin, that turns to meet the eye of the viewer. He is wearing a fedora hat, and stands in front of a bespectacled profile of a man in a black top hat (look off-center to the

right). Every individual that appears in the mural represents a member of Mexican society: from the intense revolutionary with sombrero and cigar (left on mid-line) to the hoop-braided *Indio* (Indian in Spanish) woman whose humble back is turned as she prepares food on an outdoor grill. Mexican multiculturalism is as much a theme for this mural as is the subject of the Day of the Dead—a holiday that itself combines specific and ancient pre-Columbia belief with the European All Souls Day and Spanish Catholicism. Notice the variety of the skin tones celebrated by Diego's brush—he loved his culture and his people. Larger than life, Diego Rivera embraces the Day of the Dead festival with the mural-scale monumentalism for which he was known. Mural art is public art; Diego Rivera was an unabashed social activist whose political ideas were presented in paint in a manner both tender and bold. In this mural detail, the space is packed with activities that commemorate the occasion—the stacked *calaveras* (skulls), reminiscent of practices of the ancient Maya and Aztecs . . . the masked papier-mâché skulls (at front) are shown as typical emblems . . . while Mexican crafts for sale line the streets. As all eat and make merry, the articulated puppet *calacas* ("dancing bones") jump and play their tunes, as constant and fleeting as life and as certain as death. It is a painting rich in detail, humor, color, observation, and irony. Diego Rivera paints a big statement that presents with pride the people and spirit of Mexico.

27. **MIXTEC CODEX: OAXACA, MEXICO. PRE-COLUMBIAN, CA. 1400, DETAIL.**
Ancient Mexican texts packed mythology, history, prophesy, codes of social behavior, belief, calendars, and a Pantheon of gods and goddesses into the form of an accordion-folded book called a *Codex*. A strip of cloth, fig bark, or animal hide would allow the crafting of folded books by gluing end sheets to thin wooden back and front covers. The codices that were produced by this method were painted by trained scribes and artisans and were plentiful. Codices flourished until the Spanish conquest, at which point they were all but destroyed. Several prime examples remain of Pre-Columbian codices, which have a distinctly different appearance from those produced under Spanish rule. The page in the slide would have been immediately recognizable to the eyes of earlier *Mexicanos;* gods and goddesses are identifiable through specific appearances and attributes. Small glyphic representations round out the meaning of the text—in this case, the small skull at the center left edge denotes Mictlantecuhtl, the god of death; jaguar, a powerful transformation symbol, accompanies the figure in the upper right corner. It is clear that there is a sequential story; note the repetitive figure, shown in an almost "story board" manner. Gestures of authority articulate action. The profile presentation allows the reader to see elaborations in a detailed account—each element has specific connotations. Art history may suggest a comparison between the figurative representation found in Mexican codices and stylistic features of early Egyptian dynastic art. The same decorative, profiled images that appear on the *Codex* are also found on clay vessels. Mexico has a long tradition of the book and mural arts. In its grandest scale, this country's pictorial art covers the surfaces of tomb walls in its ancient pyramids.

28. **THREE FIGURES OF TEOTHBURACAN, CERAMIC. LA VENTILLA, TEOTIHUCA A.D. 350–650; OVERALL HEIGHT 7.5 CM.** The city of Teotihuca flourished in Mexico from 1200 B.C. to A.D. 700 Believed to be the place where the Sun and Moon were born, a great ceremonial center developed with the Pyramid of the Sun at its core. Monumental architecture was one prominent feature of this stratified and complex civilization that appeared around 750 A.D. near present-day Mexico City. Teotihuca, "the city of gods," had layered society in which farmers, artisans, merchants, and political officials held a place. Nobility enjoyed palace life; both men and women occupied honored roles. One vestige of Teotihucan culture exists in figurative pottery where these three figures exhibit a high rank. Women typically wore a *quechquemitl,* or short cape with a long skirt. Wide headdresses indicate importance—the bigger the hat, the greater the authority! Other signs of status include ear spools and ornamental collars. The three figures wear capes, earspools,

and plank-sized headdresses. The early ceramic style is understated—minimized features, yet evocative in quiet expression. Forms are simplified. The standing figure at the right shows no earspools—she is of slightly different appearance, with the suggestion of hair that frames her face; the central figure wears trousers and is seated; the figure at left leans into the space, hands shown from under her cape. Note the artistic prop built into the base of the standing figure at right—a well-designed means of support. Her headdress, like the others, may have at one time been red, white, and yellow (traces may still be seen). Everything the well-dressed Teotihuacan wore seems to attest to the fashion statement, "dress for success!"

29. FRIDA KAHLO, SELF-PORTRAIT (THE FRAME) C. 1938. OIL ON ALUMINUM AND GLASS. MUSEE NATIONAL D'ART MODERNE. CENTRE GEORGES POMPIDOU, PARIS. Frida Kahlo (1907–1954) was an artist with affiliations to her folkloric Mexican heritage as well as to the world of European painting. For Frida, the brilliance and intensity of Mexico forever interested her; Western painting traditions, particularly Spanish colonial devices, provided a convenient means of confluence. Frida honored Mexican popular arts along with the spiritual mythologies and belief that infused creativity; she was nevertheless a studio painter who synthesized a multiplicity of ideas, even some of Asian origin. Recognized in Paris by Picasso, Miro, Kandisky, and by Andre Breton, who called Frida a "Surrealist" to which she objected with, "I paint my own reality." Her sophistication, held in place by a fantastic and magical Mexican sensibility, has made Frida Kahlo one of the most mysterious, vibrant women in the history of art. Her husband (twice) Diego Rivera also held a dual artistic citizenship—in love with a past and present Mexico while developing his work at the side of emergent Western Modern Art. Diego is a large part of Frida's work; he even appears in her self-portraits. In *The Frame*, Frida Kahlo is fully present as a Mexican woman dressed in a traditional manner. The look of *Tehuana* is favored by Frida who carefully orchestrated the art of costuming itself to the point where it became her signature. *The Frame* portrait is not suggestive of the stoicism and suffering seen in her many other self portraits; here a placid figure is surrounded by an arch of bright, symbolic flowers. Two birds anchor and balance the composition as they interact between figure and frame. The materials chosen for *The Frame* echo folk art—the aluminum of the delineated tin of retablos and milagros. The hot pinks and yellows of floating garden design are often seen embroidered on Mexican women's white blouses to create a border. A yellow flower tops off Frida's braided hair. There is a tentative joy suggested by a Frida who is comforted by the decorative and natural elements of Mexico, which help her to construct "her own reality."

30. "ANGEL DE LA GUARDA" FABRIC APPLIQUÉ MOLA, CA. 1960. KUNA ARTIST, SAN BLAS ISLANDS. PANAMA. The bright and distinctive cotton appliqué art known as *mola* is the specialty of the Kuna Indian women of the San Blas Islands, Panama. The electrical color and vivacious motifs of the *molas* bear a certain resemblance to the energy found in the sacred Huichol yarn paintings of Western Mexico; powerful command of textile pattern repetition recalls, to some degree, Peruvian design. In the language of the Kuna, *mola* means *blouse*. Seen most often as blouse panels, the mola became a popular craft around the early years of the 20th century. Today, molas are highly sought by collectors as well as by outside visitors to the islands. The themes of mulas range from abstract design to symbolic narrative, and they are ever evolving. Kuna women hold an esteemed place in San Blas society for it is their work that contributes to economic stability. The woman stitched into the *mola* pictured here is an angel; her face and *mola* (blouse) are treated as a separate unit within the symmetrical shape that represents both the skirt and wings. A typical linear grid activates the "night magic" of the moon, stars, and mythical creature extending from one wing. A magic wand helps this guardian to fulfill her role as protector, a task for which she appears quite capable. There is a sense of connection between the invisible and the everyday world. The favored *mola* color field of red adds to the solidity of this unique and visually stimulating work of vision, cloth, and artistry.

31. STORYTELLER HELEN CORDERO, CA. 1970, ADOBE GALLERY. Helen Cordero of the Cochiti Pueblo in the American Southwest used to say that her work came from her heart. A Native American artist, Cordero began her ceramic storyteller dolls out of a love for her grandfather, Santiago Quintana, and the wonderful stories he told to his many grandchildren. Mother Earth supplied the clay to Helen, who was born into the Southwestern pottery tradition. Never much of a potter, Helen was surprised to see her little figures spring into existence at a point in her life when her own children were grown. As a result, Helen Cordero would revive an earlier tradition of the Singing Mother and invent a new form of art: the Storyteller figure. In her work, Helen's central figure is male, like her grandfather. Adorable children are positioned on the body of the storyteller, yet each has its own particular response to the tale and its telling. In the instance of the slide image, the storyteller himself seems to be having trouble staying awake. A child on each shoulder, with one at the back of his head, the group of three at the top are seen in various stages of wakefulness—one boy, curved into his ear, is out like a light! Dad places an easy hand on another threesome on his leg, who look as if they are riding the story out on a toboggan. Of the two children on the opposite leg, one child grooms the smaller one, who rubs the sleep in his eyes. Where are the hitchhikers on his back planning to go? Notice the economic use of pattern motif along with suggestion of jewelry. Earth tones are traditional to Pueblo pottery—storyteller figures follow suite. Helen Cordero's work expanded widely to include animals such as turtles. Fortunately, she lived to see her work widely honored. Born in 1915, Helen Cordero died in 1994 with a legacy of clay storytellers that would inspire so many others, sprung from a simple vision and devotion that formed in Cochiti, one of the smallest pueblos of New Mexico.

32. JAR; ACOMA PUEBLO, NEW MEXICO. SLIPPED AND PAINTED EARTHWARE, 14″ DIAMETER. CA. 1920. The round and graceful vessel with the dramatically reversed curvilinear design is among the finest examples of Acoma pottery. When a pot is good, it is so for many reasons. From an artistic view, the pot is in perfect balance—its full volume rests almost weightlessly on a tapered black base. The swirl- and lightning-bolt motif plays both against and with the exterior curve of the vessel. It is the counterbalance between pot and pattern, between gravity and weight, light and dark, stillness and movement, that allows the pot its beauty and countenance. The Native American world view acknowledges the harmony within the clay, its ancient bond with Mother Earth, its vitality as a source of life. It is said that in Native America, there is no need for a word such as art. Why should there be? The pot speaks for itself.

33. INTERIOR OF CHIEF KLART-REEK HOUSE, NORTHWEST COAST. LATE 19TH CENTURY. PHOTOGRAPHY: WINTER AND POND. ALASKA STATE LIBRARY. The crest or totem pole is the most identifiable emblem of a culture blessed with generous forests and rich in mighty red cedar trees. Nature's bounty allowed northwest coastal Native American arts to flourish during a period of trade in the 19th century, advanced by the employment of metal tools. Remarkable carvers, the northwest coastal artists were able to ply their craft as well as use the unique design vocabulary developed in this productive region. The system of *U-forms ovoid, S-curves,* and *formlines,* with their endless variations imparts an appearance that is exclusively northwestern. A gathering point for all the works of hand is the ceremony known as **Potlatch,** a competitive feasting tradition held in the home or lodge of an important person. Wealth is determined by the ability to distribute material possessions to party participants. Potlatch also provides a stage for the enactment of northwest coastal myths, such as the origin story of Raven the Trickster. In this photograph, documented by a commercial firm, all of the elements of the northwest cosmos stand for the record. The large dance screen at the back registers the bold symmetry and pattern intricacy of northwest coastal design forms. A winged Raven or bird dancer seems poised for flight in a transformation mask which is specific to this culture. *Transformation masks* articulate with the performer—beaks open and shut, often revealing an additional creature! Animal and human transformation is a common Native American theme. Other figures pose in the photo with Potlatch hats that denote the number of feasts a clan has held through the amount of rings registered upon the hat. The Potlatch lodge interior is filled with material objects that define the ceremony. Cedar boxes, that were once said to contain the moon, stars, and sun appear here. One seems to be held shut by a mysterious head! Could it be the Sky Chief? Art and important artists, such as Bill Ried, now take their rightful place in Northwest coastal cultural arts tradition.

34. ***MY DAUGHTER'S FIRST STEPS*. NAPACHIE POOTOOGOOK, 1990 LITHOGRAPH. DORSET FINE ARTS.** Printmaking is a relatively new means of artistic expression for the Inuit (Eskimo) people living in Alaska and the Arctic region. It was not until the 1950's that printmaking was engaged by artists living in Cape Dorset. The two basic techniques employed for print production were the stone cut and the stencil. In a culture so adept at incising and carving, printmaking and graphic arts were a natural development. *My Daughter's First Steps* is a lithograph which evidences a technical expansion of the medium; it is clear that Arctic artists, such as Napachie Pootoogook, bring fresh meaning to the art of the print. In this image, a universal moment of tentative joy is depicted when a daughter ventures to mother on her own two little feet. A pair of *mukluks* have been set aside, along with the child's *parka,* to perhaps allow less restricted movement . . . from a narrative interest, there are other possibilities. Artistically, the small child's personal items create a sense of the picture's motion, suggesting footsteps along with a pointed hood to provide directionality. Mother stretches toward toddler with a sweeping horizontal gesture that is in visual agreement with the mountain range behind her. An otherwise barren landscape is infused with shape, texture, curvaceous linear flow, and of course broad human values, accentuated by postures and tender interaction between mother and child. The Inuit identity of subject is assured by environment as well as clothing indicated; the woman wears a white jacket called an *amautik,* specifically used by mothers who will carry their babies in its generous hood. The event shown here assures that less demand for the carrier hood is as certain for this Inuit mother as Arctic snow.

35. **RUSSIAN LACQUER BOX OF VASILISA. SOURCE: CORNERS OF THE WORLD.** Russian lacquer painting is an art that has been passed from one generation to the next since the late 18th century. There are specific lacquer painting production centers in Russia, of which the village of Palekh is the best known. The themes for Russian lacquer ware are numerous and narrative, from the beloved *bylinas* (legends) to history, nature, specific countryside landscapes, towns, horses, knights and castles, and to little village scenes. It is, however, the fairy tale that most often appears on the black lacquer boxes, bringing along the Russian love of folkloric tradition. Many great ballets, operas, poems, and literature are inspired by these stories. Icon painting, a long-honored Russian art tradition, also found opportunity for survival on the lids of lacquer boxes after it was banned by the Revolution. In this painting of Vasilisa, the Russian equivalent of Cinderella, the traditional elongated icon is recognized and is very much intact. The icon style of spacial manipulation, verticality, and poised gesture is frequently seen in lacquer ware painting. On this box, Vasilisa holds a little guardian doll, much like a Matrioshka, with magic power. She will need its help, for Vasilisa is sent by her mean step-sisters to the secret forest of *Baba Yaga,* a hideous witch! The witch's house is unmistakable—it stands on chicken legs and is marked by a skull. The appearance of a fine knight on a white horse offers the hope that Vasilisa will indeed overcome her difficulties and, unlike her mean-spirited sisters, live happily every after in Russia. Please notice the extraordinary night garden of the enchanted forest, its decorative treatment, and the means by which the visual activity is achieved in the long vertical picture space. Observe the embellishment of details!

36. **BOOK OF KELLS, INITIAL "L" MANUSCRIPTS.** The Book of Kells is one of the most magnificent examples of illuminated book arts in the Western World; it may also be considered a masterpiece of Celtic ornamentation. It is essentially a book of Christian religious text, written and illuminated by Irish monks over a protracted

period of time estimated between 760 and 820. During these years, there were many invasions and, as a result, a number of influences may have contributed to the richness of the work. It has been suggested that the Book of Kells owes less to the Roman book script than it does to the *runes* of an ancient Celtic past, since Ireland was isolated from much of Europe for many years. The Book of Kells has a unique resemblance to illuminations found in Islamic calligraphy. The visually stunning ideas originated in this Irish work have an identity that is their own. Devices, such as multiple spirals, are important elements in the initial letter "L." The wheel-like swirls convey a movement much like clockwork; an eternal rhythm is visually created. Humans, sometimes humorously representing the monk illuminators themselves, often appear within the curves of the letter. Try to locate a face (or two)! Decorative techniques are symbolic; included are *interlaced knots, key patterns* which are labyrinth-like repetitions, and *cruciform* and *zoomorphic* manuscript creatures. Each component of a manuscript offers certain artistic possibilities, from border to initial letter illuminating. In the end, the Book of Kells bears stunning testimony to craft, skill, technique, and, of course, creativity.

37. **THE STATUE OF LIBERTY. NEW YORK HARBOR.** She is a colossus, a feat of engineering, a Beaux-Arts classical statue, and an emblematic staging ground for every political demonstration imaginable. She has appeared as an official symbol for civic organizations, and as a logo for labor unions and women's rights groups. One might even describe her as "Goddess" of Liberty, who heroically appears to crush *"the broken shackles of tyranny"* beneath her feet. This National Monument, a gift from the country of France, is also a sculpture, one that has inspired many artistic interpretations. Even Dada artist Marcel Duchamp revamped her resolute face with a portrait "mugshot" of Surrealist Andre Breton! Countless posters, advertisements, paintings, and souvenirs bear her image. She is an American Mona Lisa, a philosophical ideal who stands fifteen stories tall. You could call her an impervious, highly recognizable celebrity, the lady in New York Harbor, who is a mere half mile from Ellis Island. To the millions of immigrants who came to America in search of a new and better life, The Statue of Liberty was a beacon of hope and reassurance, a sign of courage, and a protector of liberty. Who is the Statue of Liberty today? She is a constant reminder of what the United States of America promises to be—a welcoming, tolerant society that values diversity and honors all heritages.

38. *TAUFSCHEIN FOR MARIA ANN TRANSU. HAND-DRAWN, LETTERED, AND COLORED ON LAID PAPER. ANONYMOUS ARTIST. NORTHHAMPTON COUNTY, CA. 1825.* Fraktur is a form of folklife expression that is described as "illuminative writing" with roots in 16th and 17th century Europe. An unassuming manuscript art, Fraktur has the countries of Germany, Austria, and Switzerland as its source. Pennsylvania-Germans, Mennonites, and Amish are among the New World communities who produce Fraktur. Fanciful and symbolic birds, flowers, and hearts appear in a variety of Frakturs that have classifications: *Vorschiften*, an illuminated Bible passage; *Traufschein*, a marriage certificate; and *Taufschein*, a Baptismal certificate. There are other Frakturs that include the memorial Denkmal and the House Blessing. The *Taufschein for Maria Ann Transu* features the wide heart symbol frequently seen in Pennsylvania-German folk art. The birds, flowers, berries, and plants that accompany the heart may be considered humble representations of divine creating. This Taufschein serves as a birth certificate . . . *"For Maria Anna, daughter of Isaac and Margretha (Fehr) Transu, born June 19, 1817, in the sign of Leo, in Williams Township, Northhampton County, baptized by Pastor Stohr. Sponsors, Samuel and Maria Butz."* Pencil notation on reverse: March 20, 1840 married. Died September 17, 1886, 69 years—2 months—28 days. Frakturs state simply and poignantly the times of life and mark its occasions.

39. **MARDI GRAS MASK.** Every year in New Orleans, Louisiana, there is a big festival, a grand parade, an outrageous masquerade, a wild street party, a carnival, a pageant, and they all have only one name—Mardi Gras! The costumes, divisions, and annual time of

the Mardi Gras are much like those of other world-famous carnival celebrations. The Court Jester wearing the silver mask and holding a Pierrot baton would broadly be considered a *"Fancy Dress"* character, for he is a product of European theater, courtly life, and masquerade balls. The costume, surrounded by plumage, would also fit right into the Venetian Carnival. Characters from the pages of history, literature, the Italian Comedia dell'arte are alive and well in Mardi Gras! In New Orleans, French heritage counts in Mardi Gras—so the African, Spanish and Amerindian traditions that comprise this distinctive Creole culture. New Orleans is the only place in the United States—outside of the Caribbean Islands—that enjoys this dynamic and vibrant Creole society. Out of New Orleans heritage come not only fantastic street theater and merriment; the American origins of the Blues and Jazz were born right here on Bourbon Street a contribution of African-American musicality. Even the playful jester isn't fooling about this proud American tradition . . . *C'est magnifique!*

40. ***THANKSGIVING*. DORIS LEE. AMERICAN (1905–1983). OIL ON CANVAS. 28″ × 40″. THE ART INSTITUTE OF CHICAGO.** Doris Lee offers the viewer a slice of American life as tasty and comforting as homemade apple pie. The artist grew up in a small Illinois town that clearly provided her with a wealth of homey memories to invest in her charming "slice-of-life" painting. The intimacy of the busy Thanksgiving kitchen is made more cozy by the compositional "shoe box" effect, with depth of space suggested by the peek offered into the adjoining dining room. The viewer's eye is lifted back through the house by the perspective of the ascending checkerboard linoleum floor tile. It is an everyday scene of food preparation for a holiday that celebrates family, friends, and home. The women appear absorbed in their homemaking tasks of bringing in fresh vegetables, rolling out pie dough, selecting table settings, and checking on the turkey in the oven! Children, pets, and a guest, admiring herself in a hat, fill the picture with charming detail. With so many little pleasures to admire—such as the dishes on display and the calendar on the left corner walls near the door—the painting is as delightful as a miniature dollhouse. Note the "twins" in the corner highchair, cheering everyone on! Doris Lee has created a genre interior of American domestic life, with all the warmth of freshly baked bread. If we consider the work as one of Regionalism in style, based on this insightful and painterly description of a country kitchen in America, we are convinced to beg to hear the cry, "Dinner's almost ready!"

Asia

Russia

Kazakhstan

Mongolia

NORTH KOREA

Turkey

Syria
Israel
Jordan

Iraq

Iran

Pakistan

Saudi
Arabia

Oman

India

Yemen

Arabian
Sea

Bay
of
Bengal

CHINA

LAOS

SOUTH KOREA

JAPAN

Pacific
Ocean

South
China
Sea

Philippines

CAMBODIA

Vietnam

Indian
Ocean

Indonesia

Asia

Asian fans express the gesture of "opening up and giving."

CHINA,
JAPAN,
KOREA,
LAOS,
AND CAMBODIA

Maneki-Neko, traditional Welcome Cat of Japan, invites you to Asia!

ART ACTIVITIES FOR BECOMING CULTURE SMART

To know the Art of Asia . . . . .

. . . . . one often begins with the world's oldest and largest continuous civilization. The name *China* comes from the First Emperor Qin—pronounced *Chin*—who ordered an army of life-sized terra-cotta warriors to guard his eternal tomb, complete with full-scale horses and chariots. First Emperor Qin unified the Great Wall of China. Paramount to cultural evolution was the advancement of arts and writing, made possible by the Chinese inventions of printing and paper. Chinese artistic achievements were in jade, bronze, stone, and wood—along with *china* itself. Consider the classic blue and white Ming porcelain vase. China was known for its early production of pottery and the crafting of small tomb figureware.

China shared with Japan and Korea an excellence in The Three Perfections—calligraphy ("beautiful writing"), poetry, and painting. Materials were simple—inkstone and brush, silk, or paper. Monochromatic painting was valued for the ability to express a range of tonal nuances using only shades of black ink. Color was used sensitively and sparingly, and brushwork was of key importance. The *Mustard Seed Garden Manual,* first published in 1679, provided solid instruction for color mixing and application, along with a brushstroke vocabulary for painting rocks, flowers, and bamboo. Various marks recognizable in brushstroke painting include Dragon's Tail, Axe Blade, Teardrop, and Watergrass. Nature is all-important in Asian art.

In China, themes are deeply rooted in Confucianism, Taoism (pronounced Tow-ism), and Buddhism, which is now practiced throughout China. Buddhism was based on the teachings of the historical Buddha, born in India, who held that enlightenment and tranquillity can be attained through meditation, release from material attachments, and with compassion for all living things. Ancient Taoists followed the Old Philosopher, Lao-Tzu, who endorsed a simple life in harmony with nature, where energy may freely flow. Balancing the opposite forces of Yin (female) and Yang (male) would assure harmony in life. Many Chinese practices today, such as the use of paper joss materials, honor the ancestors. The teachings of Confucius—a code of respectful behavior, honesty, duty, and honor for family—is the ancient basis of Chinese society.

Landscape is a favored Asian theme—Chinese misty mountains and waterfalls describe nature in monumental and mystical terms. Delicate bird and flower painting—along with peachy fruits—extend to the decorative arts. Chinese painting is atmospheric, with a great reverence for nature. Portraiture was reserved to honor Imperial rulers, scholars, and heroes. Ink painting, the soul of Asian art, reached its "golden age" during the Song Dynasty, with masters such as *Ma Yuan*. Southern Song painting is lyrical, spontaneous, and poetic. In the more formal painting and decorative arts, composition and design in China is often symmetrical and orderly. The Song Dynasty, also called "Literati," anticipated the "broken ink" and "boneless" painting of Japan. Also known as Sumi-e, Japanese ink painting is considered a calligraphic expression of Zen Buddhism—brought to Japan by Asian monk *Bodhidharma*, along with tea plants! The master of Semi-e was Zen monk artist *Sesshu* (1420–1506). As any Zen painting master knows, the use of white space is of equal importance to the brush and ink.

Japan, a chain of islands, lies east to the mainland of Asia, is tiny in comparison to China. Yet, Japan has proved a mighty artistic force! Japanese painting formats, consistent with those of China and Korea, conform to **the vertical scroll, the hand-held horizontal scroll, fan, and album leaf.**

Japanese art has distinctive elements: asymmetry, love of nature, narrative content, earthy humor, the capture of "fleeting moments," and elegance. Japanese pictorial composition uplifts the eye and utilizes strong diagonal structure. Guiding principles of art and architecture, combined with Zen philosophy, are revealed through a single source—the Japanese teahouse ceremony—in integrity of materials, compactness of design, and simplicity.

The Japanese color woodblock prints produced during the Edo period elevated the art of printmaking to a level of unsurpassed quality. The technically flawless and brilliantly designed prints, originally a popular art, shaped the direction of nineteenth- and twentieth-century Western art. Japanese print masters such as Utamaro had a profound influence on the graphic works of Toulouse-Lautrec. Compositional devices, such as space cropping and multiple views, introduced new ideas to artists working in Paris—Monet, Manet, Degas, Cassatt, Van Gogh, and Gauguin.

The Southeast Asian art of Cambodia, too, found a European audience. France's favorite sculptor, Auguste Rodin, was awed and inspired by the graceful movements of a Cambodian dance troupe that visited Paris. The sway of the dancers brought to life the lovely chorus of *Apsara*—or *Celestial Women*—from a frieze on the glorious temple walls of Angkor Wat. Cambodian arts express a combined sentiment of Hinduism and Buddhism. Laos and Thailand, neighbors to Cambodia, are replete with Buddhist temples and images. Many find Cambodian and Thai sculpture, with its serenity and self-contained grace, among the most divine of all representations. The village arts of the region are visually stunning and filled with symbolic patterns and designs—the art of the everyday world brings the spirit of evanescent joy.

ACTIVITY 1

Happy New Year Dragon

Three-Dimensional Paper Sculpture

Chinese dragons are considered benevolent, wise, and lucky. They embody natural forces and—like their counterparts in Western mythology—are powerful indeed! Please note that Chinese dragons are not loathsome nor are they vicious and destructive. No knights are needed to slay these creatures.

▲ Figure 1-1. Gung Hay Fat Choy! New Year's greeting for prosperity and health.

On the contrary, Chinese dragons invoke good fortune and may be relied upon to chase evil. For thousands of years, the Eastern dragon has been a vital element of Chinese culture. The dragon is, among other things, a symbol of the Emperor and the court. This is why you will find dragons all over imperial robes!

Dragons were believed to dwell in the heavens, mountains, and seas. They have not only influenced royal decisions—they are also thought to control weather and seasons! With such a long cultural history, it should be of little surprise to find that dragons often appear in Chinese art and offer a grand centerpiece of the Chinese New Year Parade!

The Chinese New Year is based on the lunar calendar, which means it can occur anywhere between mid-January and mid-February. It is a five-day celebration. On the third day, the mighty dragon will burst on the noisy scene, bringing good luck to all in its path!

◀ Figure 1-2. Dragon's head made of papier mâché; the body is a long train of cloth. Some men hold the head, while others— usually twelve—become "dragon legs"! Can you find another dragon in the firecracker smoke?

MATERIALS

- pencils
- 36″ × 26″ color Kraft roll paper
- 12″ × 18″ color construction paper
- 9″ × 12″ color construction paper (assorted for legs, tail, and details)
- red and orange tissue paper*

- scissors
- tempera paint
- oil pastels
- glue
- pipe cleaners
- plastic wiggle eyes (may substitute with paper circles)

* Red is considered particularly lucky for the Chinese New Year!

TEACHER PREPARATION

You might want to cut 36″ × 26″ color Kraft paper for students' selection. For classroom discussion, it's helpful to access sources of Chinese dragon images. **Stress that a Chinese dragon is the sum of many parts:** Its head is said to be shaped like a camel's; it has magic creature eyes, fins, horns, pointed beard, tusks; a snake's neck, fish scales, belly of a clam, eagles' claws, and the paws of a tiger! You will want to discuss the attributes of Chinese dragons with your students before they explore their own "beastly" interpretations!

DIRECTIONS

1. **Gung Hay Fat Choy!** How do we celebrate the New Year? The Chinese have the traditional Dragon (or "Lion Dancer") to bring in the year with gusto! Students' answers to these questions should give the teacher an opportunity to introduce the dragon in this particular context.

2. Students select color Kraft paper for the body of the dragon. Fold paper in half lengthwise. Fold in half again lengthwise to make crease and open this last fold only. Cut on a diagonal from the open bottom corner edge to top at mid-fold crease. *(See S.O.S., if needed.)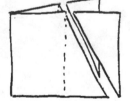

3. Select two to three colors of tempera paint which contrast with the paper body color. Open paper. Drip paint on one half of the paper and then refold and press to make symmetrical "blotto" design!

4. Fold 12″ × 18″ paper in half. Draw dragon head on fold. Cut out shape on fold. Cut out an open mouth shape with teeth. Color with oil pastels, making sure to add details, but no "eyeballs."

5. Draw half of the tail shape on folded 9″ × 12″ construction paper. Cut on fold and then decorate with textural design.

---

*S.O.S. (SAVE OUR SCHEDULE, i.e., "schedule saver" or shortcut) . . . "The Paper (Bag) Dragon" may be created by decorating a paper lunch bag in lieu of steps 2 and 3.

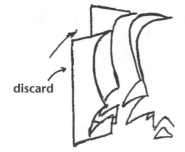

6. Draw half of a leg shape on 4 pieces of 6" × 9" construction paper that has been folded in half. Cut on fold and open legs to decorate with textural designs using oil crayons.

7. Make body into tube by overlapping side edges of now-dry painted Kraft paper. The body will be wider at head and narrower at the tail end. Scrunch tube by carefully pushing open ends together.

8. Attach head, tail, and legs with glue or staples.

9. Use construction paper to add details such as horns and dimensional scales. Fire shooting from the dragon's mouth can be created by using tissue paper and pipe cleaners, etc.

10. To conclude the project, fill the empty eye shapes with eyeballs (cut paper or plastic wiggle eyes) to express the dragon's spirit. According to the Chinese dragon painter's tradition, when the dragon's eyes are put in, the dragon will fill with energy and fly away . . . *such is the magic of art!*

Figure 1-3. Souvenir hand puppets. (May be purchased in the "Chinatown" section of many cities.) Simple classroom version is the brown bag (or "colored" lunch bag) which enables articulated mouth. Add pom-poms. ▼

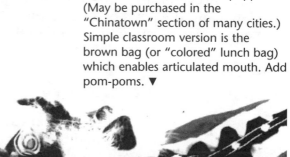

▲ Figure 1-4. Another alternative to the more ambitious version is the hand-held dragon, easily assembled as shown.

◄ Figure 1-5. You know you're in China when . . . you are standing at the Great Wall! China's world wonder is more than 1,500 miles long and is formed of endless sections, much like the art-room version detail shown here. Ours boasts the "Legend of Ch'en Jung the Dragon Painter." whose artistic powers enabled the painted dragon to break free! The student mural was made from a computer-based "blueprint."

ACTIVITY 2

Chinese Acrobats and Calendar Animals: Arts and Entertainment in Ancient Clay

Chinese Tomb Sculpture: Clay "Mingi" Figures

E X T R A : CHINESE ANIMAL TRAITS—A BIRTHDAY CHART

▲ Figure 1-6. A real balancing act!

The history of Chinese clay figure sculpture stretches back farther than the length of the Great Wall of China! Time has unearthed a variety of subjects that vary in size as well as characterization. The range of ceramic expression includes full-scale clay warriors of the Third Century B.C., elegantly glazed horses of the Tang Dynasty (618–906 A.D.) . . . and the delightful *mingi* figures of ancient China! These little clay characters were intended to appease ancestors in the afterlife; most often, the recipients of their charms were the emperors. Quite understandably, acrobats, artists, wrestlers, jugglers, and musicians would make for good company.

The favorable attrributes of small-scale Chinese tomb firgures include the twelve animals that represent the Chinese Lunar Calendar. Each has specific traits that define their animal personality—from the skillful monkey to the steadfast ox! Chinese animals were not only good afterlife companions; they remain important enough to individually identify each year of the Chinese calendar in any twelve-year cycle. People are optimistically believed to possess the attributes of the "animal year" in which they were born! Check our chart on page 10 and see if you agree.

Figure 1-7. A class of calendar animals! Left to right: Clever monkey writes a poem; one lovelorn rat holds his heart in his paws while a couple of other rats tell each other big news; a tiger in the corner dreams of friendship. ▶

MATERIALS

- clay (See Teacher Preparation.)
- modeling tools
- plastic covering for workspace
- paper towels
- plaster bats (or boards covered with plastic)

- smocks
- water bottle sprayer
- kiln
- glazes or underglazes
- paintbrushes

TEACHER PREPARATION

Cover the work area with plastic or Kraft paper and be prepared to distribute tools, paper towels, smocks, etc. Have a pile of pre-wedged balls of clay stacked in the front of the room. Set up another table with books containing quality reproductions of Chinese tomb sculptures. The type of clay you select will be determined by your own personal art classroom situation; kiln-fired clay is shown here. Substitute as needed. Please be aware that Chinese clay contributions to art history include stoneware and porcelain.

DIRECTIONS

1. Teacher may discuss how archaeologists uncover thousands of tombs from ancient China and are able to learn many things about Ancient Chinese beliefs concerning art and society through these discoveries. Explain the role of *mingi* as noted in the introduction.

2. Tell students that they can make their own mingi and/or calender animal. They are to think about what they would take with them to the afterlife. Would it be a favorite animal or pet? A magical genie to protect them? Or an object or figure that would give them special powers, for example, a bird to give them the power to fly and soar in the heavens? Distribute clay about the size of a mandarin orange.

▲ Figures 1-8 and 1-9. Two of the Four Accomplishments: art, music, poetry, and literature. ▼

3. Go over tips for working with clay—to pull shapes out or to roll out clay "egg rolls" as core shapes. Tell students that they can work with their fingers or with the tools provided. They can pull out their forms from a central mass of clay and/or add pieces together. Demonstrate if needed.

4. Consider the costume, the posture, and the interrelationship of the figure group. Students should also think about surface texture, possibly carving, or pressing objects into the clay. Depending on the thickness of their object, they may want to hollow it out, to allow it to dry more easily, to shrink more evenly, and to keep it from exploding in the kiln.

5. Store and let sculptures dry until next week. Sculptures will be glazed during the next lesson. If possible, bisque-fire first.

6. Upon next meeting, color will be applied in accordance with materials available. For example, during the Tang dynasty the traditional colors were amber, green, and yellow. Green is especially desirable beaaause it can represent jade which is considered very auspicious and magical! **Safety tip:** Teacher should direct glazing.

7. With small brushes the student will use glazes or underglazes to decorate their sculpture. If glazes are used, be sure at least three coats of the glaze are applied. Fire pieces in kiln when thoroughly dried.

8. Consider your "cast of characters" as a cooperative class grouping—animals, after all, may represent students' own personality traits. Display in showcase if available. Note: Teacher may want to combine this activity with Activity 3: "Happily Ever Afterlife."

▲ Figure 1-10. Jump for joy!

Chinese Animal Traits: A BIRTHDAY CHART

Students and teachers may want to find their animal year just for fun, and see if the traits seem familiar. Remember, your animal year will occur once every 12 years—that is supposed to be a very lucky year for you indeed!

R A T : (1948, 1960, 1972, 1984, 1996)

The lovable rat will charm you off your feet. Imagination and ambition are part of the rat's irresistible charisma!

O X : (1949, 1961, 1973, 1985, 1997)

The steadfast ox is strong, patient as the day is long, and likes to say, "a job well done." The ox plans well.

T I G E R : (1950, 1962, 1974, 1986, 1998)

Loyal tigers don't change their stripes! They make excellent friends.

R A B B I T : (1951, 1963, 1975, 1987, 1999)

Lucky rabbits play well with others. They know their way around money matters.

D R A G O N : (1952, 1964, 1976, 1988, 2000)

The mysterious dragon feels things very deeply and is most energetic too!

S N A K E : (1953, 1965, 1977, 1989, 2001)

Splendid snakes understand, for they are wise and beautiful. Snakes are sure of what they want.

H O R S E : (1954, 1966, 1978, 1990, 2002)

The popular horse works hard, wins friends, and influences people! Horses are handy for sound financial management!

R A M : (1955, 1967, 1979, 1991, 2003)

Artistic ram does not like to be pushy. Rams are diplomatic decision-makers and may appreciate the advice of others.

M O N K E Y : (1956, 1968, 1980, 1992, 2004)

Skillful monkey, what a genius! Monkeys are willing to hang upside down for others, but need lots of hugs.

R O O S T E R : (1957, 1969, 1981, 1993, 2005)

Ambitious rooster! If there is a job well done, rooster sees to it.

D O G : (1958, 1970, 1982, 1994, 2006)

Faithful dog has strong opinions, but will bury your secrets like a backyard bone. Dogs respect rules and may be trusted.

P I G : (1959, 1971, 1983, 1995, 2007)

Clever pig is strong in ways we'd never suspect. Pig is willing to stand up for the right thing. Pigs are brave!

ACTIVITY 3

Happily Ever Afterlife

"Joss" Paper Collage

Can you have too much good luck? The Chinese tradition of "Joss" seems to suggest that good luck is always a good thing. To ensure "Good Joss," a variety of papers are available. You may see bright red streamers printed with gold characters, make-believe money or paper "suitcases," complete with Mandarin-style pajamas and lounging slippers!

Actually, the "joss materials" are primarily intended to be burned in the manner of incense in order to honor one's ancestors and their households. Families will also burn joss-paper currency to "deposit money" in ancestors' "bank" in the afterlife—to provide a little spending cash! Up until the end of the Sui period (A.D. 617), genuine articles were burned for the ancestors! The replacement of paper gifts that represent the real-world objects

▲ Figure 1-11. Student joss kit collage seems to have thought of everything—including spending money!

became a logical and quite an artistic alternative. Gifts that "go up in smoke" include elaborate paper palaces, airplanes with pilot, small appliances, wardrobe items—anything to make the afterlife more pleasurable. It is a tradition that is in fact shared, in one way or the other, by many cultures. Certainly Ancient Egypt comes to mind.

In China, joss paper is popularly used during the New Year's celebration, festivals, initiations, and processions. It is used for good fortune on the first day or the middle of the month. Some say it's a new start for your best wishes!

MATERIALS

- 12" × 24" white paper
- 12" × 18" white paper
- colored markers/crayons
- variety of metallic/colored papers
- scissors

- white glue/glue sticks
- watercolor paints (optional)
- magazines (optional)
- reproducible page: "Chinese Symbols"

TEACHER PREPARATION

Teacher may want to appropriate samples of Chinese printed papers. One source is the food labels you might find in the imported specialties aisle of a well-stocked supermarket. The addition of Chinese papers adds a certain special touch. How about the "fortunes" of fortune cookies? That would be truly auspicious!

Prepare paper sizes as needed. Gather magazines for students' selection of objects.

◀ Figure 1-12. Popular joss paper kit from Philadelphia's "Chinatown."

▲ Figure 1-13. "Real" paper objects . . . paper replaces clay: ancient ceramic tomb concept carried in papercraft.

DIRECTIONS

1. Discuss what objects would be useful to ancestors. Brainstorm gift suggestions: A favorite video game? Rollerblades? What objects are practical? Recreational? Thoughtful? Representations of houses and even furniture and household appliances should be considered. Think about a favorite chair!

2. Distribute materials.

3. Have students fold up the 24" length of paper at ten inches and then fold the remaining 4" over the top to make a folder-style envelope to arrange their paper joss articles inside. They can decorate the front of the suitcase/ envelope with a greeting, Chinese good luck symbols, or other decorative designs using colored markers and crayons. (Teacher may want to make reproducible pages available to students at this time.)

4. The students can begin to create paper treasures they plan on sending to their ancestors. Perhaps a glittering mansion! They may experiment in creating their objects and the composition of the "collage." Children may cut, paste and glue using a variety of papers, shapes, and images. Consider *inside* of suitcase/envelope for contents.

5. When students have completed all their articles, they "store" them in their beautifully decorated envelopes. Gently fold into the decorative "kit."

6. These objects are much too beautiful to really burn! Display and discuss!

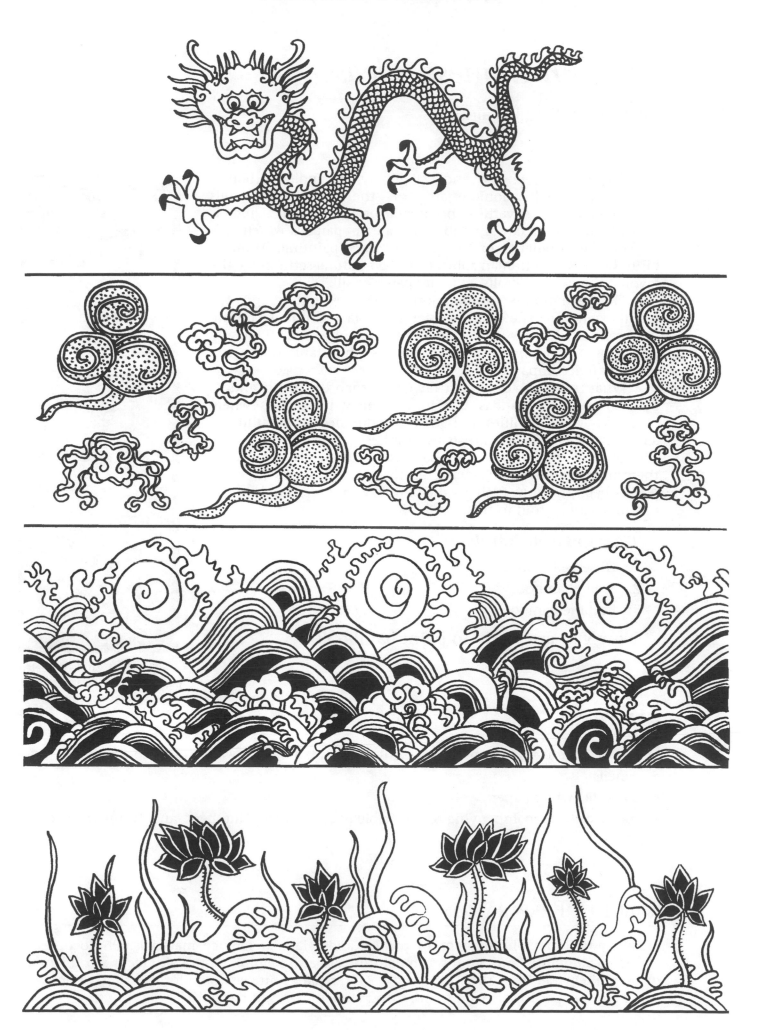

ACTIVITY 4

Say It in Chinese, Please

Calligraphy Scrolls/Painting

Chinese painting, poetry, and calligraphy are endlessly bound together in one harmonious art form—the scroll. Asian scrolls most often appear as vertical, horizontal, or "album leaf," which is shaped much like a fan. Art and nature are inseparable, which may explain the popularity of Chinese landscape painting. Animals, birds, flowers, and human subjects in their natural settings are the favored themes for scrolls, whether paper or silk!

The harmonious combination of pictures and calligraphic words exemplifies the ideals of Asian art. In fact, Chinese painting has been called "the voiceless poem." Calligraphy—which literally translates as *beautiful writing*—is just as important as the ink painting it accompanies.

What better subject to portray China than the panda and its beloved bamboo! Pandas live in the misty mountains where bamboo—which signifies strength and endurance—is plentiful. As a matter of fact, Chinese artists use brushes with bamboo handles.

To serve the range of Chinese artistic and literary expression, there are more than 3,000 characters that you can select when the poems begin to flow. Perhaps the best way to understand the art of China can be told in this simple way:

How to Paint Bamboo

1. Observe bamboo.
2. Study bamboo.
3. Become bamboo.

Now you are ready to paint bamboo!!

▲ Figure 1-14. Student-created panda scrolls with days of the week . . . and signed by the artist!

MATERIALS

- any black non-toxic water-based paint, such as tempera or water color blocks
- pencils
- 18" × 24" white paper
- copies of the accompanying reproducible page "Chinese Numbers" and "Chinese Days of Week"

TEACHER PREPARATION

Obtain additional photographs of pandas and related reference materials. Photocopies of Chinese calligraphy and Sumi brush painting are also helpful. Optional: Precut scroll lengths or cut white paper from 18" × 24" to 12" × 24". Prepare your classroom for painting lessons with water cups, paper towels, and so on. Cover student desks, if desired.

DIRECTIONS

1. Introduce the love of nature as Chinese painting expresses it, using pandas and other reference materials you may have gathered as your guide. Discuss with students their ideas for Chinese scroll subjects. Remind students that they will be using calligraphy (or calligraphic brush strokes) as part of their scroll design.

2. Point out to students that "simplicity" of idea and line are essential. Students should think about scroll-page design that will convey the feeling of their poetic subject, whether it is pandas munching bamboo or birds on a branch.

3. Distribute painting materials. Encourage students to adjust density of black paint with their water as needed. References to Chinese days of the week and numbers will enhance pictorial design. (Teacher may want to make these reproducible pages available.)

4. This is a Chinese painting experience. It is more valuable for students to learn to trust the "ink" and their instincts than it is for them to produce a perfect representation. Chinese painters believed that black ink is all you need to express complex ideas simply! Some even felt that color was unnecessary.

5. Dry paintings should be displayed in the "home"—the home is where the heart is! Note that scrolls are viewed from many points of view and are a common form of ornamentation throughout Asia. Scrolls are intended to provide continued happiness and prosperity—we wish this to you.

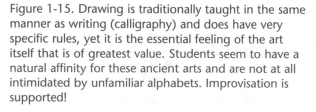

Figure 1-15. Drawing is traditionally taught in the same manner as writing (calligraphy) and does have very specific rules, yet it is the essential feeling of the art itself that is of greatest value. Students seem to have a natural affinity for these ancient arts and are not at all intimidated by unfamiliar alphabets. Improvisation is supported!

Left to right, please note "Danny's" scroll uses a top and bottom bracket device to frame his calligraphy (wallpaper samples may be used here). Right scroll offers another view of bamboo. ▶

Chinese Numbers

CHINESE NUMBERS

1	一	6	六
2	二	7	七
3	三	8	八
4	四	9	九
5	五	10	十

© 1999 by Prentice Hall

Chinese Days of the Week

SUNDAY	MONDAY	TUESDAY	WEDNESDAY	THURSDAY	FRIDAY	SATURDAY
日	月	火	水	木	金	土

ACTIVITY 5

Chinese Good Fortune Mirrors

Moon Festival Hanging Discs

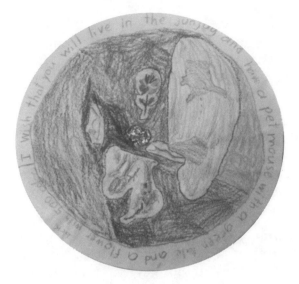

▲ Figure 1-16. This circular moon mirror reflects wishes for . . . "a pet mouse with a green tale" . . . ! Animal friend, the bunny, is regarded as "the Rabbit in the Moon"—you probably have only to study the moon imaginatively to see!

The first full moon of the New Year is a cause for Chinese celebration. Moon magic is by no means limited to early calendar days; there is an Autumn Festival to anticipate. This is a time for "moon appreciation" parties! Special desserts known as mooncakes are served . . . and children receive paper lanterns that are shaped like fish, birds, and bunnies! Did you know that in China, there is a legendary "Rabbit-in-the-Moon"!?!

Mirrors are given as gifts on these holidays as a symbol of well-being and family togetherness.

Both mirrors and full moons are the circular universal symbols of unity. They are considered sources of luck and goodness. In fact, the benevolent Kuan Yin (Kwahn-Yin), known as the Goddess of the Moon, is also considered the protector of children.

The tradition of giving mirrors dates back to 1200 B.C. Mirrors are supposed to counteract bad days and are especially useful in sending good wishes.

MATERIALS

- 12″ × 12″ white paper
- colored pencils
- foil paper
- reproducible page from Activity 3: "Chinese Symbols"

- scissors
- white glue
- hole punch
- cord

Figure 1-17. The ancient Chinese wish for "large happy families" is translated into student's own world in the Good Fortune mirror. ▶

TEACHER PREPARATION

Provide template or precut circles. "Flat-style" paper plates may be used!

DIRECTIONS

1. Introduce the lesson by discussing the festivals that are held to celebrate the harvest and other occasions. Explain that the mirrors are round to reflect the round harvest moon and bring good luck wishes to the recipient. Students will be creating their own "wishful thinking" gifts! These will be given to family and friends.

2. Student will cut the basic mirror shape from paper or receive precut circle. With pencil, draw a smaller circle within the large circle. At this time the student should be thinking of a wish that could be inscribed within the border. The Chinese message used many years ago was "may you have five girls and five boys and may there be music playing wherever you go."

3. Specific symbols can be drawn to illustrate the written wish. Ask students to draw symbols in the center of the mirror with colored pencils. Review symbols on reproducible page that represent longevity (mountains, peaches, clouds), health (the leaf), and happiness (Fu symbol). In keeping with tradition, the symbols should reflect towards the center. (See page 13 for "Chinese Symbols" reproducible page.)

4. To add the reflective touch to the mirror, the students will cut a circle of foil paper to make the reverse side of the mirror. Punch hole for cord insertion.

5. Reflect! Discuss students' wishes and the thoughts behind them.

6. Hang "mirror moons" where they can catch the light. Moons may be used as special-occasion ornaments.

Figure 1-18. Five Chinese brothers? (fifth brother "on assignment") What a clever idea for a school hallway! They certainly "back up" our hanging moon mirrors with pluck! ▼

ACTIVITY 6

Great Imperial Robes!

"Celestial" Self-Portraits/Dynastic Garments

Everything about a portrait reveals a great deal about the sitter and the society in which it was made. Chinese commemorative portraits speak first and foremost of the elevated rank of the courtly official they feature. These stately portraits were painted on silk with rare and precious mineral-based colors, including gold. Actual robes worn in Dynasty portraits were ornately embroidered, conveying great wealth and prestige.

Chinese commemorative portraiture follows a specific style of composition which places courtly rulers "front and center." To further denote positions of importance, celestial robes contain all the natural elements of the heavens and the earth.

Once again the dragon reigns supreme for it is the dragon robe that is most often used to represent the emperor. In fact, certain dynasties claimed direct descendance from Dragon Thrones!

There are endless codes and symbols of power contained in these Chinese Dynasty robes, yet it is the dragon—the national emblem of China—that is unmistakable in its enduring majesty. The dragon robe is actually a "cosmic diagram" of our universe! It reads from *bottom to top:* water, land and sky. Emerging above the garment is the head of the Emperor or Empress who reigns! In the language of imperial garments, the dragon says it all!

▲ Figure 1-19. Universal Symbols: The dragon robe is a diagram of the universe. At the bottom of the robe are diagonal bands and tossing waves which represent the water. Sections of mountains and land emerge from the water. Above is the sky, filled with dragons cavorting in the clouds.

MATERIALS

- white paper (12″ × 18″)
- gum erasers
- fine-tipped non-toxic black markers
- examples of royal court painting of Ming or Quin Dynasty (see Teacher Preparation)
- chart or examples of symbols used in identifying royalty (see Teacher Preparation)

- examples of Chinese dragons
- optional: gold foil and black construction paper
- pencils
- watercolors
- paintbrushes

TEACHER PREPARATION

Teacher might gather portraiture images and reproductions that can be compared with Chinese dynasty portraits for composition, costume, and other elements.

DIRECTIONS

1. Discuss the Chinese portraiture. How do we identify rank of individuals? Ask the students to identify symbols and discuss why they may have been used. Discuss the role of the dragon in Chinese society and suggest that they may use it on their clothing. *Note:* The *five claws* identify the emperor as well as other attributes, i.e., position of hands and facial expression.

2. Ask students to note the formal pose of the figure. The figure may be seated or standing. Review figure drawing techniques, if appropriate.

3. Distribute materials. Students will lightly sketch their figure and the robe worn, and may add the celestial symbols to the robe. At the bottom of the robe should be water symbols. Land symbols should be above the water. The sky may be drawn above using creative cloud symbols. *Most important should be the dragon cavorting in the sky!*

4. The students will add objects to the background which also identify the subject. They may also include carpet motifs on the floor and scholars' tools.

5. When they are satisfied with the drawing, painting will begin! As paint dries, students can begin to draw a black contour line to delineate figure against background, as well as accentuate details.

◄ Figures 1-20 and 1-21. The Dragon: One of the most important symbols found in formal court robes was that of the dragon. It was the national emblem of China, and the Chinese considered it a symbol of power, authority, and good fortune. A dragon with a pearl symbolized a wish for wealth and good luck. Only Chinese emperors could have a dragon with five claws embroidered on their clothing. All other dragons have only four claws. ►

6. When finished, mount on stately black paper. Decorate the black paper border with tiny royal gold lines and glue a black string to each top corner and display. How heavenly!

▲ Figure 1-22. Alison wears an antique robe that may not be imperial but is beautiful nevertheless! It tells a story much like the Blue Willow pattern. Note the student-made necklace. Is it a Chinese medicine box?

ACTIVITY 7

Japan to a Tea!

Tea Ceremony and Tea Bowls

▲ Figure 1-23. Japanese show respect for the commonplace—everyday objects show integrity. The reverence for them is an important element of the Art of Tea.

The tea bowl is an especially treasured object. It should represent high-quality workmanship and be decorated simply yet beautifully—the less pretentious the better. It is the essential element of the time-honored Japanese tea ceremony where nothing is without meaning. Simplicity and humility are felt at once—the ceremony, which revolves around the teabowl, traditionally begins after the visitors enter through a very low door. Shoes are left outside. All gestures show respect and promote harmony.

Tranquillity is experienced through the meditative gestures of the tea ceremony: Tea is poured into the bowl, the host and guests slowly turn the bowl around in their hands, admiring the shape, the glaze, and the texture. There is appreciation for the integrity of all the materials used in the tearoom—from tea bowl to architectural design. The function of the object is to serve the precious tea. The tea bowl is more than an ordinary container. Basic respect for the nature of the material from which it is made shows in its craft.

It is said that the tea ceremony began to gain its place in Japanese culture when weary scholars and samurai sought a place of refuge from the demands of the outside world. Monks also regarded tea drinking as a useful aid to meditation. The form of the tea has since evolved to the point where it has become a metaphor for Japanese living. To understand Japan, one needs to study *Chanoyu,* or the Art of Tea—the whole Japanese culture is held in a teacup!

MATERIALS

- clay (see Teacher Preparation)
- water bottle sprayer
- plaster bats (or plastic-covered boards)
- smocks
- paper towels
- paintbrushes
- plastic covering for work space
- modeling tools
- kiln
- glazes/underglazes

Figure 1-24. The essential items for the tea ceremony—bamboo tea whisk and its holder, tea scoop, and the lacquer tea caddie that holds the powdered tea. ▶

TEACHER PREPARATION

It is ideal if you are able to conduct this activity with water-based clay since it is authentic to the concept of natural materials endorsed here. Your own situation will of course determine your standard clay usage guidelines. Be sure clay is moist and malleable, and again, glazing (kiln firing) and/or painting are discretionary.

Teacher may want to make "snowballs" for individual students in advance of lesson. Prepare classroom for clay lesson.

Suggestion: How about a classroom teahouse? You might want to decorate a corner of your classroom to resemble a Japanese tea house. Cut Kraft paper on the floor becomes tatami mats; seasonal scrolls can be made by students and hung along with an asymmetrical flower arrangement (Ikebana). Upon completion of the bowls the students could have their own tea ceremony—although "tea" should be the "invisible" variety or be replaced by juice for safety reasons.

▲ Figure 1-25. A snowstorm captured in a bowl! Both inside and outside of the container are in harmony. If you think you see calligraphy, you are not wrong.

DIRECTIONS

1. Discuss the nature of the clay. How does it feel? Why do we enjoy using it? How can we help the clay become a little bowl?

2. Distribute clay "snowballs."

3. Press thumbs into the center of the ball.

4. Keep pressing the thumb down while slowly turning the clay in the palm of the hand. Try to keep the walls of the pot even—about a half-inch thick so it will be sturdy. **Hint!** Sometimes closing your eyes helps you concentrate.

5. Let the clay air dry. (Dried clay may be fired as determined.)

6. Glaze it with simple earth-colored glaze or paint it with acrylic earth tone paints. Again a kiln firing may be in order. One or two letter-style characters could be painted on with a small brush after the background color dries. Simple patterns—lines and even squiggles—are encouraged.

7. Title bowls. Discuss them quietly and respectfully.

8. Have a tea ceremony. May your teabowl always be full.

▲ Figures 1-26 & 1-27. Take a moment to admire the individual artist tea bowl. There is a world captured in this cup . . .what do you think the title might be? ▼

◀ Figure 1-28. A degree in tea! Yes, there are Schools of Tea. It is considered both art and scholarship to elegantly present the tea ceremony. Note the various-sized tea bowls that are in use.

The tearoom itself could not be designed with more purity. Once inside, you sit on your legs and admire the lovely painted scroll hung in the alcove of the tearoom, called *tokonoma.* There will be an arrangement of seasonal flowers (Ikebona), carefully selected to accompany the scroll. Everything is placed in unity within the tea house. All decorations and utensils are simple yet elegant. The servers must be schooled in the Art of Tea.

Figure 1-29. The mass-produced cup proves the point that commercial objects can still retain simple elegance. Keep this cup shape in mind for variation on the tea bowl activity. ▶

ACTIVITY 8

Daruma: A Doll to Wish For!

Popular Folk Hero Doll/Papier Mâché

Daruma (Da-ROO-MA) is a mighty popular folk hero. How popular? When Japanese children build a snowman, they usually make it in the shape of a Daruma! And who is Daruma? He is a roly-poly character based on the first of the Zen masters. Daruma is *Bodhidharma* in Chinese. Bodhidharma was an Indian monk who brought the practice of Zen Buddhism to China in the 6th century.

▲ Figure 1-30. Typical Daruma "souvenir."

People like to tell amusing stories about Daruma. Favorite tales explain that Daruma, who loved to meditate, once sat in the same spot for thirty years! When he awoke from a too-long meditation, he was so angry that he pulled off his eyebrows and threw them on the ground below! And guess what? From these eyebrows grew the first tea bushes! And we all know how important tea has always been to Japan and the world!

How to recognize Daruma? He has a characteristic appearance. In paintings, he is shown with big, bushy eyebrows, bulging eyes, full beard, and one earring. More commonly—as a folk figure—Daruma is made of lacquered papier-mâché and is usually painted scarlet red and decorated with gold and black calligraphy. Darumas come in many sizes—from about four inches to more than several feet high. The face is applied simply—save the eyes! The idea is that you make a wish and paint one of the eyes. Then, if your wish comes true, you paint the other eye! He is good luck. Darumas are especially popular at the New Year and are loved by politicians for luck in elections!

MATERIALS

- wheat paste or other papier mâché recipes (see Teacher Preparation)
- masking tape
- water containers
- newspaper
- paintbrushes
- acrylic paint: red, white, black, gold, peach

TEACHER PREPARATION

Some of the newspaper will need to be cut into small strips about 1" × 3" for the students to handle easily. Water containers should be easily accessible for students to dip strips in the wheat-paste mixture. (A reliable papier mâché recipe: equal parts of flour and water mixed in bowls.) Cover tables with paper to facilitate clean-up.

Asia: China, Japan, Korea, Laos, and Cambodia

Figure 1-31. Student work: A Daruma "get together." Commercial statues of Daruma can be readily purchased just about any-place in Japan. There are many Daruma interpretations that represent different regions in Japan—in short, Darumas abound! "Talking Daruma" can be bought in malls or from vendors—eyes mechanically open and close, too! ▶

DIRECTIONS

1. Tell students about Daruma, the papier-mâché doll that is a symbol of good fortune and luck in Japanese culture. Daruma has big, bulging eyes and bushy eyebrows and is very important! He is both comic and hero. He brings good luck to the beginning of a New Year. At that time, one eye is painted and a wish is made for good luck. When the wish has been granted, the other eye is painted as a sign of gratitude.

2. Roll up two balls of newspaper. Make one ball the size of an orange, the other the size of a grapefruit. Tape them so the balls don't come undone, and then tape the small ball on top of the larger ball.

▲ Figure 1-32. Note the expression of these diminutive Sumo wrestlers. Don't they remind you a bit of Daruma? They are another example of wit and humor in Japanese folk art.

3. Cover the newspaper balls with three layers of newspaper strips soaked in the wheat-paste or papier mâché mixture. Let dry thoroughly (usually 3–7 days). Be sure the children flatten the bottom somewhat so the Daruma will stand up by itself.

4. Paint the face. Paint circles for eyes. Use the detail brush to paint the nose, mouth, and whiskers.

5. Paint the rest of the Daruma bright red. Add some gold and black calligraphy as a finishing touch.

6. Children may choose to make their wish and paint one eye. When their wish comes true, paint in the other eyeball and thank Daruma. Now he has a reason to smile!

26

ACTIVITY 9

The Tale of Kimono

Cut Paper Kimono "Stories" and Traditional Ideas

The kimono is not only the national garment of Japan; it is the woven history of a culture that celebrates art and tradition. The kimono is made so there is no waste and it is efficiently designed. It is actually made of six rectangles of cloth that allow the gorgeous kimono to transform from full ceremonial display to a folded square that will fit in a box. One size fits many: It is the individual who defines the personality of the kimono.

The kimono serves not only to mark the important occasions of life, it provides a perfect vehicle for storytelling. One legend that many a kimono will tell is *The Tanabata Tale*. The story has several versions, but the meaning is essentially the same.

Heavenly Star Princess Tanabata was said to live on one side of the galaxy where she was known as, appropriately, The Weaver of the Skies. On the other side of the River of Heaven—the Milky Way—lived the Celestial Herdsman Altair. Princess Tanabata, the patron deity of weaving, was also the daughter of the King of the Sky. She was the weaver and seamstress of the gods. Weaver or not, the princess fell in love. She implored her father to allow her to join her true love, the Celestial Herdsman, so that they could be together forever. Her father eventually gave in.

So in love were these two that they spent all their time staring into each other's eyes and playing music while the weaving fell off the loom and the herds wandered away. The Sky King grew so furious that he sent them back to their opposite sides of the universe where they could resume their heavenly duties. However, on the seventh day of the seventh month—July seventh of each year—a celebration known as Tanabata takes place. At this time it is believed that the lovers are able to reunite. A bridge is formed by the interwoven wings of a thousand magpies that allows the two lovers to meet, if only briefly, yet completely. Today the Tanabata Bridge Festival is enthusiastically enjoyed by the people of Japan.

▲ Figures 1-33 and 1-34. Two young students show us their own individual interpretations of the Tanabata tale. Both students respect the Japanese concept of simplicity, nature, balance, and harmony. ▼

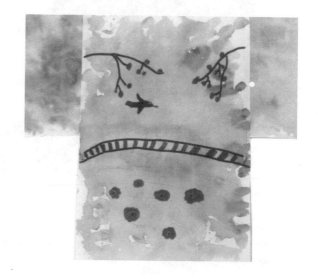

MATERIALS

- watercolors
- paintbrushes
- two white 18" × 24" paper per student

- pencils (optional)
- glue
- erasers

Teacher Preparation

These kimonos are "prewoven"; in other words, we will make the *paper* kimono version. Note: The teacher may want to precut kimonos in one piece. (See Figures 1-33, 1-34 and 1-36 for shape.)

Teacher is encouraged to tell the *Tale of Tanabata* or any other Japanese folk story, including (for scholarly and ambitious teachers) excerpts from the *Tale of Genji.* Seasonal motifs such as the plum blossom (hope), pine tree (longevity), bamboo (strength), and the chrysanthemum (Japan's imperial flower emblem) will enhance your visual kimono. (See photos for thematic ideas.)

▲ Figure 1-35. This bride and groom are able to spend all the seasons together upon the occasion of their wedding. The bride wears traditional Japanese wedding kimono, while the groom is handsomely attired in a formal tuxedo.

Directions

1. Discuss with students that a kimono was both officially and commonly worn until the end of the last century. Today the kimono is mostly worn only on special occasions such as New Year's Day and weddings, but other kimono variations like the cotton *Yukata* are still popular.*

2. Teacher will demonstrate watercolor techniques of working "wet on wet." Distribute materials and paint! Allow students to first apply water to large white paper before the cool or warm colors are used. What season might your kimono be worn in? That will influence the choice of colors used for the background. These kind of questions guide creativity.

3. When the paper has dried, encourage students to discover landscapes, waves, or even the Tanabata Bridge within the fluid colors of the watercolor. Remember those birds! Tell your story.

4. Assemble paper kimono with glue rather than thread!**

5. Display kimonos together. Feel free (with student participation) to embellish watercolor with poetry as thoughts flow!

---

* Japanese fashion today is as contemporary as any other in the modern world.

** Authentic kimonos are made of four equal-size cloth squares (for the body) and two for the sleeves (the inside of which serve as pockets!).

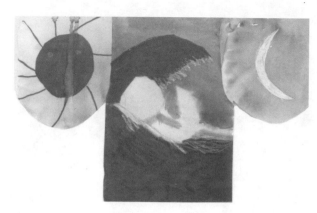

▲ Figure 1-36. Student-made kimono has important elements of moon, sun, air, and water. Note upper left top sleeve where paint has run. The teacher was wise to allow the "spontaneous" accident to remain—it is very much in keeping with Japanese thought. Imperfection is desirable. As one ancient scholar wrote, "I do not like the full moon in a cloudless sky."

▲ Figure 1-37. This young girl's kimono marks coming-of-age. Even sleeve length represents age, as does color—bright colors for kids!

◀ ▲ Figures 1-38 & 1-39. This scarf (note the folds) contains calligraphy above, along with a picture from world's first novel, *The Tale of Genji,* written by a courtly woman named Lady Murasaki Shikibu. It is a reproduction of the epic Japanese story. The maiden is shown in an abundantly layered kimono, typical of the period in which the novel was written. The teacher may be encouraged to use classic Japanese stories to motivate student kimono themes. **Note:** These ideas may be carried over into **horizontal scrolls,** which unfold *each* scene of the tale.

Figure 1-40. Our young student models a kimono that features the national flower of Japan—the chrysanthemum! ▶

Figure 1-41. This flock of Japanese girls is a beautiful and theatrical reminder of the Festival Arts of Japan, which often honor children. Don't these children look like the landing of little birds? ▼

ACTIVITY 10

Oh My Gosh, It's Suminagashi!

Marbleized Paper Technique/Printmaking: "Water Prints"

BONUS: JAPANESE LUNCHBOX LEARNING KIT!

It may surprise us to know that the artistically rich heritage of Japan was in utter isolation for hundreds of years. Not until the mid-nineteenth century—when U.S. Admiral Perry's black ships arrived in Yokohama harbor—did Japan open itself to the rest of the world. The strongest singular announcement of a unique creative vision was the Japanese print. Suddenly a beautiful distant culture appeared in elegant images throughout the Western culture. Nowhere were these exquisite prints better received than Paris, France—the worldly artistic epicenter—where appreciative master artists were forever influenced by fresh perspectives. Impressionism, Post-Impressionism, and the new art of photography all responded by assimilating Japanese artistic ideas: Japanese woodblock prints literally changed the history of modern art.

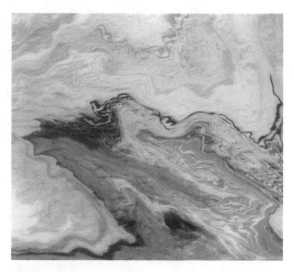

▲ Figure 1-42. Is it a great wave, or a sacred mountain? An oyster shell? Or is it simply—"surf's up!"

In addition to lively subjects, courtly scenes, nature studies, and theatrical portraits, Japanese themes attempted to capture the "fleeting moment." This important concept of life's transitory qualities is well expressed in the floating ink technique of suminagashi (sue-min-ah-gah-she). When you print from the surface of water, you have indeed captured the moment forever!

MATERIALS

- colored drawing inks or watercolors (Drawing inks, such as the Dr. Martin brand, are best)
- Photoflo 200™ (Kodak brand suggested—see Teacher Preparation)
- watercolor brushes (Of course, bamboo brushes are best here)
- block printmaking paper (substitute typing or photocopy paper)
- plastic trays with 2"–3" depth (two or three trays are great)
- drying rack (see Teacher Preparation)
- watercolor dish (Direction #1) or facsimile (i.e., watercolor cups)
- eyedropper
- rubber gloves
- tongs
- optional: coffee filters (white—any size) and other "experimental" papers if desired

TEACHER PREPARATION

To ensure success of this lesson, try to obtain suggested ink listed in "Materials." The use of Photoflo 200™ is essential to this activity; it separates the colors to make print patterns. **Note:** This is a *chemical* so *teacher* must supervise the mixing and wear rubber gloves. (Teacher should also read product label!)

Teacher will set up classroom with Suminagashi print station. **Note:** The number of trays will determine the number of students printing at the same time. Teacher may want to provide alternative "wait" activity, such as "practice" calligraphy on 3 × 5 cards.

DIRECTIONS

1. Teacher will assemble all materials on demonstration table as shown (brush stand optional).

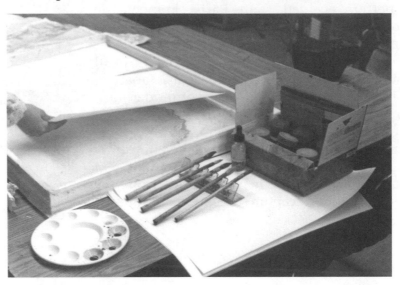

2. Teacher will use eyedropper to mix one or two drops of a colored ink with one drop of Photoflo 200™ in mixing tray. Mix a *different* color in each area of the mixing tray.

3. Touch surface of water with paintbrush that has been dipped in ink. Delicate contact with surface of water is important. Alternately use one brush and then the other. Note Ms. Choi's light touch as ripple effect takes place.

4. Mr. Dan takes over for a closer look at pattern that is now appearing on water's surface.

5. A small fan is made and used to help pattern flow.

6. Ms. Choi has plucked a single "magic" hair (Students may volunteer!) to further activate design interest before printing. Note how she pulls the hair directionally to create variety in surface patterns.

7. Printmaking begins with teacher demonstration! Paper has been gently floated on surface of water and carefully lifted as shown. (Also refer to Direction 1 phot;, note upper left.)

8. Allow finished print to dry in standard printmaking manner. Student partners may follow the same procedure as indicated.

9. Finished prints (Figure 1-42) will spontaneously suggest numerous subjects—often nature themes. Discuss student responses. For further applications of Suminagashi, see Bunko Box (Figure 1-43) . . . and use your own boundless imagination!

▲ Figure 1-43. Bunko is the Japanese word for letterbox. One would store writing materials—ink, brush, paper—in this beautiful, simple box. What could be a better way to apply your suminagashi—either inside the box, as stationery, or both. This is "noteworth"!

▲Figure 1-44. The basic calligraphy and drawing kit contains brush, ink stone, grinding stone, and bowl with tiny little spoon. Why not write a letter and/or draw a picture on your suminagashi! After all, they are entirely compatible.

B O N U S : JAPANESE LUNCH BOX LEARNING KIT

Japanese mothers are known as world-class caregivers, exemplified by their lunchbox preparation skill! It is therefore appropriate that we present teachers with the lunchbox learning concept—which may be used as a universal learning center activity. This box highlights Japanese heraldry—crests known as **mon** (kamon)—in the upper right corner. Center right and bottom shows the armor, a sword, and repoussé, "sword shields" of the Samurai. This idea respects the Japanese concept of compact and portable design and may be adapted as a teaching kit to any culture in this book. The kit is "teacher-made"; students may certainly develop their own!

▲ Figure 1-45. Japanese Lunch Box Learning Kit makes learning an art form!

The Emperor's Crown

"Sweet" Head-Dressings/Papercraft

▲ Figure 1-46. Joy is her name and joyful is this student-made Korean crown! The "surprise gems" are a sweet touch.

Korea is very close to China and Japan geographically, yet it has a distinct and age-old national identity. The Three Kingdoms—known as Silla, Paek-che, and Kogu-yo (37 B.C. – 668 A.D.)—form the foundation of Korea's history. In the Asian tradition of ruling dynasties, Korea throws its own dazzling Emperor hat in the ring!

Yes, Korea wears many hats. It was during the Silla Dynasty in the 6th century that certain elegant crowns appeared. Concurrently, Buddhism was introduced in Korea. Many believe that the Silla dynasty was unique in its Korean character; this era was not influenced greatly by China and Japan.

The Royal Crowns of the Silla Period were decorated with twisted gold wires and "magatama"—meaning "crooked beads." At the crown wearer's ears, long jeweled drops fell. This ornamentation was opulent, yet classic! An emphasis on simplicity and elegance characterizes Korean art. Ceramics, especially celadon, painting, costume design, and crafts all convey a plain, yet exquisite tradition. Korean art and design has an immediate appeal.

Korean art, like its Asian neighbors, is dictated by custom and traditional symbols—these are most evident in ceremonial attire and accessories. You will find stylized dragons, waves, flowers, birds, calligraphy, and a curious use of a treadmill to symbolize strong legs!

The colors most often seen are the Five Directional Colors of Chinese Cosmology: blue (east), white (west), black (north), red (south) and yellow (center). Strong color defines Korean design and will be recognized in its traditional national garment—the *Hanbok!* Stunning headgear tops it off!

MATERIALS

- 2" × 18" strips (assorted colors) of construction paper
- cereal, i.e., Cheerios® or Fruit Loops®, colored mints, marshmallows and/or strips of candy buttons (optional, but wonderful!)

- scissors
- crayons
- colored markers
- glue sticks
- stapler

TEACHER PREPARATION

Paper will need to be cut into strips ahead of time. One strip must be long enough to fit around the student's head, so be prepared to have some strips longer than 18 inches (or two strips can be cut and stapled together to fit). Examples of Korean traditional dress, including a traditional headdress, may be found in this activity and used for introduction for basic structure of (Silla) Emperor's/Empress's crown—which will likely be a compilation of styles. You might realize that European crowns and Korean crowns share a similar structure and appearance.

Teacher will want to have "grocery shelf treasures" on hand for the application of "jeweled" accents.

▲ Figure 1-47. Historically, marriages have been arranged by matchmakers. There is an old Korean saying that roughly translates this way . . . "A matchmaker of a satisfactory marriage is thanked with many gifts; a poor matchmaker is *not* thanked *three* times." Traditional costume is reserved for special occasions of festivity, especially the holidays, and New Year's Day, or Chu-sok (Harvest Moon).

Leo and Kathy are wearing authentic wedding costumes. The groom wears a blue ceremonial gown and a Black Scholar's hat. In ancient times, only court officials and scholars were allowed to wear this gown and hat. The bride wears a bridal gown (Hwal-ot), and a ceremonial hat (Hwa-gwan). Wealthier women's *Hwa-gwan* are made out of silk, gold, pearls, and precious stones.

DIRECTIONS

1. Discuss Korean costume, choice of color, and ornamental accents (your grocery shelf jewels). Ask students why a crown makes a person look important.

2. Give each student five paper strips. The student will decorate each strip using crayons, colored markers, and other miscellaneous material to create patterns, textures, and designs. Apply "jewels" accordingly. (**Note:** If colored paper strips seem likely to sag, reinforce back of strips with same-size paper or with tape.)

3. One paper strip is wrapped around the student's head and stapled (or taped) to form the main headband. The student then glues the other strips on from the front to the back and side to side. The other strips may be cut to form additional shapes such as those on other traditional Korean crowns or they may continue gluing from one side of crown to the other.

4. Students may want to borrow design variations on their crowns from the Scholar's hat and/or the Korean Bridal crown (note the pleasing and distinct elements of both in Figure 1-47). It's fine to improvise! Attach "ear drops" as indicated in Figure 1-46.

5. A royal class gathering of these sweet crowns is in order. How tasteful!

◄ Figure 1-48. Here is our teacher Ms. Choi, who is Korean-American, surrounded by a lucky court of third graders wearing traditional costumes. Look for student-made crowns mixed in!

ACTIVITY 12

How Now Pa Ndau?

"Flower Cloth" Paper Vests/Tribal Design

The Hmong (pronounced *mung*), an ancient tribe of "hill people," live in upper mountain regions of Laos, Thailand, and North Vietnam. In spite of seclusion from outside influences, Hmong women developed a beautiful household folk-art called Pa Ndau *(pond-owl)*. This evolving art form established a strong community tradition. Translated from oral history (Hmong did not keep written records), Pa Ndau means "flower cloth." It now may be a term used to refer to any textile decorated in a similar manner.

Pa Ndau designs are influenced by nature and have names such as Snailhouse, Star, Spiderweb, and Elephant Foot. There are also geometric shapes that virtually represent a textile garden! Hmong children are given black ceremonial vests that have horizontal strips of reverse appliqué, embroidery, and dangling gold coins to mark coming-of-age and that are worn only on special occasions. Pa Ndau is a wonderful "investment" in keeping culture alive.

MATERIALS

- black kraft paper (from roll)—substitute over-sized black construction paper if necessary
- oaktag
- white oil pastels
- craft foil—metallic gold or silver (substitute tin foil, if necessary)
- scissors
- yarn
- white glue
- reproducible page: Pa Ndau Designs

TEACHER PREPARATION

Teacher may want to create a "one size fits all" Hmong vest (pre-cut vests may be considered with very young and special needs groups). Teacher may also wish to pre-cut metallic foil into small squares to wrap around oaktag circles—these may also be pre-cut—to create "coin" decoration. Paper coins used in math activities can be substituted here. Precut lengths of yarn may

▲ Figures 1-49a & 1-49b. Simple design motif yields powerful visual results. Note the strong horizontal bands that typify Hmong designs. Snailhouse, Elephant's Foot, and Hearts are all embraced by an everyday culture that, in turn, embraces our children. Very good, very Hmong!

expedite activity. This is an integrated curriculum opportunity; symmetry in Hmong design relates to science (patterns in nature) and coins to basic math!

▲ Figure 1-50. Hmong cloth is actually a reverse appliqué technique. . . ("MOLA" . . . *see Section 7, Activity 7 . . . is a similar but not identical method.*) Does this remind you of an American quilt with its lyrical yet symmetrical pattern motif?—- and could that be a Dragon's Tail???!

DIRECTIONS

1. Doesn't everybody like to get dressed up for a special occasion? Introduce Hmong vests with a discussion about favorite outfits. How does it make you feel to wear them? Describe various costume details—drawn from your own experience and those apparent in clothing of the Hmong. Compare and contrast!

2. Distribute materials. Please note: White oil pastels are the most successful drawing material, yet they are very soft and "consumable." Substitute with white crayons if indicated by teacher's own supply availability.

3. Students will design their vests by first drawing horizontal bands, in which designs will be placed. If students' skill can manage it, traditional Hmong design asks for symmetry. Provide students with the reproducible page, Pa Ndau Designs, for a reference when creating their designs.

4. Attach coins with yarn. Glue under horizontal bands.

5. The completed vests provide the perfect photo opportunity for our arts community!

◄ Figure 1-51. The artroom tribe! So proud of their handiwork. Traditional Hmong vests are embroidered on black velvet to signify "coming of age"—this youthful group is our kindergarten!

B O N U S : ADORABLE CAMBODIAN ADORNMENT AND DANCE MEDALLION

Why not continue with costume design and create a simple Cambodian medallion? Cambodia is the next-door neighbor to Laos and Viet Nam.

The Cambodian art of adornment can enhance the Hmong vest and help capture the characteristic form of Cambodian performing arts. One way to celebrate Cambodia's art treasures—in this case, costume pieces that are gold leafed, jeweled, and intricately carved—is to try a "faux" carving. You will need gold doilies—apply small pieces of gold doily to a precut, shaped board weight paper, and decorate, using symmetrical application. The adornment, representative of those that appear in Cambodian dance costume, can be taped to shirt or blouse, or added to a Hmong vest! "Armor" pieces may be made with these super-supermarket gold treasure doilies! If you are "highly" motivated, create the "temple tower" headdress—they look much like South East Asian temples! Do both, and you have a bit of Cambodian art, dance, and architecture!

▲ Figure 1-52. Cambodian medal.

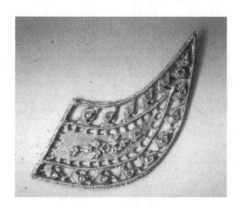

▲ Figure 1-53. Cambodian armor— Wings!

▲ Figure 1-54. Cambodian headdress.

PA NDAU DESIGNS

Elephant's foot

Pinwheel snailhouses

Sunshine and circles

Broken hearts

Africa

North
Atlantic

Black Sea

France

Spain

Turkey

MOROCCO

Canary Islands
(SPAIN)

Mediterranean Sea

Tunisia

Iraq

Iran

**WESTERN
SAHARA**

Algeria

Libya

EGYPT

Saudi Arabia

MALI

Mauritania

Niger

Red Sea

Yemen

Senegal

Chad

Sudan

Djibouti

Gambia

BENIN

Guinea
Bissau

Guinea

NIGERIA

Somalia

Sierra
Leone

GHANA

Cameroon

Central
African Republic

Uganda

Ethiopia

Liberia

Togo

KENYA

Ivory
Coast

GABON

Democratic
Republic
of Congo

Indian Ocean

Congo

Rwanda

Cabinda
(ANGOLA)

Burundi

South Atlantic

Tanzania

Malawi

Angola

Zambia

Zimbabwe

Mozambique

Namibia

Botswana

Madagascar

South Africa
(Walvis Bay)

Swaziland

SOUTH AFRICA

Lesotho

Africa

A message of hope from South Africa. This Zulu love letter is made of small beads that convey a specific message through color and shape.

NIGERIA/BENIN

KENYA

GHANA

MALI

GABON

SAHARA/WODOABE

EGYPT

NORTH AFRICA

On the Savannah and in the plains, lion is still king!

ART ACTIVITIES FOR BECOMING CULTURE SMART

Activity 1
Oba and the Queen Mother: Benin Bronze (Nigeria/Benin)
"Bronze" Portraits/Metal Tooling Repousse

Activity 2
An African Story Cloth: The Fun of Fon (Nigeria/Benin)
Appliqué Banners

Activity 3
Animal Talking Box Safari! (Kenya)
"African Story Boxes"
BONUS: AFRICAN STORYTELLER HATS

Activity 4
The Language of Kente Cloth (Ghana)
Paper Craft

Activity 5
The Mudcloth of Mali: Can You Resist? (Mali)
Fabric Resist

Activity 6
The Guardians of Gabon: Bakota Protective Sculpture (Gabon)
"Additive" Assemblage

Activity 7
About Face!: African Facial Mystique Unmasked (Sahara/
  Wodoabe)
Portrait Collage
BONUS: FLIPPING OUT FOR AFRICAN MASKS!

Activity 8
Meet My People: Ancestral Screens (Nigeria)
Mixed Media Assemblage

Activity 9
My Personal Walking Stick: Royal Regalia
Paper Craft
BONUS: WALKING POUCH

Activity 10
Eternally Yours, Egypt: Splendid Temple Tablets (Egypt)
"Panel" Painting
BONUS: PRINT YOUR MAGIC GOLD CARTOUCHE!

Activity 11
Hands Across Africa: Reaching Beyond Morocco (North Africa)
"Henna" Hand Painting/Decorative Body Art
BONUS: HANDS OF PEACE MOBILE

To know the Art of Africa . . . . .

. . . . . *is to realize that* it was on the continent of Africa that human life began, a fact supported by archaeological discovery. Rock painting and engraving in the mountainous Sahara regions and elsewhere on the African landscape reveal a wide scope of subject and style. Africa is an expansive continent with diverse geography, climate, culture, and spiritual belief. The diversity is reflected in art production—from Morocco, Egypt, and Sudan to the southern edge of the Sahara and the countries of Mauritania, Mali, Burkina Faso, Niger, and Chad. Africa north of the Sahara is primarily Islamic. In the sub-Saharan region, naturalistic beliefs honor cosmological forces, spiritual gods, and the ancestors. There is a presence of Christianity from European contact. The practice of art is born of honor, belief, and societal tradition; individual expression is marked by originality, mastery of craft, and the efficacy of object.

Ancient African arts were a rich source for the themes and methods that would later emerge. In ancient Nigeria, the *Nok* culture produced terra-cotta heads that may have forecast an evolution of royal portrait heads, dance masks, a visual language of geometric abstraction, and a preeminence in sculpture production. Great kingdoms such as Ghana, Mali, Yoruba, Songhai, and Dahomey, brought forth great African art. The Republic of Benin (c. 1100) produced commemorative portrait heads for its kings (*Oba*) and queens (*Iyoba*) that were naturalistic in appearance and cast in bronze with technical expertise. Although far less abstract than the whole of African art, the Benin bronzes suggested the idea of the head as the dwelling place for wisdom and as the container of the soul. African ideology is based upon life forces, expressed through simple, yet awesome, means; art is a vehicle for conveyance of ideas.

African art history has been carved in sculpture. Sub-Saharan Africa has often been identified as the art-producing region, although art is created throughout Africa. The sculptural objects, carved from the readily available wood of this forested western region, have indeed resounded with great authority and influence worldwide. The African carved art of masks, objects, and figures is purposeful, an aesthetic intended primarily for ceremony—as in dance— and for observance of ancestral devotion. Masks are designed to dance within the context of accompanying costume ornamentation, as well as to move to music and drumbeat; the display of masks was not an initial African concern. Masks and figures allow the occupation of mythological and spiritual ideas. Many statues are found at ancestral altars—for protection and to evoke guardianship. African dimensional art utilized a mixture of materials, creatively and intentionally. Mirrors, for example, are considered a means to deter evil; metal-iron use has particular connection with certain spiritual forces. The forms of African art are so direct and forceful that they will arrest the eye of any viewer, and meanings are often as complex as the mask structures themselves. African art delivers a symbolization of beauty through reduction and abstraction. The geometric simplification developed in African dimensional art interacts dramatically with the surrounding space; visual rhythms and sensations created by jutting angles bring to mind another distinctive art from African sources—jazz. African sculpture evokes further rhythmic activity through surface texture, animated patterning, and selective exaggeration. The subjects presented in sculpture, screens, royal stool sculpture, and drums generally conform to themes: seated couples, mothers and children, twins, equestrians, and sometimes "foreigners," or strangers. Animals are, of course, an important and constant theme.

African art and design extend to textile production, gold casting, metal work, and architecture. The mud mosques of Mali strongly align with repetitive attributes found in the region's Dogon masks. The patterned Islamic art motifs of North Africa and the ancient funerary art of Egypt show the connection between the everyday and spiritual worlds. One of the greatest strengths of African artistic expression—personified in the mask carving—is the ability to make physical and tangible the forces of the unseen, imagined worlds. This vitality of vision was not lost on Picasso and Braque, who experienced its impact and immediacy with their development of Cubism and Western modern art. African art has shaped European, Caribbean, North American, and South American cultures.

Akua-ba (pronounced Ah-Kwah-bah) is the doll carried by West African women in a wrap at the small of the back, just as a real baby would be placed. Akuaba is hoped to ensure the birth of a wise and beautiful child. Notice the similarity between akuaba shape and the "ankh," the Egyptian symbol for life.

ACTIVITY 1

Oba and the Queen Mother: Benin Bronze

"Bronze" Portraits/Metal Tooling Repousse

▲ Figure 2-1. The Queen Mother, also known as Iyoba, wears a pointed conical headdress. This cropped student "portrait bronze" focuses on her face and head itself. In ancient Benin society, the head was believed to hold the mystical powers of the person's soul.

The great kingdom of Benin ruled in full glory for hundreds of years. This royal empire—located in the land now known as Nigeria—engaged in world trade, with Portugal in particular. Benin, a great art-producing region, was just as grand as any European court, and was a major city-state. The culture itself dates back to one of the oldest known African sculptural traditions, known as *Nok* (500 B.C.). The ancient Nok custom of terra-cotta sculptural heads may indicate an early source for what would become, a thousand years later, a world-class art form: Benin portrait sculptures.

The imperial choice for the royal art of Benin was bronze. In this mighty society, the king, known as *Oba*, and the Queen Mother, *Iyoba*, would have their likeness cast in bronze using a highly technical lost wax method. The bronze casters—who were guild members—were forbidden by threat of death to create commemorative heads of any personage other than the appointed rulers! However, guards, warriors, and court attendants could be depicted in statues and plaques.

Females most often appear in Queen Mother Iyoba sculpture wearing "chicken beak" style headdresses. You will find Queen Mother heads with pointed crowns that extend into classic braids below; these frame Iyoba's face, while many bands define her long neck. When seen in a bronze plaque, Iyoba is often noted for her talent in diplomatic matters. As for the chicken symbol, according to African legend, the first *Oni*—the spiritual king of neighboring *Yoruba* people—created the earth by using sixteen chickens to scratch it up from the sea! Earthly rulers, male or female, clearly possess extraordinary land and sea powers, symbolized by diverse creatures from the humble scratchy chicken to the majestic leopard. Look for these representations of the many magnificent forms of Benin bronze!

◀ Figure 2-2. The King, or Oba, is most often seen wearing a crown that is low fitting to the brow. Shown here is a "bronze" interpretation of a famous Benin ivory crest head, topped by a circle of side-by-side Portuguese miniature figures. Mudfish may also be seen in decoration to signify the power of the Oba, realized by the awesome electrical charge they deliver! Water deities were worshipped during the reign of various Obas, so they may also appear in plaques and statue motifs.

MATERIALS

- 9" × 12" lightweight tooling "bronze" sheet (substitute brass, aluminum, etc.) per student
- orange sticks (manicure sticks)
- magazines
- newsprint
- steel wool
- erasers
- pencils
- heavy-duty scissors for cutting metal sheets
- masking tape
- black permanent ink (nontoxic)
- butcher paper

TEACHER PREPARATION

The teacher will cut the "bronze" sheets (or substitute any other metallic art tooling foil) into convenient 9" × 12" sizes for each student. The newsprint should be cut to the same size as the copper sheets to allow the students to trace their pictures directly from the newsprint onto the "bronze." Magazines or newspapers will serve as padding for tooling.

DIRECTIONS

1. Discuss the history and information about ancient Benin bronzework. Show examples and have students identify the symbols used in the artwork and discuss the significance. Do the leaders appear worthy of their important position? Describe qualities that portraits and postures convey.

2. Students will draw ideas about their own ancestral leaders—real or imaginary. What symbols would be used to identify this leader? Draw ideas on newsprint in pencil. Draw large and fill the paper!

Figure 2-3. Warriors, messengers, and attendants served the Obas who were, for a time, the most powerful men in the world! Plaques such as this student-produced detail covered grand palace architecture, demonstrating strength and mighty rule. Statues were chiefly ceremonial. Bronze heads, used as ancestral pieces, were produced between the late 15th century and 19th century. Individual features reveal the period in which the bronze was cast; these are the Early, Middle, or Late periods of great Benin bronze. ▶

3. Students will place their drawing on top of the "bronze" sheet and tape the edges to keep the paper from slipping. Now place the bronze with attached drawing on top of a magazine (the magazine acts as a pad).

4. Demonstrate how to use the orange stick to tool the "bronze," pressing into the lines of the image. Show how to make various textures, patterns, and relief areas.

5. Interpret the demonstrated technique. When finished, remove newsprint.

6. To *antique* the "bronze," paint over the entire sheet with black ink. When dry, use steel wool to scratch away excess ink. Ink will remain in the grooves and indentations, while a small residual amount will provide the raised surface with an ancient look.

7. When finished, mount the plaques on butcher paper—or wooden pillars as did Oba and Iyoba—to adorn the school. Your school is your palace!

▲ Figure 2-4. The leopard is the single most important animal associated with Oba, with its characteristics of speed and prowess. Oba is referred to as leopard for possessing extreme qualities of divine power. Student-made; glazed ceramic.

ACTIVITY 2

An African Story Cloth: The Fun of Fon

Appliqué Banners

Fon story banners and hanging cloths are pictorial history lessons. Both legends and actual events are represented in colorful symbols, which are specific and recognizable. The origin of this bright appliqué is Dahomey, a dynasty found within the Republic of Benin. The lively animals, figures, ships, and birds are all parts of Dahomey history. Children still learn from these cloth pages! Boats tell of Portuguese sailing ships, buffalo may symbolize a specific king, while fish with teeth recall a monarch with the ferocity of the predatory shark. The indigo pot (resembling a mortar and pestle) represents an old story, one with the intrigues of a Shakespearean drama!

Dahomey story cloths may appear as banners in vertical or horizontal shapes—or in a rectangular shape, not unlike a quilt. Traditionally, the appliquéed cloths have gold or black backgrounds with black, red, yellow, and white figures. However, tourism influenced banner appearance. Bright colors have grown brighter and fierce animals more friendly! The story cloth symbols indicate sayings that are immediately recognizable to those who are familiar with the history of this region. "The fish that escapes the net will not be caught again" is one such lesson, shown by a fish and corresponding net symbol. Many other equally wise and humorous quotes, such as "a buffalo wearing clothing is hard to disrobe," appear in Fon banners. Legends, sayings, and proverbs pop up in many African textiles; Fon banners or Dahomey cloths are especially colorful and pictorial in their own dazzling way.

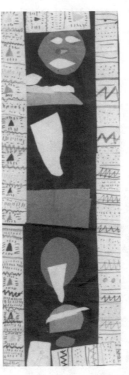 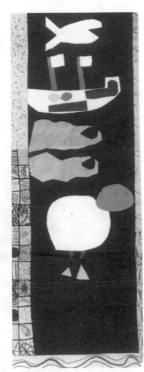

Figure 2-5 (left). Student paper appliqué banner, Fon-style. Simple abstract shapes tell an original story, offset by energetic patterned borders. Could that be a Sky King rising above a sea of clouds? There's always an inside story when it comes to art!

Figure 2-6 (right). The pictorial shapes that appear in Fon story cloths were once as recognizable as alphabet letters—all had a particular tale to tell. Here, as always, the story will change with the storyteller!

MATERIALS

- various colors of felt (squares of colored paper may be substituted)
- 2' × 6" black felt (or black construction paper)
- needles and thread (sufficient for class size)
- white glue
- markers and crayons (for use on paper banners)

TEACHER PREPARATION

Teacher will want to decide whether felt (recommended) or paper will suit classroom needs. Prepare for sewing activity as you would do normally. Threadless felt banners are another option. Use white or fabric glue. All are generically "appliqué." Cut lengths and squares will expedite your lesson. **Note:** Energetic teachers may wish to produce a mock Fon banner example in advance of class as indicated by visual in Figure 2-7. Use of traditional Dahomey symbols is encouraged if only as a point of reference. Vertical banners (as shown in Figures 2-5 and 2-6) are popular.

◄ Figure 2-7. Aishatu and Jeremiah, both lively storytellers, display a beautiful example of a big Fon story banner also known as Dahomey story cloth. For many years past, Fon handicrafts abounded under the dynasty of eleven Dahomey kings. Magnificent artwork was produced in the kings' courts: state banners and cloths, wall hangings, festival tents, hats, umbrellas, and more! Symbols were heraldic as well as legendary. Today, crafts-people may be found applying old patterns in inventive ways, some still sitting in what was once the royal palace of a king!

DIRECTIONS

1. Discuss the various ways a story is told: through books, by word of mouth, and through pictures. Ask students what traditions are carried out in their family to keep memories alive.

2. Consider the tradition of the Fon banner and what it may mean to the Dahomey (Benin) culture. Show students the various Fon symbols and allow time for them to attach a meaning to each symbol. At the end of discussion, tell students the perceived meaning of each symbol.

3. Students will begin by cutting various symbols out of colored felt (or paper) that they will use to tell their story. Consider traditional colors and strong contrasts. Encourage students to cut directly—to dive right in! Ask students to think about telling details such as teeth, spiky hair, and fur—pointy objects as opposed to friendly ones—and how these will serve the meaning of their tale.

4. Before gluing or sewing, give students a chance to consider sequence. Affix symbols to surface.

5. The finished Fon banners will be hung in honor of tradition. Upon completion, you have an oversized African history book. Students should tell tales in their own voices. Sayings, especially original ones, will be appreciated! *"The bright banner thrills the eye."*

Figure 2-8. Fact or fiction? Dahomey story cloth banners give us facts that have all the flair of a lively historical novel! Fanciful creatures and objects have specific meanings. Here's a quick guide, top to bottom.

There are more Fon banner symbols than those pictured here, and many more ways to receive them!

Bird and Drum "The chief is a great male bird . . . announced by the beating of the drum." ▶

"Mortar and Pestle with Antique Iron" (seen sideways) is actually **Overturned Indigo Pot with Flint.** The flint is likened in pronunciation to the name of a King who caused his mother-in-law's death while she was dyeing cloth! ▶

Net and Fish are taken to mean that "the fish who escapes the net will not be caught again" in direct regard to the harrowing escape of a 17th-century African King from the clutches of an enemy. ▶

The Boar (shown here without a customary sword) is associated with Fon King Akaba. ▶

Sailing Ship is quite specific since it marks the beginning of trade between the Fon people of Africa and Europe in the 18th century. ▶

Buffalo Wearing Tunic—"Buffalo wearing clothes is hard to disrobe" is a historical reminder of an 18th-century Fon king whose brothers tried to dethrone him by filling his clothes with poisonous leaves. ▶

Lion—A 19th-century Fon king quote "I am the lion who 'sews' terror as soon as teeth are grown." ▶

Shark and the Egg tells us of 17th-century King Behanzin, who tried to resist a coastal attack by the French. Shark, a fierce water animal, signifies this king's valiant efforts; the egg beneath the shark is a visual metaphor that may represent earthly matters, yet—as in all Fon symbols—it begs creative interpretation. ▶

ACTIVITY 3

Animal Talking Box Safari!

"African Story Boxes"

BONUS: AFRICAN STORYTELLER HATS

▲ Figure 2-9. This fine bird firmly grips the sun as delivery begins to its proper place in the sky. Birds have many meanings in stories, mythologies, and in overall belief. In the Pacific Northwest, North America, it is the "trickster" Raven who steals daylight from the box in which it is kept to give it to all the people. African birds are often considered magical messengers between Earth and heaven. To fly is an extraordinary attribute that is also deeply tied to the achievement of human freedom.

In a universal way, we might all be considered African—does that surprise you? This idea comes from a widely-held belief that Africa is the place where life as we know it began. While theories may support this idea, we do know one thing for sure: All cultures on Earth have time-honored stories about how things started and the way living creatures shaped our world.

The formation of the sky, earth, and sea—the appearance of the sun, moon, and stars—have been explained by the roles that animals played in often-fanciful tales. We may think about the story of Noah's ark. Other stories describe how daylight came to Earth, and how many creatures great and small, from spiders to lions, helped to orchestrate the event! These stories have endless versions that are changed by the places in which they are told, and by who tells them. They feature basic characters. Some stories, known as **trickster** tales, have common themes. From the vast Serengeti Plain of Africa to the frozen ice floes of the Arctic, we can find a story that tells us that daylight has been stored in a box! The sun then requires release! Who can do it? Usually it is the mischievous, crafty fellow—the "trickster" who becomes the catalyst in this universal drama.

Tricksters are often monkeys, spiders . . . or even birds. Usually it is the nature of the animal that suggests its role. You may meet a Sky King through a messenger bird or a brave and clever mouse. Animals may even have had the ability to talk in these old stories, passed down through generations of oral history. They possess as much life and charm today as they had . . . *"so many, many rains ago."*

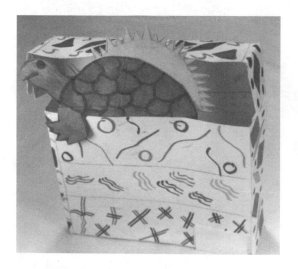

◄ Figure 2-10. Turtle may be a slow-moving creature, but surely one who knows the Earth! The shape of the turtle's shell provides a perfect fit for the sun! When Turtle appears on African walking sticks (see Activity 9), there is assurance of good health. At one time, Native American people believed that the whole world was formed on the back of a turtle shell.

MATERIALS

- 9″ × 12″ and 12″ × 18″ oaktag (large size for box, small for animal)
- rulers
- glue
- colored markers
- scissors

TEACHER PREPARATION

The teacher may want to borrow children's books that fall into the category of origin or creation myths, also known as "how" and "why" stories. Books will provide an immediate reference for students; additionally, teachers are encouraged to develop an ongoing animal picture reference file. Old calendars, magazines, and postcards that bear images of animals (preferably in their natural habitat) are a "basic" art classroom aid for this lesson, and for many others to follow.

The device of a *story box* that holds daylight is an important universal story idea. This lesson will be based on a pop-up style "book-box" (Figures 2-9 and 2-10). Teacher may want to assemble box form in relation to individual student needs. "The way the story goes" is at the teacher's discretion. In other words, select a real story, such as *The First Morning* or *Ananzi the Spider,* or ask students to create their own myth. "Teacher as storyteller"—reading stories to the students—can only bring pleasure before and during the lesson!

---

*S.O.S. (SAVE OUR SCHEDULE, i.e., "Schedule Saver" or shortcut) . . . Teacher may purchase (or save) plain boxes which can still tell tales without the box-making step.

DIRECTIONS

1. Teacher will introduce lesson with either a selected story or a *story starter.* Here are suggestions for students' own stories:

   "A long time ago, when the sky was always blue and the earth was covered with green grass . . ."

   "Many, many rains ago . . ."

   "Long ago, when the animals could talk . . ."

   "Long ago, when the heavens would send down rain and the Earth would soak it all up . . ."

2. The development of the story will be illustrated with the African paper box construction.

▲ Figure 2-11. How did the zebra get its stripes? Can a leopard lose its spots? Good questions to "jump start" a story box! These zebras roam freely on the plains of Africa, their home. The silhouettes of *wildebeests,* also known as *Gnu,* are behind them, another African animal that travels in herds. It is a quiet moment. Yet, if, in the next "scene," a prowling lion should appear . . . my, how things could change!

3. Make a box pattern (see diagram) and trace it onto 12″ × 18″ white oaktag.

4. Cut tabs and crease box on dotted lines.

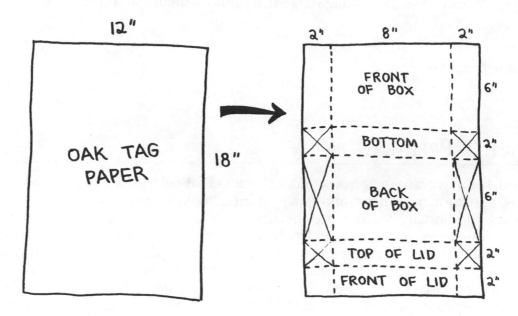

5. Using a 12″ ruler, students divide box shape into linear sections.

6. Students use markers to create an African linear pattern design. Using a limited color scheme can sometimes produce visually dramatic results.

7. Assemble box (see diagram) and glue tabs together.

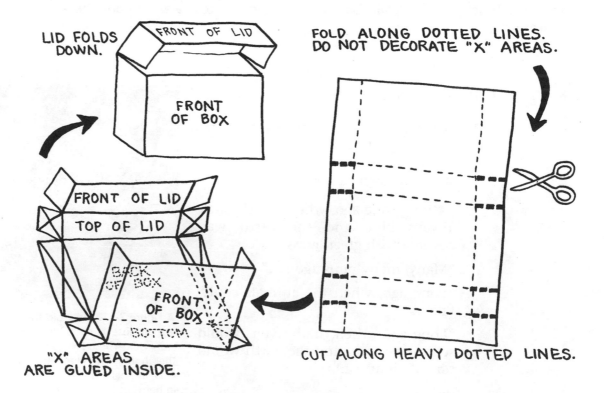

8. Students will want to consider the attributes of the animal they select to illustrate their story and its role in the selected tale, which may be as simple as the answer to "who let the sun out of the box?" According to "The First Morning" . . . Rooster is a good choice!

9. Make a cut paper animal that students have selected to represent to fit inside the box out of 9″ × 12″ white oaktag and decorate with markers. The animal should be carrying sun, moon, or stars in a telling way. **Remind** students that the box is the book and is also the container of the tale!

10. These colorful boxes will certainly illuminate your art classroom! Display the dazzling array in any manner that best tells your story.

BONUS: AFRICAN STORYTELLER HATS

To tell your story, each child may want to wear a **storyteller hat** while he or she holds the important title of *griot* (gree-oh)—the African word for the honorable position of *storyteller.*

The griot keeps the tribal history alive and passes it down from generation to generation. The oral history of a people told in stories, songs, and proverbs is as important as a written one. Dynamic African patterns that symbolize the natural world can do more for a story than words, and can speak volumes when they decorate a hat, a container, a drum, or calabash!

All you need for a storyteller hat is paper plates, oaktag, or other stiff paper for a band. Cut the paper in a manner that provides tabs to attach band to top. The inspiration for your designs will come from African fabric pattern motifs, story ideas, and the imagination!

African proverbs are plentiful and are often represented by the symbols found in patterns. You may want to carry this idea over in the storyteller hat design.

▲ Figure 2-12. As any storyteller knows, the one who wears the hat tells the tale! Hats, caps, and crowns are a clear means to signify specific roles and status. In Africa, storytelling is a highly interactive process, using a "call and response" method. Stories are intended for telling, embellishing, and traveling! Like Spider of the *Anansi* trickster tales, we weave them so they can go from here to there! Then, as Jeremiah the Storyteller would say, "When elbow bends, story ends." Try that statement for classroom group-story closure.

ACTIVITY 4

The Language of Kente Cloth

Paper Craft

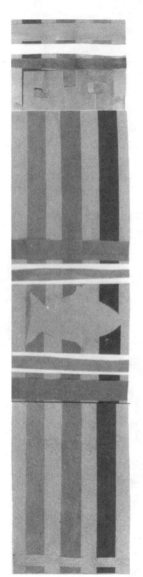

Kente cloth today has an immediate and recognizable association with African art and society. Its origins are with the Ashanti people of Ghana in West Africa. Traditionally, Kente cloth is a brightly colored narrow-weave technique of dynamic patterns that often have proverbial meanings. Specific colors are used—sunny yellows, lively reds, and vivid greens—in bold combinations.

Garments made of Kente cloth have been historically associated with royalty and status, although use is now wider and more popular among Africans as well as Americans! The construction of Kente clothing is unique: It is formed of bands that are woven, traditionally by men, on portable strip-weaving looms. Kente cloth, when worn by men, is wrapped around the body, then passed over the left shoulder, much like a toga. Women's Kente clothing is assembled as smaller wrap-around cloths that form a two- or three-piece outfit. Cloth may also serve as a headwrap or as a comfy sling to carry a baby!

The quality of the cloth itself may range from silk or even gold thread, which is associated with royalty and courtly attendants, to the more common cotton or cotton blend. Both the Ashanti and neighboring Ewe (a'-wa) societies are distinct in both their ceremonial and everyday use of Kente cloth, although appearance may vary. Either way, Kente cloth is a brilliant language of pattern, design, and texture—symbolized by personal and social meaning. The tradition of Kente is as proud as the people it represents—the word *Kente* itself is a statement of strength and has been noted to mean that "whatever happens . . . it (Kente) will not tear."

◀ Figure 2-13. Our paper Kente strip cloth emphasizes the vertical shape of the long band which—if it were the actual woven cloth strip that inspires our interpretation—could readily be joined to other strips to form a garment. This Kente activity asks for bright, contrasting colors and mindful placement of personal symbols. Could an original legend or saying be implied? How about, *"Smart fish swim far away from frisky kittens!"*

MATERIALS

- 6" × 18" assorted colored paper
- 6" × 6" assorted colored paper
- 1" × 18" strips of assorted colored paper
- pencils
- glue
- scissors

▲ Figure 2-14. This dazzling length of Kente from Ghana, West Africa, seems to have a life of its own. African history reveals that Kente patterns with specific names were "owned" by the Paramount Chief who could dictate its right of use. Kente was not unlike a "coat-of-arms."

TEACHER PREPARATION

It would be ideal to have on hand an example of actual Kente cloth or a printed version, such as wrapping paper or reasonable facsimile. Since Kente has become widely known and quite fashionable, a closer examination of the woven cloth and its multiple pattern vocabulary should be artistically stimulating! Again, tourism and import needs have affected Kente production . . . so remember, the Kente of Ashanti kings is not the same as the Kente of the marketplace! Nevertheless, all have a measure of artistic merit.

DIRECTIONS

1. Discuss with students the various characteristics and uses of Kente cloths from West African cultures. Note how they are woven on very thin looms and sewn together to create larger fabric pieces which are then used to make clothing. When discussing the Kente cloth, special notice should be taken of the symbols that are shown on the cloth and how each symbol is directly related to the wearer. Pattern, color, and vertical and horizontal lines are emphasized to the students. (See Figures 2-13 to 2-17.)

2. Distribute materials. Students may glue the 1″ × 18″ strips of paper onto the 6″ × 18″ paper in vertical and horizontal bands to create a "faux" weaving.

3. When this has been completed, the idea of Kente symbolism can be used to motivate the students to create their own personal symbols. Are you a cat person? If so, a mouse or fish would be nice!

4. Students should draw and cut out simple outline shapes of their symbols on the back of the 6″ × 6″ paper squares. These shapes are then glued onto the "faux" weavings at approximately 6″ intervals.

5. Assemble each student's finished project together into one large Kente cloth! As an "extra" for this project, students can write on the back of their Kente what each symbol stands for and how it relates to their own life.

▲ Figure 2-15. Art teacher Joyce Mathers proudly displays her students' work, on exhibit for all to see. She has employed a paper weaving method that acknowledges Kente as a woven process. Individual student "weavings" have been joined together in the spirit of Kente!

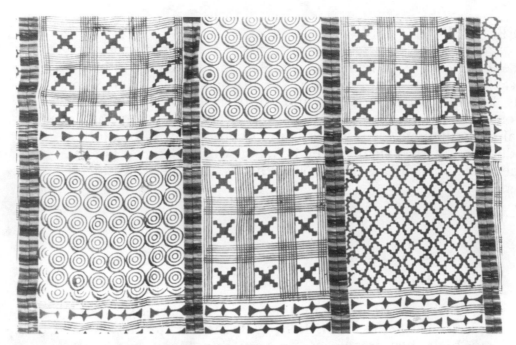

▲ Figure 2-16. Africa is a source of many striking textiles, so it is helpful to note their distinctive classifications. The stamp-printed symbols hold a codified meaning in this cloth from Ghana called **Adinkra.** In spite of its woven bands, Adinkra is *not* a form of Kente cloth. Customarily, Adinkra is used for somber occasions such as funerals; Adinkra, in fact, means *farewell.* Another well-known cloth with a similar-sounding name is called **Adire.** It is identified by its indigo blue color and crafted by the Yoruba people of Nigeria. Learning to compare and contrast these wonderful textiles—upon recognizing their unique characteristics—is both educationally and artistically rewarding!

◄ Two young girls proudly display their African heritage through their costumes and their smiles.

Figure 2-17. Kente does indeed speak a visual language. Can you find the "broken pottery" pattern or "centipede" in this piece? Many such descriptive terms are used to define the intricate Kente weaving motifs. ▶

ACTIVITY 5

The Mudcloth of Mali: Can You Resist?

Fabric Resist

It's hard to imagine a place on earth more visually stunning than Mali, West Africa. Here, as in the surrounding regions, art seems to be everywhere! Walls of family homes, which are made of clay or mud, are hand-painted by women wearing garments of fabulous patterns and colors. The design motifs are spectacular: They combine the natural world of animal and plant patterns with dynamic geometric forms. Earthen surfaces are brought to life by the powerful shapes and colors that emblazon them.

House decoration—like fabric decoration—is a community affair! Distinctive motifs of criss-cross bands, linear zig-zags, curvy arabesques, dot systems, and oppositional diamonds are applied by women. A great specialty of the region is bold mudcloth painting. The technique is a specific mud-resist technique which requires a sequenced process that women learn from generation to generation. It is the men who first weave the cloth that village women will then transform into exceptional abstract textiles.

How do they do it? The recipe goes something like the following. The cloth is spread on the ground. A dye, which is made from boiling the bark of the *wolo* tree and the leaves of the *n'golama* tree, is then painted onto the cloth with a *toothbrush.* After it has dried in the sun, the women wash the cloth, and the *mud* process begins. A coating of gray-black mud is added on the top of the pattern which has been drawn with the toothbrush. It is then washed and dried again. This process is repeated two more times until the final pattern is pitch black. After a final wash, the fabric is ready to be worn or sold. As in any artistic process, the outcome will reveal the originality of those who create it—whether the final product is a lovely mudcloth garment or the dazzling earthen wall of an African dwelling.

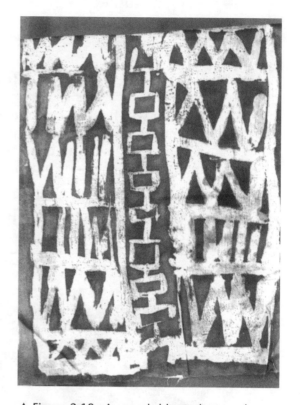

▲ Figure 2-18. A remarkable student-made mudcloth is reminiscent of an architectural facade you might encounter in the West Sudan region where the Dogon people live—and where Mali still stands today. In this region, architecture, textile, mask . . . all share a kind of African-Arabic geometry that is stunning to the eye!

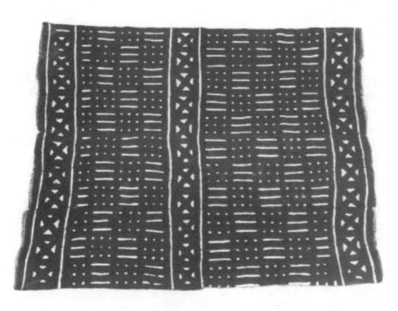

◄ Figure 2-19. Actual mudcloth, made in Africa. Note how the articulated darks and lights keep the surface rhythmically alive.

MATERIALS

- unbleached muslin
- flour
- permanent non-toxic black ink
- toothbrushes
- wax paper

- flour and water
- charcoal drawing sticks
- examples of mudcloth design (see Teacher Preparation)

TEACHER PREPARATION

Teacher will have to cut one length of cloth per student (size is teacher's discretion). A mixture of "mud" must be made by mixing flour and water to a thick creamy consistency and then adding the black ink until the flour mixture turns black (not gray). A demonstration sample, made by Teacher—or purchased fabric example—is recommended.

---

*S.O.S. (SAVE OUR SCHEDULE, i.e., "Schedule Saver" or shortcut) . . . See Figure 2-21.

◀ Figure 2-20. Student mudcloth patterns literally dance before us!

DIRECTIONS

1. Show examples of mudcloth. Tell students that it is made in a country called Mali in the continent of Africa that is famous for its art and architecture. We will be creating our own Mali-style mudcloth using a similar technique, but with "fake" mud!

2. Ask students to practice creating designs for their mudcloth using design motifs similar to those found in the examples. Pick a favorite design to transfer to the cloth.

3. Students will draw their designs on the cloth with charcoal drawing sticks. When finished, place the cloth onto the wax paper to prevent the "mud" from soaking through to the table.

4. The student will then paint the "mud" onto the drawn lines. Set cloth aside to dry.

5. When the cloth has dried, the "mud" can be easily washed out using plain water. Another coat of "mud" can be applied while the cloth is still wet and set out to dry again. After the second application, the mud is washed out and left to dry. **Note:** To save time, only one application of mud can be painted on the cloth. This layer does not have to be washed out. It looks quite nice and has an interesting texture as is.

6. When finished, the cloth could be used for many other projects, such as creating African costumes for dolls or puppets, wrapping the cloth around the figures in the traditional manner. They also are beautiful pieces of art in their own right and can be hung and displayed. Mudcloth may also be considered to cover pillows or to adorn a picture frame. The mud is the message!

▲ Figure 2-21. This S.O.S. activity will allow a "crayon resist" paper "fabric" method when the more traditional process cannot be readily employed. It is simple, effective . . . and, yes, "personal", since the motif is based on repetition, of the student's own initials! As you may note, the letters "K.M." comprise a horizontal mirror design format. Paper may first be folded in half lengthwise, then folded in opposite direction(s)—twice or three times—to create "design unit" rectangles (optional). Black crayon is recommended for borders, letters, and linear boundaries. Sections should be used to contain a variety of directly applied marks and linear design in crayon. Watercolor paint may then be engaged. Vary colors. Use simple patterns . . . the results speak for themselves!

The Guardians of Gabon: Bakota Protective Sculpture

"Additive" Assemblage

▲ Figure 2-22. Consider this heart-shaped sculptural figure for its dynamic use of the features of the human face! Where are the eyes? The marks for the cheeks? Are the "wings" that surround the head actually serpents? It is rich with meaning in the unique manner of African art!

The history of African art, it could be said, is "written in sculpture." Objects of enormous visual power have contributed to world art appreciation. The terms of African sculpture have both artistic value and social meaning. Consider this icon: the Bakota guardian figure. It is an identifiable form produced by the people who live in a rainforest region known as Gabon. As in European society, where reliquary boxes and chests contained relics of saints, this African sculpture preserves the memory of ancestors who will protect and guard the generations that follow. Bakota reliquaries are traditionally placed in sacred spaces in a village where they may perform their protective duty.

Gabon guardians, which sit atop reliquary container bundles and baskets, have a distinctive shape. Their heads are often crowned by an inverted crescent and oval faces are encased by stylized wing forms. Importantly, sculptures end on a lozenge or diamond base that economically combines the representation of arms and legs! While these Bakota figures do share identifiable features, they are actually quite original in their individual use of these conventions. What are some of the most important artistic ideas we see here and in other African sculpture?

- Multiple meanings and view in one single piece
- Figures may have "split faces"
- Dynamic thrust of geometric angles
- The simplification of form with the diamond shape representing arms and torso

Does this sound like cubism? It is no coincidence. The impact of African sculpture transformed modern Western art.

MATERIALS

- 12" × 18" oaktag
- aluminum foil
- tissue paper
- brushes
- black ink

- cardboard scraps
- scissors
- cotton balls
- white glue

TEACHER PREPARATION

This project is wonderful for teaching symmetry. It would be a great help to the students to have examples of symmetrical and asymmetrical objects to compare. Examples of Picasso's cubism—for example, images that show figures with arms akimbo—will bring out the relationship of African sculpture to Modern Art.

Figure 2-23. Two Gabon-style figures, side-by-side, each with its own personality. The first figure (left) is powerfully abstract, with an expression that invites discussion; the second sculpture (right) may represent an animal form, certainly consistent with subjects in African sculpture and masks. ▶

DIRECTIONS

1. A familiar heart or animal or a "diamond head"? Students will want to decide the shape of their "protective" sculpture before cutting of cardboard begins (see Figure 2-23).

2. Students will find and identify similarities between (metal-overlay) Bakota reliquary figures and the angular figures painted by Picasso during 1907. See slide 9.

3. Distribute materials. Students will draw their symmetrical faces on cardboard, incorporating symmetry and overlapping (Figure 2-24). Plan to cut the important lozenge/diamond shape beneath the head!

4. Decide which features will be raised in relief. Glue accordingly.

5. Cut foil to cover sculpture. Wrap foil around form; wrap excess foil around to the back. Fix in place with tape or glue. Smooth down with cotton ball so as not to tear foil and use fingers to pick up angles and small designs.

6. Paint ink over aluminum and wipe off with tissue according to desired darkness. You are now protected!

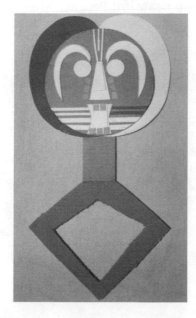

Note: Reliquary figures—which are "additive" sculpture—represent the powerful dynamics of African sculpture design ideas. We should remember, however, that it is the wood carving that is most often regarded as "African Sculpture," using a "subtractive" technique. If the teacher wishes to provide a carving experience, consider using a *block* of modeling clay. Clay tools or plastic knives will enable students to carve their own African figures. The "dynamic thrust of geometric angles" will be your guide!

◀ Figure 2-24. This Gabon assemblage has departed from the traditional metallic representation to which we've been introduced in this activity. Does it not bring to mind the abstracted, multiple equation of a cubist work? This is, after all, the source—the African sculptural mask.

ACTIVITY 7

About Face! African Facial Mystique Unmasked

Portrait Collage

BONUS: FLIPPING OUT FOR AFRICAN MASKS!

▲ Figure 2-25. This Philadelphia student creates an almost uncanny Wodoabe double through his striking portrait. We know the Wodoabe are nomadic, but it's a mighty long way from the Western Sahara to West Philadelphia! Closer neighbors to the nomadic Wodoabe are "the Blue Men of the Desert"—the Taureg people—whose work with indigo dye has earned them this intriguing name. Taureg men and women are also known for their love of beauty in the everyday object. Other tribal societies of the region include the Berbers and the Moors.

In a place as far away as Timbuktu, handsome nomadic herdsmen of the Wodoabe (Woah-dah-be) people gather for an ancient festival of dance, song, elaborate costume, and make-up! Yes, this tradition climaxes with "gerewol," which is a highly artistic, masculine beauty contest where men are awarded prizes based on their ability to apply the most engaging facial decorations. Winning smiles attract attention, too!

Imaginative costuming is a fine way to celebrate life's important events. In many cultures, the more costuming effects, the better! Feathers, shells, beads, paint, jewelry, and patterned fabric add to the occasion. It should come as no surprise that, above all, the face counts! By extension, the art of the mask is related to the art of facial decoration. What is accentuated usually tells us what is important. With the Wodoabe, heavily stained lips offset the gleam of a flashing smile. The objective of this festival is to win the heart of a village maiden through irresistible attire and dance.

In a much larger sense, these Wodoabe men and women are taking part to ensure the continuity of their society through the celebration of courtship. Important cycles are demonstrated through festival and dance—if face and body are covered, emphasis is often given to the mask. African masks are widely admired for their powerful abstract designs. We should remember that masks come in many forms and embody spirited forces. Representation of everyday life such as animal and human archetypes, as well as natural and phenomenal events—and the protective spirits of ancestors—are found in masks and personal adornment. Ideas about beauty are both individual and universal—"The Beautiful People" are everywhere!

Figure 2-26. How expressive are these eyes as they emerge through an original beaded portrait adornment! ▶

MATERIALS

- magazine pictures of faces or photographic portrait of student (see Teacher Preparation)
- colored construction paper
- black, white, and earth-tone crayons
- reddish-brown tempera (wash)
- string/yarn (teacher may precut—see Teacher Preparation)

- miscellaneous notions (see Teacher Preparation)
- brushes
- glue
- scissors
- copies of accompanying reproducible page: "MASKS! Ten Faces of Africa"

TEACHER PREPARATION

Teacher may ask students to bring photos of themselves, specifically "head shots" that the teacher can then enlarge through photocopy for each student. Ask for smiles! This is an opportunity for teacher to keep this headshot for other future lessons dealing with portraiture. Magazine photos may be substituted. Teacher may consider the issue of gender in terms of this desert community. Remember, it is the *men* who adorn themselves for the women. You are encouraged to present this lesson in a "gender-free" manner. If you wish your female students to assume a traditional female African garb as an alternative, Figure 2-27 will help provide your solution. (This beautiful portrait, it should be pointed out, is not necessarily based on Wodoabe costume; it is traditional to West Africa.

Teacher may want to gather notions such as beads, buttons, and scrap jewelry if available. Ask students in advance to contribute! Teacher may cut yarn lengths for "hair." Teacher may also want to mix a tempera wash for paint consistency—a little water added, goes a long way.

Figure 2-27. We travel again—this time to a portrait that may be favored by fashion-conscious "village maidens." The tie dye is African, the garb more typical of West Africa than Saharan lands. Does the pattern behind our young girl not vibrate with African textile vitality? Especially winning is the stylish head wrap. ▶

DIRECTIONS

1. Let's talk about the universal idea of appearance—how do peoples of the world prepare for special occasions? Even though specific ideas about beauty may vary, we all have our own ways of bringing attention to our best features. Men and women alike enjoy looking and feeling good!

2. Students will select images they plan to use: either self-portrait or magazine headshot. Distribute all materials, except paint, with the direction that students should consider how they wish to decoratively enhance the face.

   Note: This lesson focuses on the exceptional Wodoabe dancer. However, feel free to interpret facial motifs. See the reproducible "Masks! Ten Faces of Africa," for inspiration. Distribute copies to students, if desired.

▲ Figure 2-28. In this "About Face!" activity, we bring you an appearance by yet another elegant romadic individual: a beautiful Masaii woman from Kenya in East Africa. This author had the good fortune to admire Masaii accessories "up close and personal" . . . which included an elaborate beaded collar called the "Masaii Wedding Necklace." Her great sense of style did not go unappreciated!

3. Students may now delineate the features with selected colors and, if they wish, decorative patterning. White will dramatize eyes and teeth! Remember, dark lips are a sign of Wodoabe beauty. Vigorous use of crayons will prepare the surface that will resist tempera wash.

4. Distribute tempera wash. Note that the red-clay coloration is favored by our herdsmen. Gently apply paint and watch facial decorations appear!

5. It's time for hair (yarn) and accessories. Students may want to *trade beads*—this is, after all, a time-honored way among Nomadic peoples. Assemble portrait collage accordingly—braiding is encouraged.

6. Cut out portraits and glue decorative portrait directly onto colored construction paper. A border and/or background comprised of confetti-like mosaic squares will add the festive touch.

7. Completed portraits may be displayed as a group—your beautiful "Art Tribe"! Aren't they gorgeous? Right down to their very souls!

B O N U S : FLIPPING OUT FOR AFRICAN MASKS

Beauty has many faces. Now is your chance to try a masking technique! Refer to the reproducible page, "MASKS! Ten Faces of Africa," for a mask of choice: share with your students, who then create a mask "cover" by drawing and painting their selected mask style on a separate paper. Fit for size of photo face. You might want to do more than one mask, each to be layered on the other. Attach the mask(s) in the manner of a flip-card on top of photo portrait. Now you are truly nomadic, for you have sampled regional styles of masks and traveled the great continent of Africa through the art of masquerade. **Note:** Eyes can be cut to open and close as can lips to "speak . . . African has many faces."

MASKS! Ten Faces of Africa
(key: mask, society, region, origin or purpose)

(**1.**) Bundu Association Helmut Mask, Mende people, Sierra Leone. Mende girls' coming-of-age mask. Wood. (**2.**) Lumbu Mask, Gabon. Fang. Spirit mask, associated with afterlife. Wood, painted white. (**3.**) Kuba Mask, Zaire. Royal female, sister or wife of *Woot,* the First Ancestor. Beads, wood, cowrie shells, raffia, paint. (**4.**) Butterfly Plank Mask, Bobo and Bwa peoples, Burkina Faso. Representation of deity, *Do.* Rain and harvest ceremony. Wood. (**5.**) Benin Courtly Mask. Nigeria, 17th century. Ornament of *Oba* (king). Crown of figures represent Portuguese traders. Orig. carved ivory. (**6.**) Basonge Mask. Zaire. Ancestral spirit mask. Wood with holes for raffia attachment. (**7.**) Bambara Mask, N'doma Association. Dogon people, Mali. Boys' coming-of-age mask. Wood. (**8.**) Yoruba Mask. Multi figure sculpted headpiece. Yoruba people, Nigeria. Painted wood. (**9.**) Kota (or BaKota) Reliquary Mask. Protective Guardian. Kota people, Gabon and Cameroon. Brass and/or copper, metal alloys: application to wood. (**10.**) Luba (or BaLuba) *Kifwebe* (word meaning mask) Association. Derived from Basonge motif. For use in chiefly ceremonies. Wood.

MASKS!
TEN FACES OF AFRICA

ACTIVITY 8

Meet My People: Ancestral Screens

Mixed Media Assemblage

▲ Figure 2-29. A group portrait that defies boundaries with legs courageously extending beyond the frame. In art—as in artrooms—traditions are always evolving! African patterns of animals and abstract geometric shapes provide a strong backdrop to a family that shows us their particular likes in the form of "favorite things." Some of the attributes that function as pendants include a basketball, a car, and an ice cream cone! Notice how faces respect the African mask presence found in ancestral screens.

The Kalabari screen is a good example of how African society presents its ideas about itself—family, ancestors, village, friends—in a bold, straightforward, yet imaginative manner. The purpose of the screen is to honor the ancestors who are depicted with a scale that is consistent with their importance. One might find an all-important head of household flanked by two other family members. There may be additional figures who are not part of the clan since it is believed that greater numbers may convey greater status.

Screens are shown in specific places. Often they appear at trading posts! As a result, screen objects may be a mixture of "imports and exports." However, the objects that leadership figures carry are symbolic of authority—such as canes, tusks, gongs, and even rattles and paddles! It is the central figure for whom the screen altar is made. This individual may wear a specific mask with which he was identified when he was alive. The top of the screen frame (as well as the base) may be lined with smaller mask heads.

Essentially the screen is an ensemble of "social perspective" that denotes past and present community leaders. Do not be surprised to find the initials of a family or group as part of the screen design! After all, it's *"all in the family."*

Figure 2-30. Party time! This first-grader wishes his screen to honor a great hero with a great ceremony—his very own birthday party! The birthday boy is flanked by two somewhat less exuberant siblings! ▶

Africa: Nigeria/Benin, Kenya, Ghana, Mali, Gabon, Sahara/Wodoabe, Egypt, North Africa

MATERIALS

- brown construction paper or brown kraft paper
- oil pastels
- wood
- lightweight balsa wood strips (substitute: cardboard)
- oaktag

- paint (brown acrylic or tempera)
- scissors
- feathers
- glue
- markers
- miscellaneous materials (see Teacher Preparation)

TEACHER PREPARATION

Our ancestral screens will be constructed as individual panels; therefore, teacher is encouraged to gather lightweight balsa wood rectangles in quantity for each student. If wood is not a feasible choice, cardboard may be substituted. Also, wood strips, or precut oaktag strips, will be needed to define panel division and will be used to frame the panel.

Are you "game" for a new idea? Miscellaneous materials such as buttons, shells, fabric scraps, and so forth may be made available to students at work stations designated as a "Trading Post," where exchange is encouraged!

DIRECTIONS

1. Who are the important people in your life? Students will consider family and friends whom they wish to "honor" with their Kalabari screen. Teacher may want to compare screen design with family or group portrait.

2. Distribute screen panel and strips along with oil pastels. Students decide on three-part screen division which will be defined by the strips. Glue to surface. Decorate frame and panel with geometric African designs and patterns.

3. Distribute paint, brushes, and oaktag. Lightly apply brown paint to oaktag to suggest wood stain. When dry, create figures of importance and any special possessions that identify them. Who will be the central figure(s)? Students—don't forget about yourself!

4. Mount figures on ancestral screen in desired arrangement. Encourage students to create majestic crowns and to use mixed materials. This is a good time to apply those trading post "finds"!

5. Display screens next to one another as your own classroom "trading post." Fill your walls with family, friends, and the things you love.

▲ Figure 2-31. Another early childhood interpretation of the Kalabari screen tradition. This one appears to be wearing more of a chiefly cap than a party hat. The mood is clearly upbeat.

ACTIVITY 9

My Personal Walking Stick: Royal Regalia

Paper Craft

BONUS: WALKING POUCH

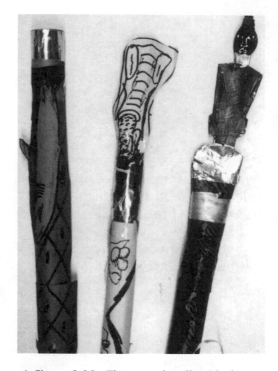

▲ Figure 2-32. Three royal staffs with three different personalities are emblems of power. The staff on the left may be "fit for a king"—it is capped with "gold" for ceremonial use. The middle staff appears to be a serpent and may, therefore, refer to "cane symbolism"—reptiles denote appreciation! The staff on the right is a figure—it is wearing chiefly adornment. Some staffs even have multi-figure finials! One can conclude that staffs—which may also be held by royal attendants—not only walk, but talk!

The object we generally define as a cane may be interpreted in many ways—from the walking stick that assists the traveler to the divine regalia of a reigning king! In its role as a courtly accessory, a staff may also be considered a scepter that denotes great status— West African courts may be replete with intricately carved royal staffs, even staffs of gold! In this setting, it is most certainly a recognizable symbol of the great chieftains. Other accessories may include fans, fly whisks, and umbrellas.

The wide variety of artistic expression that is seen in the staffs of Africa is impressive. They are often coded to represent rank. Above all, staffs convey specific and personal meaning about their owners' identities. The use of certain symbols helps to establish the power of the staff's design as well as insure its intended purpose. Whether you travel to Nigeria or Zaire, or south to the Zulu Nation of South Africa, rulers of rank can be identified by their scepters! For instance, Shaka Zulu chiefs would be known by the design of the staff they carry.

Imagine how symbols may be used on the staff. A snake, for instance, lends itself to the basic form of the stick, yet conveys its own meaning in nature. Just as artists everywhere create personal symbols based on tradition as well as their own beliefs, the African staff may be regarded for its personal meaning in one's own world. As it has been said, *"You can talk the talk, but you must walk the walk!"* A beautiful walking stick is a useful guide on any journey.

Figure 2-33. An S.O.S. alternative filled with pictures, signs, messages . . . and possibilities! Emblems have various associations, as do objects themselves. The incorporation of beadwork, metals, shells, and so forth gives an appearance of authority! ▶

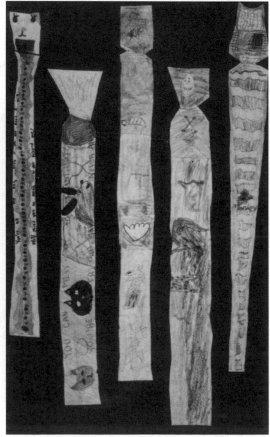

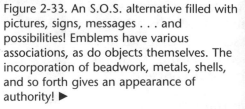

MATERIALS

- cardboard tubes from wrapping paper (see Teacher Preparation)
- colored construction paper (assorted sizes)
- foil paper
- markers

- masking tape
- glue
- cardboard scraps
- scissors
- flower pots (optional—see "Directions," step 4.)

TEACHER PREPARATION

Teacher is encouraged to save those wrapping paper tubes and household wax paper or paper towel cardboard rolls. These can be joined together with tape to create walking stick lengths. Wrapping paper rolls are ideal for walking sticks! **Note:** Slide #8 may be used for introduction of items to represent status.

---

*S.O.S. (SAVE OUR SCHEDULE, i.e. "Schedule Saver" or shortcut) . . . Flat facsimile canes will convey walking-stick ideas when cardboard tubes are unavailable. See Figure 2-33.

DIRECTIONS

1. Discuss the various roles that a walking stick or cane can represent, from royal regalia to traveler's aid. Consider that nomadic cultures may be particularly fond of canes, which are standard gear for everyday travel. The staffs of kings and queens may be more "opulent." Which do you want your staff to be? Your cane will reveal the answer.

2. Distribute materials. Students will design personal symbols based on African motifs that express their own ideas about their symbolic "journey."

3. Students will want to take into account the cylindrical form of their walking object when designing canes. **Note:** S.O.S. facsimiles (flat canes) also require specific format consideration. In both cases, canes have a top and a bottom—the symbolic story is revealed between the two!

4. Top off your walking stick with an appropriate symbol from nature or everyday life that best suits you. Fantastic elements are welcome! Display canes (as shown in Figure 2-32) or create a "cane stand" *(flower pots work here)* that will really show off the full array of student cane regalia.

▲ Figure 2-34. Look closely and you will see a cane—or a walking stick—in the hand of a witty man. The author and her cheerful friend share a moment of mutual amusement under the East African sun. Masaii people are known for their herding skills, where sticks are essential; they may also offer assistance on long journeys across the savanna where it is not uncommon to encounter irritable wildlife! Canes and sticks may be used for protection—although in the East African plains, animals of many stripes have coexisted with humans since the beginning of recorded time. Sticks can lead a practical life.

B O N U S : WALKING POUCH

As long as you're out and about, let's give you a pouch to carry your "valuables"! Students may enjoy creating this additional walking gear, favored by African nomadic desert peoples like the Wodoabe. The designs students choose may complement walking-stick motif or be original to the pouch itself. Simply create pouches by folding brown paper wrap in half (brown lunch bags are perfect). Pouches inside of pouches may be created in the same manner by reducing the size of your folded paper and inserting into larger pouch. Do as many as you like—one size contains all! Attach with string to wear over shoulder or as personal adornment. Ambitious teachers could do tooled leather pouches, or even paint leather directly if "authenticity" is desired!

▲ Figure 2-35. The Bonus activity will complement any traveler's accessories! A travel pouch may be inspired by Taureg nomadic design. These patterns "multiply" the geometrics of nature. Visual and physical space is compartmentalized—inside and outside—and ideal for portability!

ACTIVITY 10

Eternally Yours, Egypt: Splendid Temple Tablets

"Panel" Painting

BONUS: PRINT YOUR MAGIC GOLD CARTOUCHE!

Egypt and its ancient dynasties have been with us a very long time, since 4500 B.C.! Today, as ever, Egypt is located in northeast Africa, positioned between the Mediterranean and Red Seas. The geographical proximity of this unique country to the Arab and Mediterranean worlds has contributed to its rich cultural heritage. Yet, Egypt is—and always has been—on the African continent, with the great Nile River running through it. Important kingdoms have ruled nearby, then have ceased to be; one such Egyptian neighbor was the land of Nubia.

Monumental architectural triumphs of Egypt are worn by the centuries and still stand tall on desert sands. Inside the temple walls are the painted records of an ancient yet vital civilization. Much of what we have learned about these Egyptian "good old days" has been taught to us by its art. What exactly do the painted walls reveal?

Egyptian art speaks volumes. Here we can track the Egyptian development of written language—the one we know as hieroglyphics—that shows us the evolution from picture to symbol to alphabet sign! Egyptian figurative painting, which is clearly depicted in stylized profile, readily includes hieroglyphics as part of its compositional meaning. Mythology? Architecture? Interior design? Ancient belief? From pharaohs and queens to everyday life, all may be identified in the eternal art of Egypt which was, in fact, intended to last into "the forever." It has survived. Far beyond the brief time in which the works were painted, Egypt and her art endure to this very day!

▲ Figure 2-36. Meet Horus . . . "God of the Sun!" Upper-right and lower-left space contains a cartouche, complete with "magic rope" that ends in an ornamental base. Interior temple architecture boasts stunning details, such as the column's capital which is, in fact, a lotus, the symbol of rebirth. Scepter (or staff) balances the sun; flower below seems to repeat this joyful and relevant motif. Note: Horus is also symbolized as a protective eye!

◄ Figure 2-37. A student artist has handsomely portrayed Anubis. He is the jackal-headed "Lord of the Embalmers," a critical task in ancient Egypt. Egyptians believed the body had to be preserved or "mummified" in order to be recognized . . . then on to the boat journey to the next world. Notice how Anubis holds an *ankh*, the Egyptian symbol for life, in his right hand. This identifies him, along with the scepter in his other hand, which is a symbol of well-being. Another important symbol that may be used is the scarab which actually replaced the heart in the mummification process and is representative of renewed life. The descriptive character of the architectural setting and Anubis's garment have been admirably achieved! The great sun burns near a secret cartouche, no doubt containing wonderful symbols and secret signs.

MATERIALS

- posterboard—assorted colors (option—see Teacher Preparation)
- wide brushes (see Teacher Preparation)
- permanent nontoxic black markers
- rulers (optional)

- kraft paper
- white glue
- tempera or acrylic paint
- paint brushes
- pencils

TEACHER PREPARATION

Cut kraft paper to size of posterboard—teacher should allow border as indicated in Figures 2-36 to 2-38. Plan on using one posterboard per student; if quantity is a budgetary issue, cut boards in half to maximize your supply. Teacher may want to mount cut kraft paper directly onto posterboard: Spread white glue with wide brushes (or substitute with edge of 3″ × 5″ card). Smooth paper surface with hand and/or flatten with books. Allow for some drying time before distribution.

◄ Figure 2-38. Who is she? Perhaps the Egyptian girl is a student self-portrait. It is sometimes a pleasure to simply imagine ancient life with ordinary household members. Many still feel today that a home is not complete without a pet or two . . . cats in Egypt were not only enjoyed but often worshipped, even mummified for eternal life! If the cat's name is *Bastet,* we know she was divine Egyptian goddess! The cartouche (upper left) is both decorative and visually convincing.

DIRECTIONS

1. These panels may be considered architectural "finds" from some great Egyptian temple! They will tell us—with both mythological and hieroglyphical characters—secrets and telling details. Students will want to include in their panels some or all of the following: architectural elements, a mythological animal, and/or human being in appropriate attire and an interior or exterior. Single scenes should include at least one **cartouche** (explanation below) that will contain hieroglyphs. The hieroglyph may be a reference to an actual hieroglyph, an invented glyph, or a combination.

2. Distribute boards and pencils. Students will plan their Egyptian composition. Remember, figures are shown in stylized profile. Inclusion of ancient symbols and amulets is encouraged.

3. Distribute paints and painting tools along with black markers when drawing is complete.

4. The aim is to "paint a picture of ancient Egypt." Students should not be concerned with issues of perspective since Egyptian art is essentially a flat, decorative representation.

5. Finished works should find comfortable architectural niches in your own "classroom temple" where they can be admired as painted memories of ancient Egypt.

B O N U S : PRINT YOUR MAGIC GOLD CARTOUCHE!

What is a cartouche? In general architectural meaning, it is a scroll-like, ornamental shape that serves as a feature or detail. In Egypt, the cartouche is found on monuments, yet may be an independent figure used as ornamentation. The **cartouche** contains the name of an important deity or ruler, and provides a **magic ring** that will encircle and protect the name it enclosed from harm. **Note:** The ring of the cartouche evolved from a rope!

To create your own magic cartouche, you will need gold kraft foil paper. This is a printmaking experience which requires newsprint, styrofoam trays, brayers, and printing ink. Student first draws his or her name onto the newsprint using Egyptian hieroglyphics. Don't forget to surround the name with the magic ring! Our artist included palms and pyramids. Students may use cartouche shapes with closure bar at base, like those shown in our "eternal" panel drawings (Figures 2-36 to 2-38). Place the newsprint onto the styrofoam tray and trace the drawing. The pressure of the pencil will indent into the styrofoam. To create an "ancient" look, cut the edges of the styrofoam to resemble an ancient cartouche rediscovered! Print in usual manner using printing ink and brayer; yellow and white on gold foil paper yields stunning results. Mount prints on black paper. *"May eternal joy follow you!"*

ACTIVITY 11

Hands Across Africa: Reaching Beyond Morocco

"Henna" Hand Painting/Decorative Body Art

BONUS: HANDS OF PEACE MOBILE

▲ Figure 2-39. A boy with bright hands and dazzling ideas! Is it the sun or a wheel of life that we see? The meaning may be personal, or you can make it "simply spontaneous." Note how well his fingers, thumb, and palm are dynamically designed. The front of his hand, we can bet, is as exciting as his open palms!

▲ Figure 2-40. A circle of friends share hand, heart, and mind!

Since the beginning of recorded time, the mark of the hand on painted cave walls has served as our first signature, an early symbol of who we are. What could be more human than our hands, and more worthy of appreciation? In Islamic North Africa, women have painted their hands and their feet with patterns for centuries. It is a tradition that travels beyond Morocco and other North African countries to the Middle East. In the Arabian country of Yemen, women apply geometric and curvilinear designs with dye made from a dark berry; sometimes, patterns extend from wrist to elbow, and from foot and ankle to knee!

Wherever painted hands may be found, henna is often the medium of choice—particularly in India, where the process is known as *mehandi.* Henna paste is applied and removed, leaving an often elaborate and lacy pattern. For the most part, hand-painting style selections are subject to tradition, as well as personal taste. Besides delightful decorative value, are there other reasons to paint one's hands?

Indeed, painted hands help to celebrate life's joyous occasions. Splendid painted hands at weddings appear after a group of women have helped for hours to prepare the bride for her special day. On the Muslim occasion of **Eid-el-Fidur,** which marks the end of **Ramadan,** a painted hand may greet you, too!

Painted hands are appreciated when they complement garments that cover and veil face and body. The painted hand and foot also enhance the natural shape of hand and foot anatomy—especially in the gesture of dance! To "draw" attention to hands and feet through design pleases many senses. And as if all this were not enough, the painting of henna is believed by some to have medicinal value—perhaps it may even bring good luck! In any case, let's give North Africa a hand!

Figure 2-41. Hamsa means five in Arabic. This piece would most readily be found in Israel with The Star of David at the center setting the circular pattern. Hands are used as symbols of protection, from Africa to where we stand! In the Islamic world, the Hand of Fatima ensures benevolence. ▶

MATERIALS

- nontoxic, washable markers
- henna (optional—see Teacher Preparation)
- 9" × 12" white or manila paper (oaktag suggested for Bonus activity)
- pencils
- scissors (optional)

TEACHER PREPARATION

"Body painting" materials may be substituted for nontoxic washable markers at teacher's discretion. Henna is a nontoxic, red paste made from powdered leaves. When applied traditionally, it is a long process that takes hours to apply and then remains for *at least* 24 hours on the body. After, it is washed off and the bright stain remains. ("FYI"—The ancient Egyptians used henna as a cosmetic to dye their lips.) Actual henna paste ingredients may still be purchased today, for henna painting is still popular in Asian-Indian, and Islamic cultures and is gaining new audiences!. The teacher who desires "authenticity" will need access to stores in communities where the prepared mixes are available. The Islamic look of hand painting may or may not be suggested by the use of "classroom henna" (brown *washable* color marker); other colors may be used as well—particularly berry-blue! A warm soap and water source is always appreciated, but let's not rush it!

Teacher may also wish to have on hand examples of African patterns as well as Islamic calligraphic motifs (see Middle East and Turkey section).

DENISE CHENG'S HAND
Second grader from Downingtown, PA.

▲ Figure 2-42. A hand can hold so much meaning. A student-traced hand (see Step 2 of Directions) has used the royal circular motif of royalty on the palm. The thumb, with its moon and stars, symbolizes faithfulness; below, the eye represents the universe. "Patient" heart marks the pulse, while the ring finger shows a star of "dependence." We all do need each other after all!

DIRECTIONS

1. Consider your own hands. Aren't they unique—dare we say handy! Discuss with students the many ways our hands serve us in friendship, in daily tasks, in love and creativity. Do our hands protect us? Let's celebrate our hands.

2. Distribute pencils and paper. Trace hands—students may assist each other in this step. Refer to design motif samples if desired. See Figures 2-39, 2-41, and 2-42.

3. Students will now draw motifs that they select for their hand painting. Imagination counts, too! If desired, traced hands may be cut away from paper and decorated with pencil on both sides. **Note:** Teacher may wish to save these hands. (See Bonus activity on next page.)

4. Distribute washable markers. Apply washable color selection(s) directly, considering individual shape. Do front and back!

5. When completed, hands may be displayed to honor, friendship, love, and peace.

▲ Figure 2-43. Authentic Moroccan wedding tent reminds us that hennaed hands and feet mark life's important events . . . tent designs are based on natural plant forms and are typical of Islamic surface pattern.

◄ Figure 2-44. Mishou, who is Lebanese, displays the sweet *bastilla,* a pie that would be served in a "many course" Moroccan meal. The word "Fez" appears as decoration, which represents both the imperial city in Morocco and the name of a great Philadelphia restaurant! As a matter of fact, eating with one's hands is part of the delicious ceremony that is a Moroccan feast!

Bonus: HANDS OF PEACE MOBILE

Here's your chance to assemble the "practice hands" (see Step 3 of Directions) into a Collective Peace Mobile! Individuals or groups may assemble the cut oaktag "henna hands" which may now utilize both sides to send wishes for peace. Assemble and display.

The Middle East, Turkey, and Greece

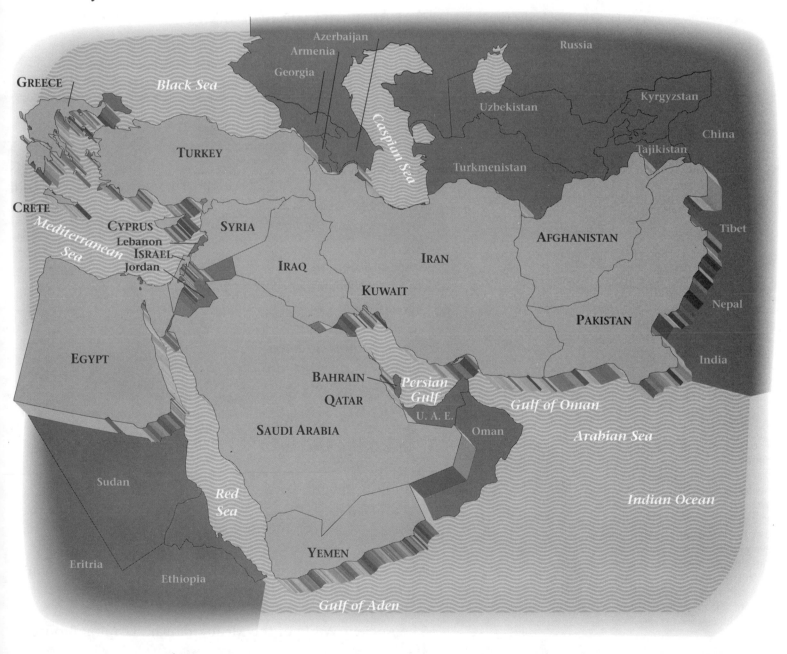

GREECE
Black Sea
CRETE
Mediterranean Sea
CYPRUS
Lebanon
ISRAEL
Jordan
TURKEY
SYRIA
IRAQ
KUWAIT
EGYPT
BAHRAIN
QATAR
U. A. E.
SAUDI ARABIA
Sudan
Red Sea
Eritria
Ethiopia
YEMEN
Gulf of Aden
Azerbaijan
Armenia
Georgia
Caspian Sea
IRAN
Persian Gulf
Oman
Gulf of Oman
Arabian Sea
Indian Ocean
Russia
Uzbekistan
Turkmenistan
AFGHANISTAN
PAKISTAN
Kyrgyzstan
China
Tajikistan
Tibet
Nepal
India

The Middle East, Turkey, and Greece

Desert palm trees frame the old city of Jerusalem. In the center is the Hebrew word *mizrah*, meaning east—symbolic of directional worship. Israeli papercut art. ▶

▲ "Spun from the heart . . . woven from the soul" . . . is the poetic sentiment written on the reverse side of this lovely Persian picture of two young women weaving. Painted on vellum. (Courtesy of Woven Treasures, Phila., PA.)

The child who wears the fez is content! It usually appears in red, this fez that once was the national headgear for Turkish men. Women in Turkey often wear a scarf called *oya* that "speaks for them": the colors, patterns, and even how it is worn communicate specific messages. "Come to the mountain top," says the *oya* scarf with the wild tulip design! The *oya* is an example of fine Turkish folk art. ▶

ART ACTIVITIES FOR BECOMING CULTURE SMART

▣ **Activity 1**
To Go By the Book: 1001 Arabian Nights and Days!
"Manuscript" Art/Book Cover and Content Design

Activity 2
The Camel Trade: Tents, Towns, and Great Bazaars!
Pictorial "Assemblage"/Syria to Yemen

▣ **Activity 3**
Architecture of the Islamic World: The Marvel of the Mosque and Its Minarets!
Architecture/Alahambra to Arabia

Activity 4
Spice-of-Life Box!
3-D Spice "Aromatic" Clay Container

▣ **Activity 5**
Windows on Israel
"Stained-Glass" Windows
BONUS: CHICKEN SOUP TO DREAM FOR! PAPER SCULPTURE INCLUDES REAL RECIPE, TOO!

▣ **Activity 6**
Tabriz or Not Tabriz? Persian Tote Bags
Carpet Design Tote Bags

Activity 7
A Turkish Delight: Iznik Dishes
"Faux" Plates
BONUS: "COLLECTOR" DISPLAY STAND

Activity 8
Me and My Turkish Shadow: The Puppet Crafts of Istanbul
Crafty Turkish Shadow Puppets/Theater Arts

▣ **Activity 9**
The Ancient World of the Mediterranean: Leaping Bronze Bulls!
"Archaeological" Metalwork
BONUS: FINDS OF LONG AGO *AND* INSTANT ARCHAEOLOGY!

To know the Art of the Middle East, Turkey, and Greece . . . . .

. . . . . one must first understand that the region known as the Middle East lies at the juncture of three continents—Asia, Africa, and Europe. The countries to the north meet the Aegean and Mediterranean seas. To the south stretches the vast desert of Saudi Arabia. Turkey, long ago called Asia Minor, is located north of Syria, Iraq, and Iran (formerly known as Persia). It is a culturally rich and politically complex group of countries. The early Aegean and Mediterranean cultures include Minoan, Cretan, and Greek societies where the Fertile Crest thrived in ancient days. Greece is further known for its identity with Europe and the formation of the Classic Age in Western civilization; Turkey is half Asian and half European. Borders have been disputed in the Middle East since biblical times. Jerusalem, in Israel, remains a holy site for Christians, Muslims, and Jews. The importance of the art and culture that grew from the historically prominent Middle East—home to the world's three most eminent monotheist religions—is profoundly acknowledged.

The land once called Persia (now Iran) is an empire with its own dramatic history. In the period from 1200 to 1800, Persia developed the bookmaking arts—to include manuscript illumination, calligraphy, and poetry. In the early sixteenth century, Shah Ismail declared Tabriz the capital of Persia. This ancient city held a *Kitabk haneh,* or "place of the book," which received the full patronage of the Shah; it was an active workshop as well as a library for collections. Another book-producing city, Herat, was located in present-day Afghanistan. Not only were beautiful book folios created, but elegant carpets—Persian rugs—were woven there as well. Artistic ideas flowed. Multicultural exchange with other influential cultures, such as China and Europe, took place on the Silk Route. Shah Tahmasp commissioned the poet Firdousi to write the lyrical *Shah-Namek* or *Book of Kings* to commemorate the history and legend of a Persian dynasty.

Turkey was also supportive of art production. Beautiful books, metalwork, textiles, garments, carpets, and architecture flowed from Turkey (also known as Anatolia). The Byzantine Empire was founded in Constantinople, now Istanbul, and St. Sophia, or *Hagia Sophia,* was built during this time—with glorious mosaic icons of Empress Theodora and Emperor Justinian. During the rise of the Ottoman Empire in the fifteenth century, the hub of the empire under Suleyman the Magnificent, who brought Islam to Turkey, was the Topkapi Palace, located right behind St. Sophia. Topkapi served as a city within a city—complete with housing for craftspeople, a seat of state, a harem, a museum, a zoo, and a mosque for the sultan. The Blue Mosque, in old Istanbul, rivals the Topkapi Palace for magnificence, with its dazzling Iznik tile.

Islamic art, with its patterned design and quality, is present in the Middle East, Turkey, India, Pakistan, and Indonesia. Islamic art is intended to uplift and inspire the viewer. Calligraphic expression of the Quran (Koran), the holy book that reveals the word of Allah, is visually stunning. Mosques all over the world are covered with calligraphic verse from the Quran, with arabesques, plant and flower motifs, and tessellated geometry to accompany text. A splendid example of Moorish architecture in Spain—and witness to the spread of Islam to that country—the Alhambra presents the Quran as architecture. Calligraphy appears in *Kufic,* an early script; there is no figurative representation. The motifs that appear on walls are also revealed in carpets, manuscripts, and other works of hand. Human and animal forms proliferate in the court arts, but are not usually seen in mosque architecture. This is a consideration that has created some general confusion regarding Islamic art. Similarly, the figurative art that one might find in a Jewish synagogue is not likely to occur in an Orthodox Jewish temple. The brilliant stained-glass windows of Russian Jewish artist Marc Chagall depict the Twelve Tribes of Israel in a Hebrew chapel near Jerusalem. It may be said that there is wide interpretation, diversity, and expansion of expression in human belief.

Make three wishes? Peace. Creativity. Love.

The Near East and Middle East have intrigued and inspired man artists, writers, travelers, and pilgrims. European painters, from Eug Delacroix to Henri Matisse, have been greatly moved by the people, landscape, light, and artistic inventions of the Orient. In the cradle of Christianity, Judaism, and Islam, one cannot help but respond to the depth of human experience. The Quran was written here . . . the Old and New Testaments were written here . . . in these ancient biblical lands that have shaped world civilization and history.

ACTIVITY 1

To Go By the Book: 1001 Arabian Nights and Days!

"Manuscript" Art/Book Cover and Content Design

▲ Figure 3-1. Arabic book arts are world-known and widely admired—inside and out! The poetry of the written word in calligraphy is believed to represent a divine spirit. Splendid illuminations grace the pages within, while the design of the book is a work of art in itself!

The Thousand and One Nights or *Arabian Nights*—enormously popular in Europe and America—are traced to Persia in the 9th century. Not at all surprising, for Persia (now Iran) was ever a fountain of art and literature. The many Arabian Night tales . . . Sinbad the Sailor, Ali Baba and the Forty Thieves, Aladdin and the Magic Lamp . . . are, in fact, told by possibly the world's greatest fictional storyteller, Scheherezade (shh-hair'-ah-zhad). It was she who kept herself and others alive by enchanting a misguided Sultan with her dramatic and engaging nightly tales. She not only intrigued the Sultan with her inventive "cliff-hangers" and was spared her own life, but Scheherezade charmed this menacing monarch into a kinder, more agreeable listener who became a better ruler.

Wise books of the Arabian world contain history, poetry, science, knowledge, and, of course, beautiful, highly decorative art. They are often resplendent with calligraphy! One other very famous book from Persia is called *The Shah-nameh* (Shah nah'-may) which is literally *"The Book of Kings,"* for *Shah* means *king*. This book, composed by Iranian poet Firdowsi in the 11th century, vividly illustrates an epic of recorded history in loving detail. It also contains some magic, such as the "simurgh," a mythical bird entity well recognized by many Arabic children! The hero of *The Shah-nameh* is named Rustam-Zal, also a leading man. There are many characters. *The Shah-nameh* is almost a *who's who* of Persia—a majestic marriage of myth and history, it is the national epic of Iran.

From the *Tales of the Arabian Nights* to *The Shah-nameh,* and from Tabriz to Baghdad, Arabic book art is meant to be read and admired—inside and out! It may be said, in the best sense, that in the Middle East one may want to "judge a book by its sumptuous cover" . . . and a "picture is definitely worth a 1001 words!"

◀ Figure 3-2. Books take many forms: albums with splendidly designed covers that effortlessly overlap and enfold the contents; folios held in exquisite slip cases and marvelous accordion pages to delight the beholder.

MATERIALS

- two 6″ × 9″ sheets of aluminum tooling foil
- two 5″ × 8″ pieces of heavy posterboard
- two 8″ × 20″ sheets of white paper
- two 5″ × 8″ pieces of newsprint
- pencils
- scissors
- white glue

- sequins
- masking tape
- ruler
- colored, nontoxic permanent markers
- hot glue gun (optional)
- 24″ colored ribbon
- reproducible page: The Middle East Patterns and Designs

Figure 3-3. Portable? You bet! These small books travel well across desert sands. This one is a sketchbook of arches found in traditional architecture, East and West! The pointed and "horse shoe" arches are specifically Arabic. ▶

TEACHER PREPARATION

This is a teaching opportunity for storytelling. A selection from *The Arabian Nights* would be ideal. Think what storytelling did for Scheherezade! The focus is on the book cover—simple elements work best! Suggestion: Teacher will want to construct a book example in advance of lesson (see "Directions, Steps 1–10 and Figures 3-1 to 3-3). Teacher will supervise her glue gun if used with student.

DIRECTIONS

1. Teacher will show students the sample product at the start of the lesson; this provides both clarity of purpose and stimulation of interest. Demonstrate the following basic steps:

   Step 1. On two 5″ × 8″ pieces of newsprint, have students design front and back covers of their book in pencil.

   Step 2. Measure and draw a 1/2″ border around each 6″ × 9″ sheet of aluminum with ruler. Cut off corners of aluminum above drawn border.

   Step 3. Place newsprint design on top of aluminum sheets and tape in place. Be sure to place newsprint within border.

   Step 4. Place aluminum with attached drawing on newspaper pad and trace design with pencil. This will leave the indentation of the drawing in the aluminum.

   Step 5. Decorate the surface with permanent, nontoxic colored markers. Hot glue sequins where desired.

▲ Figure 3-4. Calligraphy is found everywhere, not only in books. Students may want to try their hand at Arabic-style calligraphy or the Islamic-style shown on this plate, which means Mohammed, *"Peace Be Upon Him."*

The Middle East is filled with calligraphy: poetry, verse, and beautiful manuscripts. Popular tales range from the epic saga to the wise and witty folktale. When one imagines the richly detailed stories of Arabic origin, stunning illuminated manuscripts often spring to mind. It is understandable, for these vivid paintings are emblematic of Islamic visual art. However, the Arabic literary tradition itself is not only pictorial, as well as written; it is also one that was orally told. Storytellers for centuries entertained in cities and towns—at festivals, coffee houses, public baths—and in desert tents! Many literary achievements stem from the Islamic classical age, which reached its zenith in the 9th century. Stories told are stories remembered: Among the most beloved fables was **Kalila wa Dimna,** an animal tale widely enjoyed for more than 1,200 years! Of course the Muslim sacred text, the *Quran (Koran)*, is the best-known and most widely studied book of the Muslim world. This Islamic book of wisdom brims with quotes and proverbs about family, education, relationships, and everyday life. Here are two:

"Paradise is under the feet of mothers."

"Learning is a treasury whose keys are questions."

Step 6. Hot glue 5" × 8" heavy posterboard on backside of aluminum and fold border edges of aluminum over posterboard. Set covers aside.

Step 7. Fold both 8" × 20" pieces of white paper in half (10") and in half again (5"). Open up paper and refold accordion-style on these creases.

Step 8. Glue these two sheets together with white glue by overlapping one of the end pages. This will create one long accordion-pleated sheet.

Step 9. Glue one end of this sheet to the assembled front cover.

Step 10. Place 24" colored ribbon on the back cover, leaving 8" of ribbon on top and bottom of cover. Glue other end of accordion-folded paper on top of ribbon and back cover.

2. Now it is the students' turn to become book designers! The same above-mentioned steps will be followed.

3. Distribute materials as indicated.

4. This is a technically sequential activity; teacher will want to monitor each step as it occurs.

5. Upon completion of Steps 1–10, the beautiful yet blank book is finished. Will it become a personal journal? A sketchbook of observations of people, places, and things? Try your hand at calligraphy! Or an original interpretation of a classic tale, say, *The Arabian Nights*. There are 1001 ways to fill your book!

▲ Figures 3-5a and 3-5b. The exquisite pages from an ancient manuscript shown here are not the *Quran,* yet express the importance of books, learning, and "the geometry of the spirit"—calligraphy.

ACTIVITY 2

The Camel Trade: Tents, Towns, and Great Bazaars

Pictorial "Assemblage"/Syria to Yemen

Many diverse societies form the fabric of the Middle East. Since days long ago, it is a place where people have traded artistically crafted goods—along with news, ideas, and wise words. From the home of the Queen of Sheba in the country of Yemen and along ancient routes . . . whether in Cairo, Marrakech, Istanbul, or Jerusalem . . . you can always expect a fabulous bazaar! They may appear in spacious buildings that have been designed as trade centers—the very early form of the shopping mall—or may simply occupy town squares on specific market days.

In the Islamic world, the Arabic name for the market is *Souk;* in Hebrew, the same word is *Shuk* (pronounced *Shook*). Yet no word can convey the vitality of the Middle Eastern market: brass-hammered trays stacked with figs and dates, the clip-clop of camels and donkeys on ancient roads, razzle-dazzle patterns, and many animated hands and voices—a cacophony of sounds. The Middle Eastern bazaar is indeed a multi-sensory feast! In some souks, the crafts people identify themselves by incorporating the "tool of trade" into their own personal appearance. For instance, a carpenter may place a wood chip behind his ear, or a tailor might display a threaded needle on his or her lapel or bodice. Merchants are not expected to be shy and retiring!

Are you in the market for a Bedouin silver and turquoise necklace or a burnoose (a long, hooded Arab robe)? Better yet . . . a *kaffiyah* (cah-fee-ah)—a printed (or plain) scarf-like headcovering

▲ Figure 3-6. Sean, age 13, offers a scene of trade that is at once eye-pleasing and mysterious! The man at the outermost edge of the picture is a familiar figure in the Middle East marketplace—a "tea seller." You will find "water sellers" in the souk, too!

▲ Figure 3-7. Mike's desert outpost seems very exotic. Even in the cloud formation, one can find a "genie" (*jinni* is indeed a legendary Islamic magical being) and a magic lamp! Also, meet a snakecharmer (yes, they do indeed exist).
Note: Mike has signed his name in Arabic in the lower right of his picture.

traditionally worn by Arab men and boys to keep cool in the desert sun? For women, a particular scarf or headcovering is traditional attire—it is further considered proper dress in certain Islam regions. Marketplaces themselves utilize shade for comfortable shopping. Tented coverings are both logical and colorful. Also be prepared to bargain—give the merchant a chance to win your shopper's heart! Bargaining is an art and a trade, a matching of wits and melodrama! Ah, the joy of shopping—is truly timeless!

MATERIALS

- 12″ × 18″″ white paper
- assorted sizes and colors of cut paper squares (see Teacher Preparation)
- scissors
- glue sticks or white glue
- colored water-based markers
- fine-tip markers (optional)

- gold and silver pens (optional)
- crayons (to include human skin colors)
- corrugated cardboard scraps
- pencils
- reproducible page: "The Middle East: Patterns and Designs"

TEACHER PREPARATION

Teacher may want to precut assorted paper squares, including white, for expedience of lesson. Various cardboard box flaps will provide the necessary scraps for dimensional assemblage or "relief" effect. Available pictures from references that feature desert people and the environment, camels, tents, and so on will spark student imaginations. Also, if teacher and students have any objects from the Middle East, now is the time to bring them to class. Consider the use of the following "shopping list" for display and/or classroom distribution:

▲ Figure 3-8. "Ships of the desert" are the way camels are usually regarded. They can travel great distances without water and are of hardy constitution. The dromedaries are a favored vehicle of transport, and are worthy of further study. The Middle East has been for centuries a "camel culture," although rugged terrain vehicles have certainly affected desert travel. Taking your dromedary to market? There is an old Arabic saying: *"Trust in Allah—but tie your camel."*

SHOPPING LIST
Can You Picture This?

THE ARAB MARKETPLACE
Your Checklist Includes:

_____ 1. <u>Tents</u>—where clothing, craft objects, and food are sold.

_____ 2. <u>Camel</u>—with saddle made out of carpet!

_____ 3. <u>People in Arab clothes</u>—interacting with one another.

_____ 4. <u>Desert Environment</u>—sand dunes and palm trees.

_____ 5. <u>Fabric</u>—lots of patterns and designs.

This will really help to organize the lesson.

DIRECTIONS:

1. How would the class like art to take us shopping? The people of the middle eastern desert communities need and enjoy shopping . . . from the purchase of food for the household to a new carpet saddle for a camel! Discuss what objects and products might be found in the "Arabian Shopping Mall." How would one travel to the desert market? What might be found at the souk when you arrive?

2. Provide students with reference materials. Selections will be made from the "Shopping List." Teacher may require that all items appear in the pictorial composition in given numbers; for example, "three tents minimum" . . . or "at least one camel"!

3. Distribute materials. Ask students to think about the elements they wish to add. Do we want to draw the basic picture first, then attach specific items and objects? A certain amount of "scenery" seems to offer a foundation for the attachment of raised figures to picture.

4. Encourage students to use Islamic design elements on their "shopping goods." (See accompanying reproducible page for this activity.)

5. Keep it colorful! Add dazzling touches—a gold or silver pen will make "metalware" shine! Decide what exactly will be mounted on the paper. Remember the concept of "picture space." Cut out selection(s), glue to cardboard scraps, then affix to paper surface.

6. Have you filled your pictures with all that they need to convey your ideas of the Nomadic market? Great! Then let's go shopping!

THE MIDDLE EAST: PATTERNS AND DESIGNS

WOMAN'S HEADCOVERING

MAN'S HEADCLOTH

MENSWEAR: GAZA DRESS

KUFI CAP

WOMENSWEAR: FEMALE CHEMISE

SLIPPERS

ORIENTAL RUGS

Lotus and Palmette Pattern

Tribal Geometric Design

Donkey Sandle Bag Carpet

Tree-of-Life or Garden of Paradise

Mihrab or Directional Prayer Rug; Architectural Design

ACTIVITY 3

Architecture of the Islamic World: The Marvel of the Mosque and Its Minarets!

Architecture/Alahambra to Arabia

To discover great landmarks of famous world architecture, one may look at once to Islamic design. Magnificent Arabic monuments may take the form of a palace or, more often, a place of learning and reverence. The single most impressive Muslim-built achievement is intended as a "house of worship": It is the mosque.

The plan of the mosque is basic—a square foundation with an open-air courtyard that conveys the Islamic concept of the Garden of Paradise. A fountain may also be expected nearby. The mosque's most distinguishing feature, however, is its central dome. Towers—called *minarets*—flank the structure; these enable a "caller" or *muezzen* to be heard near and far, echoing a "call to prayer" five times a day. Tall minarets are symbolic of the supremacy of Allah, which translates as "the God." Inside the mosque, a *minbar* serves as a pulpit. The interior is generous yet contains small spaces, too. The "prayer niche" or *mihrab* is particularly important: It faces the worshipper in the direction of Mecca. Mosques are spiritual and practical, expressive of devotion and the mystery of the divine.

Early mosques were likely to be modest structures made of combined natural materials. Brick played a major part as the mosque evolved to its full architectural identity. The art of the potter allowed the sparkling ceramic surfaces, immediately associated with mosques, to emerge. Intended to inspire through their infinite calligraphic patterns, mosques are considered marvels of geometry, poetry, and design. It is good to remember that from simple red clay, great domes and minarets grow!

▲ Figure 3-9. A simple statement in clay describes basic mosque form—a central dome flanked by minarets.

MATERIALS

- 9" × 12" newsprint
- pencils
- ceramic clay (terra-cotta) or airdrying clay
- rolling pins
- canvas, oil cloth, or paper matcover
- brushes
- plaster bats or cardboard (see Teacher Preparation)
- 1/4" × 12" wood slats or wooden rulers (two per student)
- clear glaze (acrylic varnish for airdrying clay)
- metal L-brackets (option—see Teacher Preparation)
- hot glue gun (Teacher Supervision)
- popsicle sticks (or tongue depressors)

▲ Figure 3-10. A student interpretation of Islamic style, embellished with playful surface design that suggests several basic architectural elements. Sun-dried brick and clay commonly appear in Islamic architecture, although glazed decorative ceramic tile surfaces are generally associated as a dominant mosque characteristic.

▲ Figure 3-11. The Dome of the Rock in Jerusalem is revered as the place of the Prophet Muhammad's rise to heaven. Although not actually a mosque, The Dome of the Rock is called *Mosque of 'Uman* and is a holy site for Christians and Jews as well. It is where The Church of the Holy Sepulcher is built, where Christians believe Christ is buried. The nearby Wailing Wall is what remains of a first century B.C. Jewish temple which is today an international place of Jewish prayer. Most holy in the Islamic world is The Great Mosque in Mecca (Makkah), now Saudi Arabia, where the Prophet Muhammad was born in the year A.D. 570. Other important mosques include The Mosque of the Shah in Isfahan, Iran; The Blue Mosque in Istanbul, Turkey, an achievement of the Ottoman Empire; The Great Mosque in Cordoba, Spain; and the Muhammad Ali mosque in Cairo, Egypt. Mosques, like churches and other temples of worship, vary in appearance and are found all over the world.

▲ Figure 3-12. A colorful tile from Jerusalem, created by an artisan in the city's Armenian quarter. The architectural skyline pictured here reveals the lively diversity of the region!

TEACHER PREPARATION

If your classroom is already set up for working with clay and/or you have a slab roller, you will not need the following suggestions.

Teacher will need to cut clay into approximately 1"-thick slabs with clay wire-cutting tool. If wood slats are unavailable, two wood rulers per student can be used to roll clay to consistent thickness. Popsicle sticks or tongue depressors are excellent substitute clay tools. The project is similar to clay tile construction and should be dried on a flat surface such as a plaster bat; however, heavy cardboard (from boxes) also works well. Cover clay working surfaces with oilcloth, canvas, or heavy paper.

DIRECTIONS

1. Discuss architectural features of Islamic mosque design, such as the use of domes, minarets, towers, and pointed arch windows.

2. Draw an idea for a mosque on 9" × 12" newsprint. Be sure to include above architectural features in the drawing. Design may be horizontal or vertical. Do not make minarets too thin or they will tend to break off.

3. Distribute clay and supplies.

4. Place slab of clay between wooden slats (or rulers). Press down clay with hands and then roll slab with rolling pin to 1/4" thickness. The slab should be at least 9" × 12" wide. Place slab on plaster bat or cardboard.

5. Place newsprint drawing on top of clay and lightly trace lines in drawing with a pencil. Lift newsprint. The lines will be etched on the clay surface.

6. Using popsicle stick, cut the outside shape of the mosque, being careful not to cut off minarets. Do not cut out windows as this may make clay too thin and fragile. Remove extra clay.

7. Use the stick to gouge out clay arch windows and to incise other designs onto the clay.

8. Let clay dry. (Fire at appropriate cone temperature, if vented kiln is accessible.)

9. Glaze with clear glaze and refire. (Airdried clay may be sealed with acrylic varnish.)

10. To make the mosques stand up, use the hot glue gun (teacher supervised) to glue two metal L-brackets to the back of the structure. Another option is to poke two holes into the wet clay surface before firing. A cord can be attached that will make the structure suitable for hanging. Either way, mosques stand for inspired design!

▲ Figure 3-13. This beautiful wood inlay concisely endorses the Islamic love of pattern detail. The central square could just as easily represent a courtyard as the inside of a backgammon game box. Tesselations, geometric repetitions, and symmetrical balance appear in all aspects of Islamic design. We may know this game as backgammon; in Persia/Iran it is known as *Nardi;* and in Hebrew it is *Shesh-besh.* Students can fashion their own game set from joined shoe box lids and recycled bottle caps. Are you game?

ACTIVITY 4

Spice-of-Life Box

3-D Spice "Aromatic" Clay Container

▲ Figure 3-14. Spice containers, made by students' own hands, are precious ceremonial objects that hold aromatic delights! There is no rule to limit the imagination when it comes to spice boxes—they can take any number of shapes. Note the fish that floated into our spice box grouping. Is it a grouper, a trout . . . or *gefilte* fish?!

The Middle East is a multicultural society: It is considered the homeland for Christians, Muslims, and Jews. The Jewish people of Israel are proud of their heritage and often bring with them time-honored traditions of Europe, and of the other cultures where they have lived over many centuries. Jews worldwide share a weekly observation of the Sabbath, called *Shabat*, which begins at sundown of Friday evening. To begin, the greeting "Shabbat Shalom"—which means "Sabbath of peace"—is sung. The items present on the Sabbath table are: two candles (the twisted kind are often favored); grape juice (or wine); a braided bread called Challah, and spices! This festive occasion marks the end of the work week: All five senses are engaged. Candles are usually lit by household women. It is a time of joy, rest, and peace.

Among the most lovely of ceremonial Sabbath objects is the spice container. It is part of *Havdalah,* the close of the Sabbath on Saturday night. Havdalah is Hebrew for "separation," meaning that observers will separate from the ceremony and bring its sweetness with them into the following days. Shabbat ends when the second candle is lit—and when, some say, three stars appear in the evening sky.

Spice containers are beautiful to see, smell, touch, and experience—for they may contain nutmeg, cinnamon, and cloves. They most often appear as medieval towers, due to the European influence! Fish, flowers, windmills, houses, and animals are also included—as long as there is filigree (or other openings) for spicy aromas to be enjoyed. You don't have to be Jewish to love the spice and sweetness of life!

◀ Figure 3-15. Traditional spice box. Note the convenient little compartment for the aromatics! This container is a metal filigree. The Middle East is renowned for its metal craft.

MATERIALS

- Crayola® Model Magic™
- scissors
- rolling pins (see Teacher Preparation)
- sequins
- caps from small markers

- white glue
- gold tempera paint (optional)
- spices or potpourri
- 4" × 7" rectangular template (option—see Teacher Preparation)

TEACHER PREPARATION

The amount of Crayola® Model Magic™ needed per student will depend upon the size of the spice box you plan to make. They may be only two inches tall or as large as eight (larger is unwieldly). You may wish to have a rectangular template available in the desired size for the cylinder section of the spice box. Make a sample to decide on amount of clay needed and the size of template. If rolling pins are used, be sure they are clean. Crayola® Model Magic™ is so pliable that large markers could even be used as rolling pins for smaller spice boxes.

   A variety of pictorial (or dimensional) references that represent ideas for spice box shapes may be gathered—from castle tower to seated lions that roar!

▲ Figure 3-16. Detail from our spice box group. *Little* works quite well, don't you think?

DIRECTIONS

1. Distribute materials. Roll Crayola® Model Magic™ on a clean surface into an oblong shape. Place rectangular template on top of clay and cut out rectangular shape. Ask students to decide on the form their spice box will be and imagine the basic form.

2. Lay the clay flat and use caps from small markers to press into clay to create circular openings into the rectangle. (This will allow the aroma of the spices to escape.)

3. Roll thin coils of clay and press around opening in a coiling or spiraling manner. This enhances the filigree.

4. When the coil designs are in place, take the rectangle and curve it together into a cylinder shape by pressing short edges together.

5. To make a bottom on the cylinder, place the cylinder on another piece of clay and trace around the bottom (circle shape). Cut out this circle with scissors and press onto the bottom of the cylinder.

6. To make the stand (or stem), form clay into a stem shape and press onto bottom of cylinder.

7. The top is made by forming a small pinch pot that is slightly larger than the opening of the cylinder. Do not place on top of the cylinder until it has dried.

8. Paint with gold tempera paint and glue on sequins with white glue, if desired.

9. The spice container is now complete. Fill with potpourri or large spices and enjoy the aroma. All your senses will be pleased!

▲ Figure 3-17. Compare the architectural appearance of the spice container with the entrance to this European-styled synagogue. Some of these elements may inspire design ideas. A seated lion with a roaring (or yawning) mouth could serve our spices!

ACTIVITY 5

Windows on Israel

"Stained-Glass Windows"

BONUS: *Chicken Soup to Dream For! Paper Sculpture Includes REAL recipe, too!*

Dazzling Jerusalem! It is a place where the ancient and modern worlds converge. To Christians, Jews, and Muslims, Israel is a living illumination of the Holy Land. In a diverse society filled with many strong beliefs, there is also contradiction, conflict, and passion. A painter who felt drawn to the pulsations of this land was a Russian Jew and colorful French artist. Marc Chagall was to form a personal and artistic bond with Jerusalem through the light of his brilliant stained-glass window. In 1948, Israel was officially declared a Jewish State by the United Nations. A great many Holocaust survivors joined the existing population of Palestinians, native Jews (called *Sabra*), and many other diverse groups. The new Israeli citizens brought with them their rich European traditions, further shaping the complex and compelling identity of Israel.

The sense of a Hebrew homeland beckons large numbers of visitors in all forms of spiritual pilgrimage. For the Muslims, Jerusalem is one of three holy sites. As a Jew, Marc Chagall made his own artistically holy visit to Israel more than once. Each time, his feelings—like this place itself—would hold different meanings.

A culminating event for Chagall was a commission he received near Jerusalem for twelve synagogue windows. Perfect! Here he could bring to life with color and light the Twelve Tribes of Israel! Chagall used a visual vocabulary of signs and symbols that float in dreamy emotional space. The Jerusalem stained glass allowed Chagall to do what he did so well—bring together separate elements in glowing harmony. Art can certainly spark the hope of peace.

▲ Figure 3-18. This dazzling window is one young student's interpretation of a familiar Jewish ceremonial object, the *menorah,* used for the Chanukah Festival of Lights. Another symbol is the Star of David, accompanied above by the Hebrew letter styles.

MATERIALS

- 18" × 24" white paper (may substitute with 12" × 18")
- pencils
- colored watercolor markers (see Teacher Preparation)
- paintbrushes
- scissors (see Teacher Preparation)
- watercolor cups

Figure 3-19. Birds are universally uplifting and are regarded in many cultures as a kind of heavenly messenger. The bird is also a symbol for peace. Artist Marc Chagall used hopeful, loving images as well as religious icons—although not exclusive to his Jewish identity. He believed that art in itself was spiritual. ▶

▲ Figure 3-20. Our hand-crafted clay object is called a *mezuzah*. It is placed at the doorway as blessing to the home. Hebrew sacred text can be found within it. This mezuzah has the right shape for our activity, and is packed with symbols translated into "stained-glass" windows!

▲ Figure 3-21. This Jewish worshipper at the Jerusalem Wailing Wall is exactly the kind of figure Chagall remembers in his paintings, particularly those that describe his life while growing up in a small Russian village. Look for the prayer shawl—or *tallis*—in Chagall's art, too. While this man's hand gesture is widely recognizable as one of faith, the man himself is an "Oriental Jew" (of Sephardic origin, generally refers to Jews of Moorish Spain—Sephardic means Spanish in Hebrew). There is timeless and universal praise for tradition in all cultures.

TEACHER PREPARATION

In order to achieve the desired symmetry of the arched window, teacher may wish to precut the shape. A template can first be made by simply folding one paper in half, then curving the scissors along the edge of the paper's upper top section. It is not recommended to ask students to use these directions for their own direct work because the fold may distract the flow of their designs. Teacher can use template to precut student windows or provide templates for them to share.

Good news: a practical use for those colored markers that have lost their full color saturation. Old markers can create the illusion of light through shading application! Keep water cups on hand for variations in translucency. (Note: Be sure the black markers are in working order.)

DIRECTIONS

1. Discuss the way light looks as it passes through a colored glass window. How many students have seen stained glass? Ask for verbal descriptions. Stained glass brings shapes together and holds everything in place with unifying black lines.

2. Talk about artist Marc Chagall and his particular knack for bringing stained glass to life. What might give us some good subject ideas for these windows? Stars, sun and moon, creatures that fly; signs and symbols that lift our spirits on special times of the year.

3. Distribute paper and pencils. Students will sketch their personal window designs directly on the arched window-shaped paper.

4. Student may now receive markers and water cups. Create window "glass" by applying markers in varying shades and tones. Note: Chagall rubbed color with a rag to vary his stained glass! Students can achieve this look through thoughtful blending using all markers, brushes, and water.

5. As design is developing, think about where black contour lines will appear. Apply black line when most of the other colors are in place.

6. Remember to use the black line as a design element that will "imitate" the fragments of colored glass held together. Finish with black line drawn around entire outside contour.

7. Your sparkling vision is complete! Windows "installed" in hallways, offices, classrooms, and lunchrooms will add a very special touch, transforming a closed area into a beautiful light-filled space. Art shines through once again!

B O N U S : CHICKEN SOUP TO DREAM FOR!

Finally, you've earned your chicken soup! In the classroom you can whip up a bowl of paper soup in no time! Curl your paper noodles with good wishes, wise sayings, and notes of love. This soup includes a chicken that Chagall would adore!

For *real* "Chicken Soup to Dream For," try Bette's Homemade Chicken Soup (Mrs. Jean Star's Chicken Soup)—with Matzoh balls! *Such* bliss!

Bette's mother's Chicken Soup is a treasure, handed down from generation to generation. We are honored to present you with this delicious and special recipe from the Russian-Jewish American household in which Bette grew into adulthood. Bette is now a mother herself and appreciates the true powers of a big pot of chicken soup—it fills the home with joys and comforts both past and present.

MRS. JEAN STAR'S CHICKEN SOUP— FROM SCRATCH!

"FOR GROWN-UP HANDS ONLY TO MAKE"

Cooking time: 4–5 hours! (In a hurry? See "S.O.S." Chicken Soup)

Supplies: two large pots, fine strainer, long fork or tongs

Ingredients:

3 quarts water
6–8 pieces chicken (remove skin and fat)
8–10 carrots, cut in large chunks
1 large onion, quartered
1/2 teaspoon dried thyme or several sprigs of fresh thyme to taste
4–6 celery stalks, chopped
fresh dill, chopped (begin with 3 sprigs, then increase to taste)
salt/pepper (to taste)
one parsnip, peeled and cut into quarters
fresh Italian parsley, chopped (to taste)
1 pound thin or thick noodles or matzoh balls (optional)

Directions:

Boil water. Add chicken carefully. Note: Amount of water should not be more than one-half inch over chicken. Cook 20 minutes in boiling water. Remove chicken with long fork or tongs and set aside on a plate. Pour broth through a fine strainer into a second pot. Rinse first pot and replace chicken and strained broth. Cook another 30 minutes on medium heat. Repeat straining process.

Add all other ingredients except noodles or matzoh balls and cook for several hours, checking seasonings to taste. Add noodles or matzoh balls 30 minutes to one hour before serving. After soup is completed, refrigerate. Fat can then be skimmed off the top.

BETTE'S MOM, JEAN STAR, ORIGINATED THE "FROM SCRATCH" RECIPE

THIS IS BETTE'S ANSWER FOR BUSY TIMES

Bette's "S. O. S." Chicken Soup—Short Cut

Ingredients:

3 boxes (more or less as quantity desired) Lipton™ Soup Secrets® (no meat)
3–5 pieces chicken (your choice of parts), fat and skin removed
salt/pepper (to taste)
vegetables and herbs (from "From Scratch" recipe)
matzoh balls (optional)

Directions:

Follow directions on box of soup. For clear broth, do not add the noodles.

Season chicken with poultry seasonings, sage, and pepper. Bake or boil in a separate pot of water until done. Cut into bite-sized pieces and add to soup.

Add all the vegetables and herbs from "From Scratch" recipe. Simmer 2–3 hours. Season to taste.

Add matzoh balls or noodles 30 minutes to one hour before serving.

HOW TO MAKE HEAVENLY MATZOH BALLS!

Ingredients:

1 cup matzoh meal (will yield 8-10 matzoh balls)
4 eggs
1/3 cup margarine, melted
1 teaspoon salt, and dash of pepper
1/2 cup water

Directions:

Beat eggs. Combine water, butter or margarine, salt and pepper. Mix well into water. Add matzoh meal and mix thoroughly. Refrigerate one hour. Boil large pot of water. Make balls the size of golf balls. (Tip: Keep a cup or bowl of water handy to keep hands wet between rolling. This will keep the mixture from sticking to your hands.)

Gently drop balls into boiling water. Reduce heat to low boil. Cover and cook for 40 minutes. Using a slotted spoon, drain each ball, and drop into hot soup. Cook another 15 to 20 minutes.

HOW TO RECOGNIZE A READY-TO-EAT MATZOH BALL

- At least double original size
- Plump and spongey

Bette recommends that you eat matzoh balls in your soup at least once in your life. Cholesterol alert: eggs! Otherwise, the matzoh is a miracle. You should only know from this!

ACTIVITY 6

Tabriz or Not Tabriz? Persian Tote Bags

Carpet Design Tote Bags

Persia sits like a cat in the middle of a map within a region known as The Rug Belt—with Turkey to the west and China to the east. Tabriz was once the capital city of Persia (now called Iran) during the 15th-century Safavid dynasty. An important center of trade along the great Silk Route, Tabriz was also known for manuscript production. Tabriz was important but not the only city of splendid carpets. There is so very much to know about Oriental rugs that classification is helpful. Geography is a good way to get started.

There are five basic rugmaking regions: Persia (Iran); Caucacus (Russia); Turkey (Anatolia); Central Asia; and China/East, Turkestan/Tibet (unified stylistically). Carpet appearances vary in color, weave, format, and design; yet they are categorically identifiable. The lands of India, Pakistan, Afghanistan—and "significant others"—are praised for their rug artistry. Still, in the world of carpets, the Middle East is at the summit.

Carpets are produced in cities, towns, and small villages. Many fine weavers are either settled or nomadic, such as the Kurds, who are experts with color, design, and quality. Even though Kurds may live in Iraq, Turkey, Syria, and elsewhere, Kurdish rugs are considered Iranian (Persian). They are known as tribal rugs. The more you learn about rugs, the more there is to enjoy. Ever since the rug discovery of a 4th century B.C. woven fragment called *Pazyryk*, carpets continue to intrigue us. Rugs are not just rugs: They serve as prayer mats, desert tent doors, luggage, camel bags, table cloths . . . even maps. No wonder carpets can make us happier than a Persian kitten with a new ball of wool!

▲ Figure 3-22. Kristin, age 12, chose a central lotus or palmette pattern to surround with traditional and personal motifs for her Persian tote design. The colors and symbols express her theme. "I picked colors to match my ideas . . . to make my symbols stand out." The rug is an original. Kristin explains, "It shows my feelings on different things like love and anger, peace and war." She understands that Oriental carpets hold many meanings.

◄ Figure 3-23. Persian tote tucks in handles and transforms to carpet magically! The Egyptian vessel and Moroccan slipper make it even more convincing.

MATERIALS

- plain brown or white paper shopping bags (see Teacher Preparation)
- pencils
- colored markers
- oil pastels
- 9" × 12" manila paper
- thin-tipped, nontoxic permanent black pens

TEACHER PREPARATION

The ideal format for this activity will be found in a sufficient quantity of plain paper shopping bags with handles for your students. There may be a paper goods and/or packaging supply outlet, craft store, or a friendly merchant for the lucky teacher to discover! If this is not the case, brown bags without handles will do (yarn may be substituted for handles). Shopping bags can also be approximated with brown kraft paper, cut the shape of shopping bags with handles, and stapled or otherwise reinforced.

Students will appreciate examples of the basic Oriental rug formats to assist their own rug interpretations. Again, resourceful teachers can find basic rug designs in advertisement flyers that often appear in weekend newspapers for rug sales. Likewise, houseware catalogs may include Oriental rugs in their pages (for the record, these are usually the machine-made variety, but their designs will serve the purpose). Provide symbols and signs; photocopies will help. Basic rug design frameworks include central pattern(s), divided units, overall repetition, and compartmentalized symmetry. These are curvilinear as well as geometric in appearance and should be made available as examples for students. (See Patterns and Designs reproducible page in Activity 2.)

DIRECTIONS

1. Teacher will want to be assured that students see and understand basic Oriental rug design types before they begin the lesson. Distribute photocopies of design elements page from Activity 2 of this section. Compare rug patterns for their visual impact. What makes one pattern more interesting or dynamic than another? Where does personal taste enter into it? When the time seems right, distribute pencils and manila paper.

◀ Figure 3-24. Rugs are woven, hand knotted, and even pressed felt, as are these carpet objects. Twigs for a happy couple's wedding tent will be gathered and placed in the beautiful bags shown here, following their ancient nomadic Turkoman custom.

2. Students may want to experiment with several possibilities and combinations before they reach a final decision for their tote bags. Include borders—they are essential to Oriental rug formats! Remember, Oriental rugs love the interplay of many design elements!

3. Upon student decisions, distribute all other materials and the paper shopping bags! Students will approximate design transfer with pencil on the paper bag surface.

4. Encourage marker usage for most of the initial color application. Oil pastels will suggest the textural quality and may be used gingerly (oil pastels have powerful coverage capability and can just as easily cover linear drawing if not used carefully!). Use the black markers as needed to delineate contours, boundaries, and details.

5. Animals, plants, geometrics, and arabesques should be sprouting up all over the artroom at this point! Students can certainly invent their own symbols as well. Remember, Oriental rugs are not merely decorative; they express ideas. Ask students to consider the meaning their rugs have for them. For example, if a *title* was to be given to the rug, what might it be?

6. Rugs take patience. Coach students along—we want to transform paper into wool and silk—weaving our own universe of symbols and ideas! Students should know that the "restful" areas are just as necessary as the visually active ones.

7. Are we finished yet? Think about this—we are in fact doing what is only the very first stage of making a loom-woven carpet by creating the paper design. Oriental rug weavers use a paper "cartoon" to reproduce the rug design through memory. When paper surfaces appear fully articulated, students are probably done.

8. Now you have a fabulous shopping bag. Take it to the "souk"!

◄ Figure 3-25. This classic Yomud carpet is generally seen in an overall red field. Parviz, an experienced carpet connoisseur, tells of the surprising use of this carpet as a tent door! His wonderful rug gallery in Philadelphia, appropriately called Woven Treasures, is filled with collectible earthly lights. Clearly, rugs are more than just rugs. Since there was a particular rug section to represent every day of the year, the king knew the day by the rug. The royal rug was, in fact, a calendar!

▲ Figure 3-26. Just a boldly decorative carpet, you say? Look again. This rug is a map of Herat in Afghanistan. Unfortunately, this region has struggled to survive terrible conflicts. Parviz points out the symbolic invasion of tanks and artillery. The trees stand for the lives lost in war.

ACTIVITY 7

A Turkish Delight: Iznik Dishes

"Faux" Plates

BONUS: *"Collector" Display Stand*

▲ Figure 3-27. Flowers, plants, and the natural world are a beloved theme for these plates that favor the colors of turquoise blue, green, and tomato red. The tiled city that is Iznik today is the source that illuminates Istanbul with "miles of tiles." The beautiful plates are, like Turkey itself, both poetic and hardy. The height of Iznik production continued its popularity into the 17th century. Lucky for us, Iznik dishes still provide a feast for the eyes!

Whom should we thank? "Suleyman the Magnificent" or "Selim the Grim"? Both men ruled in Turkey. Suleyman the Magnificent was infamous and mighty; his vast territories were known as the Ottoman Empire. Under the Ottomans, it was Selim the Grim—a historically lesser-known figure of Anatolia (Turkey)—who sent 500 Persian potters to a small city by the ancient name of Nicaea. The name of this city, which grew out of Byzantine and Roman ruins, became Iznik. Near Istanbul, Iznik is synonymous with its tiles and dishes. In the 16th century under Ottoman rule, Iznik itself functioned as a great palace workshop. A Chief of the Potters supervised busy ceramic production that was held to only the highest standard.

The splendid Iznik ceramic works have an unmistakable appearance. Dishes, bowls, tiles, and mosque lamps of Iznik show creative interpretations of the courtly artists' favorites decorative features. Ceramic ware was exported beyond Turkey and into Europe. The blue-and-white Chinese glaze, as well as Asian floral motifs, are also a signature of Iznik. Not surprisingly, Persian artisans would have been geographically and culturally influenced because Persia (Iran) is located between China and Arabia. In Turkey, Iznik plates display their impressive origins.

MATERIALS

- paper plates (see Teacher Preparation)
- polymer varnish glaze (see Teacher Preparation)
- pencils
- colored markers
- brushes (if acrylic varnish is desired)
- reproducible page: "Iznik Dishes"

▲ Figure 3-28. This *Simurgh* landed on exactly the right spot—a Turkish Iznik plate. You can also find the *Simurgh* in the *Shah-nameh* or *The Persian Book of Kings*, an illuminated manuscript history of Iran. This *Simurgh* is the Queen of birds: She nurtured an important prince named Zal on the top of a mountain and then let him go, according to one of many legends.

Figure 3-29. This luscious palmette is encompassed by the poetry of the written word, repeated like a chant around its edge. ▶

TEACHER PREPARATION

Select plain white paper (not plastic) plates. Teacher may want to first "test" the drawing surface with markers if there is any question about the porosity of the paper plates to be used.

Polymer-based varnish or a similar nontoxic medium may be used as a "glaze" for a glossy finish. Again, test a completed patch of plate design with applied varnish to avoid unwelcome surprise. Note: The finish may be one of a runny glaze. Teacher may or may not want this effect; it is entirely discretionary. Reference material on Persian and Turkish design as well as Islamic pictorial symbols is suggested on page 104.

DIRECTIONS

1. Consider the perfect circle of the plate! Teacher will discuss the design possibilities with the class. Motifs will run in circles around the rim; the center will contain larger figures. Reproducible pages may be used for reference.

2. Distribute pencils. Students can experiment with their sketched ideas directly on the plates. Rims function as circular borders to offset central activity. Subjects from the natural world are welcome here.

3. Markers may be given to the class for selective use. Blue, green, and red are dominant in Iznik dishes. Decorate!

4. Students may want to indicate "authenticity" of plates by drawing linear "cracks" into the surface in one or two places. Complete dish designs.

5. The finished Iznik plates may be "glazed" if effect is desired (see Teacher Preparation). Teacher supervision is important—follow directions for the water-based finish as indicated.

6. Dish display can fill us with delight!

B O N U S : COLLECTOR STANDS!

Show off your stunning collection of patterns with collector stands. All it takes is a sheet of 9" × 12" construction paper or oaktag, folded in half. Cut from top crease diagonally towards corner of open end. Before getting to the end, curve upward. See how a plate can stand "on its own"!

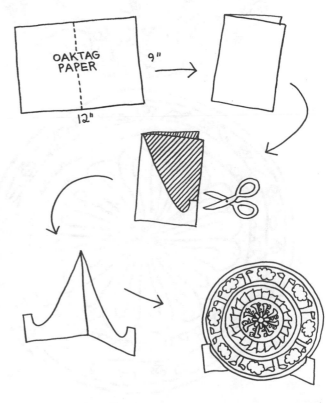

IZNIK DISHES

ACTIVITY 8

Me and My Turkish Shadow: The Puppet Crafts of Istanbul

Crafty Turkish Shadow Puppets/Theater Arts

So a rabbi, a Turkish Orthodox priest, and a puppeteer are walking across a bridge over the Bosphorus. On one side is Asia; the other, Europe. And the punch line is . . . ? The punchline—as in *Punch and Judy*—is the ongoing script of this Turkish puppet show, known to young and old alike for centuries. *Karagoz,* the shadow theater of Turkey, is still a cherished cultural tradition. Yes, the diverse list of stock characters is long and *does* include an Orthodox Turkish priest, a Jewish rabbi, an Albanian, a night watchman, a magician, a Kurd, a coffee grinder, a musician . . . to name but a few. The two leading stars of the show are *Hacivat* (Ha-dji-vat) and *Karagoz* (Car-a-gerz)—the one for whom the shadow play is named!

It is said that the *Karagoz* puppet theater was brought to Istanbul from Egypt in the 16th century when Sultan Selim I sought to entertain his son, the young prince Suleyman, who would become the grand Caliph of the Ottoman Empire! Turkey, also known as Anatolia, was a multi-ethnic society under Suleyman the Magnificent—a great patron of the arts and a ruler of vast territories. As people attempted to adjust to a wide variety of customs and beliefs, *Karagoz* provided them with comic relief. Political satire, everyday events, magic, history, mythology, and cultural miscommunications were fuel for Turkish Shadow Theater.

Karagoz himself, who represents "the little man," is a pugnacious fellow with a definite set of behavior problems! Hacivat, his foil, is well-respected and mannerly. He is an educated man (also a little pretentious), considered by all a kindly problem-solver. Between these two, anything can happen! Their misadventures and antics are as endless as the laughter they have evoked from centuries of performances. Ladies and gentlemen, let's welcome Karagoz and Hacivat!

▲ Figure 3-30. The Shadow Play! Karagoz is popular for festivals and throughout *Ramadan*, a period of days of fasting in the Muslim calendar that ends with the feast of Eid-el-Fidur.

Figure 3-31. Turkey is filled with a kaleidoscopic variety of ethnic origins and beliefs. Did you ever wonder where one might find the *Whirling Dirvish*? In Turkey! The Whirling Dirvish is a worshipper who evokes religious ecstasy through a spinning dance. Dervishes are *Sufi,* a mystical and quite poetic Islamic order that seeks a closer experience with God. Sufi dancing is considered an expression of high devotion. Dancers, magicians, merchants, artists, kings, fools—the Karagoz stage is a mirror of the world we live in, filled with timeless types and characters. ▶

MATERIALS

- oaktag
- paper fasteners
- pencils
- colored markers
- scissors
- masking tape
- flashlight (see Teacher Preparation)

- hole puncher (for paper fastener)
- wood molding (see Teacher Preparation)
- white roll paper (see Teacher Preparation)
- reproducible pages: Puppet Forms of "Karagoz" and "Hacivat"
- Plain white fabric sheet (see Teacher Preparation)

TEACHER PREPARATION

The puppet will measure approximately twelve inches in height, comprised of three sections. Teacher may want to precut oaktag for body parts: head to waist to include arms, hips, legs, and feet. Prepunch holes for fastener attachment, if desired. Students will have reproducible puppet references.

Puppets will require a stick for mounting. Teacher will cut with a saw (in woodshop, if available) strips of wood molding. Size the stick length to accommodate students' hands. Other suggestions for puppet sticks include recyclable rulers and/or paint can stir sticks. Note: Hardware stores and building supply/lumber yard outlets can cut strips to required lengths and numbers.

The puppet shadow theater screen may be sized at approximately 36" × 48". This "theater" will be supported by a table surface (see Figure 3-30). All that is needed for the stage lighting is a good flashlight! The screen may be made of white roll paper or of plain white fabric sheet—to be held by "stagehands".

RABBI, a Jewish
scholar and teacher

MAGICIAN

DIRECTIONS

1. Who are Karagoz and Hacivat? Teacher will explain the origins of the two puppets. Do you know other stories and real-life situations that provide comic characters? Discuss.

2. Familiar literary references can help young imaginations to develop ideas. Distribute paper and pencils. Students may find that the measuring of oaktag into three sections helps to organize the puppet body. Have you decided how many character types the class will represent? Teacher may want to turn into a "casting agent": Ask certain student groups to create specific stock characters. While it is not essential to conform to all the exclusively Karagoz "players," do be sure to at least include him in this play!

3. Think about the concept of figures shown in profile as they are being produced; puppets will ultimately serve as silhouettes. Even so, the costumes should be considered for their own worth. Traditional Karagoz puppets are made from animal hides, yet are translucent and often appear as filigree or "cut paper" figures. All sorts of "scenery" is provided. Teacher may want to ask select students to be in "scenery" to create the moveable stage sets.

4. These puppets are very basic, so feel free to embellish. Note: If "script writers' block" occurs, refer to "Karagoz in a Jar." How did he get there? How will he get out?

5. Distribute all other materials, but withhold the "theater."

6. Once the cast of characters is well underway, along with scenery, begin cutting and connecting the body sections. Use paper fasteners as indicated.

7. Attach wood strips to the backs of the figures and scenery. Do you have a script yet? This may or may not be written as such—improvisation is probably your best bet!

8. Let the show begin! Students will need to support the screen. You will also need a stagehand for "lighting." Unroll the white paper or stretch the sheet and pick up the flashlight. Are you ready? Lights, camera, action!

KARAGÖZ
IN A JAR

◀ Figure 3-32. The lady next door? Maybe. These puppets have "optional" articulation. Traditional Turkish shadow puppets are made of detailed filigree. The props include all kinds of scenery—from local architecture to sailing ships! Pets are welcome.

KARAGÖZ
THE TURKISH SHADOW PUPPET

HACIVAT
THE TURKISH
SHADOW PUPPET

ACTIVITY 9

THE ANCIENT WORLD OF THE MEDITERRANEAN: LEAPING BRONZE BULLS!

"Archaeological" Metalwork

BONUS: *Finds of Long Ago* and *Instant Archaeology*

▲ Figure 3-33. Here we have the fragment of an ancient bull that brags of metalsmithing and ancient symbols. All that is missing are the acrobats, which could certainly be the next artroom project.

Do you know that many beliefs that formed the origins of civilization grew alongside the Mediterranean Sea? Yet it was only in the last one hundred years that the discovery of the Minoans as the first people to inhabit the culture we now know as Greek was revealed! These early Mediterraneans lived from 2500–1450 B.C., forming the basis for the following Mycenaean society. In this same place, one would have found Knossos, the awesome city, where King Minos of myth and legend dwelled. It is said that Minos proved the right to his throne by asking the gods to make a bull emerge from the sea. And it was done. But Minos failed to meet his end of the bargain. He had promised to slay the bull, but he kept it instead. Out of these circumstances come the famous myths of the Minotaur—half man, half bull, and son of the wife of Minos—the basis for "The Bull in the Labyrinth." Minos secured this monster in a puzzling labyrinth palace where only its architect knew the way. Heroics followed, by mythological Greek gods and goddesses who have since become recognizable in the pantheon of ancient mythology.

The ideas formed at Knossos were only a "bull's leap" away from the rest of the ancient world—which stretched into an area known as "The Fertile Crescent." An agricultural oasis, nature was in full abundance. No one loved nature in her many aspects more than the Minoans, who expressed their devotion to the human form of a mother goddess. Bull-leaping was one way to please and honor the lovely Mother Goddess of Nature! Bull-leaping was an entertaining and highly dangerous activity, undertaken only by "trained professionals"—courageous acrobats—both male and female. The bull and mythical minotaur have remained with us as symbols of raw masculine strength and highly charged vitality. As in all powerful life forces, the bull's authority may be heroic, yet brute strength requires good control. Monitor those minotaurs!

MATERIALS

- one 9" × 12" lightweight tooling "bronze" sheet (substitute brass, aluminum, etc.) per student
- orange sticks (manicure sticks)
- magazines/newspapers
- pencils
- acrylic paints
- erasers
- paintbrushes
- 9" × 12" newsprint
- masking tape
- scissors

Figure 3-34. Is it Agamemnon, Minos, or a student's own invention of a newly rediscovered mythical hero? If students want to give a specific identity to their metalwork portrait, they will want to research clothing and hairstyles of the civilizations that interest them. ▶

TEACHER PREPARATION

Teacher will cut the "bronze" sheets (or substitute any other metallic art tooling foil) into convenient sizes for each student. The newsprint should be cut to the same size as the copper sheets to allow the students to trace their pictures directly from the newsprint onto the "bronze." Magazines or newspapers will serve as padding for tooling.

DIRECTIONS

1. Discuss above information regarding the importance of the bull and Minotaur symbols in ancient civilizations. Show examples (slide) and note the flowing lines of the bull's posture. The student may do the bull by itself or with leapers, or may instead choose to create the Minotaur—half beast, half man.

2. Distribute materials. Students draw their idea on the newsprint paper which is the same size as the "bronze" sheets. Draw large enough to fill the paper. If acrobats are included, one must be in contact with the bull in some way.

3. Students place their drawing on top of the "bronze" sheet and tape the edges to keep the paper from slipping. Now place the bronze with attached drawing on top of a magazine (the magazine acts as a pad).

4. Students use the orange stick to tool the "bronze" by pressing into the pencil lines of the image on the newsprint. These lines will incise into the metal sheet beneath the newsprint. Students may press various textures, patterns, and relief areas into the metal if desired.

5. When finished, remove newsprint.

6. Paint ancient motifs with acrylic paint. See slide #14 for some ideas.

7. When paint is dry, the student may carefully cut out the design. Be careful of sharp edges and leaping bulls!

Figure 3-35. Speaking of ancient times, this menorah (the Chanukah candelabra) is made of "Jerusalem Stone." All public structures are made of this material, which—at dusk—creates the "City of Gold." The menorah pictured here very much resembles early Judean pottery, although the artisan who crafted it is contemporary. ▶

BONUS: FINDS OF LONG AGO: ANCIENT BRONZES

Can you recognize these authentic archaeological finds of long ago?

- Bell for Goat
- Knot Holder for Rope for Horse
- Chicken
- Stamp
- Bottle Stopper
- Pomegranate—"Fruit of Heaven"
- Horseman Figure

Why not try making some "original" archaeological objects of clay in your own classroom? Dig it!

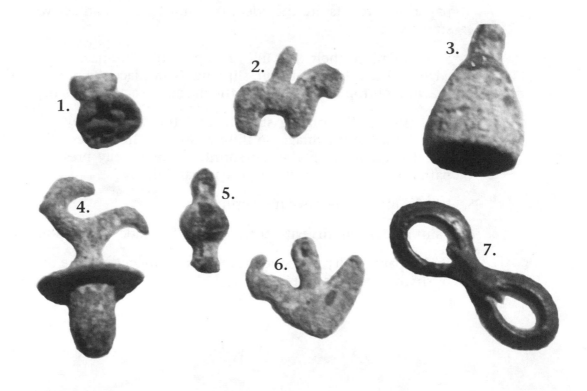

The finds are: 1. Seal Stamp, 2. Horseman, 3. Ancient Bell for Goat, 4. Bottle Stopper, 5. Pomegranate—"Fruit of Heaven," 6. Chicken! 7. Knot Holder for Rope for Horse

B O N U S : INSTANT ARCHAEOLOGY! A MODERN "FIND"

A take-out cup (from a Greek restaurant in the U.S.A.) turns into a classic Amphora! The Greek portrait vase is constructed by mounting an empty beverage container upon a small disposable water cup, turned upside down. Oil pastels create the design and surface; curled paper strips (as shown) make marvelous handles for this ancient Greek "figure ware." It's an . . . *arty-fact* all right!

India and Tibet

Tajikistan

Turkmenistan

Nepal Bhutan

Afghanistan TIBET

China

Iran

Pakistan

INDIA

Myanmar

Laos

Vietnam

Arabian
Sea

Bangladesh

Thailland

Bay of
Bengal

Andaman
Sea

SRI LANKA

Kampuchea

South
China
Sea

Malaysia

Indian Ocean

India and Tibet

Ganesha is Lord of New Beginnings and The Remover of Obstacles; he is also the patron of Learning—and students! He is usually found at doorways. This image is terra-cotta. Sculpture is a vital art form in India. ▶

A dancing figure, depicted in soft-sculpture. Her position is traditional to Indian dance—feet contact the earth as a source of energy. Hand gestures suggest various meanings. ▶

◀ Shiva, a mighty force, is represented in bronze; he is shown as the Lord of Dance. Many Indian dancers honor Shiva before their performances. Here he is shown dancing in the Endless Circle of Flames, which represents the cycle of time.

ART ACTIVITIES FOR BECOMING CULTURE SMART

◼ **Activity 1**
Everybody Loves Ganesha: Our Lucky Elephant Boy! (India)
Paper Doorway Ornament
BONUS: CLAY SCULPTURE

◼ **Activity 2**
India's Great Legends: A Gallery of Delights! (India)
Illustrated Storyteller Prop Box/Portable "Gallery" Box Construction
BONUS: TEMPLE HANGINGS OR "PICHHAVAI"

Activity 3
What's a Goddess to Wear? (India)
"Animated" Figures/Mixed Media
BONUS: VESTS OR "CHOLI"

◼ **Activity 4**
The Taj Mahal: A Monument to Love (India)
Paper Architectural Construction/Landscape Architecture
INCLUDES: REFLECTING POOL

◼ **Activity 5**
Mughal Miniature: Little Portraits of India (India)
"Frames"/Mixed-media Assemblage
BONUS: A PARADE OF FESTIVALS

Activity 6
Rangoli: Art Underfoot (India)
Village Arts/Floor "Threshold" Painting
DOUBLE BONUS: THE "WARLI" ON THE WALL . . . INDIAN "WINDOW DRESSINGS"

◼ **Activity 7**
Princess Tara of Tibet "Thanka": A Special Someone Tribute (Tibet)
"Thanka" Scrolls/Mixed Media and Painting
INCLUDES: TIBETAN MANDALA . . . AND MUDRAS

Thanka is the name of scroll painting from the land of Tibet. Meet Tara, benevolent princess, who symbolizes Tibet. ▶

To know the Art of India and Tibet . . . . .

. . . . . one must know that India is the largest country in Southern Asia, which identifies it as the Indian subcontinent. It is densely populated, with 22 percent of the world's total population, one billion people. Hindu belief began in India with the historical Buddha, Siddhartha Gautama. Siddhartha Gautama was born a prince in Northern India (563–483 B.C.). He was pampered and sheltered in the palace until the age of twenty-nine, when he left for a mission to understand death and human suffering. He wandered and fasted for six years. One day, as he sat beneath the *Bodhi* tree, he meditated until he became the Enlightened One. From that point, he understood the nature of suffering and would teach what he now knew to be true. He became known as The Buddha, or "Enlightened One." Buddhist images in art are recognizable: The Buddha is most often seen sitting in full Lotus or in a posture of ease, wearing a simple robe. His elongated earlobes signify the absence of the heavy earrings he wore as a Prince. His hair is a cap of curls, said to be a gathering of snail shells that protected him as he meditated in the hot sun. At the top of his head is a Wisdom bump or top knot *(ushnisa),* one of the thirty-two signs of his superhuman qualities. A dot between the meeting of his eyebrows is called *urna.* Placed as it is, the location refers to the "Third Eye of Enlightenment" and, with the *ushnisha,* marks Buddha with Superior Wisdom. Hands are held in *mudras* or specific gestures: His right palm up signifies reassurance, a message of "fear not."

While numerous other religious groups exist in India today, India is a Hindu subcontinent, with a basic belief that all reality is one with the universe. Hindus believe in the power of the life cycle to destroy and renew itself, over and over again. This is symbolized by the lotus, a water plant that rises from murky swamps, blooms into a pure and perfect flower, then returns to the watery, muddy earth. Lotus symbols appear throughout Buddhist and Hindu art.

It is impossible to separate Hindu art, belief, and mythology from daily Indian life. In the Hindu culture, there is endless involvement with the mythological beings who are constant, sacred, and accessible. Home and temple worship utilizes objects and ceremonies that often provide delight in their aesthetic values. Bringing a level of pleasure to the senses is not considered wrong, and Dharma—the fulfillment of one's ultimate purpose or duty—is an important aspect of living a mindful, balanced life. Appreciation for human nature exists in Hinduism, along with reverence. When the playful flute-playing, blue-skinned Krishna is seen in Indian painting or sculpture, he is usually pictured as a handsome, young male god with a mischievous, yet lovable, personality. Every Hindu knows Krishna, his great love Radha, and their many adventures. Stories of belief, mythology, and cosmic events—along with images of the gods and goddesses—fill Indian art. The Hindu Trinity (called *trimurti,* consists of: *Brahma the Creator; Vishnu the Preserver;* and *Shiva, the Destroyer,* the Lord of Time and Dance. Each god has a goddess wife; all have specific physical features and carry identifiable objects, called "attributes"; each has a favorite animal companion, called a "mount"; and sometimes Divine Children are born. It all becomes wonderfully complicated when the gods take their other forms—and there are many! Krishna, for instance, is one avatar of *Vishnu the Preserver of the Universe.* There are *nine others* including *Rama*—also shown as blue-skinned and as the Ideal King. He is shown with bow and arrow and is the hero of the epic *Ramayana.* Rama is married to Sita; and his animal companion is the monkey general Hanuman.

Indian art has a rich time line of many periods—each with its own school of art. It is a history told in temple architecture, sculpture, and painting, as well as in textile and village arts. Temple sculpture, along with its representation of the god and goddess pantheon, has its own classic style. Figures are robust, full-bodied, and filled with vitality; sculptural work must appear to "breathe."

Indian painting may sometimes look very much like Persian manuscript illumination as a result of Moghul occupation in India and shares some of the compositional devices of the Islamic manuscript. Indian visual art directs itself to the emotion the painting will evoke. The name for this Asian Indian theory of art is *Rasa,* which means "essence," in the sense of the essential expression of juice from a ripe peach. Rasa is used in Indian performance arts—song, dance, music, and drama. Indian art is in every way a living art.

The art of nearby Tibet presents a striking system of images and iconography influenced by both Hinduism and Chinese Buddhism. Tibetan Buddhism endorses ethics such as mindful self-reflections, peaceful coexistence, and compassion, along with an insight into the cosmic world view. Tibetan art is distinctively recognizable and culturally expressive: the cloth scrolls, or *thankas,* and the sand painting of *mandala.*

117

ACTIVITY 1

Everybody Loves Ganesha: Our Lucky Elephant Boy!

Paper Doorway Ornament

BONUS: CLAY SCULPTURE

▲ Figure 4-1. Ganesha, who also loves to dance, is typically shown with four arms. Sometimes he carries a radish in one hand and lotus flowers or holy beads in his other hands. Ganesha is almost always holding sweets, which he clearly enjoys!

Ganesha is the Remover of Obstacles! He has the strength of an elephant, the beloved Indian animal he represents. Ganesha is extremely popular all over India, where great festivals are held in his honor—and why not?

This rotund fellow has a special friend—the pet rat. Many believe the rat is a sign of prosperity, for rats go where there is usually plenty of food! Ganesha clearly loves to eat and is shown with a broken tusk. How did he break his tusk? Here we blame food as the culprit. Ganesha was said to be at a banquet one night when the table was upset by his rat friend, causing quite a stir. Ganesha fell and broke his tusk and when he looked up at the sky, the moon seemed to be laughing at him! Our otherwise happy fellow became angry and hurled his broken tusk at the taunting moon. This is but one explanation for the question. Another more widely held belief about Ganesha's broken tusk is that he broke it off himself to use as a writing instrument, one that would pen the great Indian epic, the *Mahabarata* (Ma-hah-bah-rah-tah)—India's equivalent to Homer's *The Iliad*.

Ganesha is the son of the goddess Parvati and her husband, great lord Shiva. There are stories about them as well and—as we will learn—many stories with fantastic individuals for us to meet in the gorgeous lands of India. Namaste!

MATERIALS

- 12" × 15" oaktag paper
- paper fasteners or staples
- scissors
- fabric, felt, fake gems (option—see Teacher Preparation)

- crayons (see Teacher Preparation)
- markers
- white glue
- glitter pens (optional)
- hole puncher (optional)

TEACHER PREPARATION

The teacher may wish to have pictorial references of elephants on hand—particularly those of Indian elephants that are often shown as painted and in decorative costumes, ready for gala events! Material preparation need only include felt or fabric, if desired. Note: India is a great source for the fabric arts; many of the English and American textiles, such as chintz and calico, may be attributed to Indian origins. Perhaps there is an Indian print garment or bedspread that could be recycled through this activity. Note: Fabric and scraps may be saved for Activity 3.

◄ Figures 4-2a & 4-2b. Interpretations of Ganesha are made in various styles as well as materials. These two dancing Ganesha figures appear quite festive. September is the birthday of Ganesha, which is celebrated nationally in India. He is known as the "remover of Obstacles," the "Destroyer of Sorrows," the "Lord of New Beginnings," and the "Lord of Learning"—this makes him quite popular with business owners and students. Happy birthday, Ganesha! ►

DIRECTIONS

1. Has anyone in the classroom ever met Ganesha? Should you have Asian Indian students, the answer would likely be affirmative! Otherwise, you may describe Ganesha through the information offered in the introductory material. Here's a traditional account for Ganesha's appearance:

> A very long time ago, the Hindu deity Shiva, a very holy man, went to a retreat in the woods leaving his wife, Parvati, all alone. Parvati grew lonely and longed for a child. So one day, Parvati decided to model a baby from river bank clay. She, too, had magical powers and turned the baby into a little boy she named Ganesha. She played with her new child and after a while, sent him to stand guard for her as she took a bath in the waters.

> Who should suddenly return but Shiva! He knew not who Ganesha was, or why he was guarding him from seeing his own wife! Shiva, outraged, lopped off Ganesha's head. Parvati rushed to the scene, only to be horrified to find what her husband had done. Shiva then understood the problem. He would immediately return to the woods to find an animal that could be used to replace Ganesha's head. The first creature he encountered was an elephant. An adjustment was made—and Ganesha now had a new elephant head! Parvati was delighted, for she loved the cute little elephant boy even more than before—and Shiva was relieved, too. Everyone, you might say, lived happily ever after.

(**Note:** As in many myths, biblical stories, folklore, and fairy tales, an element of forceful action or danger exists. You must determine the age-appropriate content of classroom literature—adjust accordingly.)

2. Students will have the opportunity to create their *own* interpretive Ganesha figures (also known as Ganesh). These will be used to decorate doorways and entrances, and to learn about Ganesha's "attributes"—the objects held by celestial beings. (See reproducible page 129.)

3. Distribute all materials. Students will consider that Ganesha loves sweets and radishes. He is also shown holding shells, beads, and lotus flowers. Ganesha also has one broken tusk, which he damaged at a feast (see introduction). The snake often shown wrapped around his great waist holds in his big tummy (and is a symbol of his father, Shiva). Sometimes Ganesha wears a jeweled turban.

4. Encourage students to fashion their Ganesha figures. Oaktag will be cut by students to size. Arms (four) and legs—as well as the objects Ganesha will hold—must be included in their planned cutting.

5. Elephant proportions and features such as trunk, tusks, and ears should be pointed out—along with the scale of the human form—to support the head. (Suggested height for the figure is 12 inches.) Ganesh is often shown with the body of a child.

6. Students will decorate their Ganesha figure with Indian design details (printed fabric is useful here as a reference). Turbans, jewelry, garlands, and *dhoti* (comfortable Indian pants) may be developed.

7. If moveable arms and legs are desired, students will punch holes in Ganesha bodies at "joints" and attach limbs with paper fasteners. **Alternative:** Staple parts onto main form.

8. Apply fabric, glitter, and other finery as desired. Trim.

9. Cut objects selected for Ganesha to hold. Attach to his hands with glue or staples. Students may use their own choices as to the importance of objects in their own lives. Pets and favorite foods, for example, are quite acceptable for Ganesha!

10. Completed Ganesha figures may be "installed" around entry areas, especially doorways. Good luck with new ventures is sure to follow . . . . Ganesha is, after all, the Lord of Auspicious Beginnings!

B O N U S : CLAY SCULPTURE: GANESHA BOYS!

Clay is a natural material for little seated Ganesha boys. An inverted pinch pot will provide the round body; a second smaller pinch pot creates the basis for the head. In India, sculpture is highly regarded for its ability to capture the spirit of the figure it represents. Elephants themselves are so important to Indian culture that they almost parallel the dragon presence in China. Elephants are considered "bringers of rain" and good luck. White elephants are very special; they are often known as "Earth Clouds" that attract rain right out of their companions, the "Sky Clouds"!

Ganesha, as "Remover of Obstacles," is perfectly suited to elephant strength and dexterity. Like his friend, the rat, nibbling and chewing can also help to penetrate great barriers. Elephants are wise, respected, and mighty talented!

▲ Figure 4-3. Wouldn't these student-made Ganeshas look perfect in any setting as a reminder that each day is a "new beginning!"

ACTIVITY 2

India's Great Legends: A Gallery of Delights!

Illustrated Storyteller Prop Box/Portable "Gallery" Box Construction

BONUS: TEMPLE HANGING OR "PICHHAVAI"

India has kept its history and mythology alive through painting, sculpture, dance, music, and theater—most of which takes the form of the story! Among the most important Indian epics are the *Mahabharata* (a heroic tale of ancient kingdoms and conquests) and the *Ramayana* (translated, it means "way of Rama," a beautiful victory of love over evil that features handsome Prince Rama, his lovely wife Sita, and monkey general Hunaman).

Other well-known stories comprise the arts of India. In Indian painting we find representations of the life of *Krishna,* who appears as a graceful blue man. He is often seen playing his flute in the forest of his sweetheart Radha. Krishna is depicted as a romantic hero as well as a naughty child. Scenes of Krishna's childhood reveal his early divine and magical powers. The Asian Indian viewer will recognize a mischievous little blue boy who steals butter from his mother, teases the cow herdresses (called *Gopis*), and uproots mountains effortlessly!

To Asian Indian people, heroic figures and their adventures are familiar and alive. The difficulties and triumphs of Krishna and his lover Radha are experienced by one and all. In India, Ganesha and his parents Shiva and Parvati are almost family members. Art not only imitates life in India, it is life itself! Interest in these vital story manifestations never ends—they are carried from village to city and town. Our box of mythological

▲ Figure 4-4. The storyteller's prop box, the *kavadh,* is still produced in the region of Rajasthan. The tradition is kept alive by craftspeople who also create these small theaters for tourists. At one time, objects such as this one predated the cinema. It may startle us to learn a grand-scale film industry, outside of Hollywood, U.S.A., is often identified as "Bollywood," in Bombay, India! NOTE: These small structures are also referred to as portable temples in many regions of India.

treasure is called a *kavadh* and resembles a small-scale model of a household cabinet cupboard or tiny temple. Inside the doors of the *kavadh* are scenes that may or may not be sequential in nature. They can show scenes from a mythological hero's life; the compartmentalized spaces function very much like elaborate storyboards. Each "box within a box" gives us another element of the fantastic yet familiar tales of India we can now recognize and enjoy.

MATERIALS

- boxes (see Teacher Preparation)
- pencils and erasers
- white drawing paper (see Teacher Preparation)
- scissors
- colored markers (fine- and regular-tipped)
- colored pencils
- paint (tempera and/or acrylic)

- brushes
- paint mixing trays
- glue sticks or white glue
- gold and silver pens (optional)
- scrap gift paper or greeting paper
- practice paper (manila or newsprint)
- rulers

TEACHER PREPARATION

The teacher will want to begin by saving small cartons, the kind that are often used to ship books. (If a shipment of textbooks arrives at your school, you're in business!) Cardboard cartons are the best choice for this lesson; they have the necessary flaps that will become the doors as well as the decorative top (and bottom) of the storyteller prop boxes. In calculating the number of boxes needed for a class, note that 2–3 students will "team" for the production of *one* box; this is a "buddy" project!

The preparation of the cardboard box with white gesso will provide a brighter, more inviting surface (even one coat should help). The teacher will want to set up painting supplies in order to first paint the box. Additional reference materials that depict the costumes, characters, and heroes of India are always useful. Scraps of cloth and paper that are stylistically aligned to Asian Indian design would be great, too.

◀ Figure 4-5. On the right side of the box door is romantic leading man Rama, and main leading lady, wife Sita. The deer in this story, *The Ramayana*, may not be so innocent as it appears (see the story sampler). Is that the "tree of life" below? Do we recognize the friendly trio above? It is Ganesha, flanked by his mom, Parvati, on the left, and his dad, Shiva, on the right.

Figure 4-6. The many-headed villain is called Ravana. He is an evil force and one to be loathed and feared. Fortunately, Prince Rama turns out to be quite the hero, but why should we tell you the end of the story? Read the story sampler! ▶

DIRECTIONS

1. Congratulations, teacher, you have just been appointed Royal Storyteller! It will be your pleasure to recount or tell, in synopsis form, four or five short stories that students will imagine and illustrate. See "Tales of India: A Short Sampler" on page 124. Don't be afraid to dramatize—your students will appreciate it. Remember, the boxes your students are about to make were carried from town to town, where story episodes were pointed out, sung, and told with gusto.

2. Assign student "teams," two or three students to a box. Seated together, these students will *quietly* discuss the stories and scenes they wish to illustrate. A division of labor may be useful.

3. Distribute practice materials—pencils and paper along with visual aids.

4. Distribute boxes and painting supplies. **Note:** Depending on age of students and thickness of cardboard, cutting the storyteller cabinet shape should be determined by the supervising teacher. (See Figures 4-4, 4-5, and 4-6 for box shape.) Students will make an agreed-upon selection of one basic box surface color.

5. Select color of paint and apply to the *entire* box surface. Let dry.

6. Distribute white paper. Students will now decide whether they wish to apply their chosen story scenes directly to the box surface—or to illustrate them in predetermined sizes of white paper (which may be approximated or sized with rulers). Cut to the sizes needed to install in storyteller prop box. The images may also be individually cut out and glued to the box surface (see Figures 4-5 and 4-6). Combinations of direct and applied images are also fine.

7. Have the students decide who will "crown" the "marquis" of their theatrical story box. "Are we clear on who's who? Are the story scenes shown as descriptive pictures?" Each should function as a self-contained unit; the use of Indian architectural arches is also encouraged. If it all looks complete, add decorative elements to help define and accent boundaries and other areas. Here is where gold and silver pens really come in handy! Feel free to add any cloth or paper scraps at this time.

8. The final "look" of the storyteller prop is one of diversification and unity. If these stories are ready to be retold, then it is time to take our "show on the road." You may arrange scheduled times for students to travel as small groups to other classes so that they may keep the great Indian storytelling tradition alive!

1. *Hanuman,* the monkey general

2. Naughty little *Krishna* stealing butter from his mom

3. Embroidered *chakla,* traditional textile

4. *Shiva* as Lord of Dance

5. *Radha* and *Krishna* meeting, while a friend stands nearby

6. The castle in the golden city of *Lanka* where *Sita* is captured

7. Evil king *Kauravas* pulling the virtuous *Draupaudi's* sari

8. *Shiva* and wife *Parvati* with son *Ganesha*

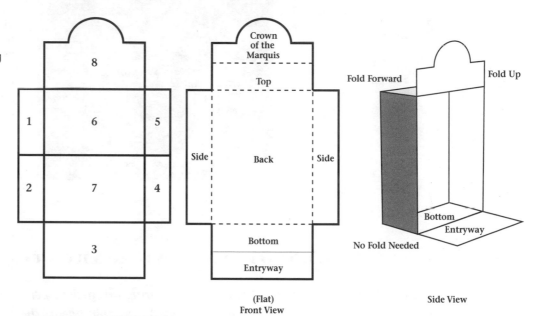

◄ Figure 4-7. A storyteller box tells all! The accompanying illustration explains what scenes are shown.

BONUS: TEMPLE HANGINGS OR "PICHHAVAI"

Have students select a chosen scene from their story box that they can illustrate on a vertical section of paper to create a scroll-like hanging. Paintings of Krishna like this one are called *Pichhavai* and often hang behind sculpture. They are usually on cloth; but that doesn't mean you can't use paper to do a temple hanging. Think of how enchanting a display of Pichhavai scenes would look behind sculpture groups of Lucky Ganesha boys! (See Activity 1.)

◄ Figure 4-8. An authentic cloth temple hanging illustrates a scene in Krishna's life that may also be found in storyteller props and manuscript painting. Our romantic Lord Krishna is charming the Gopis (cow herdresses) with his melodic flute. Note that Krishna may appear in different time frames within the same image!

TALES OF INDIA: A SHORT SAMPLER

The Ramayana: *The story, composed during an ancient period known as the Vedic Age, is one that tells of the adventures of Prince Rama. As an epic poem, the Ramayana has been popular for thousands of years and is very much a part of Indian culture.*

Noble Prince Rama, son of a great king, lived happily in the forest with his lovely wife Princess Sita. Fragrant flowers and friendly animals surrounded them. Each time Rama left Sita to search for food, he would draw a magic circle around her for her protection. One day, Rama drew the usual magic circle and cautioned Sita as always not to step outside of it.

Rama left Sita alone. She began to play with a little squirrel. The hideous Ravana saw beautiful Sita and fell completely in love with her. He realized that he must trick her so that he could carry her away from Rama. He quickly turned himself into a sweet deer who innocently coached Sita from inside the magic circle. Once beyond protection, the deer disappeared—and poor Sita was overcome by the villain Ravana, with his ten heads and twenty arms! The squirrel tried to fend him off, but Sita was taken away in Ravana's golden magic chariot and flown across the ocean to his castle fortress on the island of Lanka.

Rama returned to a crying squirrel and a missing wife! "Where is my beloved Sita?" he cried. The animals assisted in a search of the forest. Sita was spotted by Jatayus, the bird, who flew over Lanka and reported back to Rama. Something had to be done at once, for Sita was to be forced into marriage with the hideous Ravana! An emergency council was held by the animals of the forest with Rama. How could they rescue Sita? Hanuman, the wise and strong general of the monkeys, had an answer! He would assemble the monkey army, gather many stones, and create a floating bridge to Lanka! The bird would lead the way.

Everyone worked tirelessly. The completed floating bridge allowed Rama and his friends to enter Lanka. A terrible battle between the monkey army and Ravana's forces ensued. In the end, Hanuman was victorious as was Rama in defeating the demon Ravana. Rama finished Ravana off with his sacred bow. Sita would now return to her home and her loving husband. All would live happily ever after—and monkeys would forever be held sacred in India!

The Mahabharata: *A 3,000-year-old epic tale of India, eight times longer than the* **Odyssey** *and the* **Iliad** *combined!* It is the story of two great families known collectively as the Pandavas and the Kauravas, who struggled for supremacy. The Pandavas, led by Prince Arjuna, were basically kind and trusting. Five Pandava brothers were married to one woman named Draupaudi, which was common in ancient days. The mean and wicked Kauravas tried to steal her away by cheating in a Game of Dice. When the dishonest Kaurava dice player attempted to abduct the virtuous Draupaudi, he began to pull her towards him by grabbing a length of her *sari*. Through the divine help of Krishna, the sari became endless! The more the sari was pulled, the more Draupaudi simply spun where she stood. The Kauravas were so frightened by the endless magic sari that they told the Pandavas to keep Draupaudi and, if the Pandavas all went to live in the forest as hermits for 14 years, they would give them back the kingdom they lost in the game. At the end of the 14 years, the Kauravas did not hold up their end of the bargain and a great war began. Krishna, who stands on the side of righteousness, was the Pandavas' charioteer to aid Arjuna. Their victory would come to pass. *The Mahabharata is a story with many remarkable episodes that are shown in Indian art. It is also called the world's greatest encyclopedia of Hindu legend, mythology, religion, stagecraft, fashion (this is the first record of the garment, the sari), and history.*

A Legend of Lord Krishna: Krishna is seen in many forms—as a joyful baby boy and, most often, as a flute-playing young man who charms cow herdresses in an enchanted forest setting. He is dark-skinned, which is usually expressed in art as blue or purple, and is exceptionally handsome. A destroyer of ignorance and evil, a great teacher and advisor, a daring hero who possesses both human and divine qualities—Krishna's popularity is clearly widespread. He is the chubby baby who loves butter, milk, and curd and will often help himself to these treats when his mother isn't looking! Krishna's heroic deeds are many and include his lifting a mountain to provide shelter for herdsmen and their families. Krishna is particularly loved by the cow herdresses, called Gopis, a group with which he is associated, for his mother was a cow herdress. His own favorite sweetheart is Radha, who is fourteen years older than the handsome blue hero. Radha is to Krishna what is often identified as a "soul mate"—in Indian terms, she is his *prakriti* or "his very own nature."

The "Riddle" of Narasimha: What do you do to stop a dreadful tyrant who cannot be destroyed, in neither day nor night, neither indoors nor outdoors, by neither man nor beast? You hope that Narasimha shows up to help the people! Narasimha means "man-lion" so here's how the problem is solved. The tyrant is approached by Narasimha at *dusk* (neither day nor night) on his *porch* (neither indoors nor outdoors) by a *lion-headed man* (neither man nor beast). Hero Narasimha is a mythological being whose job is to appear on Earth to make sure the good people win! *The moral of Indian stories is that evil does not pay. Always the message is that one should be dutiful and virtuous—not mean, greedy, and self-serving. Other man-animal combinations, such as Ganesha, the elephant-headed hero, function in the same way.* Narasimha, the man-lion, is an *Avatar* (manifestation) of Vishnu the Preserver-Krishna and Rama, too. There are ten Avatars of Vishnu!

What's a Goddess to Wear?

"Animated" Figures/Mixed Media

BONUS: VESTS OR "CHOLI"

▲ Figure 4-9. A beautifully expressed goddess figure, created by a student who placed in her figure's multiple arms many accessories (or attributes). Arms do help when one considers the challenges that face a goddess!

If a goddess were to have a job description, it might read something like this:

HELP WANTED

One all-powerful female to protect and preserve the laws of the universe. Multiple arms desirable for suppression of evil forces and lending an extra hand in matters great and small. Great Mother Goddess especially valued as nurturer, harvest-bringer, and female ideal. Supreme leadership qualities a must!

Goddesses take many forms, yet share basic traits such as strength, perseverance, and generosity. They are often beautiful, courageous, and benevolent, yet can be quite fierce when necessary. There are several great goddesses in the Hindu cosmic system. Principal among these is Uma, The Great Mother goddess, who is also a form of Parvati, wife of Shiva, daughter of the Himalayas—and mother of lucky elephant Lord Ganesha. In fact, every Hindu male god needs a goddess to provide him with vital female energy. Just as goddesses have many manifestations, the same is true for their male counterparts. Gods and goddesses are plentiful in India, yet can be recognized individually through their specific appearances, which include telling physical attributes, and their faithful animal companions, known as *vehicles* or *mounts*. The vehicles also provide a means of divine transportation!

It may be said in India that "every goddess is a woman, and every woman is a goddess." In this expansive culture the virtues represented by gods and goddesses are not restricted by celestial boundaries; they are experienced on Earth in thoughtful action. Every mother who protects and shelters her sleeping baby with her sari or scarf is living proof of goddess goodness!

◀ Figure 4-10. This lovely Indian bride glances downward in a manner that is traditional to the wedding day. She is a stunning manifestation of goddess elegance. She wears red (considered auspicious) and gold. She uses gold cosmetically to enhance her eyebrows, drawing our attention to the *tika* between her eyes, also encircled in gold. Note the decorative henna that accentuates her graceful hands.

MATERIALS

- oaktag
- scissors
- crayons, paint, watercolor markers
- paper fasteners
- hole puncher
- glue

- recycled trinkets of fake jewels (optional, see Teacher Preparation)
- pencils
- scrap paper and fabric (optional)
- reproducible page: "Attributes of Gods and Goddesses"

TEACHER PREPARATION

The teacher will want to have small mirrors available for this lesson. These mirrors can be found in the notions department of fabric or kraft stores (be sure mirrors or similar reflective items have safe edges). These reflective embellishments are often used in Asian Indian decorative art. Artroom kraft foil may be substituted. Students will be making articulated puppets. If student level requires, the teacher may want to cut limb and torso shapes in advance; try to vary in order to avoid "cookie cutter" look.

Goddesses have "attributes" or special symbolic items. The ambitious teacher may ask students to bring in small items they treasure on the day of the lesson so that their emotional value to the student may be discussed. Nothing breakable, please! Remind students to get parent permission if they are borrowing a household treasure!

DIRECTIONS

1. This lesson is about goddesses as well as the Hindu pantheon, if you wish. It also celebrates the notable style of Asian Indian clothing. Explain the specific physical characteristics of the Indian goddess: She has multiple arms in which symbolic items are held, is dressed in traditional garments, and is usually shown as a frontal figure.

2. In the spirit of their own creative powers, encourage students to create their own special goddess-like figure. **Note:** Male students may be encouraged to think about their moms, sisters, and other women in their family. Do these important women have favorite objects that are associated with them? Now is the time to discuss any little treasures on hand.

▲ Figure 4-11. Rama and Sita also lend themselves to articulated puppet forms. Rama wears a *dhoti* and a turban, Sita wears a *sari*. Turbans are often associated with the great maharajas. However, the belief called *Sikhism* employs a turban-like headdress, also called a *mukat*. Turbans are commonly worn by Sikhs. These two figures are dressed in real recycled Indian print fabric, tailored by the student artist.

3. Let's now turn our attention to what the goddess's attire will be. What shall she wear? May we suggest a sari—the traditional garment of Indian women. (See Figure 4-10.) There are so many styles from the various regions of India that students can interpret their own version. You will want to discuss the basic sari design: a toga-like garment that wraps around as a skirt with additional fabric to be fashionably draped, usually over shoulder or head. Before distribution of materials, be sure to convey that fabric and fashion are specialties of India—and that Indian women dazzle!

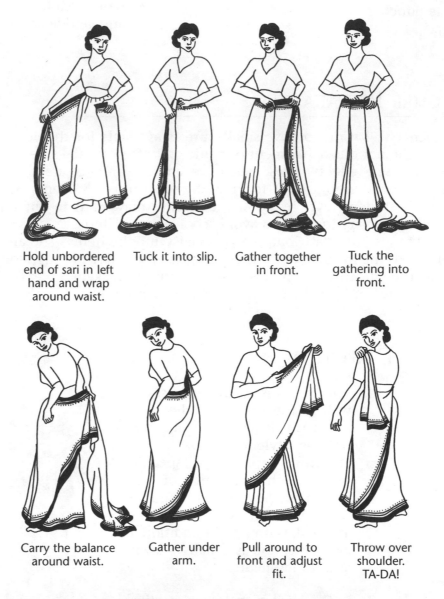

Hold unbordered end of sari in left hand and wrap around waist.　　Tuck it into slip.　　Gather together in front.　　Tuck the gathering into front.

Carry the balance around waist.　　Gather under arm.　　Pull around to front and adjust fit.　　Throw over shoulder. TA-DA!

4. Make all materials available to students. They first cut the basic figure without the arms; cut multiple arms next. Arms may be hole-punched and attached now or later—whatever works better for each class.

5. Consider the textile design of the sari along with other Indian touches. After color and texture have been applied, students may affix "sparkling" accents as well as favored attributes (in her hands) if desired. For more information about attributes, see the illustrations on page 129, "Attributes of Gods and Goddesses."

6. Few Hindu Indian women would feel complete with a *tika,* the small forehead dot usually in "auspicious" red. This fashion statement is ornamental and may be shaped into a teardrop, paisley, or a diamond. (Original meaning of the *tika,* also known as *bindi,* varies; see page 126.)

7. Completed "goddesses" may be discussed and displayed; however, Activity 2 does provide a stage for these shining stars!

ATTRIBUTES OF
GODS AND GODDESSES

SARASWATI

Goddess of knowledge, wisdom, the muses, and the arts. She is shown as a graceful woman, dressed in white, holding a musical instrument called a *Veena*. Saraswati is a River diety and rises from a lotus: her vehicle is a swan.

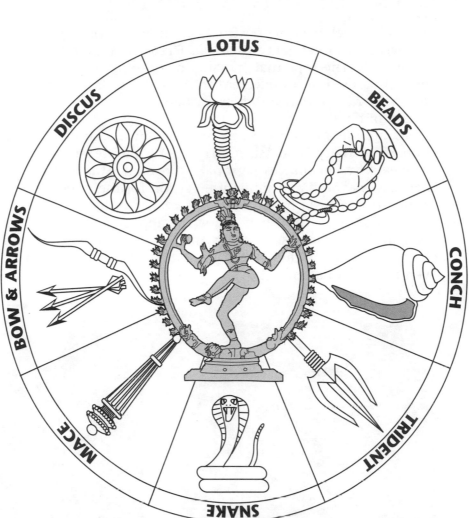

LAKSHMEI

The benevolent Mother Goddess of Wealth and Prosperity—Sister of Saraswati. She is honored during *Diwali,* the Fall Festival of Lights that celebrates the mythical return of Rama to Sita. Lakshmei is the goddess of earthly abundance and success.

THE HINDU TRINITY: "TRIMURTI"

BRAHMA THE CREATOR
who set the universe in motion

↓

VISHNU THE PRESERVER
who preserves the universe, is also known as "one who takes many forms." He has 10 Avatars, among which are Prince Rana; Narasimha, the man-lion, and Lord Krishno

↓

SHIVA THE DESTROYER
who represents the endless cycle of life, death and rebirth: he destroys to recreate. Also known as Lord of Dance and of Time.

bow and arrows—symbol of time with the arrows smaller pieces of time, also represents the power of illusion
conch shell—symbol of the origin of existence, associated with water
discus of chakra—symbol of power that creates and destroys all forms in the universe
lotus—symbol of divinity, also represents purity, source of laws, and power of knowledge
mace or club—symbol of might and power, especially power of knowledge
prayer beads—symbol of time and the continuous pursuit of knowledge
snake—Attribute of Shiva. Snake is the guardian of water, a giver of life, and protector
trident—symbol of destructive activity and power with piercing of the prongs

BONUS: VESTS OR "CHOLI"

There's so much we can do with Asian Indian fabric design and fashion that many may wish for more: hence the *choli*. The sari traditionally covers this short blouse called *choli*. The tops that Indian women wear also vary in style and design. A choli or blouse is a complement to the sari: hearts, crescent moons, peacocks (the national bird of India) and their feathers, plant leaves—even human figures—form a basis for choli design.

Our choli are sleeveless, as indicated in the photos. (For directions to precut choli, see Activity 12 in Asia on page 39.) There are strong Indian textile traditions, yet creativity encourages personal expression. Students may make one choli for themselves as well as a miniature version for their goddess: don't forget to leave room for six arms if needed!

A good-sized choli may enjoy the application of small mirrors, or reflective discs, and auspicious signs and symbols—or even be used for a playful display of characters from Hindu mythology and belief. Who knows a bouncy figure might even pop out of a pocket!

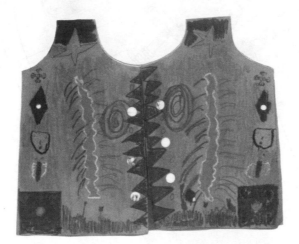

▲ Figures 4-12a, 4-12b, & 4-12c. These student-made cholis show a good sense of border design and even include pockets.

ACTIVITY 4

The Taj Mahal: A Monument to Love

Paper Architectural Construction/Landscape Architecture

INCLUDES: REFLECTING POOL

The spectacular structure called the Taj Mahal *is* a World Wonder—and for many reasons. Foremost, it is a labor of love. The Taj Mahal, a memorial, was begun in 1632 at Agra, the Mughal capital of India at the time. The year 1631 inspired this magnificent work, for it was then that the Emperor Shah Jahan lost his precious wife Mumtaz Jahan, who died giving birth to their fourteenth child. So broken-hearted was he that he immediately set about the construction of her tomb, the Taj Mahal, which is the nickname for his wife's title, meaning "crown of the palace." The marble for the monument had to be carried over 300 miles! Craftsmen were employed from Central Asia to Italy. Twenty years and 20,000 workers later, a perfectly beautiful building in traditional Islamic style was accomplished.

▲ Figure 4-13. The Shah Jahan would be very impressed with this ornate student interpretation of his Taj Mahal. What a jeweled, magnificent palace it is!

▲ Figure 4-14. Very magical is the effect of calligraphy, used as a design element in this youthful version of "Taj Mahal in the Moonlight." Calligraphy and poetry go hand in hand with Islamic architecture.

▲ Figure 4-15. The "Taj Mahal in the New Season" is a title that captures both the feeling of the moment and the endlessness of time. Note the use of natural plantings which offset the proud peacock, known symbol of immortality, and the national bird of India.

The Taj Mahal has become the architectural landmark for India. It is composed mostly of marble, with the most marvelous jewel inlays of gems as precious as sapphires, diamonds, and jade. The architectural plan of the Taj Mahal includes a royal tomb, ponds, a canal, a mosque, and a great gateway. Since all mosques have minarets, the Taj is no exception. It was, however, the first free-standing tomb to have minarets; the dome—a traditional Arabic architectural element—represents both womanhood and the Islamic concepts of paradise. The water systems continue this "Garden of Eden" idea as well as serve as a mirror for its symmetry. Yet the Taj Mahal is more than a world wonder. The Shah Jahan intended not only to memorialize the great love of his life; he made certain that he could contemplate her memory by meditating both the *direct* and *reflected* views of his realized architectural plan. He could see the Taj Mahal mausoleum from his nearby palace at just about every turn. Childhood sweethearts, Jahan and Mumtaz are remembered by the endless generations who visit the Taj Mahal from around the globe. In essence, this building—which magically changes color according to the weather, season, or time of day—has become for us a glowing symbol of the priceless product of the human heart: love!

MATERIALS

- pencils
- paint
- oaktag
- white drawing paper
- green felt (optional)
- glitter
- watercolor markers
- rulers

- scissors
- colored cellophane (see Teacher Preparation)
- white glue
- dried plants (optional, see Teacher Preparation)
- gift boxes and shoe boxes (see Teacher Preparation)
- cardboard tubes (from paper towels, gift wrap, etc.)

TEACHER PREPARATION

The Taj Mahal, its gardens, and its backdrop require having specific everyday materials on hand for completion of this lesson. This activity has several stages, so it probably works best when the "parts" are created by students, then assembled. The teacher should note the following suggestions:

ELEMENTS	SUPPLIES NEEDED
• The Taj Mahal ground plan (includes four walls and garden)	Gift box or shirt box bottom
• Backdrop (includes sky and scenery)	Gift box top (same as above)
• Grass and shrubbery	Optional green felt, thistles, pine cones, and plant materials
• Minaret towers that flank main sctructure; **note:** the actual Taj Mahal has four minarets, but teacher can get away with two with "the art of illusion"	Cardboard tubes from gift wrap or paper towels; **Note:** oaktag may be substituted
• Main building	Cut white paper rectangles to be affixed to shoebox
• Reflecting pool	Water may be represented with colored or clear cellophane or plastic wrap (which is sometimes available in aquatic colors on supermarket shelves)
• Optional	Templates for central building domes and minaret domes

The advantage of preparing the above elements in advance is that it will allow students to focus their attention on the development of the mood, atmosphere, and environment of the building and landscape architecture.

DIRECTIONS

1. Let's start our Taj Mahal experience with knowledge of the actual monument and its story. After teacher provides this information, students will analyze the elements that comprise the Taj Mahal and its environment. It is suggested that teacher distribute the "arch elements" sequentially.

2. Begin with the design of the building. Students will, after receiving appropriate materials, design the facade of the building on rectangular paper and decorate. Pointed window and door arches are a must!

3. Glue facade to the front of the inverted shoe box. Cut out the dome, the design of which must match the style of the facade. Smaller domes may now be cut to represent minaret tower tops. Design minaret tower surfaces either directly or by wrapping white paper (or oaktag) to create the form (see Figures 4-13 to 4-15). Insert and/or glue domes to the shoe box (roof) and minaret towers.

4. Next, apply paper (if needed) to exterior walls of the gift box. Consider the design of the garden; leave room for the reflecting pool. "Install" garden surface (green felt).

5. Place the Taj Mahal building and minarets on the "grounds." Use a long paper rectangle to create a three-dimensional reflecting pool. A one-inch square notch should be cut from each corner of the rectangle. Press each flap, and fold up so that four shallow walls appear. Join corners with tape. Aquatic elements (see Figure 4-17) may be added at this time. Add tinted or clear cellophane.

6. You will want to intervene at specific intervals to redirect students. Now is the time to consider the atmosphere and environment. What time is it? What season? What mood is our sky? Is there anything else in "the picture"? (See Figures 4-14 and 4-15.)

7. Students will create their own ideas for the pictorial backdrop in drawing and painting materials on the gift box edge. Leave the bottom flap to attach under the buildings and grounds section.

8. Who will stroll through these individual versions of the Taj Mahal? Goddesses, peacocks, royal children, or magical beings? Draw, cut, decorate, and install these inhabitants mindfully!

9. The Taj Mahal has so many faces that a label that titles each interpretation—with the name of the new architect—is suggested. Placed side-by-side, your class will surely have the most splendid neighborhood in the world.

▲ Figure 4-16. Certainly the most cosmic of our Taj Mahal settings so far! The sky helps us to understand why this is called the "Taj Mahal of Outer Space." The figure that stands forward in the garden, however, seems very much grounded. What a heavenly idea!

Figure 4-17. Aerial view of the reflecting pool. It is alive with water creatures and plant life. The illusion of "floating suspension" has been achieved by sensitive young student hands. ▶

SLIDE 18

ACTIVITY 5

Mughal Miniature: Little Portraits of India

"Frames"/Mixed-media Assemblage

BONUS: A PARADE OF FESTIVALS

▲ Figure 4-18. Mood, picture space, and atmosphere are established in this stylized, courtly figure, who leans back in repose. The jeweled frame suggests palace splendor.

The Islamic presence in India has a long history. The Mughal Empire, however, was most strongly felt in shaping Indian artistic ideas. The Mughals, who descended from Genghis Khan, occupied India with a zest that rivaled the Ottoman Empire. At the same time as Europe was experiencing its Renaissance, Mughal rulers held sway in lands that stretched from Persia to Pakistan. The Mughal reign set forth a colorful chronology that began with a monarch named Babur in the 15th century and went on to include the Shah Jahan, the emperor who commissioned the Taj Mahal. One more ruler followed him, marking the decline of the Mughal rule. The Mughals brought to India specific influences, particularly a revitalized interest in miniature arts.

The primary interest of Mughal-inspired Indian miniatures was one of courtly, dignified characterization. Thanks to the liberal Mughal monarch Akbar—who preceded Shah Jahan and was, in fact, his grandfather—arts in India flourished. He established studio workshops for artisans called *kar-khanays*. Akbar supported artistic production and exchange, blending Hindu, European, and Islamic tradition. Among the many styles that developed, the miniature portrait—shown either in profile or as a full-figure view—gained great popularity. Not surprising, this form of stylistic painting echoes the manuscript art of Persia.

Another major school among many in Indian art—Rajput painting—concerns the stories and brilliant scenes of Hindu belief and mythology. Rajasthan, "land of the Rajas," a ruling warrior class in west India, boasts an art tradition of energetic folklore along with elegant design motifs. Mughal influences were felt here as elsewhere, resulting in images that are often "hybrids." Sometimes Mughal art is so Persian in appearance that it is difficult to tell it is of Indian origin. On the other hand, one can find much Indian art that defies any sort of specific classification. India is a large, diversified subcontinent with many distinctive regional flairs. In any case, Indian art overall delights the senses, elevates the spirit, and satisfies the soul . . . whether it is large or small, Mughal or not!

MATERIALS

- paint and small brushes (optional, see Teacher Preparation)
- white paper (assorted sizes)
- pencils
- watercolor markers
- scrap paper
- fine-tip black markers
- scissors

- glitter (or glitter pens)
- masking tape
- "palace jewels" (assorted plastic gems)
- glue
- cardboard scraps (see Teacher Preparation)
- reproducible page: "A FESTIVAL CALENDAR— A Short List of Asian-Indian Holidays"

▲ Figure 4-19a. Miniature portrait profiles very much reflect Mughal tradition. The clear-cut line sets the figure against the background, within its four-cornered frame. An architectural element is borrowed to top it off!

▲ Figure 4-19b. This female companion piece to Photo 4-19a shows a dancer. Accentuated eyes are found in the artistic styles of certain regions—the Rajasthan school, for one. The use of the frame at the base anchors our dancer; Indian dance is very connected with the earth. This architectural element helps to make these two portraits a "pair."

TEACHER PREPARATION

The focus of this activity is small portraiture, particularly those of a courtly variety. However, the manner in which these portraits are assembled and presented is not restricted by convention. The "frames" will be more conceptual than predictable in appearance; cardboard scraps are therefore appropriate. The teacher may wish to cut paper as well as the cardboard on which paper will be mounted into a predetermined small scale. For example, students may be able to choose from a 5″ × 8″, 4″ × 6″, or other small format.

Reference materials that include a variety of portraits, particularly those showing profile and various frontal views, will be most useful. Of course, Asian Indian subjects are recommended for this lesson.

Finally, it is a tradition of both the East and West to paint miniature portraits with a tiny brush that allows for picture detail. This approach may or may not suit your students yet; it is worthwhile, to mention this technique in your introduction as general information.

DIRECTIONS

1. Discuss basic portrait composition with attention to the profile, a popular courtly tradition in India. Also, students will want to think about the space that surrounds the figure. Will it be purely decorative or dimensional? Will the figure be standing in a niche or lounging around the palace? Discuss.

▲ Figure 4-20. Another answer for a framing element. Student has created an architectural place for this stately, instructive little figure who seems to want to teach us something. The glitter takes on a whole new meaning as it replicates a constructed wall niche. Perhaps the subject of this portait is a *Mullah,* or holy teacher.

2. Distribute practice paper and pencils. Students will try their hand at several portrait ideas. When the one they like the most is selected by them—and the class is ready—make other materials available. Hold back the glitter for now.

3. Students may either transfer the drawing they choose onto the cut white paper, or re-create it. They should apply color with awareness of its effect on the clarity of the image against the surrounding area. Here is where the use of the fine-tip marker will assist definition. Simplicity is valued when space is limited.

4. As soon as possible, students will begin to incorporate the framing devices. These are not necessarily expected to appear separate from the image. In fact, it is hoped they will activate and complement the image without formality. Architectural elements may be used in sections to suggest solidarity or for decorative drama.

5. Bring on the glitter! Now is the time, along with the palace jewels (plastic gems). These gaudy materials should serve to accentuate and unify the composition. Let dry.

6. Completed and dried miniature portraits may receive their own "standing room" by the attachment of folded cardboard backing, glued and taped to the reverse side. There you have it—a courtly grouping of mughal miniatures, the collective effect of which is anything but tiny!

B O N U S : A PARADISE OF FESTIVALS! *PAT PAINTING*

Large folkloric Indian village paintings may be rolled into scrolls and called *pat.* "Pat" paper murals may run from 12 to 15 feet in length. Only the primary colors are used, with the occasional addition of green and brown. The whole family participates in the painting, which is often sold as souvenirs to tourists! Even a newspaper page, that is first painted white, can serve as the popular art pat.

If we take our cue from pat, classroom murals of parades, festivals, and holidays may be painted by small groups onto large butcher paper. The educational value of switching from small to large in itself teaches a valuable lesson about the visual effects of proportion and scale. Tiny portraits encourage individual student concentration, while mural painting promotes positive group interaction—the best of both worlds!

▲Figure 4-21. This authentic Indian painting can provide inspiration for students with its festive parade-like composition. It is reminiscent of a "pat".

In India there seems to be a festival for every occasion and community. Classroom groups can include in their festival "pat floats" that honor some or many of the heroes and characters they have met in India. (See Activity 2 and 3.) Some possibilities are actual festivals: *Holi*—the national celebration of spring, when color is tossed everywhere! This celebration is filled with flowers. Or consider *Diwali*—the fall Festival of Lights (see the reproducible Actitvity 3). You certainly can't go wrong with a goddess festival. And, of course, bring on the elephants!

▲ Figure 4-22. Detail of a festival elephant.

A FESTIVAL CALENDAR:
A SHORT LIST OF ASIAN-INDIAN HOLIDAYS*

January

PONGAL: This festival honors *the cow* and marks the end of the *winter.* In the evening, everyone comes out to watch a parade of these beloved animals, which are decorated with flowers and paint.

March

HOLI: The national celebration of *spring,* which begins with a bonfire to say farewell to the old year. It ends with red-colored water and bright powders tossed playfully among celebrants!

August

JANMASHTAMI: The national celebration of the birth of **Krishna.** Worshipers fast during the day and break the fast following a special worship called a *puja.*

September

DUSSERAH: A celebration that honors the *victory of Prince Rama's* rescue of his wife Sita from the demon Ravana. Giant paper statues appear at the festival. The *Ramayana* is performed on stage—all 48,000 lines! Dusserah begins with the **New Moon.**

GANESH CHATURTHI: A national celebration of the birthday of elephant-headed **Ganesha.** Huge and decorative images of Ganesha are paraded.

October

DIWALI: The Indian New Year and *"Festival of Lights."* Tiny oil lamps called *dipas* shine from every rooftop to light the way for Rama. The lights also lead the Goddess of Wealth and Prosperity, Lakshmi, to your door.

ABOUT FESTIVALS IN INDIA: Festivals and celebrations in India are generally joyous occasions, marked with singing, dancing, fireworks, and parades—big floats and giant figures represent heroes and villains. Some occasions, however, are more somber and require fasting, yet may end in a feast. *Id-ul Fitr* marks the end of **Ramadan,** a Muslim month of fasting. Each year Ramadan begins one week earlier than the preceding year. Id-ul Fitr begins when fasting ends. It is a time of rejoicing.

---

* Festival dates vary from community to community, region to region.

ACTIVITY 6

Rangoli: Art Underfoot

Village Arts/Floor "Threshold" Painting

DOUBLE BONUS: THE "WARLI" ON THE WALL . . . INDIAN "WINDOW DRESSING"

An ancient folk art in India, *Rangoli* is a village tradition of decorating the floor or doorstep. Temporary painting serves as a welcome mat in even the most modest dwelling. Depending on what region of India you happen to be in, the art of Rangoli has different names and somewhat different meanings; it is also called *Mandna, Alpana,* or *Kolnam.* Village women, who are artists in their own right, apply designs—which range from basic to complex—to the thresholds of their homes.

Although Rangoli may be used to mark special events—a birth, a wedding, or a national holiday—it is believed that Rangoli began as a ritual that offered thanksgiving to the Earth.

Traditionally, Rangoli is applied directly with fingers of the right hand onto a fresh, clean surface. Rice flour is the favored medium as is the bold, white pattern. Colored accents appear, often created from bright-colored dyes: Red is considered powerful and auspicious! Other media used by the Rangoli artist might be pebbles, whole grains, and flower petals. It is a craft that one generation of women teaches the next. Most commonly, Rangoli is an everyday village art. A daily ritual of washing the threshold of the home provides a fresh surface for a bright new design. When the day is finished, the design has served its purpose and is washed away. On the household threshold, the creative cycle begins in order for it to begin once again.

▲ Figure 4-23. Student displays his choice of design as well as the reference points that he selected for accent with red paint.

▲ Figure 4-24. We are very proud of our Rangoli! As you can see, designs range from compact geometric formats to free-wheeling abstractions. By joining dots or circling around them, endless varieties *can* and *will* occur!

MATERIALS

- tempera or poster paint (especially white)
- brown kraft paper
- practice paper (manila)
- brushes
- white chalk
- water containers

TEACHER PREPARATION

Rangoli is traditionally applied to the floor directly with rice paste, which we realize is not reasonable for most classes. Nevertheless, the teacher will want to recreate the authenticity of this experience by moving furniture and desks away, when possible, thereby allowing floor space for students to paint their design. The teacher may also consider, if the weather is appropriate, painting Rangoli outdoors as well.

Since this is a partner activity, the teacher will want to decide on the method for selecting student partners.

The teacher should cut lengths of kraft paper in advance to represent the threshold.

▲ Figure 4-25. Sidewalk Rangoli—what a wonderful way to spend time outdoors. Sidewalk chalk (even standard colored chalk) will do the job nicely. Find a patch of sidewalk and apply yourself. This playground Rangoli bursts with a garden of lucky symbols. The hubs or wheels represent "abundance." The leafy lotus shapes are symbols of the universe, while the vibrant heart-triangle combination is a "tree of life." Ephemeral art—or art that is not intended to last—is a universal idea that is particularly embraced in the East.

DIRECTIONS

1. Rangoli is essentially an art of pattern systems. Depending on individual teacher circumstances, personal tastes, and personal teaching styles, a highly specific pattern grid could be used. It is suggested that in keeping with Rangoli tradition, however, a grid of dots be used for reference points. These may be visually offered to students (see the illustration on page 141) or simply described them for student interpretation.

2. Discuss with your students traditional symbols and designs for Rangoli floor art (see Figures 4-23 to 4-25). Perhaps a chalkboard could serve as a visual aid.

3. Distribute manila paper and white chalk. Students will experiment with several designs using a dot-grid system. Once confidence is gained, group students into pairs.

4. Distribute white paint, brushes, water, and kraft paper. Students begin their designs with white chalk dots, followed by white poster paint.

5. Apply color as determined. Remember, color is optional—and red is very powerful. Let dry.

◀ Figure 4-26. Diwali, the festival of lights, ushers in the new year and celebrates the goddess Lakshmi of Wealth and Prosperity. To make sure the generous goddess visits your home, one may draw footprints leading in a path straight to the door! Diwali also "lights the way" of Lord Rama, insuring his return with lucky symbols. Rangoli can include designs such as these, anytime of the year, weather permitting.

6. Wouldn't it be wonderful if these threshold paintings could be used in an area where they would serve as a welcome mat, yet not be trampled? If you have such an area, try to change designs daily until all have been seen. If you do not have this sort of space, there is always the wall!

BONUS: THE "WARLI" ON THE WALL . . .

To the tribal Warli people of India, a mud wall is a perfect surface to depict simple, charming figurative scenes. Animals and people in action or at rest and at play—in swings, dancing, or working—may be seen. It is a folk art tradition that can be "saved" through painted application to specially prepared boards. This creates a permanent record of yet another precious domestic art. Typically Warli mural painting is highly pictographic—almost "x-ray, see-through"—in its depiction of interior space. It is an art of line: small marks comprise picture details. Linear expression, *not color,* is important. Note that many Warli murals are quite abstract.

▲ Figure 4-27. A student-made Warli painting.

If your classroom has dark brown display paper (if not, use brown kraft paper), your Rangoli floor painting will find itself in good company when Warli hits the walls! Students in pairs or individually can create scenes by simply joining geometric shapes to suggest figure symbols in white pencil (or white crayon), drawn directly onto the brown surface. You may want to mount sections of brown paper on the wall in advance of the lesson to provide a novel drawing surface. The teacher who yearns for authenticity may ask students to gather twigs—which will be used as a means of applying white paint (instead of the crayon). You can't get much more basic than these primal painting tools!

BONUS: INDIAN "WINDOW DRESSINGS"

Would you now consider applying decorative Indian border art around your windows and door? You can nicely "frame" with direct artistic design. If so, Indian window dressing for your classroom is irresistible. This beautiful, framed design would be found painted directly onto Indian housewall exteriors. Simple back marker, butcher paper, and scissors can dramatically enhance an existing window or create the illusion of a new one. An enlarged photograph or magazine image of scenery may be used to improve the interior design of any space, particularly small ones. Indian art will give you a whole new outlook!

▲ Figure 4-28. A student-made window dressing.

ACTIVITY 7

Princess Tara of Tibet "Thanka": A Special Someone Tribute

"Thanka" Scrolls/Mixed Media and Painting

INCLUDES: TIBETAN *MANDALA* . . . AND MUDRAS

The practice of Buddhism had its start in India when a prince named Siddhartha, in the 6th century B.C., became disenchanted with his sheltered palace life. He left behind his worldly wealth to seek truth. Under the Bodhi tree sat Siddhartha, meditating until he was able to better know the meaning of existence; and the rest, as one might say, is Buddhist history. Buddhism spread widely into the greater lands of Asia where it was established as one of the major world religions. Hinduism does include Buddhist principles but is a distinct and ancient belief system that prevails in India to this day. Buddhism traveled to the Himalayan kingdom of Tibet in the 8th century. The "roof of the world" is nested between India to the south and China to the east. The art of Tibet is itself unique, yet has absorbed both Indian and Chinese styles and beliefs.

Tibet has much to teach about honesty, mindfulness, tranquility, action, and—most important—compassion, often symbolized by a thunderbolt. Tibetan art displays virtuous principles. The unique cloth scroll, which is known as a *Thanka* (tahn-kah), may feature figurative or geometric designs. It is unmistakably Tibetan. Green Tara and White Tara are the benevolent female princesses who represent the gentle nature of Tibet. Yes, there are odious monsters, too! In Tibet, as elsewhere, art helps us to consider oppositional forces, with the hope of balance and harmony.

The Thanka contains many ideas, whether in the form of a recognizable figure or as an abstract, geometric *mandala* (circle). The meaning of the Thanka is perhaps best understood when regarded as a home for celestial beings and the ideas they symbolize. Thankas appear in temples, homes, and individual spaces. The actual design of the Thanka painting is highly codified. It is a cosmic diagram that places figures and symbols in a specifically ordered manner. The intent of a beautifully conceived Thanka is to inspire personal reflection and ensure good deeds.

▲ Figure 4-29. In spite of great struggles to maintain their homeland and their beliefs, Tibetans seem to continue to have an unswerving belief in the goodness of humanity. As this student's Thanka image conveys, there is a quiet dignity and simplicity expressed in Thanka art, which is essentially an art of contemplation. Many Tibetans no longer live in Tibet. In fact, they have relocated to India on the other side of the Himalayas.

◀ Figure 4-30. The figure occupies greater space in this Thanka. Actually, "chins" and folds along the neck have their own specific meanings in Thanka inconography. Also, in traditional Tibetan Thanka painting, the eyes of the central figure are left for last so that they can be painted on a special occasion called "The Opening of the Eyes." Eyes are sometimes found in surprising places on Thanka figures: Tara is often shown with eyes on the palms of her hands and the soles of her feet, consistent with her "all-seeing" nature. The eye in the center of her forehead generally is regarded as "The Third Eye of Enlightenment." Some trace the Indian *tika* or *bindi* forehead red dot to this origin. (See Activity 3).

143

▲ Figure 4-31. This young Thanka painter has used her own set of symbols to give her work its meaning. Note "the door," a happy statement!

MATERIALS

- colored construction paper (see Teacher Preparation)
- large white drawing paper
- tissue paper
- fine-tip markers
- glitter (or glitter pens)
- gold pens (optional, but recommended)

- scissors
- ribbon (optional)
- pencils
- mixed drawing supplies, i.e., crayons, watercolor markers
- glue

TEACHER PREPARATION

Thankas are traditionally composed of a wide silk brocade border with two smaller brocade strips that frame the image. Sometimes there is another square of brocade that appears below the painting which is known as "the door." The borders frame the "house," which is considered the home of the image. The pattern-filled brocade appears in yellow, red, and blue. The veil is usually red or yellow. The teacher may want to conform to these color and design ideas while leaving room for young imaginations to interpret their own ideas.

Brocade will be substituted with colored construction paper (unless you happen to have some lovely brocade)! Cutting strips into desired lengths may be useful for assembling the Thanka frame. Ribbon (or the substitution of small paper strips) may also be cut in appropriate lengths prior to class; these will be used to tie back the veil. Tissue paper should be sized to fit the scale of the Thanka frame, for it will be used as a curtain to both protect the image and to reveal it.

DIRECTIONS

1. Explain the definition of a Thanka and ask the students to discuss their personal heroes. What form might these everyday heroes take? Who are they? How about a parent, a mentor, a big sister or brother, a best friend—or a teacher? The Thankas of Tibet do honor great teachers (these are called *guru* Thankas).

2. Distribute white drawing paper and pencils. Students will sketch the central figure (called "lineage holder") based on the selection of "someone special" as listed in Step 1. If you wish the lesson to follow Thanka convention, the next part of the composition to be drawn would be sky elements, hills and mountains, waterfalls, and various decorative designs. Please refer to MUDRAS on pages 146-148 for ideas about hand gestures.

◄ Figure 4-32. Much like her Hindu cousins, this figure finds four hands are better than two!

3. When students have completed their preliminary sketch, distribute all other materials. Assemble the Thanka strips into the format that holds the image; these provide a frame for the house in which your "someone special" dwells. The decorative decisions about both the image and the frame may be applied simultaneously or individually. Use gold pens to enhance and accentuate linear quality. Add a "door" if desired; see Figures 4-31, happy face door, and 4-32, jeweled door, for examples. **Note:** These are artroom-produced Thankas, so formats *may* and *should* vary.

4. As composition develops, students consider how the qualities of their special image can be represented. If a great teacher is being depicted, items (or "attributes") such as a book, paint box, or briefcase can be shown. Other smaller units can surround the central figure to enhance picture meaning. Ideas may be realistic, decorative, elaborate, or simple. Freedom of expression is most valued—the students of a great teacher may even be represented as growing flowers!

5. Have students protect the "special someone" with a sheet of tissue paper, attached to the back of the construction paper with glue. Affix ribbon streamers, if desired.

6. When all students have completed their "Someone Special Tribute Thankas," display the veiled images in a grand celebration. Students will be given the opportunity to pull back the curtain, reveal their "someone special," and discuss the person's special qualities in the student's own life. To honor and value those who help and love us is a fine reason to create art.

▲ Figure 4-33. A very powerful Thanka indeed! In its youthful exuberance, our self-portrait gathers many forces of nature. The thunderbolt, as it happens, is an important Tibetan symbol, which balances the elements of this magical painting.

INCLUDES : TIBETAN *MANDALA*

The *Mandala* is a circular "cosmic" diagram shown in Tibetan Thankas and sand paintings. Mandala is an all-important representation of the inner and outer worlds. Its format is basic: a circle within a square, within a circle. The inner circle symbolizes the inner world of the self, and the dwelling place of the most essential spirit. The four-pointed square represents the Four Directions. The larger circle represents the everyday world. There are also other ways to explain the Mandala, a basic design that holds complex ideas. The Mandala could be regarded as surrounded by four gateways (the square), in the center of which is located a palace for the main and most important celestial being.

Mandalas are painted on Thankas as well as created as sand paintings—an intricate, labor-intensive process that has also been called ***particle painting.*** Sand painting can take months of extreme concentration to create, and contains infinite symbols, signs, and details. Special tools are used to allow sand colors to flow into the large, overall design. Sizes vary, yet are usually of generous scale. Upon its completion, this jewel-like elaborate sand manadala is viewed and appreciated, then swept away. The symbolic grains of sand fill a simple container, after which the contents are thrown by monks in a ceremony that returns the sand to the sea.

Wheel of Life, Wheel of Time, Endless Cycle—these are all in the circle of the mandala, which is as round as the Earth. To describe the cycle of life as a spider with its surrounding web can be applied to Asian, Eastern, and African mythologies—as well as to Native American, where the Medicine Wheel and Dream Catcher express this shared idea. (See Native America, page 284.) The circle and the square—the mandala and The Four Directions—are universal indeed!

MUDRAS

The *mudra* is a hand gesture that communicates knowledge, sentiments, and expressions of faith. It is a sign language vocabulary. Mudras are often seen in Buddhist and Hindu art. You will find mudras in sculpture and in dance—and sometimes in everyday life. Here are the meanings of twelve mudras.

▲ Figure 4-34. *Namaste* (or *Anjali*): "I respect the spirit within you," a way to greet others in India!

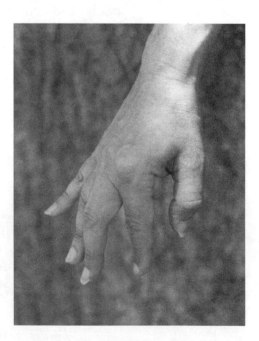

▲ Figure 4-35. Earth Touching.

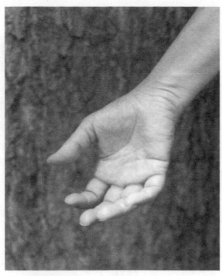

▲ Figure 4-36. Gift Bestowing.

▲ Figure 4-37. Teaching.

▲ Figure 4-38. Fear Not.

▲ Figure 4-39. Gesture of Offering.

▲ Figure 4-40. *Hamsarya:* The swan or goose vehicle of Sarasvati, Goddess of the Arts.

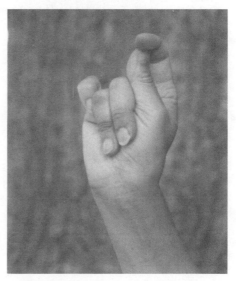

▲ Figure 4-41. *Kapitha:* A parrot associated with the Mother Goddess.

▲ Figure 4-42. *Mukula:* Lotus bud.

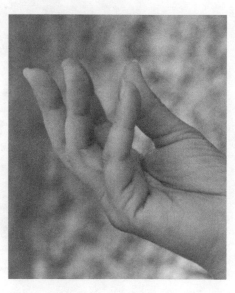

▲ Figure 4-43. *Padmakosha:* Lotus begins to open.

▲ Figure 4-44. *Alapadma:* Lotus is open.

▲ Figure 4-45. Hand Touching Tree: Although not technically a mudra, this gesture refers to early goddesses called *yakshis,* who could cause a tree to burst into bloom by a simple touch of the hand; these graceful tree spirits attest to the "powers of the feminine".

It is sometimes both educational and enjoyable to try represenations of mudra gestures in Asian art, especially when representing gods and goddesses and important "special" heroes, as in the Someone Special Thanka.

The Pacific Cultures: Oceania

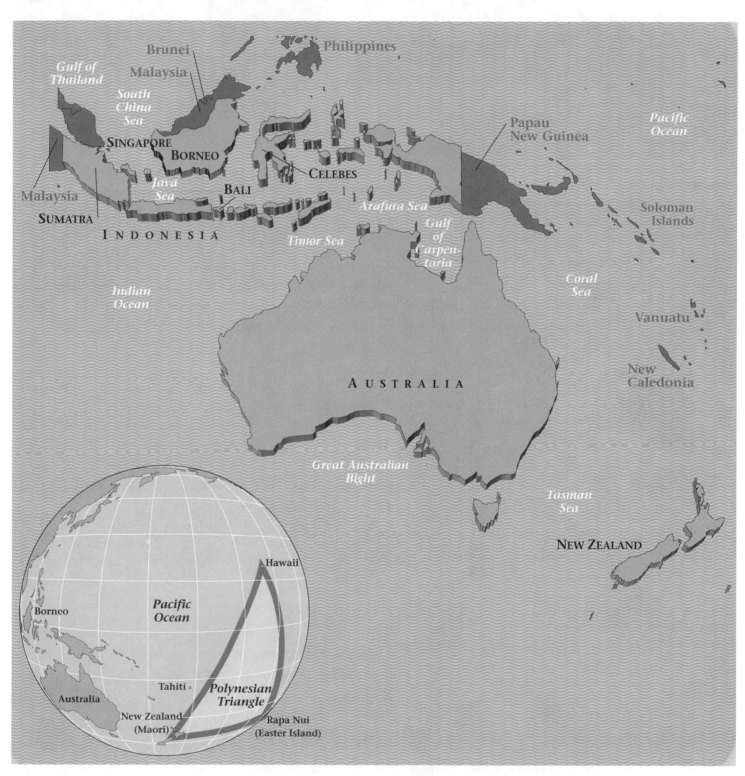

The Pacific Cultures: Oceania

In Bali, Indonesia, it is customary for women to bear offerings of fruit, piled high on their heads, as they travel to a temple. Bali has been called "the Land of 1,000 Temples."

The dance mask of Garuda, the Sun Bird of Indonesia. Garuda is also found in Indian Hindu legend and belief.

ART ACTIVITIES FOR BECOMING CULTURE SMART

Activity 1
Dance Batik! The Performing Arts of Indonesia
Batik Story Cloth/Stage Set

Activity 2
"Gunungan": A Shadow Puppet to Keep the Universe in Balance! (Java)
Tree-of-Life Puppets and the Shadow World
BONUS: WHAT'S A WIDYAHARI? A GUARDIAN ANGEL FROM INDONESIA

Activity 3
Dreamtime: Boomerangs from "Down Under" (Australia)
"Original" Aboriginal Art
BONUS: X-RAY BARK PAINTING: AMAZING ANIMALS AND RAINBOW SERPENTS!

Activity 4
Magnificent Maori: Gateways to New Zealand
"Carved" Ancestral Post
BONUS: A CALL TO ARMS! ARE TATTOOS TABOO?

Activity 5
Printing Paradise: Tapa Is Tops! (Polynesia)
Graphic Arts/Printmaking
BONUS: HAWAIIAN QUILTS

Activity 6:
Chiefly Capes (Hawaii)
Royal Feather Art

Activity 7
Aloha Hawaii! (Hawaii)
Vintage Hawaiian "Shirts"

To know the Art of the Pacific Cultures . . . .

. . . . . one starts with the island groups of the Pacific that are numerous and are often defined collectively by the term Oceania. As its name implies, Oceania is a watery continent of wide ocean that may be classified by: The central Pacific Polynesian Islands, to include Hawaii and New Zealand . . . the western Pacific cultures where Australia, New Guinea, and Micronesia are located . . . and the Asian Pacific Islands to the north which encompass Indonesia and the Philippines. Of course there are many island cultures to consider in the Pacific. Japan is geographically a Pacific island grouping, whereas Hawaii and Guam are part of the Pacific domain of the United States of America. The Asian continent and Indian subcontinent contribute to the cultures of Indonesia. Similarities exist between Buddhist Cambodia and nearby Thailand when seen in context with Indonesia. Bali, in Indonesia, is Hindu while the neighboring island of Java is Muslim. Except for Hindu Bali, Indonesia has a nearly 90% Muslim population. The Indonesian chain of islands—more than 17,000—straddle the equator and are believed to have once linked the continents of Asia and Australia.

Bali is blessed by nature and considered "a home of the gods." It is surely a paradise for the performance arts, which are conducted in accordance with the Hindu cycles of death and rebirth, ceremony and festival. Beautiful and dazzling dancers are richly robed in layers of textiles. Gold motifs flash against vivid colors, while fans, flowers, and exotic fruit offerings abound. Masked drama and dance are set in an environment that provides much inspiration for motifs. The fabric arts of *batik* and *ikat* contain symbolic and complex patternings that are as culturally rich as these Indonesian "Spice Islands."

The shadow play (*wayang kulit*) is an extended puppet performance, as appropriate for a palace as for the village square today. Java, the central Indonesian island, is world-famous for its shadow play performances. Jakarta, the capital city of Indonesia in Java, is noted for its Museum Wayang, where puppet performances are held regularly. In the shadow play, puppets tell familiar stories behind a lit screen. Hindu epics such as the *Ramayana* are told with an Indonesian twist. The *dalang,* or puppet master, is accompanied by a full *gamelan* orchestra. The stylized mythology, history, spirituality, and world view are played out through wayang kulit in its traditionally night-long presentation.

Powerful masks are used in Southeast Asian performances. The *Topeng* in Bali uses a special series of representational masks reserved for history plays. Dance dramas are a highly developed art form, and theatrical dance presentations share common expressive means. Hand gestures are consistent with classic Indian dance *mudras*—with each posture, a specific sentiment is qualified. Costumes are constructed to suggest codified virtues. The dance costume in Cambodia, Thailand, and Indonesia often appears as "moving temple" forms, recalling architectural elements. Dance is an Asian metaphor for the life cycle. Stone female figures dance in the bas relief on the walls of the Borobudur Temple at Java—considered the greatest Buddhist monument in the world. Like the Tibetan *mandala,* Borobudur is built as a three-dimensional *kalachakra* diagram, with World Mountain at its core.

Paradise is a word that has become almost synonymous with visions of Polynesia. Nineteenth-century French painter Paul Gauguin left Europe in search of a tropical Eden. Tahiti offered sun-drenched, saturated color and a people as emotionally generous as they were handsome. Much of Gauguin's painting was influenced by the original fabric design arts of Polynesia. Like Pablo Picasso, Paul Gauguin synthesized cultural tradition outside of Europe through his own artistic invention.

In Hawaii, land of dramatic physical beauty, of sea and volcanoes, the two great spirit forces that govern life are *Mana,* the positive force, and *Taboo,* the opposing negative force. Objects embody these sacred concepts. Art was best placed in the hands of the Kahuna, an artist-priest with broad knowledge. Figures were carved in all shapes and sizes, using block-like compact representations denoting power. In the textile arts, design on *tapa* cloth, made from the inner bark of the mulberry tree, uses abstract geometrics in dynamic repeated patterns with countless variations.

The Maori people of New Zealand are the "carvers of the Pacific." Like the Hawaiians, the Maori embraced a panoply of spirit gods. Ancestors remain essential to well-being; a familiar icon is *Tiki,* a representation of First Man. Intricate whirls, spirals, and filigree marked the decorative tradition of carving that appears in abundance on canoes, paddles, and ceremonial structures. *Moko,* Maori tattoo design, is deeply rooted in the culture, as is the *dendroglyph* bark carving.

In Australia, northwest of New Zealand, aborigines lived with the land for 40,000 years. Aboriginal art comes out of the *Dreamtime,* a way of life and cosmological beliefs. This art is defined by expressively unique styles and techniques that include coded symbols, dot-field systems, crosshatching, and x-ray picture devices which vibrate with the forces that the artists—The Keepers of the Dreamtime—have conveyed since earliest times.

ACTIVITY 1

Dance Batik! The Performing Arts of Indonesia

"Batik" Story Cloth/Stage Set

◄ Figure 5-1. The dance batik "story" painting tells of classical Balinese dancers and more! On the left is an offering of fruit and flowers. In front of the dancer (lower left) is a *frog bird bath*—probably symbolic of new life. Dancers flank a beautiful Balinese waterfall! Temple architecture surrounds us. What is central to this scenic display? We believe the dance and all other artistry is to honor the traditional Javanese wedding couple—Dewi Sri, (right) the Rice Goddess, and her counterpart, Sadono, (left)—who appear in a niche at the upper right. Their presence in the household promises a happy marriage and prosperity.

If one were to wish for an "art heaven on earth"—set in a land of stunning natural beauty and filled with dancers, musicians, puppets, masks, exquisite fabrics, and golden temples—just click your heels and say *Indonesia!* Within the world's largest archipelago of over 13,000 islands, tiny Bali, which is 90% Hindu, is the "jewel in the crown." For a very long time, Indonesia was closely associated with India, primarily through its Hindu belief. Although Indonesia itself is home to virtually the greatest concentration of Muslims, the Hindu legends are represented in the Indonesian performance, both in courtly and popular theater. In central Java, characters and episodes from the *Ramayana* and *Mahabharata* are eloquently portrayed in *wayang kulit*—which, literally translated, means "leather puppet." This performance is known as "shadow world" and has an accompanying *gamalan* orchestra conducted by a *dalang*, the master impresario. Without a formal script, the dalang is indispensable! *Wayang golek* is enjoyed without a screen; these puppets are carved and three-dimensional. Among other notable Indonesian performance art is the Balinese *topeng*, the Javanese word for mask, which is essentially a history play—complete with kings, queens, and prime ministers. Bali and Java overflow with spirited creativity! Art and theater truly rule.

There is a saying in Indonesia: "Things are not always what they appear to be." Objects have their own power and one art overlaps the other. There is no specific word for artist—art is life. Batik, which at first blush appears to be simply stunning fabric, holds a rich vocabulary of meaning. Batik is used for various purposes and is often seen in the popular *sarong*. An ancient Indonesian textile art, batik is still practiced today, although commercial production has made traditional techniques far more rare. Batik translates as "small, wax writing"; it is essentially a wax-resist method. Special pens, called *tjanting* (CHANG-ting), are used to apply the hot wax designs that may indicate status or clan, bring protection or good luck to the weaver, or please the spirits! Design inspiration is drawn from nature, mythology, and established ceremonial motifs: They are exquisite and mysterious! To have heaven on earth in one place . . . what could be *"sarong"* about that?

152

MATERIALS

- 9" × 12" white paper
- white crayons
- watercolors
- 12" × 18" manila
- pencils
- scissors
- 16" × 24" white shelf paper (suggested) or kraft paper

- white tempera paint
- markers/crayons (optional)
- brushes
- glue sticks
- paper towels
- nontoxic gold pens (optional)
- reproducible page: "Batik Designs"
- nontoxic black permanent marker

TEACHER PREPARATION

William Shakespeare's idea of "all the world's a stage" is not alien to Indonesia. To the Indonesian, theater is a metaphor for life itself: The stage or screen represents the universe. In this activity, students will re-create the "Indonesian Universe" by creating a stage set that includes the essential elements of daily living, fantastic landscape, and ceremonial arts. To this they will add dancing figures that represent both the real and the mythical individuals, often portrayed in puppet form. The treasured art of batik will provide the costumes and attire. It is suggested that the teacher, through the use of such reference materials as travel brochures and available visual sources, help students to "form a picture" of Indonesia. Of course, real props such as Balinese puppets are perfect.

In preparation for this activity, cut lengths of scroll to provide the "painted backdrop" for the "theatrical production." For samples of batik design, see the illustrations on the accompanying reproducible page. **Note:** It is suggested that students work in pairs.

DIRECTIONS

1. Discuss the spectacular land of Indonesia with students through verbal description and visual aid. To design a backdrop, students will want to note the difference between landscape painting and set design. The latter in this art invites curvy and fanciful design. Perhaps it is best described as an "enchanted place"—filled with magic mountains in the background, flowering fruit trees, terraced fields, waterfalls, and towering tear drop-capped temples.

Figure 5-2. This cold-resist batik is easily accomplished in the classroom with often remarkable results. The batik process is more than just a means to beautiful design: its motifs are deeply connected with nature and the cosmic universe. Names such as "light rain" and "fallen leaf" convey its lyrical meaning. ▼

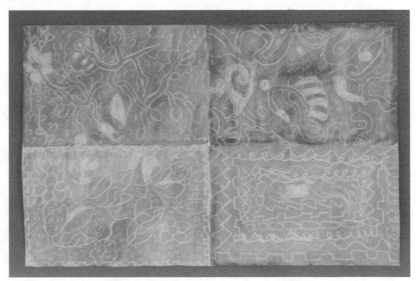

BATIK DESIGNS

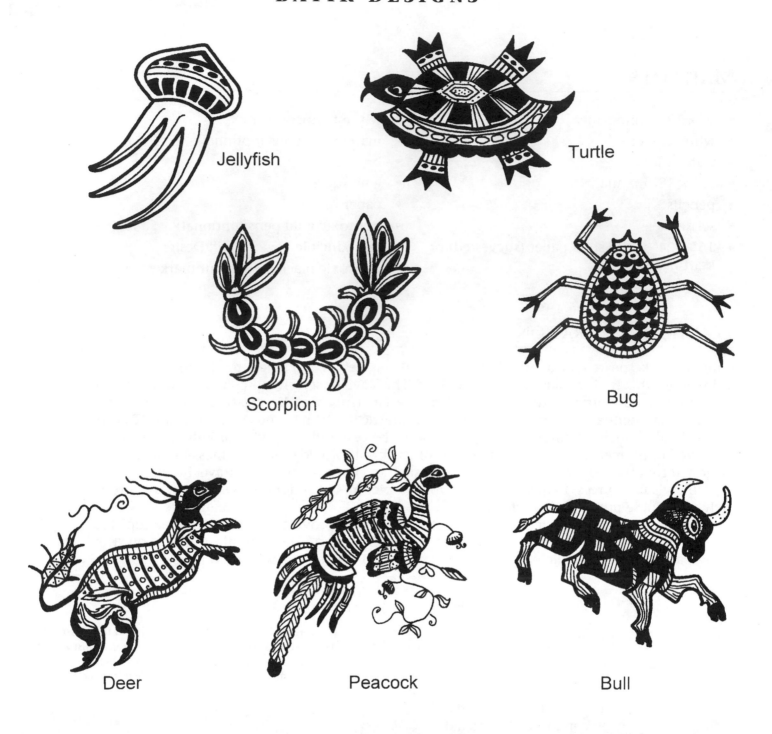

Jellyfish

Turtle

Scorpion

Bug

Deer

Peacock

Bull

Lung klewer

Delima wanta

Kirna monda

Hibiscus

2. Distribute pencils and scroll paper. Students are to sketch a preliminary idea of what this lovely land may be (figures will be added later). Put aside.

3. Now is the time to consider batik design, which is based on the motifs just described. Indonesian batik is a highly refined and technical hot-wax process, and students will create their own form. Our "cold water" version of paper batik is one with the "wax-resist" method. (See Figure 5-2 on page 153.) Batik will then be combined with Balinese painting.

4. Distribute manila paper and white crayons. Students will fold paper into four sections (either in quarters or horizontal bands). Using traditional motifs for inspiration—along with their own knowledge of flowers, waves, clouds, and birds—students will fill the paper with four different ideas. Let dry.

5. Distribute paint, cups, paper towels, and brushes. Students will apply paint to the four sections in varying colors—and be delighted as designs magically appear! Let dry.

6. Students will now turn their attention to the Indonesian dancing figure as it is so often seen on both the puppet stage as well as in dance performance. For a moment, pretend you are about to appear on stage—you will need to warm up! Students, with your assistance, may want to gently exercise their hands to prepare for the very curvy gestures Indonesian hands show. A gentle stretch back with the fingers of one hand pressing the fingers of the other (repeat) will allow hands more flexibility. Try a few hand poses! (See Mudras, page 146, India.) You may even want to stand on one leg while moving hands in curving waves, much like the flow of the curving sea. In this spirit you may sit down and begin drawing—with a pencil on white paper—a small troupe of dancers (and accompanying movements). Figures should have a height of approximately six to seven inches. (See Figures 5-3 and 5-4 for more ideas.)

◄ Figure 5-3. Meet the hero prince. The handsome and "refined" figure represents the Indonesian ideal of male beauty. He is considered a *wayang golek* rod puppet, one that is made of carved wood and dimensional. He wears traditional garments that include a gold-braided velvet jacket, offset by a batik sarong. He is flanked by *topeng* theatrical masks: Garuda appears at the left, and a familiar topeng mask at the right can be identified by the color she is painted. Behind the hero prince is a portion of Balinese story painting depicting a ceremonial village event. An Indonesian crescent moon glows above!

Figure 5-4. A wonderful Balinese dancer by Stephanie, who seems to be signing her name with the dancer's toe. She too embodies the Indonesian essentials—graceful gesture, meaningful facial expression, and elaborate yet simple textiles and accessories. Note the detailed crown, the Garuda symbol on her sarong and the "winged" arm bands. She displays on her bodice the most sacred of all Indonesian symbols—the mountain temple. ►

7. Students should know that their figures' attire will mostly be cut from the paper batik. Plan dancing costumes and sarongs as needed.

8. Just like an Indonesian dancer, students are spinning many plates at the same time—artistically speaking! Bring both scroll and batik into students' reach. Watercolor, paint, markers, and crayons will help create the reality of the figure, as well as the stage set.

9. Distribute scissors and cut out dancing figures. Retrieve paper batik for dancer wardrobe. Cut and size as needed; affix with glue stick. Hats, headdresses, wraps, and sarongs work best. Without gluing, place figures against the stage set. Determine whether original sketch requires an adjustment. A temple? A pavilion? Women carrying tall "mountains" of fruit offerings on their heads as they approach the temples? Are more dancers needed? If so, add them to the stage set. You may even want to try a "stage within a stage"—an outdoor shadow puppet performance would certainly add to the entertainment!

10. Assemble all parts in accordance with students' own "artistic universe." Linear accents such as white or gold outlines will certainly spark interest. White paint helps to carry the batik feeling of the story panel and provide visual spark. You may even wish to include flying *garuda* or other little "angels." Is life imitating life or is life imitating art—in Indonesia the difference is delightfully unpredictable. (See Figure 5-5 for a sample story cloth.)

---

*S.O.S. (SAVE OUR SCHEDULE, i.e., "Schedule Saver" or shortcut . . .) The teacher-in-a-hurry may want to review steps 3 through 8 (cold-wax batik "swatches") and go directly to number nine. The dancers may be drawn directly onto the sketched scenery along with other pictorial details (suggested in step 9). Sketch the entire composition directly onto the length of scroll. Use a "mixed-media batik" method with the application of crayon and paint, done in stages at the same time, depending on the allotment. Anyway that you do it, it will be enchanting!

◄ Figure 5-5. Detail of a story cloth. Note the women carrying offerings of food piled high on their heads as they journey to the temple. This charming image is deeply connected with Indonesian life and ritual.

ACTIVITY 2

"Gunungan": A Shadow Puppet to Keep the Universe in Balance!

Tree-of-Life Puppets and the Shadow World

BONUS: WHAT'S A WIDYAHARI? A GUARDIAN ANGEL FROM INDONESIA

Imagine yourself in central Java in a village square. You have come to see a shadow play. A wide white screen is set up in front of you while day turns to night. Flat leather rod puppet characters (*wayang*) line up to the left and to the right; in the center stands the *gunungan,* a scenic puppet meaning *mountain* or *kayon,* meaning *forest.* It is also known as "the tree of life." The graceful, fan-like presence of the gunungan signals the beginning of the long *wayang kulit* performance, with oppositional forces lined up on each side. Soon they will come into dramatic motion. The screen itself represents the universe: The role of the gunungan is to keep the world in balance.

The shadow play progresses with increased puppet activity. Evil-tempered characters clash with heroic ones. The *dalang* or narrator creatively conveys the unfolding tale. He or she is aided by the gamelan orchestra, complete with percussion instruments and a variety of gongs. Expect the gunungan to come fluttering through the set, an indication of unrest, upheaval, and change. Like its shadowy companions, gunungan is made of painted leather and is delicately crafted. It does not require multiple rods. Gunungan, with its simple shape, could not be more central to the wayang world in every sense, for it marks both stability and transition. Whether you call it gunungan, leaf, kayon (forest), or tree of life, the sight of this lotus-shaped puppet in the center of the wayang screen—when the play is over—means all is well. The play is finished and the sun is rising in the sky once again as there is harmony and balance in the universe. Applause!

▲ Figure 5-6. Traditional *gunungan* or tree-of-life puppets are made of filigree leather and often feature a powerful mask character on the reverse side. This stunning puppet by 12-year-old Jade fully suggests the filigree surface through a honeycomb pattern of small, circular design units. The main house-temple that contains The Powerful Spirit of All Things is protected by two very capable scorpions! Her curvilinear motifs have all the rhythm of the skies in Van Gogh's "Starry Night."

◄ Figure 5-7. When gunungan puppets are grouped together, they make for an eye-pleasing display.

157

MATERIALS

- 12" × 18" oaktag
- scissors
- pencils
- colored markers

- wooden paint stir sticks (or wooden dowels)
- stapler or hot glue gun (only under teacher supervision)

TEACHER PREPARATION

Teachers may want to precut the leaf shape for younger children. Wooden paint stir sticks, provided by the local paint store, are ideal for this lesson.

DIRECTIONS

1. Gunungan puppets are simple to produce, yet contain deep ideas. Discuss the symbolism of the leaf shape—sacred mountain (gunungan) or forest (kayon)—with the students. Have students place the tips of their fingers together and curve the sloping fingers inward. Hold hands at eye level, with stretched thumbs meeting at tips—a ready reference for the leaf form is "on hand!"

2. Oaktag is suggested as a substitute for leather. Distribute pencils, scissors, and oaktag. Students will fold the oaktag in half vertically and draw half of the leaf shape, being sure to touch the top, bottom, and sides of the paper. Cut out when satisfied with the shape.

◀ Figures 5-8a & 5-8b. This artist's demonstration model fashioned by teacher/illustrator Joe Baker seems worthy of its position next to an authentic Indonesian shadow puppet. ▶

3. The fold in the center of the leaf or lotus shape provides an opportunity for both symmetry and asymmetry. Students will draw the tree trunk (with pencils) to stabilize the center of their design, leaving room for a tiny temple structure that must have closed doors; this can also look like a little house or a small cabinet. Create two guardians; Balinese masks and puppets make a wonderful reference here. Draw curvy branches to extend the edges of the form. Fill with serpentine and curvy designs that contain animals and other appropriate elements.

4. Colored markers are fine for the required linear designs and details.

5. The gunungan rod or handle may be a wooden dowel or, better yet, a short paint stir stick contributed to students from the local paint store. The central rod or handle may be attached with a standard stapler or teacher-supervised hot glue gun—after the color has been supplied to the completed puppet design. The handle may be part of the design or simply a handle; use artistic discretion. This puppet may be reversible if desired, in which case students will create a "flip-side" of their own choice based on Indonesian design ideas that show natural forces. When students have completed their scenic gunungans, the play may either begin or end!

B O N U S : WHAT'S A *WIDYAHARI?* A GUARDIAN ANGEL FROM INDONESIA

Garuda is the national bird of Indonesia. Garuda seems to have flown straight to Indonesia from India, bringing along the many heroes and goddesses of Hindu belief and mythology. In India, Garuda is the *vehicle* of the great deity Vishnu the Preserver. Indonesia interpretations of Indian Hindu mythology have a distinctive flair and style that is both imaginative and recognizable. Meanings are shaped by the originality of Indonesian belief. Garuda is associated with the sun. (Figure 5-9.)

▲ Figure 5-9. Garuda, Bird of the Sun.

In Bali, the craft of carving and wooden figures is particularly valued. Encouraged by tourism, artisans have become even more adept at producing a large variety of characters from myth and folk tales. Objects such as mirrors, statues, boxes, trays, small chairs, and plaques abound. Often Garuda is shown as an explosive, figurative carving in the form of a statue with dramatic, radiating wings. *Partima,* which are small figures of Hindu gods with large animal and bird mounts (vehicles), have become popular for decorative use. Carvings serve architectural use and artistic need. A playful array of lizards, monkeys, frogs, mermaids, goddesses, deities, Buddhas, leaf and fruit sets—even pigs, cats, elephants, and seahorses—may be found.

When birds fly like Garuda, held up by strings with wings attached, these figures can be known as *Widyahari,* which translated means "heavenly nymphs." Their purpose is one of protection; they provide hanging altars to keep babies safe as they sleep. The cast of carved figures is expansive, drawn from folklore, television, Balinese legends, Hindu mythology, and contemporary culture as well as the art of other Asian societies. The carving itself is taken quite seriously and is

often generational. Balinese artists who develop new ideas are recognized for their originality, yet traditional belief seems to always play some part in the craft. And yes, even pigs can fly in Indonesia; in fact, you might even find a signpost along the road of a carving village that reads: "The Family of the First Pig Carver." (See Figure 5-11.) After all is said and done, Widyahari seem to know no imaginative limits and are certainly created for a kindly cause.

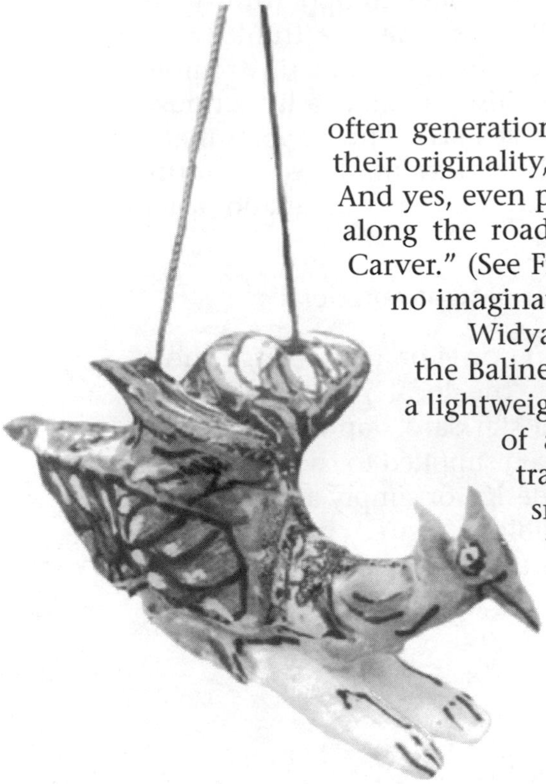

Widyahari are easily accomplished in the classroom without learning the Balinese art of carving. To make your very own Widyahari, we suggest a lightweight air-drying clay. Start with a ball of air-dried clay about the size of a small snowball. Create the animal, angel, or creature with traditional clay-modeling techniques. Wings may be added and smoothed into the figure or pulled from it. Let dry. Apply color with paint or marker. Hang in a special corner or use as a decorative ornament.

Figure 5-10. A successful student widyahari demonstrates a Balinese painting style.

▲ Figure 5-11. Pigs, elephants, frogs, and other fanciful creatures can fly! These *widyaharis* have been fashioned by Indonesian carvers. They have grown so popular through tourism and export that many traditional figures such as Garuda have given way to unexpected, more modern widyaharis, from fish to *flying classroom teachers!* Widyaharis now take many appearances.

▲ Figure 5-12. Balinese carvers create earthbound creatures, too, although this kitty seems equipped for air travel if desired.

ACTIVITY 3

SLIDE 21

Dreamtime: Boomerangs From "Down Under"

"Original" Aboriginal Art

B O N U S : X-RAY BARK PAINTING: AMAZING ANIMALS AND RAINBOW SERPENTS!

Toss your boomerang back 35,000 years and find yourself in the oldest known continuous culture in the world. You are now in Australia, where it is always *Dreamtime*—which explains the past, present, and future of the Aboriginal Australian. Known as "Dreaming," this creation story is where the explanation of worldly existence is found. The heroic characters who inhabit the Dreamtime perform both extraordinary and everyday tasks; they are known as Ancestral Beings. They are also called The Dreamings. They are realized in plant, animal, and human form; they also manifest the elements and all natural forces. The places that the Dreamings visited are believed to be transformed. The Dreamtime is the source of a striking mythology, complete with many versions. Stories have an "outside" and an "inside"! Dreamtime is the origin of all classical Aboriginal art.

To understand art of the Dreamtime, one must first learn that there is no concept of meaningless landscape. Everything has been

▲ Figure 5-13. A beautiful bunch of boomerangs display the design power of Australian Aboriginal art. The strong geometric elements of dot and line systems form patterns that are unmistakably Australian art.

"dreamed" into existence. Once the ancestral beings had completed their original creative activities, the people were told they were to be custodians of all living things. No object is without its own history or spiritual life. The same is true of the artistic marks and patterns applied to bark—and boomerangs! A spiraling line may represent a rainbow, a snake, water, lightning, or a cliff. Decoration is not merely decoration; everything has meaning. Actually, there is nothing "nonrepresentational" about Aboriginal art; all things are connected. Through the travels of the Dreamings, narratives and song lines cross the land and join people and places. Like the boomerang, the Dreamings "walk about" their map of civilization. As it is told, in the beginning of Dreamtime, the flying boomerang pulled the sun from the sky and brought the world night and day. Just as the boomerang makes its journey across the sky and returns to where it began, Dreamtime draws together all living things.

MATERIALS

- brown butcher wrap (see Teacher Preparation)
- scissors
- white paste
- white opaque paint markers (or white acrylic paint)
- black, yellow, and red watercolor markers

- black nontoxic permanent markers
- white oil pastels
- stapler
- pencils
- reproducible page: "Dreamtime Art"

TEACHER PREPARATION

Cut brown butcher wrap into 10″ × 26″ rectangles. Each student will need 4 pieces of paper. Layering 4 sheets of paper with a paste coating between each layer will create a stiff boomerang. Staple the 4 papers together in two places to keep them from shifting when students cut out the boomerang shape. Older students may be able to draw their own curving boomerang shape, but younger students may need a pattern to trace. It is important that the boomerang shape have approximately a four-inch width in the center area before tapering occurs at the ends.

Students will benefit from examples of Australian Aboriginal boomerangs and Aboriginal art that uses decorative lines, dots, and circles in a variety of symbolic patterns. (See Dreamtime Symbols reproducible page 163.)

DIRECTIONS

1. Distribute pencils, scissors, and four 10″ × 26″ sheets of butcher wrap (stapled together) to each student. Students draw a boomerang shape as large as possible on paper (or trace pattern) and then cut out shape, cutting through all layers of paper.

2. Distribute photocopies of reproducible page. Students observe and discuss the Aboriginal boomerang and the decorative use of lines, circles, and dots in symbolic arrangement. Discuss composition possibilities for student projects. As a means of organizing the overall design idea, students should consider whether they want to create a symmetrical or asymmetrical composition. For a symmetrical composition, the boomerang shape could be visually divided lengthwise with symmetrical shapes drawn on each side of the dividing line. Another symmetrical composition could begin with a large central shape and designs created symmetrically to each side of the central design. Students sketch out design ideas incorporating Aboriginal symbolism.

3. Trace design with black nontoxic permanent marker. Color selected shapes using red, yellow, and black watercolor markers. Leave some shapes uncolored to fill in later with white.

4. Distribute white opaque markers or white acrylic paint and brushes. Color remaining shapes and create white dot pattern designs around or between shapes.

5. Distribute white paste and wet paper towels (for cleaning hands). Adhere layers of boomerang shapes together with a smooth, thin application of white paste over the entire area of each shape. Caution students to make sure each layer is positioned properly on the layer below. When the boomerang shape—which has the design—is applied on top, caution students to clean the paste off their hands. Press on top of the drawing. After pressure has been applied to firmly adhere all layers together, allow boomerang to dry flat.

6. Isn't this art making a major "comeback"? Thanks to your efforts, we saw it coming!

DREAMTIME SYMBOLS

LIGHT OR SUN OR WATER	STAR	CLOUDS OR WIND	STORM CLOUD	LIGHTNING
HUMAN	MAN OR WOMAN	MAN OR WOMAN SITTING	LIGHTNING AND STARS	RAIN
EMU	KANGAROO	POSSUM	CAMPSITE OR FIRE	LIGHTNING FROM STORM CLOUD
EMU TRACKS	KANGAROO TRACKS	POSSUM TRACKS	TWO MEN SITTING	FIRE OR SMOKE
RUNNING WATER BETWEEN WATERHOLES	GRASS GROWING ON THE LAND	SITTING DOWN PLACE	FOUR WOMEN SITTING	RAINBOW OR SANDHILL
TRAVEL	TREE OR FRUIT OR WATERHOLE	POTATO OR YAM	BOOMERANG	SPEAR

B O N U S : X-RAY BARK PAINTING: AMAZING ANIMALS AND RAINBOW SERPENTS!

In the Australian Dreamtime, animals and other elements of nature are seen not only for their external features, but they are also seen simultaneously *inside-out.* These "x-ray" images are still being made today as paintings on sheets of bark from the stringybark tree, a kind of eucalyptus. It should be noted that Australian Aboriginal art has been introduced to traditionally Western art materials: oil paint, acrylic paint, canvas, and a variety of available commercial colors.

Students will be happy when you announce that everyone in the class will suddenly acquire x-ray vision! What this means is that we can now see shapes of Australian animals from the inside-outside. Student selection of individual animals will be made before the distribution of pencils, nontoxic permanent markers, and cut lengths of brown kraft paper. If our animals become see-through, what exactly will we see? The answer is defined by the students' imaginations. Successful combinations that will enable students to rise to the challenge of Aboriginal bark painting are shown in Figures 5-14 through 5-16. Basically fantastic as well as "anatomically correct" interpretations of internal anatomy— fused with Aboriginal-style dot and line systems—deliver a visual punch! Students may find that first dividing the inside of the animal into sections where their x-ray vision now penetrates will help organize internal design.

◄ Figure 5-14. An animal shaped like a boomerang approaches a dancing tree! Painting and drawing are highly honored forms of expression in Australia. Cave walls, the human body, the bark that shelters, and the sacred ground where people dance are all places where art is found. The paint is applied traditionally with the forefinger and palm of one's hand. Brushes are made from a twig of a tree or bark chewed at one end. The vision of the Aboriginal artist is entirely at one with the Dreamtime.

Figure 5-15. Turtle is so very basic to creation stories around the world. The x-ray appearance, dot and line systems, and "bark" identify this as a Turtle Dreaming artwork. ►

▲ Figure 5-16. This wonderful animal (can you guess which one?) displays the inside-outside features.

Introduce white paint as well as oil pastels once students have finished all outlining of their Australian animals. If space allows, add a eucalyptus tree, leaves, rocks, or stream. The white paint, applied with brushes (or white paint marker), will create a dazzling decorative contrast—traditional earth colors may be used to block in all other areas. If a crinkle bark effect is desired for "authenticity," crush the finished product into a ball and open! Repeat several times. Does it look like "bark" yet? If not, turn the paper over, apply water with a sponge (lightly), smooth with your hand, and let dry. Don't "bark," mates . . . your art will soon be dazzling!

Students will have a wonderful assortment of animals and plants to draw and paint when they artistically visit Australia. The ecological diversity of this unique continent—that drifted away from the rest of Asia millions of years ago—cannot be found anywhere else on Earth! Where else can you find species such as the wallaby, emu, spiny anteater, goanna (lizard), koala, kangaroo, or wild dingo? Creatures of land, air, and sea are often featured in Australian bark painting— turtles, fish, serpents, and whales. And, of course, there's . . . the Rainbow Serpent!

In the beginning of time all the world was dark. No one could see that the Rainbow Serpent slept wearing so many beautiful colors. The Rainbow Serpent dreamed of rocks, mountains, streams, and stringybark trees. She dreamed of many animals—animals that crawl, fly, jump, spin, and swim. Plants of all kinds sprung up. So did mountains, rocks, and lakes. The light came and everything in the world woke up! Rainbow Serpent was not alone in the Dreamtime. In a world filled with life, magic dreams really do come true.

Feel free to embellish this story with other versions of Dreamtime stories and their cosmological character beings, such as Barramundi the fish and Mimi the trickster.

The Dreamtime is filled with beings familiar to Aboriginal Australians, who are both artists *and* storytellers, almost by nature. The way of life has changed little since the ancient days in this regard. Aborigines love art, stories, dance, and music—which may often be heard flowing from a hollowed eucalyptus branch called a *didgeridoo*.

Would your students like to try their own illustrated version of the Rainbow Serpent story? (See Figure 5-17.) Many colors should be used—this *is* a *rainbow* serpent, after all! Watercolor markers and crayons may be mixed together; nontoxic black permanent markers help, too.

Try a "snake-within-a-snake," the sections of which will be filled with dots and lines. Wake up a plant, an animal, and a mineral (rock) to keep Mother Rainbow Serpent company and to form the whole world! Remember, every dot, line, and mark has a meaning. Dreamy!

▲ Figure 5-17. Rainbow Serpent . . . she wakes up the Dreamtime World—animal, vegetable, and mineral alike . . . by a dreaming third grader!

ACTIVITY 4

Magnificent Maori: Gateways to New Zealand

"Carved" Ancestral Post

BONUS: A CALL TO ARMS! ARE TATTOOS TABOO?

▲ Figure 5-18. Is there an ancestor in this "carving"? Approximate symmetry is used in an arresting image!

Are they panels? Are they posts? Is it a *tiki,* a form of figurative carving? Or are they masks? The art of the Maori people of New Zealand is dynamic—even startling—through use of tribal design. Objects may not be readily recognizable, nor easy to define! The appearance that Maori art takes may range from block-like (*hie*) tiki figures to curvilinear to filigree in its presentation. Much of the Maori art is of wood, stone, jade, and bone, while ceremonial body art is inseparable within this realm. All Maori art clearly displays a respect for carving.

The first Maori people of New Zealand believed that the art of carving was conceived by the great sea god *Tangaroa* (tahng-ah-row-ah), who gave carving as a gift to mankind. The link between the living and the ancestral divine is found in powerfully carved and decorated objects called *taongo* (town-gah). Representations of ancestral beings occupy art and architecture. A *tukutuke* panel is believed to embody an ancestral spirit as is the case with much of the figurative, architectural carving: Wall panels, sidepost, pendant, and mask may contain *mana*—ancestral spirit power!

If you were in Maori you might enter a *pa* (village) where you might see a protective figure in the form of a *para* (lintel). It could look exactly like a *karura* mask—fierce, artistically striking, and mysterious. These post figures may be carved from a pole or a single slab of wood. A mask face will likely be "tattooed" with patterns that identify chiefly tribal status. Such a face! Ancestral authority—ever present in Maori views—is captured in the art of carving. If the art is doing its job by protecting the village, the art is good and the art has *mana!*

MATERIALS

- kraft paper
- scissors
- oil pastels

◄ Figure 5-19. The Creation of All Things is revealed in this Forces of Nature gateway post. Can you not feel the awesome power of Tangaroa as he moves sea and sky? It has *mana,* don't you think?

TEACHER PREPARATION

Cut assorted lengths of craft paper. Teacher may want to precut shapes for gateway structures. The emphasis of this lesson is on "carving" with design, very much in keeping with Maori art. Designs draw their strength from *approximate symmetry* that, by its very nature, makes the symmetrically balanced precut format strictly optional. Therefore, teacher will want to determine the precut format on the basis of his or her students' capabilities and needs. Refer to the illustrations shown here for design ideas.

Figure 5-20. Very much the architectural element, yet very much a mask. Those teeth will certainly add to village gate protection. ▶

▲ Figure 5-21. What is so wonderful about Maori student art is the many ways in which one can interpret meaning. A "Maori Butterfly" panel, invented by Makina, age 13, conveys a somewhat friendly spirit. Still there can be a scary aspect to Maori gateway art. Don't mess with this butterfly!

DIRECTIONS

1. Discuss the mysterious and fierce appearance of Maori carving. Sometimes a mask and other times not, these "wooden" figurative structures seem to have a life of their own. Materials will be used to suggest sculptural expression along with the powers of the ancestors. They may have features like a mask or be without features—or somewhere in between.

2. Distribute all materials. Students will fold and cut paper to desired shape (if paper has not already been cut). The fold down the middle will provide a reference for the center of the structure. Before work begins, briefly discuss the use of the materials that will create a textural effect and how the use of certain dark colors will suggest the surface quality. A limited use of color in this case is not a bad thing, yet students should feel free to create their own powerful image.

3. Begin with "direct carving"—the application of the oil pastel to the kraft paper. "Pencil-dependent" students may be comforted by an initial sketch made lightly with a lighter color. Start with one strong motif or feature on one side that will be carried to the other. Encourage simple shape and design development from that starting point. Set imaginations free!

4. Remind students of the meaning of "approximate symmetry," which does not view two perfectly mirrored halves as necessary to the design. This promotes confidence in each student's own abilities. In fact, the approximate symmetry is often the more intriguing.

5. Before completion, students will want to use the white oil pastel for areas they wish to accentuate, and the black for areas to recede. Other colors are discretionary; contour outlines help with the "carved" appearance.

6. Display protective gateway structures where protection is needed. A classroom filled with these ominous images is certain to give a start to any *pekeha*—a stranger or person of non-Maori origin. No harm can come here.

BONUS: A CALL TO ARMS: ARE TATTOOS TABOO?

Is the subject of tattoos *taboo* in the classroom? Not necessarily, when understood from the perspective of this Pacific Island culture. Our intent is to understand and value world art—*not* to endorse or encourage the youthful tattoo! The Maori people use elaborate, incised linear body markings for identification of status, protection, and other social meanings. Consistent with the Maori belief in carving as a divine art form, powerful incisive body ornamentation is widely recognized as distinctively Maori in origin.

During Captain James Cook's several voyages to the Pacific Islands, the tattoo was not lost on members of his European crew, particularly on the infamous *Bounty!* The Maori people held sacred meanings for this "physically challenging" tattoo process with its role in initiation and ceremony. However, the pure decorative impact of Maori designs was admired by British sailors who brought the tattoo back to Europe! It is generally believed that this Pacific event helped launch the popularity of decorative tattoo in the Western World.

For teachers and students to value the artistic merit of Maori body design, this activity will provide a perfect format . . . it may cost you an arm and a leg, so to speak. Happily it's only a paper arm! You will need white kraft paper cut in lengths proportional to the dimension of each student's own arm. Students will position their non-drawing arm on paper to trace the outline; cooperative learning is useful here, as students assist one another in drawing those hard-to-reach spots. Using suggested Maori art patterns, students will create Maori bands of designs. Symbols and signs may be interpretive. Watercolor markers are suggested. Black and only one other color may be enough to create a strong design. Upon completion, cut out and display. Maori arms can literally appear to "hold up" classroom windows and "open" classroom doors! Just as students will be fascinated with this culturally intriguing lesson, so it was for famous traveler and writer Robert Louis Stevenson, a great Scottish literary figure who deeply appreciated many world cultures. Stevenson, author of *Treasure Island* and *A Child's Garden of Verses,* collected his own art treasures. Among his art objects is a carved arm crafted by a Pacific artisan. This sculptural piece bends at the elbow in a gesture of offering, and very much resembles the spirit of student art shown here. Stevenson was entirely right when he said, "The world is so full of a number of things, I'm sure we should all be as happy as kings."

▲ Figure 5-22. Markings form the Marquesas! The decorative bands are typical design elements favored by Pacific artists.

◄ Figure 5-23. Arms . . . and a leg, too! Traditionally, the body arts of the Maori are protective—they form a kind of "tropical armor" to keep the wearer safe. Our students did a spectacular job of it, don't you agree?

ACTIVITY 5

Printing Paradise: Tapa Is Tops!

Graphic Arts/Printmaking

BONUS: HAWAIIAN QUILTS

▲ Figures 5-24a and 5-24b. The "Polynesian print" has its own merit—yet will transform into a collage with powerful visual punch! The print does not have to be "planned" for collage parts: Allow the tapa print design to guide ideas. Figure 5-24a is a heady mix of wallpaper and printed paper shapes that create an island paradise. Note how the print (shown in Figure 5-24b) provided a sacred mountain, coconut tree bark, and a sarong for a beautiful Polynesian queen. ▼

Certainly French artist Paul Gauguin did not invent Polynesia. His sun-drenched canvases, however, serve as large colorful postcards of a tropical Eden, a land of uncommon beauty. The first known settlers, it's said, arrived at the time of Christ. One popular theory holds that they came from Southeast Asia in seven fabled canoes. The vast territory known as the South Sea Islands is often called **The Polynesian Triangle**, defined by *Hawaii* to the north, *New Zealand (Maori)* to the south, and *Easter Island (Rapanui)* to the east.

The natural splendor of Polynesia and the warmth of its people remain undisputed to this day. Of course, Gauguin's scenes of idyllic paradise were his own interpretations. Still Polynesia is visually stunning and a diverse mix of Japanese, Chinese, Javanese, and other cultural groups. It is geographically blessed with sun, sea, and gorgeous flowering plants that are showcased in colorful fabric *pareus* that people still wear. These garments wrap like sarongs and show off traditional printed fabric inspired by regional flora and fauna. All may be set off by a bright flower perched against flowing dark hair. These bold floral prints, that boast of botanical island delight, are not the only decorative contributions of the Polynesian people.

Tapa cloth—also known as "Kapa" in Hawaii—is a powerful cultural element of Polynesian life and history. Prints are created from designed stamps that were carved into printing strips. One such design stamp, known as *ohe-kaapala* (literally translated, "printing bamboos"), would typically be used as a stamping device to print motifs on bark cloth. Uses for tapa cloth are extensive, ranging from courtly and ceremonial to domestic—even sculpture may be composed of tapa cloth! Do you know that the word *taboo* (taboo) originated from *tapu*, which means forbidden? Boundaries that include taboo areas were often marked by tapa cloth. Specific everyday uses for tapa include bedding and clothing. Designs used for tattoos in neighboring cultures (Maori) are thought to have influenced tapa designs. Tapa use has ebbed and flowed over the years and is currently experiencing a resurgence in interest.

The power of Polynesian design was not lost on sojourner Paul Gauguin. A prolific carver and printmaker, Gauguin showed appreciation for tapa design in his art. Indeed, Polynesia influenced European art overall—and the proof is in the tapa!

MATERIALS

- linoleum for block printing
- lino-cutting tools (see Teacher Preparation)
- water-based printing ink
- pencils
- brayers (ink rollers)
- watercolor marker
- scissors

- plexiglass inking plates
- wallpaper books (see Teacher Preparation)
- scrap colored paper
- printing paper (sized to printing plate)
- 18" × 24" white paper
- glue stick
- black crayons
- reproducible page: "Printmaking Process"

TEACHER PREPARATION

Teacher will prepare linoleum squares for the number of students participating in this basic printmaking activity. It will be "teacher's choice" on the kind of paper that will be used to pull prints. Note that these proofs—when dried—will be cut into compositional elements, so photocopy paper is your best bet. Select appropriate cutting tools and use with caution. **Teacher supervision is required at all times.** The printmaking process is a routine one; if a refresher course is needed, refer to the reproducible page 173. Prepare your artroom for printmaking along with any bench hooks or gloves you may wish to use for safety purposes. Note: If for some reason basic printmaking is not appropriate, substitute with styrofoam meat trays that will be incised with dried-out ballpoint pens.

Teacher will want to be sure to have wallpaper books on hand, particularly those with textural wall effects. Linoleum is recommended for grades 6 and up and styrofoam for the earlier years.

It will be useful to have images of Tahiti on hand as well as reproductions of those made by artist Paul Gauguin.

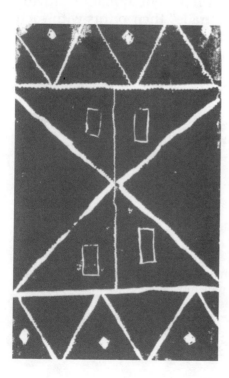

◀ ▲ Figures 5-25a & 5-25b. It almost appears as if this student's print is a magic box that contains the enchanted land revealed above! The linoleum print is shown in Figure 5-25b.

DIRECTIONS

1. Discuss the nature of tapa design with your students. A printing art that began in the Pacific, tapa (also known as kapa in Hawaii) is a traditional blockprinting method. Designs were carved from bamboo strips and "beaten" into bark cloth. Students, however, will "carve" linoleum blocks using the simple geometric elements that produce dramatic tapa/kapa designs. Chevrons, zigzags, and linear motifs work best. Combined, these will please the eyes. Avoid circles as they are hard to do and sometimes can be hazardous to the young printmaker! See illustration below for some ideas.

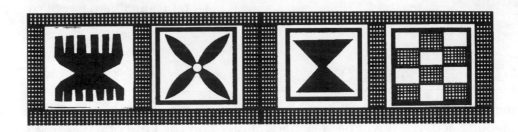

2. Distribute printmaking materials—tools, ink, brayers, papers, and so forth. Demonstrate printmaking techniques. Students will then apply direct, simple surface patterns with crayon onto linoleum block. Remind students that their prints will "reverse" in both page position and black-and-white appearance. When design is satisfactory, begin printmaking techniques. Make several prints or proofs and let dry.

3. Distribute drawing paper, pencils, wallpaper scraps, markers, scissors, printmaking proofs, and glue. Students will now draw a scene from their own island paradise! Students should consider "wallpaper helpers" for terrain and foliage as well as other decorative needs. Begin to cut proofs for framing as well as for compositional elements. Move them around, make decisions, and apply with glue. Use the drawing to enhance and unify the entire composition. Tapa can either be suggestive and representational or provide defining borders. **Note:** Students may want to "trade" their prints with each other as needed. In topping off our art with tapa, we have honored Tahiti, Hawaii, Polynesia, and European traditions and contemporary ideas.

---

*S.O.S. (SAVE OUR SCHEDULE, i.e., "Schedule Saver" or shortcut . . .) In situations where printmaking tools are not appropriate, rubber stamps combined with drawing can make a pretty nifty show, as shown in Figure 5.26.

◄ Figure 5-26. This student selected a traditional Japanese image for her rubber stamp, remembering that Japan is indeed a Pacific Island! We love the scale of this "Polynesian Rose"—watch out for those thorns! A mixed media print is fueled by the student's imagination.

PRINTMAKING PROCESS

1. Draw image on the block with a crayon (black or white) that contrasts with the linoleum.

2. Show cutting method. Place non-working hand behind the working hand. All cutting movement must be done away from the body.

3. Squeeze ink across the top of a piece of plexiglass or cardboard.

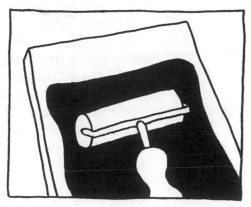

4. Use roller to pull ink over the board's surface until it becomes tacky.

5. Roll ink over the block.

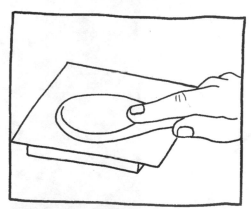

6. Place your paper on top of the block, leaving a border. Use the back of a wooden spoon to rub the back of the paper.

7. When the paper has been evenly rubbed, grasp two corners as shown and gently pull the paper away from the block.

8. You have just printed your first proof! Repeat the process for additional prints.

B O N U S : HAWAIIAN QUILTS

At first, the connection between Hawaiian quilts and tapa cloth may not be obvious. Quilts were noted in the journals of travel writers who visited Polynesia—especially the Cook Islands, Society Islands, and Hawaii—and are recorded in photographs as well. They are often identified as bedspreads and appear as an ornamental backdrop to identify high-ranking individuals. Quilts became the receptacles for motifs originally found in traditional tapa cloth design. There are native names for these quilts; the *tifaifai* is one. The colonial European and American influences on these quilts are very real. Here, as elsewhere, missionary women brought craft ideas that would meet strong existing cultural traditions. Floral and plant motifs are understandably common. As in all quilts, the Hawaiian designs are based on familiar icons of heritage and on natural forms found in the immediate habitat. The Hawaiian quilt represents old and new ideas as well as the fusion of cultures that history has brought together.

Your students' paper quilt squares (12″ × 12″) are "instant cloth" replicas of basic tapa Hawaiian symmetry. To create your own "old Hawaiian" floral quilt patch (an early style), fold your 12″ colored paper into quarters and cut in the manner of a "snowflake." (Has it ever snowed in Hawaii . . .?) The designs will be direct from the imagination—students will be asked to picture in their minds big exotic flowers as well as individual elements such as bananas, leaves, fish, frogs, and stars. Mount the cut-out colored paper with a glue stick to contrasting 12″ colored squares. If desired, roll out a length of colored paper for your ceremonial class quilt!

▲ Figure 5-27. Paper quilt squares cut in the manner of "snowflakes"—although Hawaiian snow is not in the weather forecast.

ACTIVITY 6

Chiefly Capes

Royal Feather Art

Who were the first Hawaiians? Opinions may be expected to vary. Many believe that the Polynesians came by double-hulled canoes from Tahiti to Hawaii. Pacific people were great seafarers traveling the vast waters of the Pacific Ocean. One thing is certain: Captain James Cook (who made several expeditions to Oceania) "discovered" a complete and thriving culture that existed long before his arrival in Hawaii in 1778. At that time, each Hawaiian island was ruled as an independent kingdom by ancestral chiefs. During his reign, King Kamehameha I united the islands and established the kingdom of Hawaii, which lasted until 1893. Yet, it was in 1898 that Hawaii's sovereign was transferred to the United States by official legislation.

In ancient Hawaii, kings were as powerful as gods. Even the shadow of a king could bring life and death. It is said that the only individual to gaze upon the king was the "spirit catcher"—the one designated to retrieve sacred bird feathers. Feathers were so valued that they were used to pay taxes! More important, feathers indicated status. The power of feathers in Hawaii is profoundly connected with their use in Tahitian society. So divine are feathers that they are identified in an

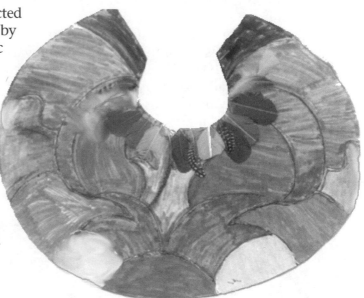

▲ Figure 5-28. Feather cloaks and capes accompanied by helmets were worn chiefly by men and women of high rank. The feather "lei," worn around the neck or as a hat band, is recognizable throughout the United States. Sometimes the lei was turned into a vertical feather rainbow that was used to mark ceremonial occasions. This student-made cape has respected the curve of the shape.

ancient Pacific creation story that tells of a red- and yellow-feathered "first being" who shook off his feathers. With that, the world burst into existence! Feathers bloomed into banana trees, lush green forests, and big bright flowers. The feather is the essential artifact of creation. It carries meaning of divine power and the cultural history of the Pacific.

Feathered Hawaiian capes were spiritual, protective, and chiefly garments; they provided the wearer with confidence as well as "tropical armor." Elaborately crafted capes could create an awesome physical presence! Feathered capes and helmets were the regalia of high-ranking individuals. Red and yellow feathers were often favored: red is the color of a fierce feathered effigy named, "Ku," a force of war, while yellow denotes wealth. Capes, cloaks, and feathered helmets eventually gave way to European styles, with red and gold uniforms often favored. Feather capes—along with helmets as well as other feathered objects—have grown to be a powerful symbol of ancient Hawaiian tradition, one that is upheld by many present-day inhabitants of Hawaii. The feather flies on the wind of power and continuity of an ancient Pacific culture that is now known as Hawaii.

MATERIALS

- kraft paper or white paper scaled to display roll (see Teacher Preparation)
- markers (see Teacher Preparation)
- scissors
- white glue
- assorted feathers (see Teacher Preparation)

TEACHER PREPARATION

Teacher will want to cut a template (see Cape Patterns below) that students may use as a template for their cape garments. Younger students may appreciate a cut cape that requires only their design ideas. Teacher should be aware of sizing the cape: A one-size-fits-all may work in individual situations depending on the students' age span. White kraft paper is suggested, as well as experimentation with size of lengths needed. This lesson also finds use for those markers that are starting to dry out.

Inasmuch as we are seeking to create a feathery-looking surface, semi-moist markers help endorse this illusion. Feathers may vary from bright, luminous colors to the natural bird patterns. **HOT TIP:** Teachers with limited time/budget will find "bouquets of feathers" in the readily available, everyday feather duster! A bunch of feather dusters is more than adequate for students, who will also enjoy watching the teacher "transform" a domestic object into a source of ceremonial art!

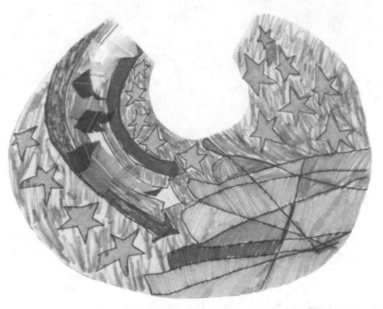

▲ Figure 5-29. A cosmic explosion of stars and stripes! As royal and chiefly power have changed over the course of Hawaiian history, capes remain as powerful symbols of both the past and present.

DIRECTIONS

1. Discuss the traditional use of capes in ceremony. Can students name people who use capes? (Kings, queens, heroes, dancers, toreadors, magicians, and sorcerers) The Hawaiian chiefs used capes that marked their status. Let's don the cape of royalty.

2. Distribute capes and markers. Consider the variety of design motifs shown (see below). Encourage students to design their own cape motifs with their own symbolic meanings. Remember to respect the horseshoe turn of the paper format in the design plan.

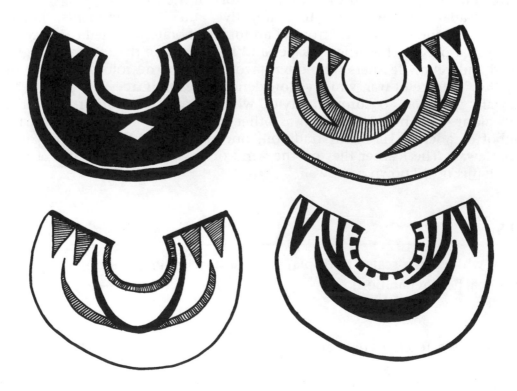

3. Students apply the marker directly to the paper (pencil is not necessary; a marker that is starting to dry out may be used instead). Think about the areas where the craft feathers will be applied. Cape designs share one "golden rule": the designs are always simple and straightforward; no need to become complex here. Once the basic format has been established, see Step 4.

4. Students will apply markers in a "feathery" manner—short, light strokes work well. Encourage students to experiment with various techniques to accomplish this appearance, i.e., varying hand pressure, selective density of application, and so forth.

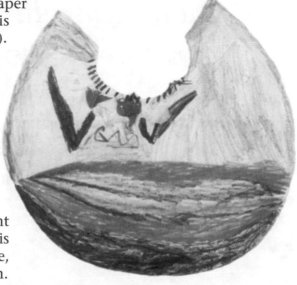

▲ Figure 5-30. A "feathery touch" with water-color markers pays off as a convincing featherwork cape!

5. Now is the time to use those feathers for the "touch of authenticity"! Assuming the quantities are limited, feathers should be placed in selective areas consistent with design flow—or may be used to accent a pectoral or necklace effect. Some feathers may be used to suggest teeth, birds, even *leis*! Mix them up, space them accordingly, and use scissors for size variety if desired. **Note:** Colors have specific meaning in Hawaii, such as red for war and yellow for wealth. Students can make up their own meanings for other colors.

6. Finished feather capes are a regal sight; perhaps a ceremony is in order. At the very least, capes together provide a royal feast for the eyes and for the spirit!

◀ Figure 5-31. A student finds a "divine" answer to the question, "What do I do with extra feathers?" This is a tiny, yet fiery feathered volcano goddess! Could it be Pele? It is likely not Ku, a war god who appears in red feather effigies with a mighty angry appearance. Feathers are extremely important to ancient Hawaiian mythology and belief. According to the Moori, Ta'aroa, "the First Being," broke out of the absolute darkness, identified Heaven and Earth, Dark and Light. He eventually shook off the red and yellow feathers from his body; these became plants, trees, and greenery of the world—as well as other gods . . . all from feathers!

ACTIVITY 7

Aloha Hawaii!

Vintage Hawaiian "Shirts"

▲ Figure 5-32. The sweeping archipelago of Hawaii stretches for over 1,500 miles. Weather and climate are excellent, yet the threat of hurricanes and volcanic eruptions cannot be entirely ignored—adding to the scope of Hawaii's spectacular personality! Hawaii is lush and verdant, blessed with a backdrop of palms, waterfalls, pineapple fields, mountains, and valleys; just as rich as the environment is Hawaiian history and culture. Jennifer, age 11, captures it all in her bigger-than-life Hawaiian shirt. Note the accessory in the pocket.

Aloha is the official nickname for Hawaii's generous spirit. Friendly and embracing of many cultures, diverse in its history, the "Aloha State" is as warm as a sunset on the island of Maui! Rarely are visitors disappointed when they meet Hawaii face-to-face. So many ideas about Hawaii's dramatic beauty precede the appreciative tourist—sweeping beaches, towering waves, fearless surfers, great volcanic mountains, exotic flowers . . . and those sweet, fragrant *leis* that await you, topped off by a welcoming pineapple. Tourists leave their Hawaiian paradise with a smile, a tan—and often with a bright Hawaiian shirt!

Perhaps the most appealing and popular format for the story of Hawaii may be found in this ingenious *and indigenous* Hawaiian fashion! Vintage Hawaiian shirts and their reproductions quite literally represent Hawaiian culture, art, legend, geography, and history. The images that appear on Hawaiian shirts range from exquisite and descriptive prints to patterns that follow the Polynesian and ancient Hawaiian *tapa cloth* tradition. Shirts can function as maps, postcards, portraits, still lifes, and landscapes! It's not unusual to find Japanese prints, Chinese motifs, and other elements that represent the rich mix of Hawaiian cultures.

Elegant masterpiece to endearing cliché—popularized through Hollywood film characterization—the Hawaiian shirt has become inseparable from Hawaiian life. The creation and manufacture of this unique art has its own history, complete with distinctive labels and graphic signatures. In fact, Hawaiian, Tahitian, and European words and alphabet designs often appear; "Aloha," meaning both hello and good-bye, is a common pattern device. If you ever spot a shirt that says "Mai hilahila," take note; it means "Don't be bashful!" Be sure to snap up the shirt that shouts "Welakahao": "Let's have fun!" *Aloha!*

MATERIALS

- white kraft paper or oversized paper (see Teacher Preparation)
- bright markers (scented, if possible)
- scissors
- pencils
- Hawaiian recorded music, if available

TEACHER PREPARATION

Teacher may choose to use precut lengths of white kraft paper that students will personalize by cutting their own interpretations of the Hawaiian shirts. Alternative is for teacher to cut a Hawaiian shirt pattern (see Figure 5-33) that all students will use. Shown in this lesson, the uniformly shaped shirts should at least show movement: for example, their flutter in the tropical breeze. Encourage students who own Hawaiian shirts to lend them (with family permission) to the artroom for observational appreciation of design and fabric quality. It wouldn't hurt to have reference materials available on Hawaiian elements—nature and associated motifs or historical figures, if desired. The idea of this lesson is to stimulate the senses (this is why fruit-scented markers are suggested) and the imagination. Above all, *WELAKAHAO*, translated "Let's have fun!"

▲ Figure 5-33. The subject for Hawaiian shirts is as diverse in possibilities as Hawaii itself. Our "student-tailored" shirts seem to say that simple "clean-cut" fashion statements are as effective as can be. Just the same, shirts lend opportunity for endless topics: surfers, volcanoes, pineapples, coconuts, ukeleles, leis—you name it!

---

*S.O.S. (SAVE OUR SCHEDULE, i.e., "Schedule Saver" or shortcut . . .) Note that Hawaiian shirts may also be fashioned with marker on kraft paper or with colored chalks on oversized colored construction paper.

DIRECTIONS

1. How many have seen or admired Hawaiian shirts? If examples are on hand, bring them forward. Discuss variety of design choices.

2. Distribute paper, pencils, and scissors. Students will produce the outline of the shape of their own Hawaiian sportswear. Cut out garment when ready.

3. Distribute markers. If possible, use bright (tropical) markers and scented markers. Hawaii is a sensuous, fragrant place, so these materials will enhance the proper mood. Play music while you direct the lesson accordingly. Themes for shirts can range from surfing to active volcanic mountains and their goddesses. You may even want to get specific about Hawaiian fauna and flora.

4. Sketch desired Hawaiian subjects onto paper garments. Think about elements that may represent nature and the environment. Don't forget to include collars, buttons, and pockets, if desired. Hold on to scrap paper on the cutting-room floor for accessories that the student may want to add later. Consider the shape for creating the flow of design.

5. A step-by-step formula is inconsistent with this lesson: Encourage students to express their own ideas in a manner that is suitable to them. Develop individual ideas until the surface is completed. Shirts should reflect not only Hawaii, but the personality of the designer.

6. Extra time? Create sunglasses, paper leis, and tourist cameras! A postcard tucked into a pocket would provide a telling detail. If any art ever begged a clothesline exhibit, it is surely these fashion masterpieces, swaying to the hula rhythm of beautiful Hawaiian days!

▲ Figure 5-34. It's true that Hawaiian shirts are cut larger than average to allow space for both artistic design and a comfortable fit. Samantha's graceful shirt seems to sway in the tropical breeze. Is that the Great Wave rolling in from Japan on the lower corner?

▲ Figure 5-35. Alison displays her interpretation of Hawaiian fashion—a shirt that also utilizes the *muu-muu* style. A loose-fitting dress that originated in Hawaii, the muu-muu was "all the rage" throughout the United States in the 1950s and 1960s. Actually, it's an old fashion with many variations, mostly floral in design. Watch out for a muu-muu come-back!

The Caribbean Cultures

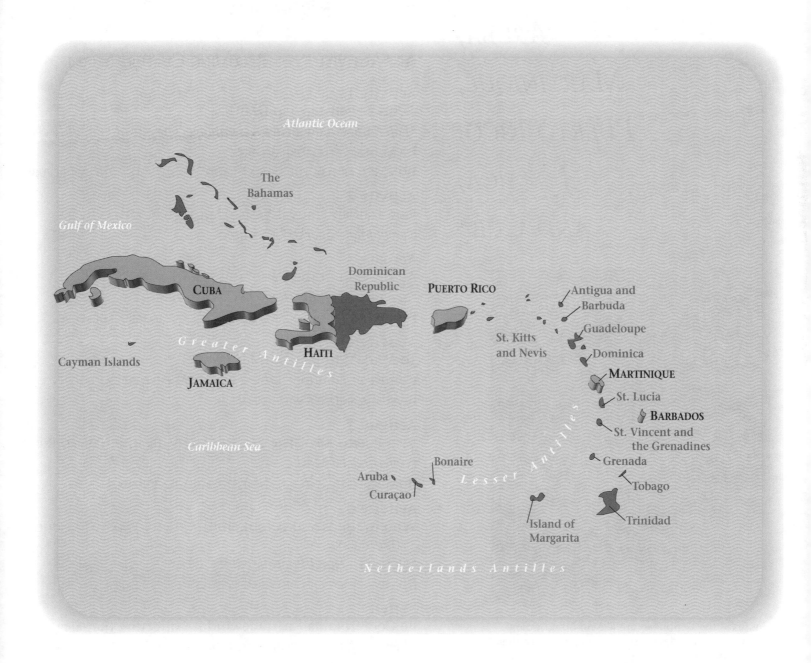

Atlantic Ocean

The
Bahamas

Gulf of Mexico

Dominican
Republic

PUERTO RICO

Antigua and
Barbuda

CUBA

St. Kitts
and Nevis

Guadeloupe

Dominica

Cayman Islands

Greater Antilles

MARTINIQUE

HAITI

St. Lucia

JAMAICA

BARBADOS

St. Vincent and
the Grenadines

Caribbean Sea

Grenada

Bonaire

Lesser Antilles

Aruba

Tobago

Curaçao

Trinidad

Island of
Margarita

Netherlands Antilles

The Caribbean Cultures

HAITI,
DOMINICAN REPUBLIC,
ARUBA,
MARTINIQUE,
PUERTO RICO,
JAMAICA,
AND CUBA

A young man sells flavored ice on a hot afternoon in Puerto Rico. ¡Que sabroso!

ART ACTIVITIES FOR BECOMING CULTURE SMART

Activity 1
A Bus Called Tap-Tap (Haiti)
"Folk" Buses/Low-Relief Assemblage/The Art of Global Recycling
INCLUDES: "STEEL DRUM" ART
BONUS: MAP TO "THE FAIREST LAND" . . . THE DOMINICAN REPUBLIC!

Activity 2
Rara Haitian Festival Vests (Haiti)
Ceremonial "Sparkle" Costumes

Activity 3
All the Fish in the Caribbean Sea (Aruba)
"See"quarium/Box Montage Construction
BONUS: NIGHT MAGIC: CARIBBEAN SCRATCHBOARD ART

Activity 4
To Market, to Market (Martinique)
Caribbean Painting/"Little Market" Masterpieces
BONUS: A SAILOR'S VALENTINE!

Activity 5
Viva Puerto Rico! The Mask of the Vejigante (Puerto Rico)
Papier-mâché Masks
BONUS: "ZEMI:" LITTLE ANCIENT CACIQUE PENDANT!

Activity 6
Who in the World Is Jonkonnu?: Pitchy-Patchy Masquerade (Jamaica)
"Dancing" Hand Puppets/Fabric Arts
BONUS: "ROOTS" SCREEN MASKS

Activity 7
Be Cool in Jamaica: Tradewind Architecture (Jamaica)
Blueprint for Caribbean Dreamhouse/Tropical Design

Activity 8
Bongo! The Afro-Latin Beat of Cuba
Decorative Musical Instrument/Drum

Houses in the Caribbean are like no other! Color and architectural design seem to have a life of their own—whether it is a house placed on a hilltop—or little painted folk art to hang on a wall.

182

To know the Art of the Caribbean . . . . .

. . . . . *is to consider how* these tropical island cultures—shaped by trade, conquest, colonization, and heritage—developed their own expressive art histories. The Caribbean, both an ocean and a group of nations, is located in the Middle Americas. The Greater Antilles, the larger islands, are located in the western Caribbean. Cuba, the largest, is less than 100 miles from the southern tip of Florida. Cuba's neighbors, Haiti and the Dominican Republic, share one island—once called Hispaniola—the second largest island. Puerto Rico lies east of Hispaniola, its closest island neighbor. South of Cuba is Jamaica— "the land of wood and water"—the third largest island. Jamaica, known earlier as *Xaymaca*, recalls pre-Columbian cultures living in the Americas. Ancestors to original cultures may be traced back thousands of years. The indigenous *Arawak*—the "Good and Noble People"—who are now extinct, once lived in the Greater Antilles. When the Arawaks traveled to the Lesser Antilles, they encountered the *Caribs*—a fierce warrior group whose name means "The People," and is the root word for *Caribbean*. Carib attacks weakened Arawak society at Columbus' arrival. The rest is the history of colonialization.

The Caribbean, also known as the West Indies, is home to many proud heritages and traditions. The natural environment is graced with sun, sea, and palm trees—a postcard vision. The idyllic Caribbean has had its share of invasions from Europe, slave traders, sugar plantation dominance, and piracy. Caribbean islands have in part gained independence and autonomy from their colonial past while others still have governmental ties to France, Britain, and the Netherlands. Their rich mix of African, European, Asian, and American cultures gives them their unique flavor.

The Lesser Antilles, located in the Eastern Caribbean, lie southeast of Puerto Rico where the southeastern curve of these Leeward and Windward islands begins. The Lesser Antilles include the U.S. and British Virgin Islands, the French Antilles, the Netherlands Antilles, and Trinidad and Tobago—which are states located close to Venezuela, South America, and are the home to calypso, carnival, and callaloo.

Each Caribbean island, state, and nation has its own distinct cultural blends and attributes. Haiti is the poorest nation in the Western Hemisphere. At the same time, Haiti embodies survival, spirituality, and creativity. Religious practice is a mix of French, African, Christian, and pre-Columbian belief. The *Voudon* practice (voodoo), brought to Haiti by slaves, has its roots in west Africa. The mystical connection with the underworld and ritual magic helps to give voodoo its dark and fascinating reputation. It was in Haiti where the first independent black Republic in the western hemisphere was won.

The Haitian spirit is apparent in its arts, where the transforming spirit of art found in common objects is enjoyed. Empty oil drums are changed by Haitian artists into magical sculpture—or "oil drum art." The industrial-sized drums are split and flattened with Haitian hands, feet—and whole bodies. Sanded, smoothed, and often painted with enamels, these empty drums come alive as animals, mythical sea creatures, and vividly painted representations of the colorful *tap-tap* buses! Haitian architecture is considered a form of folk art.

A love of life, in spite of its hardships, is manifest in the cycle of celebrations known as Carnival—or *Carnaval*. Rich in history, myth, spirituality, folklore, and custom, Carnival is an exuberant display of human creativity. All participate, regardless of age or social status. The costumes are filled with fantasy through use of available materials that are both ingenious and enchanting. Trinidad and Tobago, the source of Calypso music, hold a spectacular carnival that ranks alongside the carnival in Rio de Janeiro in Brazil for its pageantry, verve, and sheer magnificence.

The Hindu presence in Trinidad and Tobago is one-and-a-half centuries old. *Hosay,* a large Indian festival, combines Muslim, Christian, and Hindu elements. Large architectural floats, called *tadjahs,* are displayed and carried. The Hosay Festival is also held in Jamaica. *Jonkonnu,* in Nassau and elsewhere; *Rara* in Haiti; and *Jounnen Kweyal Etenasyonnal,* a Creole festival in St. Lucia enliven island cultures. The presence of African influences prevails in the present-day Caribbean in dance, music, art, language, and custom. The African sources are everywhere—from the "Ananzi the Spider" trickster tales, called *Anancy* in the Caribbean, to the best of reggae in Jamaica, to the sound of Cuban drums.

The United States and the Caribbean became one in the island of Puerto Rico. Ancient petroglyphs reveal clues to the depth of this Caribbean culture, along with the amulets of early beliefs. The Taino traveled throughout the Caribbean to find their spiritual home in Puerto Rico. This civilization was ruled by chiefs called *caciques* who sought to keep society in balance. The island shares a wealth of cultures as well as the sentiment of Jamaica's national motto, *"Out of many, one people."*

ACTIVITY 1

A Bus Called Tap-Tap

"Folk" Buses/Low-Relief Assemblage/The Art of Global Recycling

INCLUDES: "STEEL DRUM" ART

BONUS: MAP TO "THE FAIREST LAND" . . . THE DOMINICAN REPUBLIC!

▲ Figure 6-1. This student "tap-tap" seems to be bumping along the streets and mountain roads with a sunny disposition. Its destination is Port-au-Prince, the capital of Haiti.

In big ways and small, transportation is a "moving" account of the places in the world we inhabit. Haiti is a Caribbean country that shares an island with the Dominican Republic, yet has a distinctive culture all its own. The direct descent from Africa forms much of the basis for this mountainous land where French and English are spoken. To live in Haiti is not always easy, for a place of natural beauty may also be marked by struggle. The proud, resourceful Haitians have a way of turning trouble upside down; ironically, a land without great monetary riches abounds with creativity and spirit. Painting, steel-drum sculpture, architecture, and festival arts defy earthly limitations. Even an old, reconditioned school bus, through Haitian imagination, becomes a great work of art.

"Tap-Tap" is the sound these vivid working buses make as they travel the winding roads, often taking people to the busy capital city of Port-au-Prince, where tap-taps are the major form of transportation. *Tap-tap* is both the sound and the name of the Haitian buses that display social messages, folk tales, business signs, love poems, and recognizable stories. It is not unusual to find a bus, for example, transformed into Noah's Ark! Symbols, patterns, and signs comprise the exterior of the tap-tap. They may even have their own name, slogan, or point of view— "Bonjour," a French greeting that literally means "good day," might be proclaimed by a tap-tap! On top of the tap-tap, the baggage and nourishment of life is often held in precarious balance. Inside, passengers bounce to the rhythm of the bus. Expect to find just about anything on top of and inside a tap-tap—fruit, livestock, chairs and tables, sun umbrellas, straw hats, rolled mats, and lots and lots of baskets. Roosters crow and babies cry. There is plenty of activity: standing, sitting, arguing, laughing. To catch the tap-tap, you need to tap on the side of the bus to signal the driver to stop. The big destination for many Haitians on the tap-tap is the iron market at Port-au-Prince, a huge structure filled with merchants and customers surrounded by the bountiful variety of Haitian products. Where might a tap-tap take you?

MATERIALS

- corrugated cardboard (see Teacher Preparation)
- brushes
- tempera paint (bright colors suggested)
- water cups
- pencil
- white glue
- scissors
- crayons and/or markers

TEACHER PREPARATION

Teachers will want to collect cardboard boxes; those used to contain beverages in quantity work well here. This lesson will require that a 12" × 18" sized section of cardboard is given to each student. Students may assist in box collection, too! Cardboard scraps and sections will be used to create "raised" bus components. If student cutting skills are diminished or scissors are dull, the teacher may want to precut the basic bus shape. (See Figure 6-1.) The teacher may want to either plan on producing an example for the class or simply wait to demonstrate the basic assemblage for students when the lesson begins.

These tap-tap buses are simple in style and design; however, the teacher may want to elaborate on the narrative painting many tap-taps display. For example, a bus theme might easily be "Noah's Ark." Lettering that shows names, symbols, and verbal messages may also be considered—including the student's name!

DIRECTIONS

1. Discuss buses as a means of daily transportation. How many students ride a bus to school? Is it a yellow school bus or public transportation? People in the country of Haiti *really* rely on buses to transport them around the mountainous island. Their tap-tap buses are filled with passengers, packages, animals, and market goods. Actually, Haiti—as well as countries in Mexico and Central America—often use recycled American school buses! You can bet they break down on those mountainous roads! Yet, they are colorful and vivid—a moving form of folk art.

   Explain the meaning of low-relief assemblage, which is the sculptural effect that results from building up a surface. It provides a suggestion of greater dimensionality.

◀ ▲ Figures 6-2a & 6-2b. These two folk art originals are simple and sweet. Passengers, cargo, and drivers are set to go. Painted on recycled oil drums.

2. Distribute cardboard, pencils, and scissors. You may want to demonstrate techniques for cutting the basic form or provide students with an assembled sample of the bus they will make. Explain to students that the body of the bus is basically a boxy rectangle with rounded "top" corners. Wheels, roof rack with packages, windows, and driver's cab will provide the decisions for the mounted parts for the low-relief tap-tap.

3. Encourage students to sketch the vehicle and its elements in pencil directly on the cardboard pieces. Cut the cardboard shapes when ready.

4. Assemble all tap-tap parts before attaching with white glue. Let dry.

5. Distribute drawing and painting supplies and have students paint their tap-tap! Simple pattern application can be highly effective. Add lettering, such as names or the destination of the bus in Haiti. Let dry.

6. Students will bring their completed tap-taps to an area of the classroom where they may be propped up against a vertical surface. In this "bus terminal" everyone may admire the creativity that art can bring to the everyday world. It's moving!

INCLUDES : "STEEL DRUM" ART

The tap-taps themselves provide a metal surface, rather than canvas or paper, for the artists to apply their decorative ideas. Haitians are particularly adept at seeing the possibilities for transformation of everyday materials into artistic visions. Perhaps the best example of this Haitian talent is the art of cut-steel sculpture, which established its popularity in the early 1950s. The large-capacity steel drums that contain oil in quantity became the source for music and art when recycled. When hammered, pressed, cut, manipulated, and constructed, powerful images emerged. Many of these flat Haitian works are able to convey fully realized expressive forms. Subjects range from the earthly to mythological. Students who wish to "forge" steel-drum art may do so by using their own kraft paper. Symmetry is also used and very effective for chosen subjects. A pencil drawing may be applied to cut and folded paper. Cut, open, and gently crush—open again and carefully smooth with hand. To achieve the hammered or "hand-wrought" look, a tempera wash in a dark tone may be applied with a tissue. Blot as this "patina" is applied. The end result should appear more "sculptural" while the painted, cardboard tap-tap will boast of colorful surface decoration.

▲ Figure 6-4. Birds of steel can fly with their prophetic messages. When we see a bird, does it mean that land is near? This is a two-headed bird: one head for grace and one for style. When it comes to seeing near and far, two heads are definitely better than one!

▲ Figure 6-3. This mysterious and beautiful creature was created by a professional Haitian artist whose work embodies human, animal, and bird elements. Is it an angel, mermaid, or flying fish? This steel-drum sculpture makes you want to know more about its fascinating identity.

BONUS : MAP TO THE "FAIREST LAND" . . . THE DOMINICAN REPUBLIC!

Haiti occupies one third of an island known as Hispaniola. The other two thirds is called the Dominican Republic. The Dominican Republic is the second largest country in the Caribbean, after Cuba, and has a distinction of being quoted by Christopher Columbus, in 1492, as "the fairest land under heaven." In its capital of Santa Domingo, a Spanish-colonial settlement where its plazas, churches, and architectural landmarks remain intact to this day, is a church in which it is claimed Christopher Columbus is buried. Although Christopher Columbus has been acclaimed for his discovery of the Americas, history continues to view Columbus with many different eyes. While the exact measure of his contribution to world progress is often challenged, one fact remains—Christopher Columbus was an intrepid adventurer; yet, even intrepid adventurers need maps. Picture yourself preparing to leave the comfort of your familiar surroundings and heading out by sea to a distant land. Your journey will most likely be based on part fact and part fiction. Students will enjoy becoming explorers who create their own maps for adventuresome seafaring. The teacher may want to have a variety of maps on hand for reference for this activity, (which will require more imagination than fact). The concept is . . . "You are the explorer and the year is 1492. Create your own picturesque map that includes any and all details you (student) find necessary. Plan for a decorative border because map-making is a time-honored skill." Any perspective that students wish to take should be encouraged. This activity is, after all, a voyage of make-believe with a reference to actual history. Using mixed media, students will chart their course!

▲ Figure 6-5. This map indicates the possibility for attacks by sea creatures as a confident sailing ship makes its way from a country topped with a castle to one filled with mountains and dwellings. Actual distance between the countries appears to be less than one nautical mile, but who's counting? The label, generated by computer, provides the "official" look.

ACTIVITY 2

Rara Haitian Festival Vests

Ceremonial "Sparkle" Costumes

▲ Figure 6-6. This young celebrant prepares to join her classmates in their dazzling display of Rara creativity.

The festival of *Rara* is held in Haiti at the same time as so many other world festivals, in the winter to spring season that celebrates the triumph of life over death. Each spring Haitians turn out in large numbers to dance, sing, shout, march, whirl, jump, and shake their "jonc," a baton filled with noisy rattling charms! There is nothing shy about "making Rara"; it fills the streets of Haiti with all the bells and whistles imaginable. Rara is not just fun, it is also quite an ordeal, demanding that revelers understand their role in carrying out the Rara tradition. Rara may appear to be simply a carnival of sights and sounds; yet it holds complex meanings in African, European, and Caribbean traditions. Rara itself is a Yoruba-African word that means "loud and noisy." It is not the unleashed spectacle it appears to be, however; it is as organized and codified as a military ceremony, complete with specific leaders, ritual flags, and glittering uniforms that reflect role and rank. Its history is, in many ways, the history of Haiti itself. Above all, Rara reminds us that **Haiti was the first independent black republic in the Americas;** Rava sends a strong message of African pride and independence. Even the colors of the costumes and flags make reference to Haitian leaders. The signs and symbols have specific value to the Haitian people.

Undeniably, a carnival allows celebrants to leave behind their daily cares and to remember their origins. In their desire to make bright and merry, the creative Haitians again recycle common objects in combinations that ensure excitement of the senses. The noise-making, sparkling, clamorous, and glamorous details are usually provided by hardware and household items cleverly recast by Haitian ingenuity. Rara is a time of magic, exhilaration, emotion, and remembrance. Rara, for all its dazzle, is a glittering history lesson complete with heart, art, and spirit!

MATERIALS

- colored kraft paper (or fabric)
- pencils
- scissors
- oil pastels
- white glue (see Step 4)

- stiff brushes
- glitter (see Teacher Preparation)
- sequins/plastic mirrors (optional) (see Teacher Preparation)

TEACHER PREPARATION

The teacher will precut a sample vest based on the shape as indicated in Figure 6-6. In many cases it is preferable to complete the examples as shown in lieu of actual fabric examples. Again, the teacher may wish to create a template for students. Either way, the teacher will cut lengths of colored kraft paper that allow a "one-size-fits most" vest. Note that the vest will be made by folding the paper in half with a fold at the top. Held vertically, the neck opening will be cut. Alterations may be customized for individual students. This is a single-fold, seamless paper garment. No sewing required!

Glitter should be made available in a quantity-sized container, if possible. Sequins and small decorative mirrors—available through sewing supply distributors—are optional enhancements to this lesson.

This lesson will call for simple symbol design; the teacher may choose to ask for personal symbols or use African symbols—or a combination of both.

GLITTER ALERT!

Many teachers find glitter use is made less overwhelming by setting up a "glitter station" for students. Try this idea: Save the shipping cartons that hold your 18" × 24" paper. Use a box cutter or mat knife carefully to establish a 4" wall around the perforated edge of the box. Place an 18" × 24" piece of paper in the bottom of the box. Students will shake glitter onto artwork surface inside of the box boundaries. Excess glitter may then be readily contained and reused without fuss by carefully removing glitter-covered paper from the bottom of the box to pour back into the glitter container with paper folded as a soft funnel. Cure your glitter phobia!

DIRECTIONS

1. Introduce the idea of decorative vests through your own example of a glittery Rara vest. Students may better understand the role of flashy costume use when asked about their own experiences with circuses, carnivals, and parades.

2. Distribute cut lengths of paper with template(s), scissors, and pencils. Fold paper in half to create "tailor pattern." Outline with pencil, if necessary, and cut. Be sure the neck opening can accommodate the wearer's head.

3. Have your students ever thought about symbols or signs that they personally enjoy? Stars and stripes, hearts, and flowers are popular. A simple line can become a symbol with a curve or an angle. Keep it simple—a large central shape with a decorative accompaniment will do nicely. Oil pastels can be used to help emphasize shapes and suggest texture.

▲ Figure 6-7. An actual Haitian banner—filled with signs, symbols, and sequins—represents the spirit of the heart while honoring "Erzulie," Haitian goddess of love!

4. It's sparkle time! Distribute glitter in your standard manner or see Teacher Preparation. Glue may either be applied by brush (with glue in watercolor cups) or by directly squeezing through glue applicator. Curvy lines, dot, swirls, and scallops will glow with glitter. The vest may be decorated on both front and back with varying design elements. Let dry.

SAFETY NOTE:

Keep glittery fingers away from eyes and face until hands are washed.

5. Schedule a Rara fashion parade. Musical accompaniment that includes "bells and whistles" and a good steady beat will ensure a lively, lovely time! Let's all cheer . . . "Rah, Rah, Rah for Rava!"

▲ Figure 6-8. These young revelers pose for the camera, proud of the variations they discovered for their own ceremonial vests. Diamonds, hearts, stars, and flowers glitter almost as much as their smiles!

ACTIVITY 3

All the Fish in the Caribbean Sea

"See"quarium/Box Montage Construction

B O N U S : NIGHT MAGIC: CARIBBEAN SCRATCHBOARD ART

Clear water, bright sun, beaches that range from pink to black, trees bursting with tropical fruit, breathtaking mountains, and sailing ships help to form the legends of the Caribbean. Color, it seems, is everywhere. The sweep of islands we call the Caribbean—also known as The Lesser and Greater Antilles—begins in the U.S. Virgin Islands of St. Thomas, winds and curves for 1,000 miles and ends just short of South America with the so-called ABC Islands. *A* is for Aruba, the small island that marks the end of the Caribbean chain. (Bonaire and Curaçao are *B* and *C*.) Here is an unusual geography and a Dutch history. Charming small Dutch facades line the streets in town while goats and cacti may be found along the shore. Flamingos and iguanas also inhabit these islands! It is dry and desert-like, surprisingly unlike the lush tropics expected.

The land above the sea is the one on which our feet wander; when we dive the ocean's depths, another world opens. Ask any deep-sea diver and you will be told that this watery world is one unto itself. Silent yet filled with life, we can only imagine what it is like in the place that tropical fish call home. The Arubans who dwell on land announce "One Happy Island" on their auto license plates! Although there is no real documentation to support this, you can bet the silent fish of many stripes and sizes feel the same way about their expansive headquarters. They receive many tourists in wetsuits and goggles. Tides, tradewinds, and coral reefs rank the ABC Islands as top among the diving sites of the Caribbean. Water visibility is so excellent that it is simple to spot the occasional sunken ship, reminding us of the Caribbean's adventurous past—pirates, treasures, and mermaids! The Caribbean celebrates the wonder of our natural undersea world.

▲ Figure 6-9. Is it oceanography or is it art? It's both. This "see"quarium allows us a glimpse of the tropical undersea world. The student used a mixture of magazine photos, postcards, and toy rubber fish to give us an inside-out view of an aquatic wonderland.

MATERIALS

- shoe box or gift box (see Teacher Preparation)
- railroad board, bristle board, or lightweight posterboard (may substitute heavy construction paper)
- magazines and other pictorial references (see Teacher Preparation)
- white glue
- pencils
- masking tape (colored paper tape is optional)
- toy rubber fish (optional)

TEACHER PREPARATION

The teacher will ask students to bring a large shoe box or a gift box to school. Collect magazines, calendars, and postcards that show undersea life. Back issues of travel magazines, especially those that deal with island vacations, are ideal. *National Geographic* publications serve well. Railroad board should be cut down to sizes appropriate to the boxes, including a border of at least three inches.

DIRECTIONS

1. Imagine you are a diver who has just jumped off the side of a boat into the Caribbean waters. Splash! Down you go. Behind the goggles, or diver's mask, what do you think you would discover as you plunge the depths of these warm currents? That is exactly what we will try to bring back in our **"see"quarium** . . . our viewable treasure chest of the natural undersea world.

2. What is down below? Conch shells, coral reefs, brilliant tropical fish, squids, octopus, starfish, seahorses—and sharks! Students will "go fishing" for their own photographic images in magazines as well as other pictorial references provided for them; these will form their photo-montage "see"quarium. All materials on deck, please—boxes, paper, scissors, and glue. Place the box face down on the board or paper intended for the frame. Trace opening of the box onto paper and cut out. Be sure to leave a border of at least three inches around the perimeter. Set aside.

3. Students should be ready to glue images into the interior of the box. Remind students that pictures representing water should go into the box first; this is equivalent to the background or backdrop. Fish may be grouped to suggest underwater drama or simply arranged to personal artistic tastes. Use scissors to help define clearly the shape of the sea creature or element. **Note:** If students are unable to locate desired images, remind them that they may draw these pictures directly onto the magazine page. The shape itself will represent the idea in an imaginative way. Using this technique, even mermaids are possible!

4. When students' "insider-views" of the sea are completed, a shaped frame is ready to emerge. Retrieve materials for the frame (see Step 2). Cut outside edges of paper frames in accordance with the undersea life shown in each individual box. Some ideas might be sea scallops, coral reef, tentacles, sea anemone silhouette, waves or shark fins. Students may want to experiment with the overall shape of the frame.

5. Attach the frame to the box by taping the back of the frame to the sides of the box. Carry over some interior elements onto the frame to unify the "see"quarium.

6. What else is there to do with a treasure trove of "see"quariums but to proudly display them for all to *see*!

BONUS : NIGHT MAGIC: CARIBBEAN SCRATCHBOARD ART

There are many worlds within the one we inhabit—worlds of sea, air and earth. As day turns to night, the worlds we know change with it. The "nightlife" of the Caribbean also exists for creatures that quite naturally glow in the dark. The ocean is filled with phosphorescence, the rain forest filled with a thousand glowing eyes! Animals that appear at night bring with them a special kind of magic for which no electric bill will arrive. To picture this world we will need fluorescent neon crayons and a vivid imagination. The perfect way to uncover it is with a scratchboard technique.

Students will cover a 9" × 12" piece of oaktag with various bright colors of crayons in any pattern they desire. Be sure to press hard and cover all areas (no paper showing). When completed, students then make all the colors "turn from bright to night" by applying black crayon over the entire paper surface. Again press hard, blanketing the presence of all color. **Note:** A newspaper that covers a student desk will keep crayon shavings from marking desk surface.

Then try this with your students: "You are in a Caribbean rain forest at night. It is pitch black. Suddenly the full moon helps to make the creatures of the night appear. Let your pictures show us what you find in this Caribbean moonlight on this magic night." Students will need a tool to scratch away the black blanket of night. Recommended are heavy-duty paper clips folded open with one work point, orange stick, stylus, old scissors with a dull point, or compasses held lightly. **Note:** Symmetry can be very powerful, but is not required. Poetry and imagination must be included!

▲ Figure 6-10. The Caribbean night magic in its phosphorescence glows with mystical delight.

ACTIVITY 4

To Market, to Market

Caribbean Painting/"Little Market" Masterpieces

BONUS: A SAILOR'S VALENTINE

▲ Figure 6-11. This painting seems to sing "Welcome to my market!" Can't you just feel the rhythm of the marketplace day and the spirit of its people? This is a mixed media painting that holds together as an original composition and vibrates with life. Note the many charming details painted by K.C., a seventh-grade artist with islander spunk!

▲ Figure 6-12. A painting on canvas with acrylics by an aspiring eighth-grade artist. Kelly captures the style and feeling of a hot Caribbean afternoon.

Whether you live in or visit any Caribbean island, there is expectation of a wonderful marketplace—and for good reason! The personality of the Caribbean Islands may be individual and unique, yet each one is privileged to receive the gifts of nature from the earth and the sea. The open-air market will delight all your senses: sweet tropical fruit, gorgeous flowers, fish fresh from the sea—and the crafts made with the ingenuity and skill of Caribbean hands. "Let me show you a straw hat, *mon cherie*" may be heard on the French island of Martinique. Travel to Barbados where the West Indian or "Bajan" (native-born to Barbados) artisans will sew tropical fashions right before your eyes! "Bahama Mamas" carry bushels of fruit and flowers atop their heads.

The market women of the community, or "higglers," have become the mainstay of the developing town-market economy. On market day, men and women from the mountains leave early in the morning to travel into town with their produce and handmade products: island-made candy, straw hats and baskets, cassava bread, handmade clothing, sour soup, island paintings, coconut bread, and root vegetables indigenous to the islands. Bright faces of all ages fill the market with many goods and smiles—often speaking their own island's *patois* (or dialect). Islanders gather in an open area and offer their wares for sale. Most of the markets are held outside, but some are held under a large canopy of corrugated iron. The Iron Market at Port-au-Prince in Haiti is widely known.

Whether you are on Martinique or St. Maarten, one of the most joyful purchases you can make in the marketplace is the darling little folk painting of everyday Caribbean life. Folk artists keep the scale of these paintings small, so it is no coincidence that the miniature canvases will fit neatly into that straw bag you may have just purchased . . . the one with the island's name and its birds and flowers crafted upon it! *"Ah, sweetie, you make a good choice!"*

MATERIALS

- watercolors
- water cups (or similar water containers)
- assorted colored markers*
- pencils
- nontoxic fine-point black permanent markers
- marketplace props (see Teacher Preparation)
- brushes (see Teacher Preparation)

- Crayola® Tropical™ Markers (optional)
- white acrylic paint
- white paper (see Teacher Preparation)
- manila paper cut to scale (see Teacher Preparation)
- pictorial reference materials (see Teacher Preparation)
- reproducible pages "Living" Sea Life and "The Caribbean Marketplace"

Figure 6-13. Authentic island painting purchased at a Straw Market in the Caribbean. In a very basic statement, this picture captures the economic history of the Caribbean: sugar cane. Here is a field of sugar cane that is made to seem like a towering endless sea. Its importance is noted even in this tiny 8" × 9" canvas. ▶

◀ Figure 6-14. A common scene of everyday island life in a mountain village. Yes, for some it is laundry time!

---

* Acrylic paints are optional (see Teacher Preparation).

TEACHER PREPARATION

To create a Caribbean atmosphere and provide textural samples of marketplace wares, the teacher can visit his or her own local market for pineapples, bananas, mangoes, coconuts, and so forth—whatever is in season and available. Also worth gathering are straw baskets, shells, straw hats, and fresh flowers. Students may contribute their marketplace "show and tell" treasures; craft items available from their Caribbean visits are most welcome here! Some cities can even provide real sugar cane—in such areas as "Chinatowns" or other specialty markets. If you can get your hands on starfish and conch shells, you are in business (or see Figure 6-17). Party-goods stores can add some more fun to the festivity and colorful nature of this lesson with paper parrots, streamers, fishing nets, and (paper) palm trees. Travel magazines and Caribbean guidebooks would be great to have on hand for use throughout this lesson, too.

The teacher will want to precut manila paper and white paper for watercolor into actual "marketplace" dimensions of 8" × 9" (or simply use 9" × 12"). **Note:** If authenticity is desired, canvas board and acrylic paint will make splendid originals from the marketplace art classroom.

To conduct this lesson with canvas and acrylics, realize that studio painting requires that acrylic paints are set up on palettes (or a reasonable substitute); palette and canvas painting techniques apply here as well. Canvas boards in small sizes are recommended.

Brush sizes—with *either* painting choice—should vary from small (#03) to medium (#05). Standard oil/acrylic painting brushes will be needed for the canvas painting activity; however, the brushes with their stiffer hairs will assist in the application of white acrylic paint (as needed) in the main lesson of watercolor/marker painting. **Safety Note:** Ask students to be mindful of holding long-handled brushes in a manner that does not invite a poke in the eye!

Prior to class distribution of watercolors and markers, pour small amounts of white acrylic paint into watercolor cups or similar containers. (If you plan to use white acrylic paint more than once, cover the container tops tightly!)

▲ Figure 6-15. A small craft item allows attention to the all-important mother figure of the Caribbean. She is always welcoming, nurturing, and generous in her ways.

Figure 6-16. Island living for inhabitants who live in small hut-like dwellings. All is well here in this tightly composed little painting gem.

DIRECTIONS

1. Introduce the marketplace goods by allowing students to both see and touch them—but not all items at once. It is important that classifications be made among fruits, crafts, flowers, and sea creatures. Have available pictorial references as well as illustrations for The Caribbean Marketplace worksheet (see page 201).

2. Discuss how these items reach the marketplace. In the Caribbean, it is often the women who bring the goods to the market by foot or by bus, while the men farm or fish. Baskets are carried on the women's heads, while babies sit on their mothers' hips. Picturing these colorful scenes will enable students to better describe in paint their focused vision of a Caribbean marketplace. Think of the scene to describe "one little corner of the Caribbean."

3. Distribute paper and pencils. Encourage students to envision a close-up snapshot of their marketplace scenes. Where are we? What items are in the stands? What are in the baskets? How are the people standing? Are the people having fun? Students should note that the texture of a starfish is different from that of a straw hat, so their painting of these various items should reflect this understanding—along with creating a colorful Caribbean mood!

▲ Figure 6-17. A basket of Caribbean joy! Starfish, conch shell, coconut, etc., are joined by Akuaba, an African wood sculpture. The connection is natural—African presence is powerfully rooted in Caribbean history.

4. Have students sketch a preparatory design in pencil on manila paper; a 15- to 20-minute time frame should be enough. Follow this with The Caribbean Marketplace worksheet.

5. Distribute painting supplies. Ask students to consider the bright colors of the Caribbean and how blue, for example, looks even brighter when placed right next to orange; this is the moment to reinforce the concept of complementary colors. Begin painting, adding Crayola® Tropical™ Markers and all other markers to the students' supplies. After the students' scenes have been blocked in, ask them to add *textures* and *details*.

6. Encourage students to incorporate local Caribbean personalities, such as "Bahama Mama" (the nurturing, generous mother figure beloved by all). Other characters may be familiar or fictitious. Challenge students to pack color, texture, personality, and flavor into a tiny space. They can do it!

7. Have students apply white acrylic paint with small brushes to "highlight" details. If students fear they may *mess up,* then tell them to *fix up*! White acrylic paint will cover weak areas, dry quickly, and actually add a glossy look to the picture. Watercolor and markers may be reapplied, if necessary. Use black fine-point markers to define both large and small areas.

8. Display the paintings in the classroom as though the room were a marketplace . . . among the straw hats, starfish, and bright ideas. *Oh my, sweetie . . .* who would not delight in this show?

BONUS : A SAILOR'S VALENTINE!

The antique nautical craft of inlaid and applied shellwork appeared in Caribbean history with the advent of European sailing ships and their long navigations to and fro. English sailors would return home after lengthy sea voyages bearing beautiful gifts intended mostly for wives and sweethearts. The messages inside would speak sweetly of sentiments, likely to melt hearts.

Interesting to note is that the romantic image of a homesick mariner carefully crafting tiny shells while sailing lonely waters is not quite accurate; the exquisite octagonal boxes with decorated mosaic shell lids and interiors were usually produced by island artisans! It is not only the modern age of cruise ships that launched Caribbean ingenuity—early European visitors established the market for exports. Island talent responded with fine hand-crafted items. Often, valentine shell boxes were commissioned by seafarers. Messages and designs could be "made to order" . . . you have to wonder who may have received the credit once the valentines found their way to England! In any case, these are heartfelt, one-of-a-kind treasures.

▲ Figure 6-18. Continuation of the hub-and-spoke design is revealed through sponge printing repetitions and well-placed shell "inlay." This valentine contains a map and message from "Capt. Matt." So much more artistic than a bottle with a message washed ashore—and no less welcome!

For your own version of this antique craft, you will need:

- 11″ × 18″ white paper
- nontoxic black permanent markers
- squares of manila paper
- thick yarn
- white glue
- rubber stamps of sea life (optional)

- scissors
- rulers
- map "scraps" (gift wrap, road maps, copies of maps, etc.)
- cut-up sponges
- watercolors
- pencils

Access to a photocopier will allow you to reduce, if desired, the computer-scanned page of "Living" Sea Life (see the full-page illustration on page 200. **Note:** This reproducible was generated by directly scanning the arranged three-dimensional sea group of shells and creatures directly through the computer's own printing process. Rubber stamp prints, if available, would add a nice touch, too.

Students will fold the white paper in half. To create an octagon, measure a square and cut. Then draw an X from the corners, and draw a cross through the middle of the X. (See the illustration.) Using the ruler, draw the "cut in" corner and the "cut them away"; an octagon card should be the result!

Note that traditional sailor valentine boxes open from a top fold. However, students should feel free to use a traditional "open-like-a-book" fold for their octagonal "box" cards, with the fold at the left.

Begin the cover design in pencil. A central circle (see Figure 6-19) will establish the "hub" composition and will also respect the octagonal shape. Radiating "spokes" lend a nautical feel and allow for easy-to-design sections.

Now distribute the other materials: watercolor paints, thick yarn, rubber stamps (if desired), and so forth.

Students will determine the subject worthy of central interest in their boxes. Mermaids, sailing ships, and sea life all work well. Why not a portrait of a generous woman, such as "Bahama Mama"?

Students encircle their completed images in yarn. Then they paint, print, cut, and apply "shell work" (see Figure 6-19) as they wish. **Note:** The teacher may want to reduce the "Living" Sea Life page on a photocopier to help shells fit the spaces.

When the cover is finished, students open the card to decorate both sides. Map scraps and poetic messages on manila notes fit well into the interior octagonals (see figure on page 198). Sponge printing seems to resemble sea foam, so students may want to include this technique as well. Students can tint or "colorize" shells in shades that suit their fancy.

This activity has enough charm to bring a salty old pirate to his knees! *Ahoy!*

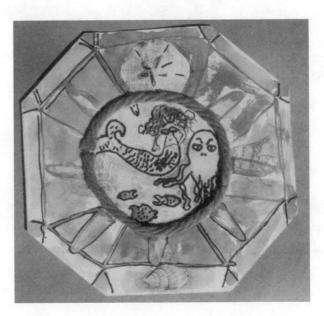

Figure 6-19. A mermaid and an octopus—surrounded by fish and topped with a sand dollar—make a fine sailor's valentine. Mythologically speaking, European mermaids are prone to sit on a rock with a comb and a hand mirror. Their songs are irresistible to lonely sailors. Comes the sea foam, alas, and the mermaids are gone. ▶

"LIVING" SEA LIFE

Name _____ Date _____

THE CARIBBEAN MARKETPLACE

Draw one item in the box next to the word. Show shape *and* texture!

SEA LIFE

Starfish

Shell

Fish

Coral

THE CARIBBEAN MARKETPLACE *(Cont'd)*

FRUIT AND FLOWERS

Pineapple

Bananas

Sugar cane

Mango

BONUS POINT: Star fruit

Name _____ Date _____

THE CARIBBEAN MARKETPLACE *(Cont'd)*

CRAFTS

Straw hat

Basket

Carved wood sculpture

Fashion item (jewelry or clothing)

Fish net

What is around and behind your market-place? Draw an example of a tree.

ACTIVITY 5

Viva Puerto Rico! The Mask of the Vejigante

Papier-mâché Masks

BONUS: "ZEMI:" LITTLE ANCIENT CACIQUE PENDANT!

▲ Figure 6-20. Student-crafted Vejiganté mask (or *máscara,* Spanish word for mask). This wide-mouthed character is really quite basic in appearance—bright Caribbean colors, pointy horns, and . . . oh those eyes!

"*La Isla*" or "the Island" of Puerto Rico sits in the middle of the Caribbean island chain next to the Dominican Republic. It was originally inhabited by the peace-loving Taino Indians and their fierce enemy, the Caribs. Life in early Puerto Rico—also called **Boriquen** (an Indian word)—was quiet and happy for the most part. Things changed, however, with the arrival of Christopher Columbus and the later settlement of Europeans. The history reveals an unrest to follow—conquests, pirates, and raiding European armies. Spain claimed Puerto Rico until it was ceded to the United States as a result of the Spanish-American War (1898). Puerto Rico became a Commonwealth of the U. S. in 1952. The decision of whether or not Puerto Rico will become the 51st state of the U.S. or an independent nation is currently under discussion and debate. Like several other islands of the Greater Antilles, Spanish culture and language is strong in Puerto Rico. Today, Puerto Rico is defined by its Spanish-Indian past and its Spanish, Indian, and African heritage—all of which have merged with contemporary American culture.

Art, music, dance, and vitality are part of island life. Nowhere is this more evident than in the festival of the Feast of Santiago Apostle which features the main character of the Vejigante (VEH-He-gan-TE). The Vejigante is the fantastic character that represents the carnival itself. He is a blend of Spanish, African, and Caribbean cultures—the three powers that comprise Puerto Rico. The Vejigante's history is a surprising one. You can even find this character within the classical Spanish novel *Don Quixote,* written in 1605 by Cervantes, reminding us that history and human nature are often reflected by literature and the arts. The wonderful fun of any carnival is that public fun may be made of ourselves at least a few times a year. The variations of the Vejigante character takes place in two specific locations in Puerto Rico, in Loíza and Ponce, at two different times of the year. The city of Loíza, an African-Caribbean community, gives us the three wonderful characters—the Knight (represents Santiago, the Spanish war hero, and Ogun the Yoruban god of war), the Old Man (El Viejo), and the Crazy Woman (La Loca). Like most plays and carnivals, meaning is constructed by the triumph of good over evil. It is a festival filled with music; the popular *Bomba* percussion keeps the beat bouncing. *Plena* is a more recent percussion that acts as a musical narrative filling the town with stories set to pulsating rhythm and non-stop news! These forms of music and dance are unique to Puerto Rico. If you want to find Vejiganté himself, then you must look for him in *La Isla* . . . Puerto Rico!

Figure 6-21. A small Vejiganté *máscara* by a Puerto Rican artisan. This one boasts of finely-appointed dots, peppered all over his mysterious face. Note the dental work! ▶

MATERIALS

- templates (see Teacher Preparation)
- masking tape
- pencils
- papier-mâché (see Teacher Preparation)
- newspaper
- scissors
- polymer medium (optional)

- brushes
- large oaktag
- water containers
- bright tempera paint (see Teacher Preparation)
- reproducible pages: "Vejigante Templates" and "How to Assemble a Vejigante Mask"

TEACHER PREPARATION

The Vejigante mask is a great character for students to produce and is most easily accomplished through templates. Patterns for mask parts (see the illustration) may be used to guide students in cutting the mask(s)' essential elements. The teacher may choose to cut templates that will be shared by small groups. Another possibility is to reproduce the page for students and distribute; they will then create their own templates by tracing and cutting directly from the sample.

Note: Teacher will determine the scale of the mask, so the size of the template will reflect this decision. Enlargement on a photocopier can be extremely helpful. Finally, the teacher may simply wish to draw on a chalkboard or display template shapes required and have students approximate these elements themselves in a freehand manner, refine, and cut. There are many ways, depending on the developmental level of the students and resources available that will result in understanding and completing the assembly of mask parts.

Likewise, there is no single, correct formula for papier-mâché ingredients. Many teachers simply use the recipe below. Commercially prepared papier-mâché is available through art suppliers.

> 1 cup flour
> 1 cup water
> black-and-white newspaper
> white glue (optional)

Mix flour and water a little at a time in a bowl. Some people prefer adding flour to water, believing that it makes a smoother paste. Add white glue, if desired. Avoid "puffs" of flour in air by sifting it directly into water. Tear newspaper into strips. Be sure to cover work surface with newspaper.

When lumps in mixture have disappeared, dip in strips. Slip excess paste off strips by pulling them through two fingers. Apply strips to mask form and build features. Add dry paper strips between very wet ones to absorb extra wetness, if necessary. Squeeze and manipulate to control shaping. When complete, let dry.

Red, yellow, and black are the traditional colors favored for the Vejigante. Caribbean colors are just as acceptable. Earth colors are also effective. Select colors accordingly. Tempera paint is recommended, yet acrylic paints may be substituted. Nontoxic acrylic gloss or matte medium may be used later to preserve the finished mask. A sample of a completed Vejigante mask would be useful—even if color has not been applied—to reveal mask structure.

▲ Figure 6-22. A little coconut Vejigante, commonly sold as a souvenir. The shape is another mask alternative.

Figure 6-23. Vejigante is a character, a mask, a myth—an idea of the imagination. Vejigante portrait masks prove mighty powerful. ▶

DIRECTIONS

1. Who is this colorful character of Puerto Rico called Vejigante? Discuss the significance of Vejigante and his companion characters (see introduction). The Vejigante is a sort of scary, yet funny clown and animal combination, that chases children until they scream with delight! Introduce the sample mask.

2. Distribute templates (see Teacher Preparation). Students will cut mask parts beginning with a circular mask foundation. Cut mask features (eyes, nose, mouth, and horns), remembering that Vejiganté is part animal and part human.

3. Assemble with masking tape according to the directions on reproducible page, "How to Assemble a Vejiganté Mask."

4. The fully-assembled paper Vejiganté mask is now ready for papier-mâché application. Use the papier-mâché mix and directions as provided in the Teacher Preparation. Use two to three layers of strips. Let dry until hardened.

5. *¡Si!* We are ready to paint! Distribute paint supplies. Have students apply a selected color to the surface of the entire mask. If reasonably dry, students may wish to delineate features with contrasting colors; dot patterns are optional. Encourage students to invent possible variations, such as teeth and eyelashes!

6. Acrylic medium may be applied to preserve the mask overall. Just be sure that the Vejiganté mask is ready in time for the big festival!

▲ Figure 6-24. In the city of Philadelphia, Pennsylvania, where the Latino community is chiefly Puerto Rican, we find several important island characters! "La Plena" is a dancing woman (left) accompanied by "Jibaro" (hee-barr-ro), which stands for the proud Puerto Rican country folk—his wide-brimmed hat is unmistakable. At the right is the unflappable Spanish Hero Conquistador. The "house fronts" behind the three figures deserve a second look . . . it's great community art! P.S. Neighborhood student artists produced the installation.

VEJIGANTE MASK TEMPLATES

FACE WITH EYES
Cut one piece.
Cut out eyes.

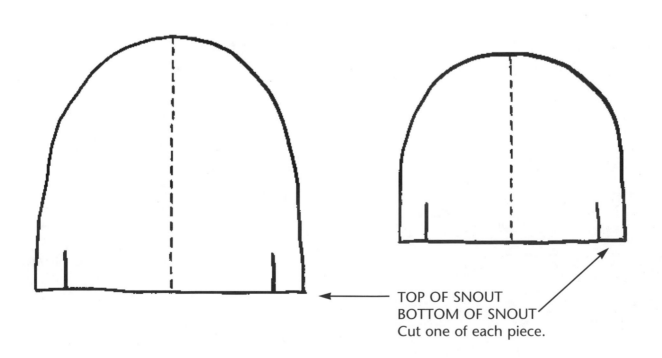

TOP OF SNOUT
BOTTOM OF SNOUT
Cut one of each piece.

VEJIGANTE MASK TEMPLATES *(Cont'd)*

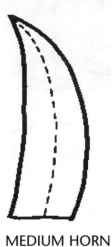

LARGE HORN
Cut six pieces.

MEDIUM HORN
Cut four pieces.

SMALL HORN
Cut four pieces.

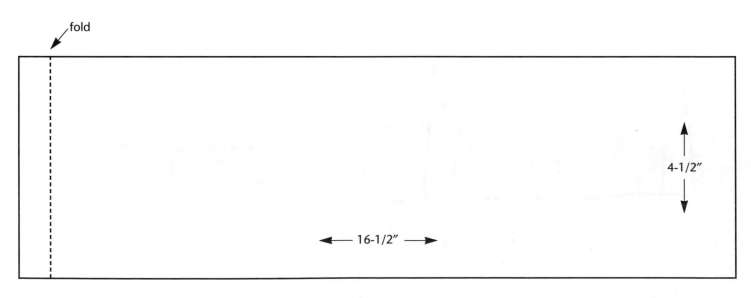

fold

4-1/2"

16-1/2"

HEAD (base)
Cut horizontal strip of paper with the measurements shown above. Note fold line
for Step 1 of "How to Assemble a Vejigante Mask.

HOW TO ASSEMBLE A VEJIGANTE MASK

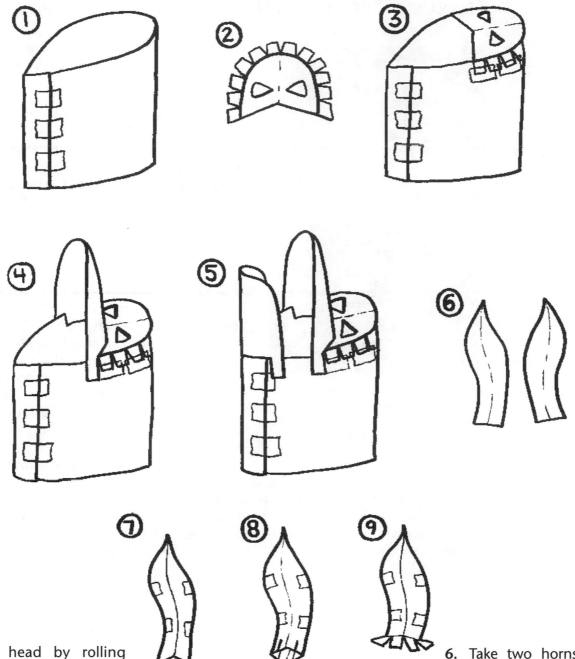

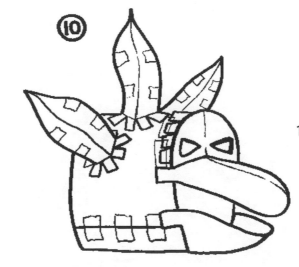

1. Create head by rolling paper. Fold flap over. Secure with tape (masking tape).

2. Use scissors to cut slits along outside edge of face.

3. Attach face to head with masking tape.

4. Attach top of snout to bottom of face. Use slits in snout to secure to side of head.

5. Attach bottom of snout to bottom of head. Use slits in snout to secure to side of head.

6. Take two horns of same size.

7. Fold each horn and secure with tape.

8. Cut four slits at bottom of horn.

9. Spread tabs out at bottom of horn.

10. Attach each horn to Vejigante mask as desired. Secure with tape.

BONUS : "ZEMI:" LITTLE ANCIENT CACIQUE PENDANT!

▲ Figure 6-25. This petroglyph pendant, also known as Guanin, is such a bright charm! Could this be the *sol de Jayuya,* a Taino sun symbol?

Puerto Rico has a long and ancient history. Wonderful petroglyphic faces and forms are part of the indigenous culture. So endearing are the little symbolic rock images that they *must* be seen, made, and worn! Depictions vary, depending on the *zona arqueológico* (archaeological zone) where they are found. Artists and craftmakers have emblazoned bowls, jewelry, plates, and other items of clay and stone with their irresistible expressions. Ancient art survives!

The cacique (cah-seek-cay), or chief, in ancient Puerto Rican or Taino society, often wore a protective pendant to attract good luck and power. Once made of gold, the amulets are now found in clay. The "Zemis" (Los Cemies) are spiritual objects, much like the tiki pendants of old Hawaii, and form broad interpretations. Specific three-pointer stone Zemis are said to represent the mountain form, sacred in so many cultures. In La Isla of Puerto Rico, the mountain of El Yunque rules—it is also the only tropical forest in America's Nation Park system!

Students will enjoy crafting their own Zemi pendants, or Guanin, of clay formed or pressed into circular disks. A hole is pierced so that the dry (and fired) clay pendant can later receive a cord. With a clay tool (or reasonable substitute), students can draw a magical insect, a little Zemi goddess, a mask (*máscara*)—or even an ancient Happy Face! (See the reproducible.) Pendants should bring good luck, sunshine, and lots of compliments!

THE PETROGLYPHS OF PUERTO RICO

1 Momia

2 Lagartijo

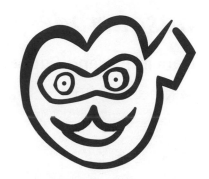

3 Máscara

4 Pulpo

5 Angel

6 Coquí

7 Mariposa

8 Cara Feliz

9 Zemi (Cemi)

Try Your Own Interpretations! Ancient Artists Did!

Who's Who?

1. Momia = Mummy
2. Lagartijo = Lizard
3. Máscara = Mask
4. Pulpo = Octopus
5. Angel = Angel or Guardian
6. Coquí = Frog, the beloved mascot of Puerto Rico!
7. Mariposa = Butterfly
8. Cara Feliz = Happy Face (and we thought the Happy Face was only a sticker!)
9. Zemi = Example of three-pointed "mountain" stone

ACTIVITY 6

Who in the World Is Jonkonnu?: Pitchy-Patchy Masquerade

"Dancing" Hand Puppets/Fabric Arts

BONUS: "ROOTS" SCREEN MASKS

▲ Figure 6-26. Pitchy-Patchy puppets welcome the company of other Jamaican characters, such as Notorious Calico Jack the Pirate and his female pirate pals. There's also the legend of the Witch of Rose Hall—and, of course, a "Rasta Imposta" may want to join in the fun!

The intensely colorful Jonkonnu Festival is traditionally held in Jamaica—one of the three largest islands in the Caribbean—during the Christmas and New Year season. It dates back to the 18th century. The word *Jonkonnu* is derived from early associations with a masquerade character named *John Canoe*. There are many, often conflicting, accounts as to *who* John Canoe really is! A performer named "Jack-In-The-Green," who appeared in a plant-like camouflage, is probably closest to the *Pitchy-Patchy* character, a masquerader who appears in the Jonkonnu Festival of Jamaica today. The speculations about John Canoe's real identity include characters such as "Jack Pudding," "Koo-Koo," and "Actor Boy"—encompassing Jamaica's British-Colonial past, along with the strong African and West Indian presence. Jonkonnu is "where old England encounters the Yoruba spirit dancer" . . . the result is the exuberant Pitchy-Patchy!

There are two essential elements within the Jonkonnu Festival: *Roots*, African heritage, and *Fancy Dress*, which emerges from European history. The Creole nature of the Caribbean, however, rarely allows one, single source for any character—and Pitchy-Patchy is no exception. Basically, the character Pitchy-Patchy may be linked with Reggae and Rasta, and even Ska, all Jamaican rhythms—as well as with marching European bands. In spite of Pitchy-Patchy's Yoruban-African dancer appearance, it has also been noted that this lively performer draws further inspiration from May Day parades in old England which celebrate plants and flowers (Jack-In-The-Green)! Add to this the clever camouflage of Jamaican Maroons, a successful slave-resistance movement. Jonkonnu is practiced beyond Jamaica; it has gained popularity in the Bahamas, St. Thomas, and Brooklyn, New York, where a West Indian community thrives today. Pitchy-Patchy dances on, *mon*!

MATERIALS

- lunch bags (see Teacher Preparation)
- scissors
- markers
- fabric scraps
- white glue

- masking tape
- miscellaneous scraps and holidday ornaments (see Teacher Preparation)
- wiggle eyes (see Teacher Preparation)
- bells and beads (see Teacher Preparation)

TEACHER PREPARATION

The teacher will gather various fabric scraps—colored and patterned felt squares, burlap, fringe, rick-rack, and recyclable garment scraps. The teacher may cut scraps into strips if students lack scissors skills. Other items that will help Pitchy-Patchy puppets to sparkle and sing are holiday tree trimmings, musical bells, wiggle eyes, beads, braided fabric tassels, and other sewing notions. One helpful hint for material resources is toy store party novelty items, such as plastic jewelry (including beads), which will provide inexpensive dazzle.

Plain brown lunch bags are, as always, fine for this Caribbean puppet. Even better are the assorted colored paper bags found in art catalogs, discount centers, and paper party goods stores. **Note of interest:** The teacher may want to use this lesson as an opportunity to hone sewing skills. In this case, socks are suggested along with appropriate sewing supplies (no need for glue). It is helpful for the teacher to create a Jonkonnu puppet sample in advance of the lesson. Audio tapes and CDs of Jamaican music, such as Reggae (Bob Marley, for example) are suggested. Substitute Calypso if Reggae is not available.

◄ Figures 6-27a & 6-27b. The Reggae culture has its base in Kingston, capital city and home of the late, great Reggae artist Bob Marley. Rasta is linked to Ethiopia and, in its pure form, is a natural religious movement that supports vegetarianism and a respectful life style. Reggae and Rasta bring to mind images of dancers with flying dreadlocks that cascade from bright, woolen caps. ►

DIRECTIONS

1. Discuss the popular Jonkonnu Festival and its characters. Introduce your students to hand puppet Pitchy-Patchy with a lively sample product presentation. Students will see and hear this dancing figure through its movement of flying fabric strips and tinkling bells! Ask students to observe the shape of the fabric and the overlapping fabric effect that emphasizes the rhythm of the puppet's movement. Shake Pitchy-Patchy to prove the point.

2. Distribute paper bags and markers. Students establish area to be used for the face and create their own Pitchy-Patchy character's facial features, which may or may not be covered with strips. The bottom of the paper bag is suggested for facial articulation.

3. Distribute all other materials. Students will cut selected fabric into strips.

4. Glue layers of strips to the body of the paper bag puppet along with application of miscellaneous ornaments. Masking tape aids in application of various elements and can be camouflaged with fabric strips.

5. It's Jonkonnu time in Jamaica! Play Jamaican, Reggae, or other Caribbean music (Calypso may be substituted), if available. Place puppets on hands and "Party on, *mon*."

BONUS : "ROOTS" SCREEN MASKS

Pitchy-Patchy is a *Roots* character. Dancing the streets of Jamaica during Jonkonnu is traditionally performed during Christmas holidays and public occasions. Pitchy-Patchy puppets are our renditions of the fully costumed (usually male) dancers that perform in the Jonkonnu parade. Jonkonnu costumes often combine painting techniques, recyclable materials, collage, and sewing.

To create the wire mesh mask as an item of Jonkonnu interest, you need window screen (found at hardware stores). Wire mesh should be cut into 8" × 8" squares; cloth or duct tape is used to cover the edges. The rest is easy: Students will apply acrylic paint to the wire mesh square "face" (similar to the box-face shape of Pitchy-Patchy puppets). Encourage students to use simple symbols for eyes, nose, and mouth. (Happy clown/sad clown ideas will provide quick visual reference.) Let dry. Crepe paper fringe or fabric cut and glued to edges can create a finishing touch.

One great joy of the wire mask activity is the experience of painting onto a completely different, highly porous surface. The wise teacher will have newspaper on hand to keep "screen painting" from becoming "desk" painting. Wire masks may be displayed against carnival-colored backdrops, or worn by threading string through wire and attaching behind the head—a fine homemade solution to all carnival and costume celebrations. Students will certainly be safe from any invasion of flying bugs!

◄ Figures 6-28a & 6-28b. Samples of wire screen masks—one with brightly colored paper streamers and the other with a magnificent smile! ►

ACTIVITY 7

Be Cool in Jamaica: Tradewind Architecture

Blueprint for Caribbean Dreamhouse/Tropical Design

In architecture as in real estate, *location, location, location* is everything! The architectural habitats of the Caribbean are already in the best earthly spot imaginable. The physical attributes of the Caribbean—brilliant sun, blue skies, endless pastel beaches, rising mountains— create the perfect scene for tropical architecture. The features of the tropical climate influence where houses are built. Tradewinds allow fresh, cooling breezes to blow through dwellings that are constructed to receive them. This is the reason why most of the architecture includes terraces, verandahs, and open courtyards. The cantilever effect of a roof on an open porch additionally creates an opportunity for shade. Shutters not only provide bright visual elements, they also enable the residence to control the entry of the hot tropical sun.

Figure 6-29. This compact little "Blueprint Page House" can catch the breeze as it wafts off the water! The student architect spells out interior elements in the upper left-hand corner of her drawing. Her "floor plan" description accompanies a fine three-quarter view elevation.

The proportions of the Caribbean architecture vary dramatically: from the popular one-story *case house* to great manors that sit atop the landscape's high ground. The smaller houses are usually the most vibrant in color; they seem to celebrate their lucky environment. Festive combinations of hot pink and turquoise, or yellow and red, beam with individual pride! These are the colors of brilliant flowers and bright tropical birds. They are modest little homes that pack a visual wallop, a friendly extension of regional folk art. Gingerbread, lattice, and grill work—usually accompanied by rolling hills and palm trees—seem to sing of the local flavor. These small rural houses nested in the hillsides are generally known as *case houses*. Understandably, they are also rightly known as the *popular* house.

On the other hand, the *plantation house* is of grander dimension and a surviving record of Caribbean history. In Jamaica, where plantation life and colonialization were dominant, there are many architectural testimonies to the period. Montego Bay is enjoyed by many tourists each year. One may either visit or stay in Rose Hall, about five miles east of Montego Bay, built around 1780. It is a sweeping estate where the great house rises far above the sea. Its legendary mistress Annie Palmer, who lived at Rose Hall around 1820, is also known as "The White Witch of Rose Hall!" She became a Jamaican legend through her notorious activities. Travel five miles from Rose Hall and find another great house that was owned by the poet Elizabeth Barrett Browning. If you can picture these transplanted European apparitions gliding through airy mansion chambers, you are probably picturing a plantation house. Many are now resort hotels offering an interior as well as exterior view. Popular houses, much like Reggae, spring from the heart of Caribbean Island spirit.

MATERIALS

- 12″ × 18″ white drawing paper
- rulers
- pencils and erasers
- watercolor markers (see Teacher Preparation)

TEACHER PREPARATION

The tradewind architecture lesson is set in Jamaica where dominant tropical breezes blow—yet, there is no reason not to select another Caribbean spot of choice (note Slide 25). This architecture lesson will wisely be designed for a tropical Caribbean place. To aid students in better understanding the environmental factors that influence architecture in its setting, the teacher will present two basic Caribbean house types. The illustrations on the following pages will allow students to make a selection for the type of Caribbean house they will feature. There is also an opportunity to present the basic architecture planning concept of a blueprint, as well as specific vocabulary: *elevation, facade, terrace,* and *verandah.* This activity will encourage students to think about the style of a home, its exterior appearance and special features, its relationship with its immediate environment, its interior accommodations, and its decorative appeal. Students will also consider the "personality" of the house by giving it a name! The prepared teacher may wish to provide visual reference materials such as *Architectural Digest* and other books and magazines on this subject. *Blueprint* refers to the floor plan. *Elevation* refers to a straightforward view. If the teacher can find examples, this will help students understand these various views. This floor plan may be simply stated in a verbal description that is noted on student art or supported by a visual sample of same.

Markers should be bright; however, it is the *popular* house that would require tropical colors, for *plantation* houses are often white with less flamboyant color usage. Tropical Markers by Dinney-Smith Crayola would come in handy.

◀ Figure 6-30. A complete facade indicates a comely Plantation House. Notice how the chimney remembers its European design origins.

DIRECTIONS

1. "If you had a home of your own in the Caribbean, would it be grand or cozy? Would it sit on a hilltop or next to a sea? Let's say you are in Jamaica where the tradewinds blow. How could you use them to cool your house? Would you have a terrace, a porch, a big front door? Will your windows have shutters or louvers?" Discuss these questions with the students.

2. Distribute pencils, paper, and rulers. Reproducible pages that show Caribbean House styles may also be distributed at this time. **Note:** Use examples of plantation and popular houses for motivation, *not* replication. Ask students to decide which kind of house they would like to draw.

3. Collect reproducible pages. Students will sketch the elevation of their chosen house with a floor plan and descriptions noted nearby, if desired. Set the details in place, including surrounding vegetation and setting. "If your house had a name, what might you call it?" Include in the sketch the house name. Some examples from literature and history are: House of the Seven Gables, Green Acres, Sam Lord's Castle (in Barbados), and Rose Hill (Montego Bay) in Jamaica.

4. Distribute markers. Students should be mindful of the colors selected and their ability to complement the house type. Include descriptive information as part of the student's picture scheme. "Is your house painted? Are your windows in place? Are you relaxing on the verandah? How does your tropical garden grow—and where?" With elevations completed and optional floor plans/descriptions included, it is probably safe to say that the house—whether a popular case house or a plantation—is in "move-in" condition! Discuss the personal meaning of each student's architecture, including and valuing all student work. Show off this delightful Caribbean neighborhood with a grand, yet cozy display.

▲ Figure 6-31. A preliminary sketch by third-grade Jenna who promises a "House of Sugar Cane"!

CARIBBEAN HOUSE STYLES

CASE OR POPULAR HOUSE

The *case house* or *popular house* is usually a modest dwelling. Many case houses consist of a single room, while others include additional rooms and special features. Case houses may be portable, for they typically have no foundation or basement. They are usually made of wood, painted in bright colors, and found in rural regions. Styles vary from region to region as can be seen by the drawings and blueprints on this page. This type of house is a work of Caribbean folk art!

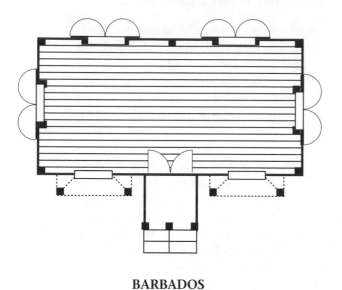

BARBADOS

BARBADOS

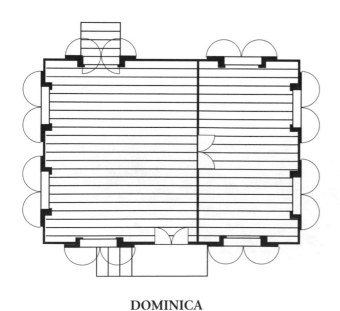

DOMINICA

DOMINICA

CARIBBEAN HOUSE STYLES *(cont'd)*

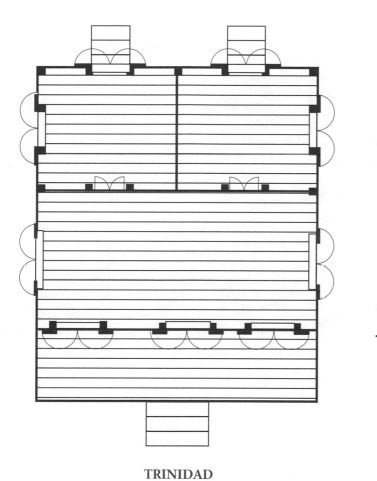

TRINIDAD

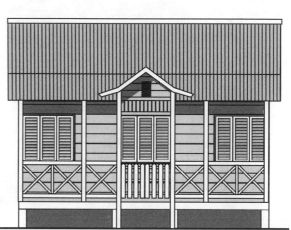

TRINIDAD

CARIBBEAN HOUSE STYLES *(cont'd)*

THE PLANTATION HOUSE

The **plantation house** is much greater in size and scale than the small case house. It recalls the days of sugar cane, colonization, and sweeping estates. Plantation houses have many airy rooms and often include great parlors, large family dining rooms, and guest rooms. Most plantation houses are located in the center of a large estate and are made of stone, brick, or another type of hard building material. What a unique picture of European architecture in a Caribbean paradise!

ACTIVITY 8

Bongo! The Afro-Latin Beat of Cuba

Decorative Musical Instrument/Drum

▲ Figure 6-32. Salsa, Mambo, Cha-Cha-Cha! In spite of Cuba's many challenges, there is much to celebrate. The spirit of the Cuban people is as steady as a heartbeat and as lasting as memory and music themselves.

Cuba, the largest island in the Caribbean, moves to the heartbeat of the drum. In the 1940s and 1950s, Cuba was world-famous for its music, dance, and song. Restaurants, cafes, beaches, and their cabanas—even the streets—filled with vibrant colors and rhythms. Bongo! Conga! The voices and flamboyant dancing stay with Cubans always, marked by the distinctive influence of the African drum. A powerful fusion of African and Spanish tradition, Cuba is responsible for the *Mambo* and the *Cha-Cha*! Think of the Hotel Tropicana and the Copacabana and you have an immediate, colorful picture of Cuba.

The size alone of Cuba—with its 11 million people—represents a diversity of lifestyles from city to farm, to mountains, beaches, and seas. Havana (La Havana) is the capital city where you will see old Baroque cathedrals alongside ancient city walls. On the long promenade in July, the *carnaval* bursts out with Conga lines of dancers. Cuba is a place of contrasts: It is very Caribbean, yet the country stands alone. Cuba is only 90 miles from the southernmost point of the Florida Keys in the U.S. Many Cubans now live in the U.S., particularly Miami, Florida, parts of which have become known as "Little Cuba."

Cubanismo is the pride of being Cuban. It is a culture that honors its past, one that is of African and Spanish roots. The "talking drum" of Africa sent its message to the vibrant and determined Caribbean people of Cuba. The drumbeat speaks: Cuba, alive and strong, live on, live on!

MATERIALS

- colored tissue paper
- white glue
- fluorescent paper or other colored paper
- 2-foot length thick yarn
- kraft paper (substitute brown shopping bags)
- Cuban music (see Teacher Preparation)

- scissors
- pencils
- large brushes
- watercolor cups
- drum-sized containers (see Teacher Preparation)

TEACHER PREPARATION

The teacher will save empty drum-sized containers, if available; perfect for this lesson is the empty Crayola® Model Magic™ container. Other options include: cylindrical ice cream containers (large size) or small plastic household buckets (purchased at cut-rate stores). **Note:** Holes will be needed at top and bottom of drum container in order to pull through yarn for authenticity. These openings may be best prepared by the teacher in advance, carefully perforating surface with a sharp tool.

The teacher may wish to precut circles to size of container opening, leaving a margin for "fringe." Cutting yarn in lenghts may also save class time. **Note:** Tissue paper application to drum surface works best with white glue that has been watered down so that it is not heavier than tissue. This water/glue combination will be used to "paint" the drum surface as tissue strips are applied. Keep the undiluted, dispensable glue container handy.

Consider the "hot" beat of Cuban rhythm: fluorescent paper can be used for application of letters to make drum designs "sizzle." Also try to have Cuban/Caribbean music available.

DIRECTIONS

1. In Cuba, the music never stops. The *Mambo, Cha Cha, Salsa*—you name it, the Latin beat goes on. Our drums will capture the Cuban musical spirit and provide an actual instrument! How many students would like to design their own Latin drum? You are encouraged to read "Nothing but Drums" by Oscar Hijuelos (ee-wey-los) to your students, either as an introduction or at other times during the lesson.

NOTHING BUT DRUMS
by Oscar Hijuelos

AND NOW NOTHING BUT DRUMS, a battery of drums, the conga drums jamming out, in a *descarga,* and the drummers lifting their heads and shaking under some kind of spell. There's rain drums, like pitter-patter pitter-patter but a hundred times faster, and then slamming-the-door-drums and dropping-the-bucket-drums, kicking-the-car-fender drums. Then circus drums, then coconuts-falling-out-of-the-trees-and-thumping-against-the-ground drums, then lion-skin drums, then the-whacking-of-a-hand-against-a-wall drums, the-beating-of-a-pillow drums, heavy-stones-against-a-wall drums, then the-thickset-forest-tree-trunks-pounding drums, and then the-mountain-rumble drums, then the-little-birds-learning-to-fly drums and the big-birds-alighting-on-a-rooftop-and-fanning-their-immense-wings drums, then a-boat-down-the-river-with-its-oars-dropping-heavily-into-the-water drums . . .

2. Distribute pencils, paper, and scissors, along with the perforated cylindrical containers. Remember, containers must be turned upside-down (top of drum is bottom of container). Students will draw and cut the alphabet letters of A, B, C, U from fluorescent or other colored paper. Students should think of letters as not just letters, but as individual shapes with a life of their own. Set these aside.

3. Hand out appropriate colored tissue paper and have students cut into patches. Distribute watered-down glue and brushes.

4. Students will "paint" the glue onto the surface of the cylindrical container *one section at a time*. Apply an overlay of colored tissue. Keep moving! Then let dry.

5. Arrange letters to spell CUBA on the curved surface of the drum using glue at full strength. Gently press in place. Students may use other words such as "Bongo" or "Musica" as part of the letter art design. Let dry.

6. Distribute thick yarn. Students will "weave" yarn in and out of the perforated openings, tying ends together. Cut away excess.

7. Distribute circular drum tops. Attach with full-strength white glue to the top of the drum. Be sure to allow margin to extend around the drum top. Smooth the drum top for an appearance that is "as tight as a drum." Cut fringe with small clipping motion, moving around the drum clockwise.

8. Play Cuban music on tape or a CD player and form your own classroom musical troupe! Gently find the beat and let the tempo of Afro-Cuban song fill your hearts!

Mexico, Central and South America

MEXICO

Caribbean Sea

Belize

Honduras

North
Atlantic
Ocean

Costa Rica

GUATEMALA

VENEZUELA

Guyana

Suriname

El Salvadore

Nicaragua

French Guianan
(FRANCE)

COLOMBIA

Panama

ECUADOR

PERU

BRAZIL

South
Pacific
Ocean

Bolivia

Paraguay

Chile

Argentina

Uruguay

South
Atlantic
Ocean

Falkland
Islands (U.K.)

South
Georgia
Island (U.K.)

Mexico, Central and South America

Powerful portrait of a Mexican *compasino*.

In the "Land of the Fifth Sun," *El Sol* is central!

A bus filled with passengers, baskets, and bundles of goods—and even a few farm animals—stops for a repair. Note the mechanic under the hood. Clay miniatures from Mesoamerica provide delightful interpretations of life as we know it!

The *retablo* opens its doors to reveal a Sombrero Shop. New hats bring cheer everywhere! Found throughout the Americas, this retablo was made in Peru—where charming little works of this kind are also called *Imagineria*.

ART ACTIVITIES FOR BECOMING CULTURE SMART

▣ **Activity 1**
Day of the Dead: A Celebration of Life
Clay Figure "Calacas"/Miniature Sculpture
DOUBLE BONUS: BINGO! *LOTERIA* MEXICO! . . . "LA CATRINA" AND "EL ZAPATISTA" DANCING PUPPETS
INCLUDES: RECIPE FOR "DEAD BREAD" (PAN DE LOS MUERTOS)

▣ **Activity 2**
The Popol Vuh: Picture Codes of Mexico
Gods, Goddesses, and Glorious Myth/Big Book Covers of the Codices
BONUS: JAGUAR KNIGHT: VIVA EL TIGRE! FULL-SCALE PAPER MASK

Activity 3
Big Time! The Aztec Calendar
Oversized Paper Sundial/Signs and Symbols/Self Portrait
BONUS: "CROWN" OF MONTEZUMA!

▣ **Activity 4**
Ladies and Gentlemen of Ancient Mexico: A Classic Clay Society
Ancient Mexican Clay Figures
BONUS: OLMEC CRYBABIES AND CHOCOLATE POTS . . . AND MEXICAN DOGS DANCE!

▣ **Activity 5**
Milagros and Retablos: Small Miracles of Tin Art
Tin Frames/Milagros

Activity 6
The Ancient Andes Is Still Tops: Tip Your Hat to Peru!
Textile Arts/Four-Cornered Paper Hats
BONUS: AMIGOS OF THE AMERICAS: A FRIENDLY MIX . . . "AMIGO" DOLL PINS

▣ **Activity 7**
Rainforest Molas: The Art of Ecology from Panama to Brazil
The Paper Mola with a Message
BONUS: THE BIRDS OF BRAZIL: PAPER RELIEF FOR THE AMAZON

To know the Art of Mexico, Central America, and South America . . . . .

. . . . . is to recognize that the geographical term *Mesoamerica*—or Middle America—is commonly used to identify the narrow land mass that connects the continents of North and South America. Mexico, in North America, geographically ends at the border of Belize and Guatemala. According to an archaeological definition, Mesoamerica begins north of Mexico City and extends south through Nicaragua to Costa Rica. Often, the term *pre-Columbian* is used to designate the time before the arrival of Columbus. Columbus, however, did not give relevance to preexisting cultures; at the time of Columbus's arrival in the Caribbean, Mexico supported a teeming city with a monumental temple complex that would easily rival any city in Europe. In Peru, a vast Incan empire of gold and silver stood tall and strong. Civilizations were well developed; ancient ruins indicate a long and productive past.

From the *Olmec* culture (1500–200 B.C.), colossal heads carved of volcanic rock—ten feet tall and weighing many tons—rise from the earth at La Venta, near Mexico City. The features are strong and massive; all wear helmets that may refer to ancient ball games. The Olmec people also built pyramid temple centers for worship. Carvings, figures, and pottery inform us of this seminal civilization. The jaguar, considered a sacred animal, occurred in sculpture as a "were-jaguar," part human and part animal.

The development of western Mexican culture is evidenced in the pottery, which depicts social activities as well as ball games. Western Mexico is a source of geometric pottery and terra-cotta dogs. The visionary yarn paintings of the *Huichol* (wee-chul) emerged from this region. With the Maya came the first city-states. *Teotihuacan* grew into the "city of the gods" around A.D. 600 in Central Mexico. North of Mexico City, Teotihuacan was the capital city of ancient Mexico; the streets were lined with palaces, temples, and about 20,000 houses. The monumental Pyramid of the Sun was central. It contained neighborhoods with workshops for potters, weavers, and sculptors. By A.D. 750, Teotihuacan was destroyed by invaders and abandoned.

Today in Mexico and Guatemala, many important pyramids remain intact—for example, Chichen Itza, Tikal, Palenque, and Copan. In some cases, post-Columbian Catholic churches have been built directly on top of ancient pyramids. The Maya, still living in Mesoamerica today, can be traced back to early times. The classical period of the Maya began around A.D. 320 in the Yucatan in Mexico, Guatemala, Belize, and Honduras. Writing systems were developed, accurate calendars were invented, and hieroglyphic symbols were created. Many spirit gods fill the art and architecture. Rain god representations are abundant, along with human and animal forms. Carvings document spiritual, imperial, and everyday life. The Maya may be considered the first Mexican mural painters. Images of figures, accompanied by glyphic elements, form tomb wall art. Mayan painting appears on walls, vessels, and codices, such as the Popul Vuh—the source book of story, belief, and social history. The Mayan profile—forehead and nose prominence with the demarcation of the epicanthic eye—is classic. The painting itself is of naturalistic style, with expressive line quality.

Aztec civilization replaced Mayan presence in Mesoamerica. In 1345, The Aztecs moved to an island in the middle of a lake called *Tenochtitlan,* "place of . . . the Prickly Pear Cactus." Tenochtitlan was located near present-day Mexico City. A magnificent palace was built. Temples were used for worship and sacrifice. Aztec art represents a pantheon of gods and emperors—who sometimes exchanged roles. A turquoise mosaic mask, which appears skull-like in its formation, is an iconic portrayal of either the rain god Tlaloc or the emperor god Quetzalcoatl. Masks were worn for ceremonial reasons. A host of spirit gods defined religion: gods of rain, wind, sun, moon, stars, flowers, breath—and many more. Representational figures appear in "stop-action" poses.

The civilizations of Peru were rich in history and vivid artistic creations. The early *Chavin* sculpture brought with it a highly geometrical and flattened animal-human motif that forecast the later multiplicity of Peruvian textile design. The remarkable ceramic sculpture of the *Moche* period has an arresting realism, particularly for this early period in the Americas. *Machu Picchu,* the ancient Inca city in the Andes Mountains, speaks of past glory—along with Peruvian mummy bundles and mysterious little silver figures who play Andean panpipes.

In modern Mexico, Mesoamerica, and South America, traditions continue: artist Diego Rivera upheld Mexican mural arts with his large-scale public works; Frida Kahlo manifested the myth and magic that combine to express everyday Mexican life; painter Rufina Tamaya also reflects European modern art in his representations of an evocative world that draws upon ancient Mexican imagery. In Mexico, the arts continue to explain the past and contribute to the future.

A brightly painted wooden rabbit hops in from Oaxaco (wah-HAH-kah)!

ACTIVITY 1

Day of the Dead: A Celebration of Life

Clay Figure "Calacas"/Miniature Sculpture

DOUBLE BONUS: BINGO! *LOTERIA* MEXICO! . . . "LA CATRINA" AND "EL ZAPATISTA" DANCING PUPPETS"

INCLUDES: RECIPE FOR "DEAD BREAD" (PAN DE LOS MUERTOS)

In Mexico each year, between October 27 and November 2, a great celebration takes place! The "Day of the Dead" or **Dia de Muertos,** is considered the most important holiday of the year. The time of year for *Dia de Muertos* is close to that of Halloween and All Saints Day. Yet, the Mexican celebration is one like no other: it serves to teach the history, belief, humor, courage, and spirit of the Mexican people. Linked with Christian Catholicism, this event is deeply connected to the roots of Mexican-Indian culture. The role of death in everyday life in pre-Hispanic Mexico existed as the central theme of early mythology and belief. Death and life are inseparable and must be equally embraced. This idea forms a way of thinking that is as true in Mexico today as it was with the Maya and the Aztec societies. "The Day of the Dead" is not regarded solely as a sad time. In fact, it is a celebration of life!

▲ Figure 7-1. "Gone fishing" . . . hope to catch *el pescado.* This fisherman is on the rock for the long haul; perhaps, if he is lucky, he will encounter *La Sirena*—the mermaid.

Dia de Muertos welcomes the return of ancestors to the Earth for a brief, joyful visit. Different days represent the return of specific souls. There is much in place on Earth to welcome the spirits back—wildflowers are everywhere, particularly marigolds. Much preparation beforehand allows for an atmosphere of intense color, filled with excitement. Plentiful *ofrenda* (or offerings), *Santos* (Catholic Saints), candy sugar skulls with names on them, fruits, candles, incense, traditional tissue paper banners or *papel picado,* masked dancers, mariachi bands playing, and toys such as *calacas* puppets abound! A special "dead bread" (*pan de los muertos*) is baked for the occasion. The craft and art are extraordinary. This is not a time of mourning; it is a time of reunion! Parties are held in cemeteries where tombstones have been color-washed in bright pinks and blues—or in colors enjoyed by the deceased. Photographs and flowers are accompanied by favorite treats. If Uncle Pepito was a chocolate lover during his life, he would be sure to find chocolate candy and other sweets awaiting him! A newspaper front page and other signs of daily life would bring him up to date.

During *Dia de Muertos* art imitates life and life mocks death. Whether one is a politician, a farmer, a mortician, a general, or a president, death is inevitable. Why not come to terms with this fact at an early age? For generations, the Mexicans seem to have found a way to better accept mortality through "The Day of the Dead."

It is a magical time, for each autumn, a sign of the approaching "Day of the Dead" appears in the sky. The Monarch butterflies (**mariposa,** Spanish word for butterfly) begin to arrive in Mexico. Believed since ancient days to give flight to the spirit, the Monarch fly by the millions to Mexico from near and far. These winged creatures of transformation, long associated with departed warriors, come at a time when Mexicans express their heartfelt fears, joys, sorrows, and hopes. The *mariposa* (Monarch butterflies) magically remind all that life and death are cyclical, one forms from the other. Just as the butterflies are sure to return each year, families, friends, and loved ones will meet again in Mexico.

MATERIALS

- air-dry Mexican clay or Crayola™ Model Magic (see Teacher Preparation)
- toothpicks
- gesso
- small brushes
- fine-tipped nontoxic black permanent markers
- tempera or acrylic paints
- white glue
- miscellaneous scraps—fabric, holiday trim, cotton balls, ornaments, etc. (see Teacher Preparation)
- reproducible page: "La Catrina" and "El Zapatista" puppet patterns

TEACHER PREPARATION

Teacher may choose the modeling material for this lesson; any standard clay that will air dry should suffice. Recommended is Mexican air-dry clay, which will require white gesso for surface coloring. Crayola™ Model Magic is ideal—it is white in color (no gesso required) and will dry quickly. **Note:** Color may be applied with colored markers when clay is dry.

"Scrap offerings" for this lesson are miscellaneous and assorted: toy fragments, fabric, lace, doily scraps, cotton puffs, holiday ornament remnants, and so forth.

Note: In regions where "The Day of the Dead" celebration is gaining popularity in the United States, the calacas or "Dead Boxes" are more available to the buying public and are not generally outrageously expensive, for they are mostly sold as souvenirs. Of course, if the teacher has access to these objects, bring them to class along with any other festival memorabilia. Also note that the calacas we intend to make may appear with or without walls. If the teacher wishes to include walls, a corner of a giftbox will work.

Consider that the subject of "The Day of the Dead" is most readily accepted during the real time in which it annually takes place—along with Halloween—at the end of October to early November. A comparison between these two celebrations provides a basis for understanding.

Note: An effective display will require a few extra materials. See step 7, page 231, to be prepared.

▲ Figure 7-2a. Two noteworthy "dead boxes," sometimes called *calacas*. These frontal-view boxes gently ridicule the passing pleasure and occupations of daily life. Artist Frida Kahlo appears in her wheelchair with her canvas of a *calavara* (skull) behind her. To the left stands artist Diego Rivera, Frida's husband and great Mexican muralist. His nickname was "the frog" because of his froglike features—Frida affectionately called him *sapo-rana,* which means "toad-frog" in Spanish. Both Frida and Diego loved the Mexican tradition of "The Day of the Dead" and all the art that accompanied it.

DIRECTIONS

1. Discuss the Mexican holiday known as "The Day of the Dead"—***Dia de Muertos.*** *Explain this is a very special time in Mexico when people remember their ancestors in a funny, yet respectful way. (**Teacher:** See introduction for information you feel comfortable conveying to your students.) Students will be constructing skeletons that will show occupations and activities, not actual people. Emphasis may also be given to skeletal anatomy.

▲ Figure 7-2b. Even calacas need a few beauty tips from their skeletal hairdressers!

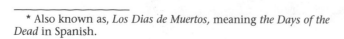

---

* Also known as, *Los Dias de Muertos,* meaning *the Days of the Dead* in Spanish.

2. Brainstorm on the board a number of activities and occupations that might be fun for our little *calacas*—beauticians, musicians, physicians! Other thoughts include movie stars, sports heroes, principals and teachers, crossing guards, postal workers, waiters and waitresses, artists, chefs, kings and queens, surfers, aerobics instructors, soldiers, and circus performers. Activities may include fishing, climbing, dancing, singing, or throwing a ball.

3. **Demonstrate** the formation of the clay figure with a ping-pong ball-size portion of clay.

▲ Figure 7-3. In this little corner, we have a man, a dog, and a duck. The man sits on a park bench and feeds a duck, while the dog observes it all. Recycled toy trees and flowers grow in this most mystical place. Time seems to stand still.

   a. Divide clay in half. Use one half for the base of the figure. The base may simply be a flattened circle or any other shape on which the figure will rest.

   b. The figure(s) will be formed from the other half of clay. Roll a small oval for the head, a larger oval for the torso. Attach the head to the torso with a toothpick (adjust toothpick to size).

   c. Roll coils for arms and legs. Attach to torso with toothpicks. Bend, twist, or shape the various sections of the figure into the action desired.

   d. Attach the "action" figure to the base with toothpicks. Use extra clay to create any additional "props" needed to convey the action or occupation of the figure.

4. Distribute all sculptural materials, withholding painting and drawing supplies. Students will follow clay-building methods for their calacas as demonstrated by the teacher. Remember to include the base. Extra clay provides such "accessories" such as hats, pets, musical instruments, and so forth. Let dry.

5. Distribute drawing and painting materials, scraps, and glue. With black fine-tipped permanent pen, students will indicate skeletal markings, such as ribs, spine, arm and leg bones, as well as skull features. **Note:** If teacher has elected to enclose figure in a small box form, now is the time to assemble with the figure.

◀ Figure 7-4. This happy bride and groom remind us that we may want to create non-skeletal calacas. It is a happy occasion that occurs in this retablo-like box.

6. Paint surroundings and objects, leaving the calacas figure mainly white. Bright colors may be used for accents on the figure, yet the "bone-quality" of the white should prevail.

7. Students' calacas may be gathered as they are done for "The Day of the Dead" in Mexico. Set up figures in an appointed area that may be complemented by tissue, flowers, doilies, and even fake food if available. Your art classroom now has an installation called an "ofrenda" or offering—where one may find calacas and other whimsical creations.

Figure 7-5. We never promised that calavara (or skulls) would *not* be scary. This "Lord of the Underworld," or "King of Death," appears with the characteristic open-mouth expression that suggests *"El Grito"* or *"The Cry,"* sometimes performed in festival activities. Papier-mâché is a popular Mexican craft material. However, actual "sugar skulls" are made and sold to the delight of one and all, especially the children who seem to enjoy seeing their names written in icing on the sugar skulls. Again, the early introduction of mortality in Mexico seems a healthy alternative to the avoidance of the subject. ▶

DOUBLE BONUS : BINGO! *LOTERIA* MEXICO!

Loteria (LOO-ter-ee-a) is a game in Mexico enjoyed by young and old alike. Considered a form of Bingo, Loteria traditionally has 54 numbered picture cards along with the *tablas,* which are the gameboards. The equivalent of Bingo chips are "rooster tokens," used in the same manner; there are repeated images that will match the pictures on the board. Loteria is so much more than a lively game . . . it is a printed art form in its own right. The objects, animals, and people used for Loteria cards appear particularly Mexican, based on the iconography of art and artists past and present. For example, *El Corazon* (see page 232) is shown not as a sweet little candy heart—it is, in fact, the bleeding heart of *El Corazon Sangrante,* a visually powerful icon to represent both the visceral organ that it is and the container of human hopes, dreams, and desires.

Loteria favors a simple and clean image. Yet, Mexican interpretation of everyday objects seems somehow mysterious. The *La Escalera* (or the ladder, see page 232), often found in Surrealist paintings, seems to have no means of support. Where is it going? We don't know. Other symbols include the hand (mano), skull (calavara), earth (el mundo), spider (la arana), and deer (el venado)—a symbol found in the paintings of Frida Kahlo. The term *magical realism* is often used to describe the writing, photography, filmmaking, and other visual arts of Mexico. Loteria cards use many of the same references as are found in *milagros* (see page 251). Other inspirations come from the immediate environment, commercial printing in the tradition of Mexican artist, Jose Guadalupe Posado, and from the people themselves.

Students will create a *tabla* along with matching picture cards (see the illustrations). It is highly recommended that the Spanish words appear on the cards; numbers are optional. The amount of cards and boards made are discretionary; our hope is for students to use the Spanish language and better understand Mexican imagery. Teachers may use a variety of visual sources (beyond those that appear here) for the cards: painting reproductions, food labels, postage stamps, currency, and photographs. Remember to keep a card looking like a card! Focus on a single object, one at a time. Colored markers are recommended. Remember, it's not whether you win or lose, but how you "draw" the game that counts!

DOUBLE BONUS : "LA CATRINA" AND "EL ZAPATISTA"
DANCING PUPPETS

A graphic artist named Jose Guadalupe Posada (1852–1913) helped to popularize the Day of the Dead fiesta through his political satire and humorous illustrations of droll scenes, events, and characters. Posada, called "the Artist of the People" by Diego Rivera, developed leaflets called *Calaveras* (translated as *skulls*) which contained witty poems, epitaphs, and sayings. These handbills were given out as favors for the living "dead" celebrants! The festival has a human side, a ghoulish side—and a strong sense of humor.

It was Posado who created the character of *La Catrina,* who appears as a grand lady in all her glorious folly, wearing a big, overly decorated hat. There were many other personalities that Posado popularized as well. His *El Zapatista* portrays a fearless revolutionary. The so-called *Zapatistas* were followers of a hero named Emiliano Zapato, who led a grassroots movement. The soldiers in his army were *campasinos* or "country people" who were defending the right to a fair distribution of the land they farmed. This puppet characterizes the look of a *Zapatista.*

On the following page these two Day-of-the-Dead stars are offered as articulated puppets. Students may change and embellish them after joining their bones at spots indicated with paper fasteners. Add musical instruments and fashion accessories as desired. Sticks may be added to the backs of the puppets so that they, too, can dance the night away! These traditional paper puppets are sold in city markets and are often pictured playing musical instruments. (**Note:** If two or more individual puppets are desired, please use page 234 templates accordingly.)

PAN DE LOS MUERTOS
(Bread for the Dead)

1-1/2 cups of flour	1/2 cup of sugar
1 teaspoon of salt	1 tablespoon of anise seed
2 packets of dry yeast	1/2 cup of milk
1/2 cup of water	1/2 cup of butter
4 eggs	3 to 4 1/2 cups of flour

1. Mix all dry ingredients together except the flour.

2. In a small pan, heat the milk, the water, and the butter. Add the liquid mixture to the dry mixture.

3. Beat well.

4. Mix in the eggs and 1-1/2 cups of flour. Beat well.

5. Put in the rest of the flour, little by little.

6. Knead the mixture on a floured board for 9 to 10 minutes.

7. Put the dough in a greased bowl, cover with a towel, and allow it to rise in a warm area until it has doubled in size (about an hour and a half at sea level).

8. Punch the dough down and reshape it with some "bone" shapes on top to decorate it.

9. Let it rise another hour.

10. Bake at 350°F for about 40 minutes.

11. After baking, sprinkle the bread with confectioner's sugar and colored sugar.

LA CATRINA AND EL ZAPATISTA PUPPET PATTERNS

ACTIVITY 2

The Popol Vuh: Picture Codes of Mexico

Gods, Goddesses, and Glorious Myth/Big Book Covers of the Codices

BONUS: JAGUAR KNIGHT: VIVA EL TIGRE! FULL-SCALE PAPER MASK

The history of ancient Mexico is most powerfully conveyed by the art and architecture that is still very much a part of Mexico today. To better understand the mythology and beliefs of pre-Hispanic Mexico, we are fortunate to have illustrated stories, accompanied by *pictoglyphs*. These are called *codices*. These important books contain pictorial records of vast civilizations that thrived before the Spanish conquest of Mexico in the 1500s. Not unlike the workshops and manuscript and illumination guilds of Medieval Europe, highly trained artisans or scribes would have been especially selected to depict the images that would appear in the handmade books during these early times.

Perhaps the most compelling codices reveal the central cosmologies from which great empires grew. The Popol Vuh (poh-pohl-VOO) of the Maya is a fantastic codex revealing a creation myth that explains how the world came to be. The Popol Vuh reveals a sacred ballgame—the ball represents the sun as it crosses the sky. Ancient heroes of the story include the figure of "The Grandmother of Night and Day," "The Twins," "Hummingbird," "Deer," "Owl," "Rabbit," and, of course, "Hunter" and "Jaguar." Great floods and many other catastrophic events occur until

▲ Figure 7-6. In this student's codex, we find two jaguar knights protecting a very important princess. She holds her hand in a stylized gesture that typifies the art of the Maya and Aztec. Male figures flank the central throne of the princess. The entire design is most certainly symmetrical, which is key to understanding the artistic design used in the Americas. Symmetry is a foundation for art and architecture. Compositional balance is important in codices as elsewhere. Great care has been given to the detail of the costumes and features of this book cover. The linear style of Maya and Aztec art is respected.

miracles allow corn to grow and the Earth becomes a safe place for the sun to rise. The codices served many purposes throughout Mexican history: classic text, prophecies, scriptures, history, astronomy, key events, tributes, and rules and regulations . . . hence, the codes and rules of behavior in society were also conveyed.

◀ Figure 7-7. Glyphic and terrific! This codex truly simulates an archaeological find. Here we see the pictographic content of the codex along with the glyphic symbols that represent words and sounds. Often seen in ancient American manuscript and wall art are the representations of speech indicated as small scrolls coming out of the mouth of the speaker. The "Flowering Breath" is a device that looks like as a cloud formation around the mouth of a figure, almost appearing as a beautiful source for the "cartoon balloon"! The Mayan/Aztec people had a wonderful sense of poetry and have left records of their lyrics for the modern world to contemplate.

235

The Aztecs, the most powerful civilization in Mesoamerica in the fourteenth century, kept elaborate records. The gods and goddesses who controlled all things on Earth, and below, and beyond were very clearly identified by Aztec artists and artisans. Most important is the Aztec god of Creation, Learning, and the Wind, Quetzalcoatl (KET-zahl-KWAH-tul), whose name means "feathered serpent," a benevolent god who created and protected humankind. The Aztec codices were composed of picture-writing with a dot system to represent numbers. It was predicted that the plumed serpent King Quetzalcoatl would return to Earth in the calendar year 1519 to the capital city Tenochtitlan (tay-NOTCH-teet-LAHN), present-day Mexico City. The mighty Montezuma, ruler of the Aztec Empire, welcomed Hernando Cortez, Spanish nobleman conqueror, believing him to be the reincarnated Quetzalcoatl coming back to protect the people as was prophesied by the Calendar of the Fifth Sun. The rest is history: Spain conquered the Aztec Empire and sadly destroyed almost all of the existing codices. Sometime later, a Spanish governor in Mexico, named Mendosa, ordered a codex to be produced as a record of sixteenth-century life in Mexico. These pictures often depict the styles of clothing, architectural plans, furniture, weaponry, ceremonial garb, and everyday details of Mexican life. The codices that appear after the Spanish conquest seem to serve more as a recorded document, while the earlier Mayan/Aztec codices allow us to know the colorful mythology and origins of ancient Mexico.

◄ Figure 7-8. Original codices, or painted books, were made by folding fig bark paper or other book surfaces into an accordion shape. Traditionally, the covers would appear at the ends, mounted onto thin wood boards. Of course, ours is a book of covers, in which every page is as important as the next, with its own unique artistic composition. This student's work indicates a scene of dramatic proportion. Eagle warrior grips the arm of a seated figure. The rest of the meaning is a good topic for discussion!

MATERIALS

- 18" × 24" white paper
- 18" × 24" posterboard
- watercolor/tempera paint (optional)
- glue
- pencils
- scissors

- fine-line markers
- colored pencils (red, yellow, green, turquoise, black, and brown)
- 3" transparent mailing tape
- reproducible pages: "Aztec Gods and Goddesses" and "Pictoglyphs and Their Meanings"

TEACHER PREPARATION

You are about to enter the mystical world of Ancient Mexican myth where you might encounter Quetzalcoatl—the "Plumed Serpent," son of the "Cloud Serpent," who helped to form all life on Earth. Do watch out for "Smoking Mirror" (Tezcatlipoca), the warrior god, enemy of the good god Quetzalcoatl. Smoking Mirror had magical powers and was absolutely up to no good. A case in point was when Smoking Mirror fooled the kindly Quetzalcoatl into thinking that his youth and power were gone when a view of a tired old man was offered to him in the evil, magic mirror. This is only one way in which the warrior god Tezcatlipoca attempted—and later failed—to overthrow the throne of wisdom and kindness, that of the feather serpent Quetzalcoatl.

The story snippet just told is the kind that one may have read in ancient folded books called *codices*. In the code called Popol Vuh, the Maya tell, among other things, their origin stories. There are many codices, many civilizations, and certainly many stories. The teacher may want to acquire some of the children's stories available in picture books that illustrate and tell ancient Mexican myths and legends. The Aztecs have tales to tell, even about their own journey into Mexico. It seems that a Sun God named The Hummingbird Wizard told the people to leave their homeland and to wander until they saw an eagle eating a snake while sitting on a spiny cactus . . . this is but one version of a familiar legend. (See the reproducibles on page 239 for Aztec Gods and Goddesses and Pictoglyphs on page 240—make available to students.)

The teacher should be prepared to start a story that will stimulate students' imaginations when this lesson is introduced. Students will be illustrating book covers in the style of many Aztec pictographs found in codices. It may also help to simply mention or list names—such as Moon Jaguar, Smoke Monkey, Hummingbird Wizard, Grandmother of the Night, The Twins. (Refer to the introduction paragraph for other names.) Encourage student visualization of story illustration. Also see the full-page illustrations of Aztec gods and goddesses. The teacher will find this lesson to be a wonderful combination of fact and fiction: Students will be able to use references of ancient Mexican gods and goddesses while inventing heroes and villains of their own.

Colored pencils are very effective for this lesson, and the colors listed under materials are quite faithful to those in codices. Essentially students will be illustrating a legendary scene of their own using the reference and format of a codex. Mounted on posterboard (one per student), the completed pictographic covers will be joined together to form one BIG accordion-pleated book. Plan to leave an area available in the classroom for this monumental display.

Jaguar

Hummingbird

DIRECTIONS

1. "Set the ancient Mexican stage" for students' pictorial storytelling. Ask students where they might find a "Hummingbird Wizard" and who might be in the picture with him/her? What would they be doing? Would it be ceremonial, ordinary, or very magical? If one of these ancient Mexican characters is important, how would we know? Questions like these are certain to help students picture illustration ideas.

2. Show visual examples of Maya/Aztec illustrations on hand. (Reproducibles are handy at this time.)

3. Distribute drawing pencils and white paper. *Hold paper horizontally!* Students will begin their compositions by either dividing the page into large compartments or by simply inserting a border outline. Keep in mind that many of the figures appear in profile and that symmetrical placement was valued by these ancient people. If students have a fairly good fix on the characters and scenes they wish to portray, preliminary drawing will begin.

4. When ready, distribute colored pencils and fine-tipped markers and any other drawing media desired according to the materials list. Remind students of the colors favored by ancient Mexican codex artists. Students block in their compositions.

5. Students are now becoming scribes. No need to dash through these illustrations; they are, after all, codices (cover art) that should be made to last. Students may also begin articulating the borders with glyphic signs and symbols. These motifs may also be products of students' own imaginations and drawn from the elements within their main picture theme. Glyphs may simply be carrots and rabbits—or spotted fur hearts to represent jaguar knights!

▲ Figure 7-9. The graphic black-and-white appearance of this codex illustration allows us to appreciate the originality each student brings to a lesson. Easily influenced by Inca design, this illustration reminds us that as artists we are free to mix Maya, Aztec, and Inca design elements to come up with our own bold statement.

6. When pictures and borders have been fully completed, posterboards, glue, and tape may be distributed. With the help of the teacher, students will mount their codex covers with glue onto assorted posterboards. Cut lengths of transparent tape to join one student's coverboard to another—partnership really counts here. Number of boards that can stand freely when joined together is probably six to eight—but do experiment! An oversized accordion book is being formed.

7. Display this great work of classroom myth and mythology, glyphs and pictographs, stories and legends wherever you can. As they might have said in the Popol Vuh . . . it's your universe after all!

AZTEC GODS AND GODDESSES

Xochiquetzal
Goddess of flowers, love, and beauty

Quetzalcoatl
God of wind

Tezcatlipoca
God of warriors

Huitzilopochtli
Sungod and god of war

Chalchiuhtlicue
Goddess of water

Xilonen
Goddess of corn

PICTOGLYPHS AND THEIR MEANINGS

crocodile
cocodrilo
Cipactli

wind
viento
Ehécatl

eagle
águila
Quauhtli

house or home
casa
Calli

lizard
lagartija
Cuetzpallin

snake or serpent
serpiento
Cóatl

jaguar
tigre
Océlotl

deer
venado
Mázatl

rabbit
conejo
Ozomatli

water
aqua
Atl

dog
perro
Itzcuintli

monkey
mono
Ozomatli

grass
yerba
Malinalli

flower
flor
Xóchitl

movement or motion
movimiento
Ollin

Note: Words appear first in English, then in Spanish, and finally in Native Aztec language. Pictoglyphs may also represent Aztec day signs.

BONUS : JAGUAR KNIGHT: VIVA EL TIGRE! FULL-SCALE PAPER MASK

Jaguar, a creature of both day and night, is considered at the top of the "most powerful" forces in Mesoamerica! Jaguar is quick, smart, fierce, brave, and cunning. These desirable qualities would be especially valued by warrior knights. Jaguar is also considered a creature of transformation. In one ancient Aztec myth, the fearsome being Tezcatlipoca (tess-caht-lee-POH-kah)—god of the night—disguised himself as a jaguar. In a battle with Quetzalcoatl—god of knowledge and wind—this Night god was struck and fell into the water. According to legend, Tezecathpoca changed into a jaguar! The idea of transformation from human to animal is a strongly held element in Mesoamerican thought and belief. With jaguar in particular, warriors aspire to this animal's distinctive qualities. There are ceremonies held by shaman, who are considered healers and wise men, that attempt to evoke the jaguar spirit. Men who participate in these ceremonies seem to turn into the jaguar that growls, crawls, and sees in the night!

What fun for students to turn themselves into jaguars—without an elaborate ceremony! First, we must consider the appearance of a jaguar, not to be confused with a leopard, yet looking very much the same except larger. Jaguar or "El Tigre" (Spanish) is a big cat with yellowish fur and distinguishing black spots. It helps to have picture references on hand of jaguars, which are found from the southwestern United States to Argentina. Students will be "transforming" into jaguars with simple grocery bags from the local supermarket (avoid printed bags). The El Tigre costume that students will be crafting may be considered a shield-like mask. You will also need yarn, scissors, crayons, markers, construction paper, and glue.

First, approximate the jaguar face by using the bag flap and marking the place where each student's eyes will fit—in order to see in both night and day. The other cat features will be interpreted by students who will also plan for the later addition of yarn whiskers. Students will use markers and crayons to suggest the yellow jaguar fur in an all-over manner applied to the bag. Add jaguar spots. Delineate features with markers and accent any other details, for example, the coat of fur. Using construction paper, cut jaguar ears and attach to top of jaguar's head. Yarn whiskers may now be glued in accordance to feature placement. Even though jaguars are mostly independent animals, our jaguar knights will band together. Wouldn't it make a *mucho grande* statement about the transformation powers of art to have our students slip into their jaguar "selves" and form a moving display? Jaguar knights on parade make a powerful sight for any occasion!

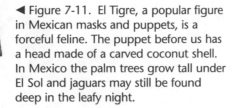

◀ Figure 7-11. El Tigre, a popular figure in Mexican masks and puppets, is a forceful feline. The puppet before us has a head made of a carved coconut shell. In Mexico the palm trees grow tall under El Sol and jaguars may still be found deep in the leafy night.

▲ Figure 7-10. Andreas, smiling with the grin of a big cat, proudly displays his own personal jaguar identity. Once inside the mask, Andreas would not be so easy to find!

ACTIVITY 3

Big Time! The Aztec Calendar

Oversized Paper Sundial/Signs and Symbols/Self-Portrait

BONUS: "CROWN" OF MONTEZUMA!

Figure 7-12. In the "Land of the Fifth Sun," this student is at the hub of the animal world. Monkeys and dogs and snakes appear alongside this moon-like face. Decoration and motif create an illusion of movement that enhances the student's calendar stone.

The Aztecs believed that they lived in The Fifth Sun and last creation of the world—as defined by a huge ancient calendar. Each creation was represented by a sun, since solar movement maintained human life. The stone calendars were monolithic! While Aztec calendars appear in codices, the authoritative command of a 24-ton stone calendar cannot be ignored! The days in a calendar numbered 365. The Aztecs based their sun disk on the Mayan calendar where the first date noted is 3372 B.C. The Mayan knowledge of astronomy and the nature of cyclical time, along with mathematical systems, was truly astounding. It was the Maya, after all, who first understood the concept of *zero*!

By the time the calendar stone was in use by the Aztecs, its effectiveness had grown uncanny. Everything seems to be predicted and revealed in the stone's iconography. It stated when the Aztec world began, how long it would continue in its cycle—and exactly when it would meet its predictable end. Actually, the Mayan sun disk was two calendars in one—incorporating seasonal changes and harvest times along with ceremonial dates and special celebrations. Two wheels comprised the ritual calendar—the large one for months, the small one for the days. All calendar dates would come together, turning like three wheels, at 52 years—thus marking a 52-year Mayan century. There were 365 days in both the Mayan and Aztec calendars, five of which were regarded as unlucky. During these "nothing days," arguments could last forever and bad fortune might be hard to undo. Festivals, offerings, and ceremonies helped people ward off the unlucky. Similar measures were taken to prevent the end of time when the 52-year calendar cycle reached conclusion; the gods must be appeased so that a cycle may begin again. Calendar symbolism was taken very seriously by all. In fact, the calendar stone is the representative symbol of Aztec and Mayan cosmology. Ancient Mexicans viewed time in terms of creation and destruction—two cyclical, yet interdependent opposites. At the time of the Spanish conquest by Hernando Cortez in 1519, the Aztec believed they were living in the fifth and final era, which the gods had predicted 535 years earlier. With the Spanish invasion of Mexico, the Aztec world did indeed come to an end. However, the heritage and contribution of past civilizations have a living history that far outweighs the markings of recorded time.

Figure 7-13. Our young artist strongly conveys a sense of what she wants, needs, and desires. The symbol she has created in her calendar stone include a cozy home, the acquisition of wealth, the hope for peace—and a skull shape that symbolizes the coexistence of life and death. This calendar stone mysteriously glows. ▶

MATERIALS

- brown kraft paper (see Teacher Preparation)
- metallic foil paper
- construction paper (miscellaneous colors)
- markers
- string (see Teacher Preparation)

- pencils
- tempera paint
- markers
- scissors
- brushes
- glue

TEACHER PREPARATION

Students will be creating their own big Aztec calendar stone self-portrait! The teacher will want to precut enough lengths of kraft paper to accommodate all students. The scale of the paper should be determined by its width (example, 36"); thus the size of the calendar surface will be established. Paired students will cut their own circle by turning into a human compass (see step 2). For this purpose, precut lengths of string will be needed. Other materials to have on hand are metallic foil paper and colored construction paper remnants, along with other materials listed.

DIRECTIONS

1. The teacher will discuss with students the design and purpose of the Aztec calendar disk—or "Stone of the Sun" as it is known today. Essentially the calendar stone contains concentric circles into which signs and symbols are placed. Whose face appears in the middle of the stone? Is it a king or a queen? Is it a Sun or Earth face? Actually, it could be either or both. Why don't we place ourselves in the center of the universe! Note that the signs and symbols that appear on the calendar disk represent various aspects of the world (see the illustration for the center part of the calendar disk).

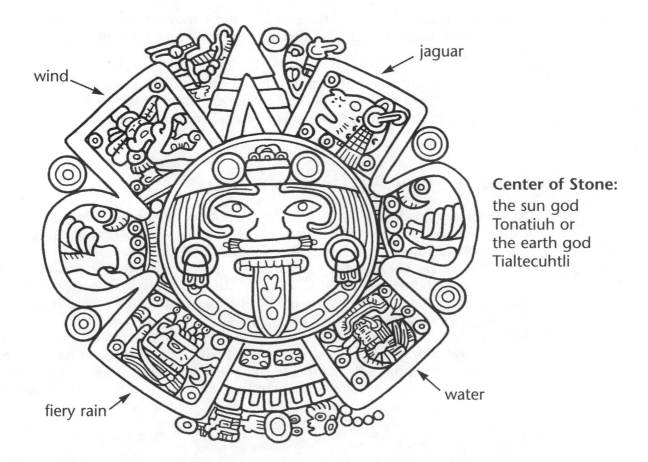

wind

jaguar

Center of Stone:
the sun god
Tonatiuh or
the earth god
Tialtecuhtli

fiery rain

water

2. Distribute kraft paper lengths, along with string, scissors, and pencils. In order to establish a circle format, two students will form a human compass! First fold the paper into quarters to form a center mark where the folds cross. Use a length of string that measures less than half the diameter of the paper. Students will tie the end of the string to a pencil. For the next step, two students will work together in establishing the "stone" calendar circle.

3. One student will hold the free end of the string in the center of the paper while the other student moves like a clock around the outside edge of the paper—marking with pencil as he/she follows the circular rotation. When the circle is complete, cut out. **Note:** The teacher may use other standard methods for cutting an (oversized) circle if preferred.

4. Students will return to their individual "stones" after assisting one another. The circle in the middle is reserved for the student's portrait; save for later.

5. Students will draw the number of concentric rings desired—simplicity is honored. A wide "X" formation behind the portrait circle will conform to calendar stone design. Students may also include "sun points." Once the framework for the design is established, discuss the nature of the students' portrait ideas along with the accompanying symbols they plan to use. (Refer to the reproducible in Activity 2 for the pictoglyphs and their meanings.)

6. Discuss what a self-portrait may reveal about a student's own likes and dislikes, hopes and fears, or wishes. Students will learn that the Aztec stone portrait has a pointy tongue that they may want to incorporate as well. The four sections of the "X" formation will contain pictorial elements selected by students.

7. Distribute all other supplies. Students will define the visual elements of their portrait with paints and markers. Other calendar stone elements may be set in the stone circle. Decorative motifs may also be used.

8. A crowning finish for the calendar stone may be comprised of alternating foil patterns to create a radiating design. This is, after all, the "Stone of the Fifth Sun."

9. Completed Aztec calendar disks should create quite a spectacle! There's nothing like being at the center of the universe and have all time revolve around you. Another day in the life of a smart young hero. Isn't it just about time?!

BONUS : CROWN OF MONTEZUMA

Montezuma (also Moctezuma) was the great Aztec ruler who held his post in the capital empire city of Tenochtitlan, which is now Mexico City. As was the case with all Aztec rulers, Montezuma was also the *tlatoani*, which means "the speaker." Montezuma was not the only Aztec ruler in the history of the Aztec nation, which existed from about A.D. 1345–1521. During this relatively short period of time, the Aztecs built a vast empire—yet were beset by a prophecy of doom. It was during the reign of Montezuma II that Hernando Cortez arrived (1519–1521), thus fulfilling the prophecy in a most unexpected way. Montezuma II mistook Cortez to be the returning of the god Quetzalcoatl (feathered serpent)—as was prophesied by the Aztec calendar. Montezuma II gave the Spanish nobleman Cortez the most precious gift of all: a headdress made of the rare iridescent feathers of the *Quetzal* bird. It was a gesture that would signify a transfer of power from the Aztec to the Spanish that—after a bloody war—would end the Aztec empire forever.

In his days of glory, Montezuma II dressed splendidly! Only nobles were entitled to wear gold, turquoise, and other elaborate accouterments. Most exquisite of all was the brilliant headdress made from the feathers of hundreds of birds. The bigger the headdress, the more important the wearer. Nothing was more telling of the high rank of a ruler than a headdress worn with great splendor.

Many say it's good to be the king or queen. We will have an opportunity to find out how important it feels to wear the Aztec crown. You will need large oaktag, scissors, oil pastels, assorted colored feathers, gold glitter, pencils, glue, and stapler (yarn is optional). Students will fold oaktag in half and draw a simple horseshoe shape with stair-stepped edges that ends with a crowning top—an inverted pyramid shape. Cut and open. Distribute drawing materials—provide feather and glitter as lesson advances. Students may now select a theme for their headdress that will reflect their power (see Aztec chart on page 239). Motif should reflect theme; for example, if student chooses to be the king of rain and lightning, the "Montezuma crown" will convey these elements. Crowns should be richly colored and geometric as well as complemented by individual motifs. Students will try on their crowns and adjust accordingly. When satisfied, add headband loop and staple in place. There's no question about it—your students have become instant VIPs of the ancient Americas.

▲ Figure 7-14. Who is this mysterious Aztec? She is Carla, otherwise known as Xochiquetzal, goddess of beauty, love, flowers, and all growing things. Her name means feather-flower, but Carla came up with the carrots on her own. Xochiquetzal was the protector of craftworkers and artisans. With a crown like this, who would doubt it.

◄ Figure 7-15. This trio of ancient aristocrats rightfully shows off their ornamental stature.

ACTIVITY 4

Ladies and Gentlemen of Ancient Mexico: A Classic Clay Society

Ancient Mexican Clay Figures

BONUS: OLMEC CRYBABIES AND CHOCOLATE POTS . . . AND MEXICAN DOGS DANCE!

▲ Figure 7-16. Jewelry created by a student who converted little balls of clay into circular hoop earrings with matching necklace, topped off by a hat clip. The hat or large headband was a sign of importance—size indicated status. A short cape (quechquemitl) is a fashion must. Braided hair would also reflect social standing.

The Teotihucan (te-oh-tah-WAH-can) people lived in the valley of Mexico between 100 B.C. and A.D. 700. In A.D. 500, Teotihuca was at the height of its imperial power: a great religious, cultural, and political center with an advanced economic system. The society of this great city was clearly defined by its nobles, priests, politicians, potters, weavers, sculptors, warriors, farmers, and trade-laborers. Here was the home of *The Pyramid of the Sun, The Temple of Agriculture,* and *The Pyramid of Quetzalcoatl*—the benevolent plumed serpent god—in Teotihuca. By A.D. 750, Teotihuca became a big "ghost town," an abandoned site. The rise and fall of Teotihuca was honored by the Aztec, who discovered these monumental ruins and considered them sacred.

Many great and awesome societies existed before the arrival of the Europeans. The *Olmec* society, which is sometimes known as the "Mother Culture" of all Mesoamerica, began in A.D. 1500 . . . 150 years before Egyptian King Tut! The Olmec people were fond of a ballgame similar to soccer for which they used protective sports gear. Along with their development of a crude writing system and the construction of ceremonial centers, the Olmec are best known through the *colossal stone heads* that honored their leaders. Who can resist the stone Olmec babies with their little jaguar faces?

The Maya and the Aztec were said to be the Greeks and Romans of the New World. They were the "empire builders" of Mesoamerica. The Maya are known for their mythologies, mathematics, picture-writing, development of calendar systems, and, of course, their art and architecture. Clay works are still being unearthed in tombs that help explain "who was who" in the Mayan physical and spiritual world—the kings, the queens, the artists . . . how they looked and what they wore. Although Mayan society is still in evidence today, the ancient Maya were overthrown by the Aztecs. A long journey of "forty generations" was kept by the Aztecs in search of their "city in the lake"—Tenochtitlan. This chosen place became their home as a result of an ancient message that predicted the sight of an eagle landing on a prickly pear cactus on an island in a lake. Their civilization was built around the heart of Tenochtitlan—a grand-scale city replete with ball courts, great temples, and a place of trade. The reputation of extraordinary Mexican craft and art was further advanced by the production of pottery, carvings, textiles, jewelry, and baskets available for export. Tenochtitlan was the "Venice of the Americas"! Clothing and hairstyles, along with "accessories," identified an individual's position in the greater society. The Aztec were as socially conscious as any other civilization. Nobility and wealth would be reflected by elaborate necklaces, heavy earrings, nose spools, and other ornaments. Jewelry was decorative and protective as well as

▲ Figure 7-17. Boy, what a ballplayer! This clay fellow seems to have survived many a rough game. Small marks in the clay indicate pattern while giving visual variety to the piece. Note the knee pads.

intended to bring greater power to the wearer. It was a serious crime for everyday people to wear the garments of those of greater status. Gold, silver, and precious stones were the mark of knights, nobles, and rulers. Fabulous feather headdresses and even masks distinguished the Aztec VIP from the ordinary person. Of course, hairstyle would tell another story about one's place and would be defined by appearance—whether a woman was married or whether a boy had become a warrior. The texture of the clothing itself made a whole other fashion statement. What a person wore in Mexican history would be worn forever in a clay likeness. The sculptures and carvings that represent individuals from years past also commemorated their place in society—leaving little chance for a wardrobe change. As they say, it was all cast in stone!

MATERIALS

- clay (see Teacher Preparation)
- pencils
- templates (see Teacher Preparation)
- rolling pins
- modeling tools (see Teacher Preparation)

- colored pastels: turquoise, red, white, earth tones
- oaktag (see Teacher Preparation)
- paper towels

TEACHER PREPARATION

Terra-cotta clay is recommended if authenticity of materials used by Mayan and Teotihucan society is desired. Air-dried or kiln-fired clay may be used according to discretion. Clay tools may range from standard wooden sticks to tongue depressors to toothbrushes, combs, toothpicks, and pencils to vary the textures of the clay clothing.

Oaktag may be used to cover desks when clay slab instruction will take place, for which rolling pins are needed. Otherwise, follow usual clay procedures. The teacher will use the templates provided here to construct clay figures. For display material suggestion, see step 9.

DIRECTIONS

1. Discuss the various roles held by people in classic Mayan and Teotihucan societies. Stress that each person's job was important and that work and play were valued in life. For example, the ball court was a central element of ancient Mexico. The sports heroes would wear certain uniforms, recovered from ancient ruins, which would make sense for a ballplayer to wear. Noble ladies wore more elaborate clothing marked by jewelry and headdresses. How would students feel about creating these two classic clay figures in art today?

2. Distribute cueball-sized portions of clay to each student along with all other materials listed, except for the pastels. Students will place clay on oaktag, press flat, and roll out slab with rolling pin to about 1/2" thickness.

3. Distribute templates. Students will place the template onto their clay. Using selected clay tool, students will follow the outline of the template by pressing the tool through the thickness of clay. Remove figure (students write their name on back) and retain excess clay.

4. Students will roll a small portion of clay to form the building of the figure's face. Join clay head to slab with usual clay method. Pinch out features.

5. With the spare clay, students plan and make specific figures' wardrobe! Female figures will need a good-sized hat and some jewelry—don't forget her little shoes. Ballplayer appreciates protective gear: helmet, kneepads, strong belt, and gloves or mitts.

6. Add texture to suggest design motifs and feeling of fabric. Hair may be plaited. Keep capes in mind for the Teotihucan or Mayan lady. Ballplayer may proudly show heroic "wear and tear" through textural markings.

7. Let dry (Bisque fire if kiln is used).

8. Distribute pastels when piece is ready. Students will rub pastel colors onto clay surfaces. **Note:** Important colors were turquoise, red, white, and earth tones. Distribute paper towels to remove excess chalk.

9. A great way to display these important ancient figures is to build a pyramid by stacking available boxes that may be covered with colored paper. Place the Mayan and Teotihucan personalities on each "pyramid" step (against a wall or backdrop that will support them) and enjoy an *ancient* fashion show.

BONUS : OLMEC CRYBABIES AND CHOCOLATE POTS . . . AND MEXICAN DOGS DANCE!

Fat little stone "babies" and colossal basalt heads appeared in ancient Mexico during the early Olmec civilization. The faces of the Olmec babies are somehow curious—they seem to have cat-like features. This zoomorphic quality is intentional, for the Olmec stone baby—known as *were-jaguar*—is a combination of jaguar and human. In the Olmec society, babies were believed to have special powers and an ability to communicate favorably with the ancestors—at least until they developed language skills. The jaguar, with its strength and bravery, was the most highly regarded creature in ancient Mexico. Put the two together . . . a "jaguar baby" is transformed by stone or clay.

Students will enjoy making these small transformation figures in clay. A lively discussion about human babies will precede the lesson. How do babies express themselves? Cry, pout, laugh, yawn, put their fingers in their mouths, rub their eyes, or simply smile contentedly. Do babies have anything in common with jaguars? Both travel on "all fours"—they both crawl, don't they? A jaguar and human baby sit on their "hind legs," open their arms (for different purposes), and reach up and stretch. Of course, there are many traits not necessarily shared. For example, jaguars and babies make different sounds. Be sure to discuss the cat's facial features—how do we describe the face of a big cat . . . turned-down nose and turned-up mouth? Oblique angle of the cat's eye? Pet cats at home will help students to define feline features—many students should volunteer descriptions of their "Snowball" or "Fluffy." Pictures of babies and felines on hand are sure to inspire, including students' own baby pictures!

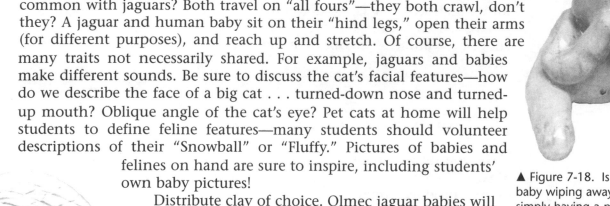

▲ Figure 7-18. Is our jaguar baby wiping away a tear, or simply having a pensive moment? Either way, it's all in a baby jaguar's day.

Distribute clay of choice. Olmec jaguar babies will be formed by rolling out two balls—one for the round-bellied body and the other for the oversized head; arms and legs may be made of fat coils. Clay tools will help to delineate jaguar features. Students may include necks and extra rolls of baby fat! The jaguar aspect of the clay figure may appreciate pointy ears. Students will add their own touches.

Completed jaguar babies will be as cute as any nursery can be. Display together in a showcase to brag about your babies!

▲ Figure 7-19. A miniature "colossal" head pops up to remind us that all crybabies shown here are inspired by the Olmec civilization. This figure, too, wears the helmet of a ruler or hero.

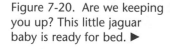

Figure 7-20. Are we keeping you up? This little jaguar baby is ready for bed. ▶

AND THE CHOCOLATE POT . . .

In the Mayan Popol Vuh, an important sacred text, it is said that . . . "Every clay pot has its own soul." The Maya were skilled artisans who captured the spirit of their civilization in distinctive pottery forms. The discovery of classic Mayan jars shows clay vessels with tubular handles—often with glyphic inscriptions. One such vessel is the chocolate jar, used to contain the precious CA-CA-WA (cocoa). Chocolate was a valuable commodity in the Americas, along with corn. Workers, artists, and nobility enjoyed chocolate in much the same way chocolate treats are devoured by many of us today. "Lord Chocolate" (Ah Cacas) reigned in Tikal, the largest and most prestigious Mayan city from 1682–731 B.C. The ruins at Tikal may still be seen today in Guatemala.

▲ Figure 7-21. These chocolate pots appear as iridescent as the feather of the rare *Quetzal* bird—or are they lined in gold? Chocolate is the sweet reward for a shiny and beautiful pot.

Students will enjoy designing a chocolate jar for Lord Chocolate or any other "Resplendent Person"—the glyphic title for Mayan king. Use a simple basket design for the clay object. A pinch pot with a rolled coil attached will do just fine. If the teacher wishes to supervise glazing, inscriptions or glyphs can be incorporated. Our jars do not have lids, yet the Maya wisely created a "locked top" for their chocolate jars, no doubt understanding how often chocolate jars may be robbed! Dried and/or kiln-fired glazed chocolate pots may be filled with wrapped chocolate candies, thus bringing archaeological meaning to this Mayan candy dish.

. . . AND MEXICAN DOGS DANCE!

Have you ever seen two dancing dogs? In the late pre-classic period of ancient Mexico, *Colima* dogs may be found dancing, playing, or guarding treasures. The often-reproduced images of the dancing dogs shows two dogs that seem to be lost in the music. Other dogs seem as fierce as jaguars. It was believed that dogs had powers to protect the lords of the underworld. The dog we see here in the illustration, with its spotted fur, would discourage any intruders. Note the bared teeth. Students may be inspired by these Mexican dogs and may want to try a clay dog effigy of their own.

▲ Figure 7-23. Everything about this guard dog seems to spell ATTACK: the curled tail, the poised position of the hind legs with ears drawn back, and those fearsome pointed canine teeth!

▲ Figure 7-22. "Shall we tango down to Argentina?" asks the dog to his dancing partner. These dogs make the clay dance.

ACTIVITY 5

SLIDE 29

Milagros and Retablos: Small Miracles of Tin Art

Tin Frames/Milagros

Mexico is a place where craft magically becomes art. The art of Mexico is the product of a rich and vibrant mixture of cultural influences. Artist Frida Kahlo grew up in the land of vivid colors, tropical birds, monkeys, and floating gardens—along with an abundance of textiles, pottery, amulets, jewelry, and fine miniature craftworks. Frida Kahlo's heritage flows through her paintings, which often show Frida in traditional folkloric Mexican fashion. She was partial to the styles of the Tehuantepec (te-WAHN-to-pec) of Oaxoca (wah-HAH-cah), a state in Mexico with an intense feeling for artistic expression. Frida loved elaborate costuming and embraced Mexican traditions. Frida herself, like Mexico, was of multiple heritage. Her beloved father was an Hungarian-Jewish

▲ Figures 7-24a and 7-24b. Our beautiful young artist deserves a place of honor in a retablo designed with a most suitable motif. The palette seems to be filled with flowers—art is a growing thing. ▼

photographer and her mother of Mexican-Indian descent. Frida's European-Catholic background fused with ancient American symbolism in her work, thus providing us with a unique Mexican vision.

Frida fully absorbed the arts and crafts that surrounded her. One folk art form with which Frida seemed to particularly identify was that of the *retablo*. By definition, a Mexican retablo—with its roots in Spanish Catholicism—is a tin painting that serves as evidence of gratitude for a "miracle" or an answered prayer. A typical retablo offering may be painted for a doctor, a saint, an angel, or any person who helped save or heal one's malady or misfortune. Writing would often appear on the painting as part of the thanks that would be given. This object is a form of a *votive* or *ex-voto*. Frames, when used, may be simple or detailed. Retablos may also appear as three-dimensional altars that open and shut with decorative panels. Retablos may be made of tin, wood, even shells.

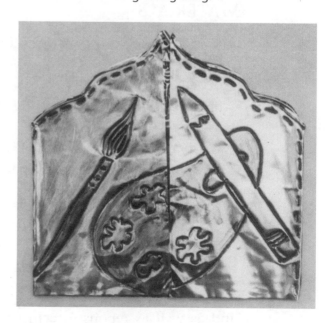

The word *milagro* (me-lahg-grows) is Spanish for miracle. Small metallic objects or charms, often found pinned to the skirts of saints in churches, have earned the name milagro. These shiny objects, often made of silver or tin, depict symbolic items such as corn, clothing, or specific animals as well as the moon and the stars. A common milagro would appear as a heart (*corazon*), hand, or eyes: Parts of the body, such as a leg, are often seen as a means to promote healing.

The milagro is one with the votive retablo: It is a means of bringing good fortune, while acknowledging one's appreciation. Milagros may indeed be seen in combination with retablo art.

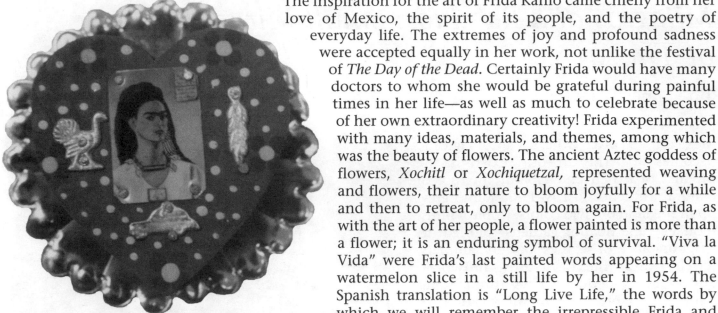

The inspiration for the art of Frida Kahlo came chiefly from her love of Mexico, the spirit of its people, and the poetry of everyday life. The extremes of joy and profound sadness were accepted equally in her work, not unlike the festival of *The Day of the Dead*. Certainly Frida would have many doctors to whom she would be grateful during painful times in her life—as well as much to celebrate because of her own extraordinary creativity! Frida experimented with many ideas, materials, and themes, among which was the beauty of flowers. The ancient Aztec goddess of flowers, *Xochitl* or *Xochiquetzal*, represented weaving and flowers, their nature to bloom joyfully for a while and then to retreat, only to bloom again. For Frida, as with the art of her people, a flower painted is more than a flower; it is an enduring symbol of survival. "Viva la Vida" were Frida's last painted words appearing on a watermelon slice in a still life by her in 1954. The Spanish translation is "Long Live Life," the words by which we will remember the irrepressible Frida and embrace the spirit of Mexico.

▲ Figure 7-25. Made by an artist to honor another artist, this original piece is a combination of retablo and milagro. In the center is Frida Kahlo, who is accompanied by several lucky milagros, and decorated with amulets. The wood is painted.

MATERIALS

- 6" × 12" newsprint paper (see Teacher Preparation)
- pencils
- lightweight aluminum tooling foil (see Teacher Preparation)
- scissors
- stack of folded newspapers (per student)
- masking tape

- nontoxic permanent colored markers
- brushes
- black drawing ink (optional, see Teacher Preparation)
- paper towels
- photograph (see Teacher Preparation)
- glue

TEACHER PREPARATION

This lesson will require lightweight aluminum tooling foil that is used for craft activities of this kind as well as repoussé techniques. Our tin retablo lesson will in fact be made from this aluminum material. The teacher will want to supervise the cutting process carefully so that students are not harmed by sharp edges. Likewise, black drawing ink, which is intended to create an antique patina, will require teacher supervision. It will stain and should be used with upper elementary and middle school classes. Inking should be conducted in a specific work station established by the teacher (near sink, if possible). Newsprint paper will be used to create templates for frames and for the transfer of design from paper to aluminum.

Cut newsprint to 6" × 12" lengths. If newsprint is not available, substitute with lightweight paper. Paper should be sized to scale of aluminum—teacher will precut length of aluminum tooling foil to accommodate each student's frame.

Note: This lesson will teach students how to make a frame with opening and closing panels which will honor anyone they wish, including themselves. A photograph may be used for this purpose; however, students may opt to draw a portrait. Students should begin looking for a photo of a friend or family member or even images that students find suitable for framing, such as baseball cards or reproductions of famous artists (the teacher may contribute these). Magazines will provide other possibilities.

Figure 7-26. Would you like an alternative to the finely crafted aluminum tooled foil, standing "tin" retablo? The S.O.S. is a sheet of oaktag on which a portrait has been drawn in oil pastel. The frame is made from humble heavy-duty aluminum foil found on the grocery shelf. Another way to create surface interest is by applying white glue with the dispenser to create a linear pattern; let harden. Retablos, like people, come in many wonderful shapes and forms. ▶

DIRECTIONS

1. Discuss the meaning of the retablo—also called *nicho,* which is considered a portable memento. Using the shapes appearing in Figures 7-24a and 7-24b, demonstrate—either on paper or chalkboard—the retablo format (open and closed) that will be used. It is important to mention that students may create variations on this shape. For a paper demonstration of retablo, the teacher should use the 6" × 12" newsprint as an example:

   - Find center, fold two ends to center to create the panels.
   - Fold again at center.
   - Cut the "roof" of the retablo to a pleasing point.
   - Open. A retablo shape should be in place.

2. Distribute newsprint, pencils, and scissors. Using the method described, students will create their own paper retablo template.

3. Discuss design motifs with students before beginning to draw designs on the template. What are some themes that will carry the feeling of the photo of the person to be honored? The retablo shown here reflects an interest in art and flowers. Now is the time to remember that a space should be marked for the later insertion of the photo. Students will design motifs for retablos on newsprint templates.

4. Distribute lightweight aluminum tooling foil and newspaper stacks. Place decorated newsprint retablo template on length of aluminum foil. Tape the paper template to foil to secure in place. Place taped paper and foil unit onto newspaper stack.

5. This is the step where the design will be transferred from newsprint to foil. Using pencil, press firmly over existing motif. Be sure to remember also to outline the "roof" on paper template. **Note:** Do NOT cut foil yet!

6. Distribute permanent colored markers. Remove newsprint template from foil and begin color application to "tin" frame. Once interior of retablo is complete, turn retablo on other side and color doors only (interior design will have transferred to front panels). Return retablo to original position.

7. Before the foil retablo shape is cut, an ink patina may be applied (this step is optional). The teacher will set up a station where a very small amount of black ink is brushed across the foil surface and quickly removed with a paper towel. Let dry. Ink that remains will create an antique effect.

8. Using scissors, students will CAREFULLY cut out the "roof" line of the retablo—watch out for points and sharp edges. Fold doors.

9. What's missing? The person whom this retablo is intended to honor. Students will retrieve their selected photos and glue in the center of the retablo frame. **Note:** Precious photos should come with permission from home or simply be photocopied and hand-colored for framing.

10. The *nicho* retablos do require their own niche. Since they are portable, they are sure to bring joy wherever they go.

◄ Figures 7-27a and 7-27b. These authentic milagros, crafted by Mexican artisans, exemplify the power of the symbol. These tin-crafted images are intended to protect and assure the wearer and may be placed anywhere that seems appropriate. Here we have Mexican "heart and hand" . . . "el corazon y la mano." ►

ACTIVITY 6

The Ancient Andes Is Still Tops: Tip Your Hat to Peru!

Textile Arts/Four-Cornered Paper Hats

BONUS: AMIGOS OF THE AMERICAS: A FRIENDLY MIX . . . "AMIGO" DOLL PINS

Peru is at the heart of a vast Andean culture that reaches as far back as 8600 B.C.! Even back that far, in those ancient days, textiles were woven by a civilization that would come to be known generally as the Inca. The country of Peru—in South America with its capital city of Cuzco—governed a vast empire uninterrupted until the Spanish conquest in the sixteenth century A.D. Within this ancient Andean civilization grew several important and distinctive cultures: the Chavin, Nasca, Moche, and Inca. Geographically, the Andean region—with the Moche on the north coast and the Nasca to the south—extended to Colombia, Ecuador, Chile, and Bolivia. The Andes, along with the flow of the great Amazon river, are the two great natural aspects of the South American continent. It was in the Andes, specifically Peru, where a textile tradition like no other emerged. To the Inca, textiles were no less precious than gold!

Weaving and dying fabric is a specialty of the region, passed down from century to century. Think about how important the concept of weaving is to the cosmology and belief systems of the Americas. Goddesses and gods charged with the creation of the universe are frequently seen as weavers. The idea of the "fabric of life" comes from the sense that all in existence has been woven intricately together. It is not accidental that the loom, the thread, the stitch, the pattern all bring meaning to the creative process of life. Weaving is associated with birth, changing nautical cycles, healing, and life itself. Inca textiles go beyond the skill and craft of the beautifully presented fabric article—they function as fragments of mythology, woven records in a society with no writing system and are representations of social standing. In fact, the tunics, hats, and capes (*lliclli*) serve as evidence of their culture as they perform both ceremonial and utilitarian functions.

▲ Figure 7-28. The four corner peaks of the Andean hat declare its unique personality. The peaks themselves suggest animal ears, perhaps a cat or llama. If there are four ears, then there may be two animals represented by the hat appearance! The hats shown here display the use of mathematically repeated designs favored in Peruvian textile arts. Note the "Pyramid of the Sun" hat at the right.

▲ Figure 7-29. Symmetry in hat form and pattern is as solid as a magnificent pyramid as Machu Picchu.

255

Textile art rules in the domain of the Andean people! Multiple patterning, reversals, checkerboards, ziggurats, and the geometry of the woven cloth is truly astounding. Peruvian textiles offer a means of understanding the many arts of the ancient American cultures. Textiles were used to wrap mummy bundles in the Chavin culture; tapestries marked the code of an emperor. Symbolic animals and specific motifs suggest ancient meanings. To know the architecture and mathematics of the Andean civilizations, turn your attention to the patterns of a poncho and you will find a pyramid!

Even the most modest mountain community seems to have a splendid sense of fashion. One essential clothing element is the Andean hat. This whimsical and practical item appears in a variety of spirited shapes. The traditional *"pancake"* hat, emblazoned with colorful yarn, is favored by mountain dwellers. The *Chullo,* a knitted cap, is sometimes worn beneath the "pancake." Variations of the *Chullo*—with its familiar earflaps—have found their way into the winter wear of the USA! What would otherwise appear as a man's English Bowler hat is seen in and around Peru and Bolivia particularly on women, usually with a pigtail peeking out below! The Andean hat variety is delightfully endless. The heartbreaker is the Andean four-cornered hat: Tassels or pointed knots mark each corner. These four-cornered hats with their tapestry patterns even appear on ancient clay effigy figures, thus securing their place in the textile history of the Andes. The hats are as solid as any four-walled architectural structure, roof included—with perky little peaks. The materials from which the hats were produced include the basics of tapestry makings, as well as featherwork and rug design. Hats may or may not have deep pile. Once again, a hat with four corners may proclaim authority of the weaver, yet the design and use—even though researched—are still up for interpretation and imagination. Hats off to . . . four-cornered Andean hats!

MATERIALS

- 12" × 12" assorted colored construction paper (see Teacher Preparation)
- pencils
- rulers
- templates
- oil pastels (see Teacher Preparation)
- white glue
- masking tape
- scissors
- 9" × 12" manila practice paper
- yarn, pompoms, fuzzy pipe cleaners (optional, see Teacher Preparation)
- reproducible page: "Peruvian Patterns"

TEACHER PREPARATION

Each student will be making his or her own four-cornered Andean hat for which a template will be needed (refer to scaled-down template shown on page 256). The teacher will enlarge the given template pattern to fit a 12" × 12" sheet of colored construction paper. The teacher may want to cut template to its shape, depending on the students' capabilities.

These hats will combine design with geometry and architecture—think of hats as wide paper pyramids for student head gear. The four corners of the Andean hats are topped with points or tassels. This lesson will conform to the "animal ear" style; however, the teacher may substitute the paper points with tassels, pom-poms, yarn, pipe cleaners, or any other ornamental materials. Four-cornered Andean hats are made from textiles and, for this reason, we will use oil pastels on construction paper, which provide the feeling of textural surface. However, if visual clarity of design is the goal, substitute with colored markers.

The teacher will want to make Peruvian design samples (see the introductory photos) available for this lesson. It is strongly suggested that the teacher create a finished product of the four-cornered Andean hat in advance of class.

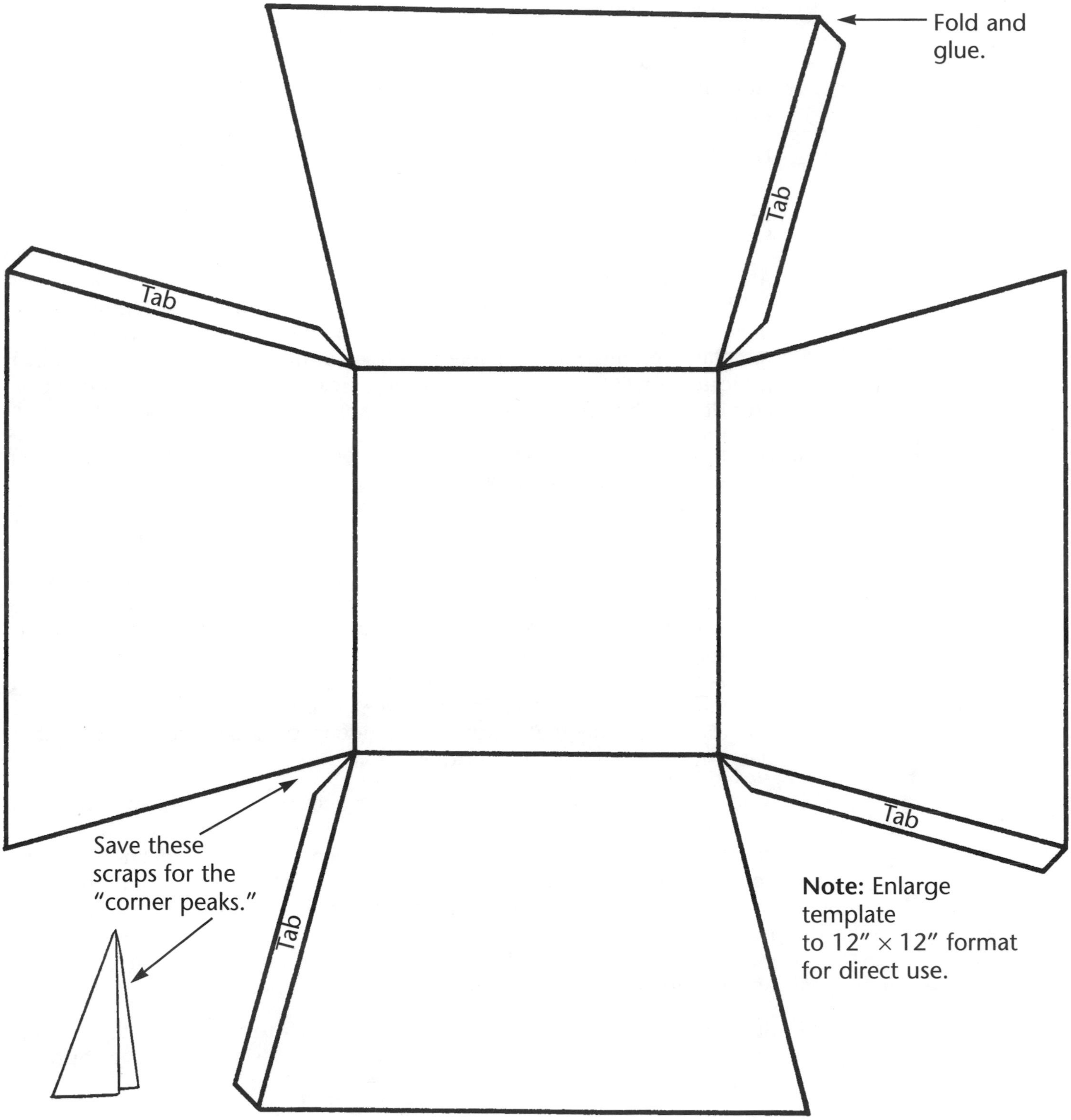

Fold and glue.

Tab

Tab

Tab

Tab

Save these scraps for the "corner peaks."

Note: Enlarge template to 12" × 12" format for direct use.

DIRECTIONS

1. Have examples of Peruvian designs on hand (see the reference illustrations) to begin discussion about four-cornered hat design. Students will note the geometric nature of design motifs which seem in many cases to conform with a "block" design. Students will see how bird, figure, and animal representations can be suggested with abstracted geometric patterns. Let students know that they will be constructing a hat that will stand as proud as a pyramid—only much more colorfully!

2. Distribute manila paper, pencils, and rulers. Students will practice hat design geometry by dividing their practice paper into sections with the ruler. Simple divisions of squares into which patterns will be placed is a good warm-up for the hat activity.

3. Are we ready for the real Andean deal? Distribute templates, adjusted to 12" × 12" size, along with assorted colored construction paper. Templates that have not been precut by teacher should now be cut out by student. Place template on construction paper and trace outline with pencil. **Note:** Areas indicated for TAB will not receive design treatment—designs should end on area defined by dotted line. Remove template from work area.

4. A simple four-squared grid drawn from one edge of the hat to the other, repeated on both sides, will provide a simple guideline for geometric patterning that students will develop for hat design. This pencil line will guide the balance of symmetry favored in Andean art and architecture.

5. Distribute oil pastels (or markers). Students will begin design constructing the center block, which will become the top of the hat. It is best to have a plan for the manner in which individual pattern motifs will appear. For example, if a large "X" grid is used for the top-center, one might plan to use checkerboard pattern grids on the two opposite sides—alternating with design bands on the remaining two sides. This is not mandated; however, it is a design structure that is fun to try. Students should be free to design their hats with motif alternatives of their choice.

6. Students will have selected motifs from reference materials provided as well as using their own ideas for symbols. Diamond patterning, as well as checkerboard and block grids, are very popular for Andean hats. Also consider sawtooth, stair-step, split-triangle, fish hook, and pointed-star patterns. The key concept in creating a four-cornered Andean design is *repetition*—with simple geometric patterns. Remember, the geometric patterns may be simply decoration or may be based on human, plant, or animal forms—llamas and alpacas, Andean animals, are often represented.

7. Students will use oil pastels in a "wooly" manner to suggest the tapestry-like quality of Andean hat design. When the overall design covers the entire hat surface, hat will be ready for assemblage.

8. Distribute scissors, white glue, and masking tape. Students will cut out the hat form—be sure to *save the corner scraps*! Apply "just enough" glue to TAB areas, fold, and glue TAB areas to hat sections. Close four sides of hat together. The teacher may want to help students reinforce inside hat seams with fitted lengths of masking tape.

PERUVIAN PATTERNS

9. The scraps you saved will define this colorful construction as a *true* Andean hat. Students will fold scraps in half lengthwise to form *triangular hat corner peaks* (see template). Repeat folding and cutting until four triangular peaks have been shaped. Students will "borrow" a design element and color from their hat to decorate the peaks, which will blend with the hat form and motif when joined to the four corners at the top of the hat. Glue bottom of triangle discreetly to outside corner of the hat on all four sides. Be sure the hat peaks dry upright. **Note:** Teachers who wish to use alternative materials such as pompoms, yarn, pipe cleaners, or tissue may experiment with application to hat corners at this time.

10. Hats are made for wearing. Students will want to show off their spirited four-cornered Andean hats—and why not? Any Inca would be honored to wear these "up-to-the-minute" yet ancient designer statements. Fashion prediction: Watch these hats!

BONUS : AMIGOS OF THE AMERICAS: A FRIENDLY MIX . . . "AMIGO" AND "AMIGA" DOLL PINS

▲ Figure 7-30. Three new friends for a young girl are tokens of affection that will not soon be forgotten.

The Americas are rich in resources, both natural and artistic. Mexico, from ancient to modern times, has gifted the world with an eternal flow of art and craft that amazes and inspires. One cannot think of Guatemala, Mexico's neighbor to the south, without picturing an explosion of brilliant color. Streets and marketplaces are filled with gorgeous purples, vivid reds—and blues, greens, and yellows the colors of tropical birds. This classic Mayan region extends through Belize and Honduras. A tradition of art and craft that has existed for thousands of years continues south through other Central American countries . . . Nicaragua, Costa Rica, and to Panama, after which the continent of South America begins. These great artistic riches and resources fully inhabit the continent of South America, right down to the tip of Tierra del Fuego!

In South America we have the cultures of the Andes and of the Amazon—mountain, river, rainforest. Environmental diversity has an inseparable relationship with the arts of the Americas, in all regions. Animals provide the wool for the textiles, tree branches become sculpted figures, stone transforms into monumental carvings, feathers of birds become headdresses, and—although reserved for *Resplendent Persons*—turquoise, gold, and other precious metals abound. Wouldn't it be a fine idea to honor our American amigos with friendship dolls that combine the crafts for which the arts of the Americas have been rightfully recognized? All that is needed for the Amigo pins are wooden clothespins (the one-piece, nonspring type), lightweight paper (optional, geometric giftwrap), markers, glue, scissors, recycled doll hair (substitute yarn), and pin backs sold in bulk in hobby stores (may substitute safety pins). We will be crafting simple little figures that will be wrapped in a "textile" of choice manufactured by the students' own hands on a small paper square (if appropriate, gift paper patterns are available—go for it).

Have you ever made "a friend at first sight"? These little amigos and amigas (friends) are just that kind of a doll—to be made spontaneously. Mark simple faces and apply patterned paper (either student's own or commercial) around clothespin form. Attach pin back to reverse side of clothespin and glue. **Note:** Teacher may want to make sample patterns available to students to help with their handmade paper textile ideas.

It's a quick lesson, but a very friendly one indeed. It is hoped that students will appreciate, through the joy of their own handiwork, the happy combination of "textile-patterned paper" and wood put to good use. "A pin in need is a friend indeed."

▲ Figure 7-31. Friendship doll pins with all their finery seem to be in chatty conversation that one might observe in a Guatemalan marketplace.

◄ Figure 7-32. A rag doll from Ecuador with a sweet/sad little face reminds us that a simple serape may be created by folding a paper rectangle, cutting a hole for the neck, and slipping it over the neck of a friendship doll. We hope his friends come along to join him soon.

▲ Figure 7-33. Here we may have the luckiest doll in South America. This souvenir figure is armed with lucky charms and amulets that represent life's basic needs and wants—all tied around his neck in little bags. He has it all—corn, herbal medicine, rich soil for planting, and, of course, a thousand-dollar bill extends below. He wears a knitted wool cap and seems to be announcing his wares. Lucky guy also provides us with ideas for further embellishing our friendship dolls. Feel free to add play money and charms.

261

ACTIVITY 7
Rainforest Molas: The Art of Ecology From Panama to Brazil

The Paper Mola with a Message

▲ Figure 7-34. A poignant paper mola crafted by a young artist from Springfield, PA. Captured in art only, this "lounging lizard" is having its moment in treasured, familiar surroundings—the rainforest home. Every creature plays its role in the living network we call Earth.

BONUS: THE BIRDS OF BRAZIL: PAPER RELIEF FOR THE AMAZON

The Pan American highway runs from Alaska to the very tip of South America, except for one section in lower Panama. There lies the thickest and most impenetrable rainforest of all the Americas—the Darien Rainforest. The nearby hub of Panama City seems worlds away. Panama, the narrowest country in Central America, provides passage between the Pacific and Atlantic Oceans through its canal. Panama is also home to the Kuna Indians of the San Blas islands—a group of at least 350 islands—in the Caribbean Seas. These indigenous tribal Americans have proudly protected their Panama homeland, called *Kuna Yala*, "Land of the Kuna." Kuna Indians have become known to the world through their extraordinary fabric appliqué art known generally as *Mola*—literally meaning "blouse." Up until the sixteenth century, when Spanish explorers first sailed along the Caribbean coast of Panama, Kuna women excelled in body painting design. These brightly colored paintings drew upon the features of their rich environment—animals, birds, fish, flowers, along with sacred and protective symbols and designs. Characteristic "skinny cigar shapes" vertically accompany the figures, creating dazzling visual vibrations! Molas today represent the transfer of body painting to fabric art, a direct result of moral codes imposed upon the Kuna Indians by Europeans. The protection of both tradition and environment remains a vital topic in today's world.

The narrow land bridge of Panama ends where the country of Colombia begins. We are now in the expansive continent of South America, where the world's largest rainforest is found, covering 2.5 million square miles, chiefly in the countries of Bolivia, Peru, Colombia, Venezuela, and, of course, *Brazil*! The Amazon, both a river and rainforest, possesses nearly two thirds of the world's living plant and animal species—along with a multitude of mineral reserves. This extraordinary tropical rainforest in Brazil may be regarded as the "lungs" of the planet Earth. The trees provide a worldwide supply of oxygen to help us all breathe easier—along with hosting thousands of medicinal plants that remain to be

Figure 7-35. An original cloth reverse-appliqué mola produced by a Kuna artist in San Blas, Panama. Note the unifying, yet stimulating effect of the vertical "skinny cigar" element. The composition of the mola is that of "form within form." Without the critical repetitive motif, a mola just isn't a mola—at least traditionally speaking.

discovered as we search for critically needed cures. The Amazon supports nature's biggest pharmacy! It is the epicenter of **biodiversity.** This great rainforest, the Earth's single greatest resource of species and forest life, however, is being destroyed at a hideously alarming rate.

The Amazon is the living home to the remaining tribal people who have inhabited this region since "the first sunrise." Portuguese explorer Pedro Alvares Cabral landed in Brazil in 1500 in what is now the Afro–Brazilian state of Bahia. At that time, there were millions of American Indians living in the Amazon Valley. Brazil itself, with its primary language of Portuguese, is a population of "The Three Powers": Indian, African, and Portuguese/European. The Amazon belongs to the Native Indian societies, very few of whom are left to defend it. Principally it is the Yanomani, an otherwise secluded society, that have come forward to protest the destruction of their natural home. Yanomani means *"human being"* in the language of these people, members of the largest indigenous tribe of the Amazon, who are now threatened with extinction. Yanomani philosophy and belief are consistent with the Native-American conscience: Tradition is sacred and all people are linked to the fate of the planet and its inhabitants. To destroy our environment is equal to destroying ourselves. Wherever a rainforest thrives—whether in Brazil, Panama, Costa Rica—we thrive, too. All creatures are precious and—as Native Indian

▲ Figure 7-36. Aren't they adorable? Who would harm them? These cute little tree dwellers need their trees—another reason why the tree is so often called by many cultures "the tree of life." Deforestation of the rainforest gives concern to one and all. We want to keep the tree sloth smiling.

beliefs suggest—it is our job to preserve them.

MATERIALS

- 12" × 18" black construction paper
- 12" × 18" white paper
- 12" × 18" assorted colored construction paper (see Teacher Preparation)
- glue sticks

- scissors and/or X-acto™ knives (see Teacher Preparation)
- pencils
- cutting boards to protect tables (see Teacher Preparation)
- reproducible page: "The Five-Step Paper Mola"

TEACHER PREPARATION

This activity is recommended for grades 4 and up; *use of X-acto™ knives is intended only for upper grades under strict teacher supervision!* **Note:** The danger of X-acto™ blades as sharp cutting tools must be taken seriously. These tools should be used in situations where teachers are completely confident that students will not harm themselves or others with the knives. Some school districts require signed parent permission before use of blades, which are then signed in and out by the teacher in the art room. For the use of X-acto™ blades, solid classroom management is a must. If an accident should occur, send student to nurse, retrieve blade with rubber gloves, and discard appropriately. The substitution of scissors is endorsed if X-acto™ use is not suited to grade or specific teaching population. Include protective boards or newspaper sections to protect desk surfaces when using these knives.

▲ Figure 7-37. Not all molas need to be pictorial, for many are symbolic in appearance. Mola designs include labyrinth maze formations, simple and complex geometrics, as well as abstractions that represent nature.

Mola art is bright, bold, and highly contrasted. Primary colors work just fine, yet teachers may take this opportunity to convey oppositional color theory, as in the visual effect of complementary colors placed in combination, such as red and green.

The purpose of this lesson is not only to introduce the art of mola, it is also to endorse ecological awareness for students as they learn about their world. Hence, the "message mola"—which could be described as "protest art" for a most worthy cause.

It is strongly recommended that the teacher prepare at least one sample paper mola prior to introduction of lesson. Of course, actual mola art, brought to class, will greatly enhance this experience. **Note:** Any Central and South American rainforest reference and reasearch that teachers and students can obtain will be most helpful when including plant and animal species on molas. There are many wonderful recordings that are found in music and nature stores that capture rainforest sounds and environment, often set to contemporary rhythms. These would be wonderful to play during your rainforest lesson.

DIRECTIONS

1. Discuss the art of the mola as well as Kuna Indian artists who originated this art form. Discuss the themes used for mola design—birds, flowers, plants, animals, and signs and symbols. For rainforest animals, see "Who's Who in the Rainforest" on page 267 for a small sampling! Also, talk about the "message" in the mola and the fact that words are often used as part of mola composition. Note that mola art characteristically contains vertical line systems (we refer to them here as "skinny cigar shapes").

2. Further discussion should focus on possible rainforest themes that will be selected by students, who will simplify their ideas into direct representations. Brainstorm!

3. Demonstrate the basic steps of mola (see the reproducible). Show the finished teacher example (as stated in Teacher Preparation). Pass the finished example around for students to examine the layering technique.

4. Students are ready to begin. Follow the illustrated directions on "The Five-Step Paper Mola."

5. All completed molas should form an ecosystem of their own. The display itself should stimulate awareness and interest in the rainforest and its precious diversity.

HOW TO MAKE A PAPER MOLA

① Create sketch.
Use pencil to draw idea.
Draw big forms.
Include skinny cigar shapes
in open space.

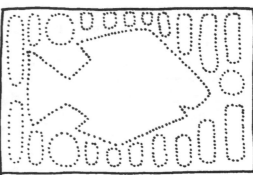

② Select bright color,
such as red.
Use sketch as guide.
Draw outline of shapes.
Use scissors or exacto knife
to cut along dotted lines.
Save scraps for last step.

Teacher:
CAUTION with
this tool!

③ Select second bright color,
such as blue.
Place beneath first color.
Draw smaller shapes
inside larger shapes.
Cut along dotted lines.
Glue beneath first color.

④ Select third bright color,
such as yellow.
Place beneath second color.
Draw detailed designs.
Cut along dotted lines.
Glue beneath second color.

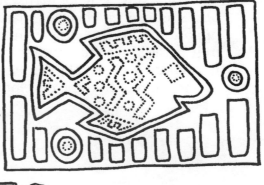

⑤ Select black sheet.
Glue beneath third color.
Use scraps to add details.
Add urgent message.

BONUS : THE BIRDS OF BRAZIL: PAPER RELIEF FOR THE AMAZON

Brilliant Brazil! It is in Rio Janeiro where the greatest carnival on Earth is performed—a spectacular show of flashing light, cacophonous sounds, constant movement, and, of course, the brilliant plumage of costumed pageantry! Although the carnival in Rio is not commonly compared to the Brazilian rainforest, there is an unexpected parallel. One may envision the Amazonian rainforest as a natural spectacle with vibrant lights provided by shifting canopies, the calls of howler monkeys, buzzing insects, and, most important, the extraordinary array of color and rhythmic song of the birds of Brazil.

Students will create a low-relief paper construction that will depict birds in their natural habitat. Yes, birds fly, but they also perch, feed their young, and go fishing! There are so many species from which to select. The focus of this dimensional view is, specifically, birds;

▲ Figure 7-38. Among the birds of Brazil is the Great White Heron. One of Ms. Divine's students in Upper Darby, PA, imagined this touching little scene, complete with waterfall. An elegant paper relief shows the heron in her watery home. Herons are considered acrobatic masters because of their grace, stretch, and agile movement.

however, other species may appear as well. Environmental features such as waterfalls, streams, and rock formations will help define student expressions. Students will need colored construction paper, lightweight board, scissors, pencils, glue, and ends of corrugated boxes to build the relief surface. Plan a simple scene; draw, cut, apply, using sections of cardboard to raise selected forms. **Note:** Watercolor or other drawing media may also be used to complete the rainforest vignette. **Hint:** Teacher may want to acquire field guides that illustrate individual bird species in a checklist manner to help with student choices. This is a great opportunity to study the wonderful diversity of "the world and everything that's in it." It is also a chance to draw attention to our endangered species. This lesson is a standout in all subject areas—science, environment, social studies, geography . . . not to mention the development of a social conscience.

◀ Figure 7-39. Have you ever met a *jacare?* A member of the alligator and crocodile family, it is found in the Amazon and the Pantanal, a swampland in western Brazil. Jacares rarely attack humans unless provoked. This family group portrait is a combination of mola and low relief. The jacares, as you can see, lay eggs and show concern for their young. The *Tupi* Indians gave the name *jacare* to these reptiles, which are threatened by poachers who sell their skins to dealers. The jacares find the piranha, a predatory fish, particularly delicious, which helps to control the population of this often mean-spirited fish!

Figure 7-40. *"You crazy bird"* is the sound of the toucan's repeated cry, which seems to sound to many as an unabashed toucan's declaration! The toucan, which has almost become a mascot of the Amazonian rainforest, seems to beg artistic interpretation. In the sculpture shown, the toucan appears dignified and reserved. Brazilian city children are responsible for this piece and other objects composed of recycled materials of the region. ▶

WHO'S WHO IN THE RAINFOREST : AN ECO-CHECKLIST!

Reptiles/Snakes

Green Iguana

Tree Frog

Red Tegu Lizard

River Turtle

Jacare Alligator

Bushmaster

Anaconda

Boa Constrictor

☑ 2,000 species of fish!

Mammals

Howler Monkey

Spider Monkey

Marmoset

White Face Capuchin

Ocelot

Jaguar

Amazonian Skunk

Tapir

Manatee

Anteater

Sloth

Collared Peccary

Armadillo

☑ 15,000 known animal species!

Birds

Macaw

Toucan

Giant Kingfisher

Parrot

Great White Heron

King Vulture

☑ One quarter of the world's bird species—and 18,000 species of butterfly!

Native America

Greenland Sea

Bering
Sea

Arctic
Ocean

Inupiats

Beaufort
Sea

Baffin
Bay

Aleuts

Yupiks

ARCTIC

Inuits
Gulf of
Alaska

Carrier

Labrador
Sea

Tlingit

Dogrib

Haida
Tsimshian

Chipewyan

Montagnais-Naskapi

Beaver

Hudson
Bay

Bella Coola

Kwakiutl
Salish
Nootka
Cowichan
Makah
Chinook

Tillamook

Tolowa

Kutenai
Dwamish
Yakima
PLATEAU
Wishram
Umatilla
Klamath
Modoc
Bannock

Blood
Blockfoot

Flathead
Nez Perce
Crow
Assibiboine

Piegan

Hidatsa
Mandan
Sioux

Ojibway

Micmac
Abnaki

SUBARCTIC

Cree

North
Pacific
Ocean

Wintun
Yurok
Hupa
Karok Maidu
Yuki
Pomo
Mwok
Yokuts
Salinan
Chumash
Luiseno
Cahuilla
Kamia
Diegueno

Washo

Shoshone

GREAT
Northern
Cheyenne

Winnebago

Ottawa

Huron

Santee
Sioux

Potawatomi

Iroquois

Wampanoag

GREAT
BASIN **Ute**

Oglala
Sioux

Ponca

Iowa

Kickapoo

Narraganset

Mohegan

Miami

Delaware

Paiute

Arapaho

Otoe

Kansa

Illinois

EASTERN

Powhatan

North
Atlantic
Ocean

Jicarilla
Apachee

PLAINS

WOODLANDS

Shawnee

Southern
Cheyenne

Osage

Cherokee

Mohave
Hopi Taos
Acoma

Kiowa
Apachee

Chickasaw Catawba
Chocktaw Upper Creek
Lower Creek

Yuma
Zuni
Navajo
Pueblo

Comanchee

SOUTHEAST

Papago

Pima

Chiricahua
Apachee

Tonkawa
Lipan
Apachee

Natchez Apalachee
Chitimaca

Timucua

Yaqui
Mescalero
Apachee

Calusa

Seminole

SOUTHWEST

MIDDLE
AMERICA

Gulf of
Mexico

Caribbean Sea

NORTHWEST COAST

CALIFORNIA

Native American
Tribes Circa 1650

Native America

Could this be a little clown family? In the pueblo communities, Kachina ceremonies are held as part of the yearly cycle. Koshari is a sacred clown who is an important part of the Kachina festival. Black and white stripes are painted on Koshari and are a highly identifiable visual feature. Mom, Dad, and the kids do not wear the traditional, double-pointed horns worn by Koshari; perhaps they just like stripes! The climbing children do remind us of the lovable storyteller dolls made popular in the Cochiti pueblo of New Mexico.

SOUTHWEST, GREAT PLAINS, NORTHWEST COAST, CANADA, AND ARCTIC

A different trickster, Coyote, was said to have brought shape to the land, according to the Native American legend of the Salish people. There are many Salish tribes in and around the Bitterroot Mountains of the Northwest. This playful child—from the region of Flathead Lake, an area said to be favored by Nature—was photographed by Edward S. Curtis. An acclaimed photographer who was born in 1868, Curtis was known for his commitment to recording and preserving Native American life with his camera. In 1930, Curtis completed a stunning book of photographs entitled *The North American Indian*. Curtis surely captured a universal moment in the day of the life of a happy, healthy child.

ART ACTIVITIES FOR BECOMING CULTURE SMART

■ **Activity 1**
Storyteller, Talk to Me
Multiple Pottery Figure
BONUS: TRADING ALONG THE SANTA FE TRAIL . . . CONCHA BELTS!

Activity 2
The Winter Count: Pictures That Make History
Mixed Media/Pictography/Brown Paper Hides
BONUS: TRAVEL LIGHT WITH PARFLECH LUGGAGE
INCLUDES: "POSSIBLE" BAGS

■ **Activity 3**
The Power of the Clay: Pueblo Pots and Spirit Bowls
Clay/Mixed Media
BONUS: SWEET DREAMCATCHER: CIRCULAR "WEB WEAVING"
INCLUDES: NAVAJO EYEDAZZLERS!

Activity 4
Mudhead! Koshari, Clowns, and Kachinas of the Southwest
Clay Figures
INCLUDES: PAPER KACHINA DANCER
BONUS: LUCKY ANIMALS: PERSONAL CHARM ZUNI NECKLACE

■ **Activity 5**
Raven Invites You to a Potlatch Party!
Chilkat Dance Blanket
BONUS: RAVEN BOX OF DAYLIGHT!

■ **Activity 6**
Once Upon a Walrus Tusk Scrimshaw
Arctic "Prints and Etchings"
BONUS: BLUEBERRY WOMAN: MASKS OF THE NORTH
INCLUDES: PRINTS IN THE SNOW: A STAMPED "ICE-SCAPE"

To know the Art of Native America, Canada, and the Arctic . . . . .

. . . . . one should know that the ancestors of the first North Americans crossed a landbridge at the Bering Straits that linked Siberia to Alaska, marking the beginning of Native America and the establishment of cultures that would grow in areas now known as the Arctic, Canada, and the Americas. Complex networking developed between tribal societies throughout North America—in the Northeast or Woodland; the Southeast, which extended to Florida; the Great Plains; the Southwest, or "four-corners region" (where New Mexico, Utah, Arizona, and Colorado meet); California and the Pacific Northwest; and Canada. Arctic regions are home to Native American Indians as well as Inuit (Eskimo) and Aleut people.

Native American culture is marked by many developments. Early varieties of maize (corn) were being cultivated in the Valley of Mexico. In the American Southwest, agricultural growth was occurring, and the Southwest pueblo pottery traditions also began. Agriculture would spread to the Temple Mound civilization of the Mississippi and Ohio valleys, home to the Hopewells and Adenas. The Hopewells and the Adenas built large earthworks; most were square or circular, but some were shaped like animals. The impressive Great Serpent Mound earthwork runs over 1,200 feet in Ohio and Kentucky.

In many world cultures, there is no word for art. Native Americans hold a holistic view that does not separate art or religion from life. There is a spiritual interconnectedness with nature; rocks, clay, and feathers have meanings that go far beyond their mere physical presence. Above all, *hojho* (harmony) and balance are sought. Much like the aboriginal people of Australia, Native Americans belong to the land. The concepts of Mother Earth and Father Sky suggest responsibility on the part of the children— inhabitants of the land. According to the great Duwamish Chief Sealth (for whom Seattle is named), ". . . every part of this soil is sacred." He asked the U.S. Government, "How can you buy or sell the sky? . . . We do not own the freshness of the air or the sparkle of the water. How can you buy them from us?" The point is further made that those who care for the land take care of one another.

Art begins with idea, vision, and purpose. In Native America, art is everything in life and art is also medicine. Art, as practiced in sandpainting, promotes healing. The Native American universe abounds with art—painting, carving, beading, metal tooling, weaving, sewing, pottery, and mask-making. The arts embody spirit, mythology, tradition, and creative force. From the twisted False Face of the Iroquois to the animal transformation masks of the Haida people of the Northwest, art has many meanings.

Themes and subjects in the Americas, Canada, and the Arctic do share stylistic treatment and motif. In both art and architectural structure, totemic symmetry is favored. The artists of the Pacific Northwest developed an advanced and original system of *ovoid, S-form, U-form,* and *formline* that offers a wider visual lexicon. Pueblo pottery carries a strong geometric tradition forward from the "Ancient Ones." Fanciful and simplified expressions of the plant and animal world appear in painting and dimensional art. The mixing of media is common; for example, incorporation of such materials as hair, feathers, and beads is common—particularly in the dance arts. The linear abbreviation on preset color fields, like those that appear in Kachina dance masks, provides an effect of mystery and drama. Throughout the Americas, animal guardians and totems, nature spirit representation, and combined human and animal forms are omnipresent. The same interests provide sources for design elements—for example, zigzag for lightning, eagle as seminal power symbol, and the multiple split diamonds that create optical effects in the Navajo Eyedazzler rugs.

Inuit art follows that of Native America in its world view. Appearances of carving and printmaking, drawing, engraving, and mask-making does differ in some respects; the use of color in the Arctic is often more subdued and limited, and white is frequently seen on Arctic masks. Minimalization of features is also a traditional Arctic feature.

Art has offered Native America a means of economic recovery. Much art is purchased and collected by interested parties outside of the immediate communities. A wider market for the arts of Native America is opening. In Arctic regions, artists have formed cooperatives under the support of the Canadian government. Recognition of the worth of Native American and Arctic art in its own terms is certainly well deserved.

ACTIVITY 1

Storyteller, Talk to Me

Multiple Pottery Figure

BONUS: TRADING ALONG THE SANTA FE TRAIL . . . CONCHA BELTS!

▲ Figure 8-1. Mother Bear and Father Bear sit the three little bears down for two different versions of the same story. No one is complaining—story variations add to the richness of the tale!

The art of storytelling is as ancient as clay. To pass stories from one generation to another is a means to keep people, places, events, ideas, and legends alive. The Native Americans have added the dimension of clay to oral tradition. Many a "little one" has sat upon a parent's or grandparent's knee to hear a tale before slipping into slumber. Ceramic artists now preserve the storytelling moments in the most charming and endearing ways. The often-seated figures are covered with offsprings: some sleepy, some curious, some attentive . . . others distracted and bored!

The arts of Native Americans are as rich and varied as the people themselves. Storyteller figures are found in certain pueblos of the Southwest United States: the Cochiti Pueblo is where one may most readily encounter storyteller figures. It may come as a surprise to learn that the development of the irresistible storyteller figures is a recent one, with clay artist Helen Cordero at the lead. Helen shaped her first storyteller doll, based on memories of her grandfather, Santiago Quintana, as she remembered him telling stories to the five grandchildren. The year was 1964. Cordero thus launched an entire new genre of Pueblo pottery.

The creativity of Helen Cordero evolved from a long tradition of figurative clay and effigy vessels that have ancient origins in Pueblo Indian civilization. Storytellers in clay may have as their predecessors an ancient sculptural form known as "singing mothers." Instead of a female figure, Cordero used Pueblo men surrounded by children as her inspiration. The male storyteller plays an important role in Pueblo society even today. Happily a large variety of clay figures tell their stories: male, female, animal, and human. Mother owls warn baby owls not to stay up too early! Big turtle tells little turtles of how the world was formed on the back of a turtle shell and how the place we now call The United States was once known as Turtle Island back in the beginning of all time. Much like a teacher, the storyteller gives lessons on life, learning, history, mythology—and throws in some wise and witty insights to help his or her charges to stay tuned! One can only hope the playful children will listen, learn, go to bed, and dream sweet dreams!

MATERIALS

- clay (see Teacher Preparation)
- oaktag
- clay modeling tools (see Teacher Preparation)
- paper towels
- plastic bags (see Teacher Preparation)
- small paintbrushes
- glazes/acrylic paint: earth tones, turquoise, orange, and white
- reproducible page: "Construction of Storyteller Doll"

TEACHER PREPARATION

Wet clay used for modeling is necessary for this lesson, which will take place over several class periods. The teacher will do well to have a kiln-fired final product; however, lack of kiln access should not stop teachers from offering this work activity! Glazing clay appears on Figures 8-1, 8-2, and 8-3, and will enhance the surface of the storyteller figures. Acrylic paints may be substituted. Clay tools, as well as standard modeling methods, will be used in this lesson. Again, the teacher may simply use tongue depressors and plastic tableware. Plastic bags, along with paper towels, will be needed to keep the clay in working order between class sessions. Recommended size: one-quart bags proportionate to individual scale determined by teacher and students. Enough oaktag should be on hand to cover students' individual work space. Visual references are always appreciated along with three-dimensional ones. If there is access to clay storyteller figures, by all means bring them forward for this experience. The teacher should prepare class for a clay lesson. Stations should be set up for glazing, if desired.

▲ Figure 8-2. To which tribe do these two belong? The scene of passing knowledge from one generation to the next through storytelling is as familiar to the tribes of Scotland as they are to the tribal nations of the United States. Note how carefully observed the musculature of the father figure is . . . and how tenderly the child listens. Actually, the kilt is worn as a Native American garment as well.

DIRECTIONS

1. Discuss the history of the Native American storyteller doll which is specific to the Pueblo Indians in New Mexico. Explain to students that seated pottery figures called "storyteller dolls" will be made in clay. Other small figures—the children—will be added. How many students can remember being told a story by an elder—grandparent, great uncle, or even big sister, mom, or dad? Students should consider whether or not their storyteller doll will be an animal or person and plan to have at least one figure attached to it.

2. Using the directions shown on reproducible page 274, demonstrate the formation of a clay storyteller figure. Distribute clay materials (excluding glazes/acrylics) to students. Using construction techniques from Step 1 through Step 4 on the reproducible page, students will create a seated figure. Clay tools will aid in delineating features. Students will use standard additive and subtractive methods to develop the form—hair, boots, vests, hats, shawls, and jewelry. **Note:** For animal storyteller figures, add ears, tails, paws, and so forth.

3. Unless the teacher has an extended art period, students will store wet clay figures by wrapping a damp paper towel carefully over the forms. Slip a plastic bag down carefully to the base of the figure and tuck ends under to prevent air from entering and to keep the piece moist.

4. When ready to resume clay modeling, remove the plastic bag and paper towel. Ask, "What good is a story, if no one is there to listen?" Students will create "miniature" versions of the larger figure already formed. It is best to place each small figure as close to the large figure as possible to avoid breakage. Keep a variety of body gestures in mind for the little ones. (See Section 7, Activity 4, **Bonus,** for starter ideas.) See Step 7 on the reproducible page. Let dry. (Use kiln for firing the clay if safely available to classroom art teacher.)

CONSTRUCTION OF STORYTELLER DOLL

① Roll clay into the shape of a hotdog.

② Squeeze top of clay to separate head from body.

③ Cut slit for legs with popsicle stick. Smooth edges.

④ Pinch bottom of legs to form feet.

⑤ Roll coils for arms and attach.

⑥ Bend legs into seated position.

⑦ Make babies using same method. Attach to storyteller doll.

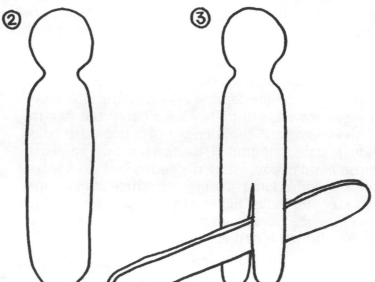
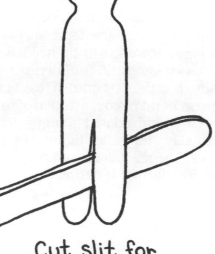
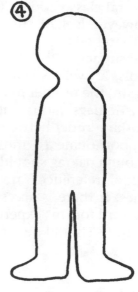
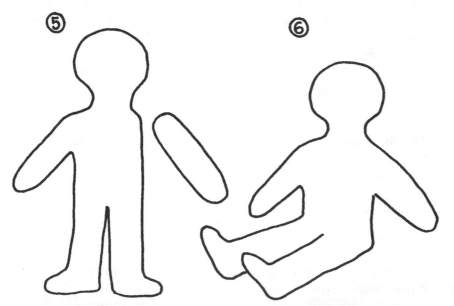
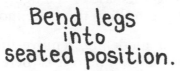

5. Air-dried and/or kiln-fired clay figures are now ready for su
   as well as details. Acrylic paints may now be applied to d
   under supervision of the teacher, may be applied to
   (acrylic paints will work here, too). The teacher will f
   figures according to standard kiln requirements.

6. The oral tradition is once again preserved in clay. Yet,
   would allow storyteller figures to keep company with cl
   that tell special stories of Native American life and traditi

BONUS : TRADING ALONG THE SANTA FE TRAIL . . . CONCHA BELTS

It was the influence of Mexicans who lived in New Mexico and Arizona—the "Four Corners" region—that enriched Navajo and Pueblo silversmithing. The Native American craftspeople were quick to process ideas that came from Mexico, Spain, and their own powerful creativity. Out of the artistic versatility displayed by Native Americans in the Southwest, many original and appealing objects were developed. One of the most outstanding of these was the *concha* belt. Concha is the Spanish word for "shell." Metalsmithing was learned and mastered so competently that objects "found a market" along trade routes. The Santa Fe Trail, which went from Santa Fe, New Mexico, to Independence, Missouri, during 1821 to 1880, provided artists with an outlet for their hand-tooled concha belts. These beautiful, shiny belts are as prized today as they were in those early days.

▲ Figure 8-3. One on the head, one in the lap, and one little boy stretched across his feet . . . this storytelling dad doll has his hands full! Children surround him, almost forming a totem pole. The family resemblance is clearly present. Note the haircuts.

The classroom version of the concha may be made simply by covering large oval shapes of cardboard with craft foil, then incising designs into the foil with a pencil. Two notches are made in the center of the ovals, held horizontally, into which a strip of cut black felt is threaded. Concha belts are sized to each student's waist and tied in the back. Consider making a miniature concha belt (or two) to fit the storyteller doll that you just made! It makes sense while trading stories to wear "belts of trade."

◀ Figure 8-4. Exquisite student-made concha belt mixes quite well with the glyphs on her bright T-shirt.

ACTIVITY 2

The Winter Count: Pictures That Make History

Mixed Media / Pictography / Brown Paper Hides

BONUS: TRAVEL LIGHT WITH PARFLECH LUGGAGE

INCLUDES: "POSSIBLE" BAGS

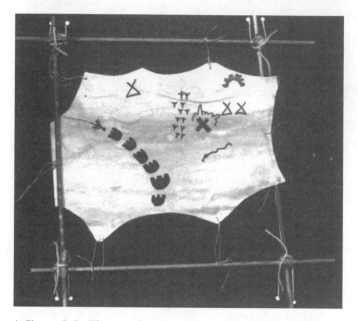

▲ Figure 8-5. The art of understatement is at play on this handsomely displayed paper rawhide account. Perhaps this story records an encounter of the great grizzly during an encampment of Plains people on a sunny day. The "X marks the spot" establishes an orientation point for the compositional direction.

The Great Plains stretch from Texas to Canada, and from the Mississippi River to the Rocky Mountains. The native people of the Plains belong to history and legend, born of rolling prairies, canyons and buttes, and wasted badlands. The destiny of the Plains Indian culture was aligned to the arrival of the horse, which was introduced in the late eighteenth century, enabling great mobility. There were spectacular herds to follow, chiefly those of the buffalo. The Plains Indian people brought a sense of great beauty with them as they traveled from summer to winter, from prairie to mountain top.

The Plains culture is consistent with Native American belief that possesses a profound understanding for the Earth and all the creatures that inhabit it. The use of rawhide was an efficient and respectful means of survival and remembrance. Exquisite buffalo robes kept people warm while displaying and recording events; rawhide *winter counts* held biographies and tribal histories—animal hides provided an indelible "canvas" for Plains Indian iconography. The pictograph was elevated in the hands of the Plains people and became an elegant expression of myth, belief, history, and authority. Great chiefs and leaders would have their own accounts graphically recorded on rawhide, with the aid of an understood sign-and-symbol system. Interpretations may be based on both fact and internal vision. The *lodge mural* appeared in the headquarters of an important ruler and was based on sacred dreams.

The art of Plains pictography has defining formats and features. People, places, or events appear on the tanned side of a buffalo hide used for the yearly winter count, so-called because it measured time by the passing of winters. Early formats were circular in design, beginning with the first symbol placed in the center of the hide. The winter count could record the events of a family or might be autobiographical in nature. For example, a winter count painter would begin with the first central symbol or himself/herself at the start of life. Traditionally the next picture would appear at the left, to continue with other pictographic recordings in a circling spiral. The way to read the symbolic picture was counterclockwise. Symbols that might appear could represent a young child, an eclipse of the sun, the arrival of a new animal, and so forth. The buffalo hide can represent one or more "winter count" calendar years. Later directionality of the winter count read linearly, from left to right, from top to bottom. Pictographic representations are often very simple, almost the same as an alphabet character. Symbols range from modest to sophisticated. Every object has its own story, whether it is a tipi, a buffalo robe, a lodge mural—or a winter count.

MATERIALS

- brown butcher wrap (see Teacher Preparation)
- oil pastels
- colored markers
- colored chalk
- newspaper (see Teacher Preparation)
- scissors

- sticks, branches, twine (optional: see Teacher Preparation)
- brushes
- watercolor paint (see Teacher Preparation)
- hole punch
- reproducible page: "Native American Patterns and Designs"

TEACHER PREPARATION

The winter count lesson may take several direction Students may have choices in format and theme. The teacher may want to guide students in the selections that include buffalo robe autobiography, lodge dream mural, or winter count. The directions that appear in this activity have "wiggle-room," yet do suggest a winter count of a "year in the life" of the student. O course, students may wish to imagine themselves in tl Plains over a hundred years ago, and report their autobiographical year from that perspective. Signs and symbols are provided on reproducible page 279. It is important that students think about their own original pictographs as well.

The teacher will need lengths of brown butcher wrap to be used as buffalo hide; brown grocery bags may be substituted. Precrushing of "hide" for textural effect is up to the discretion of teacher and students. The drawing and painting media may also be used selectively. Newspapers are used to cover desks if painting and chalk application is planned.

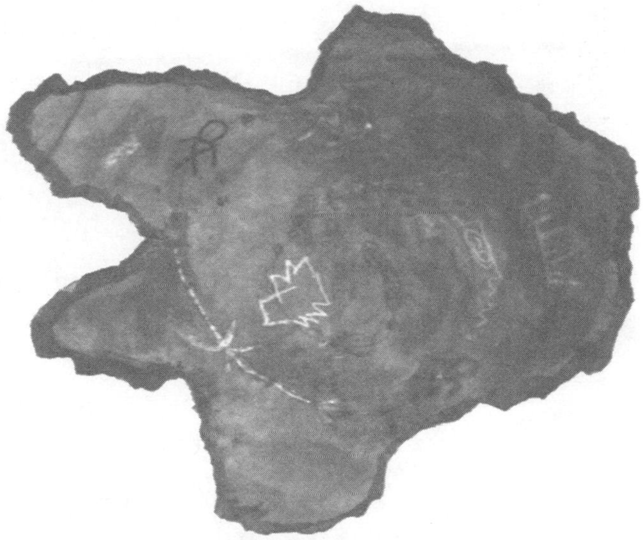

Note: A beautiful way to display completed "hides" is by constructing a branch frame, wrapped with twine. Winter count and other pictographic formats would be attached inside the frame with twine (as shown in Figure 8-5). Scale is optional. If a branch frame is planned, gather twigs and appropriate card or twine lengths accordingly.

▲ Figure 8-6. The technique for this winter count seems to be a resist method that works well visually in this counter-clockwise spiral format. Don't you think the work of this young student has a certain "primitive immediacy"? What a year it must have been.

DIRECTIONS

1. Discuss the many artistic uses for rawhide in the Plains Indian society. Be sure to explain the use of animal skins in the context of the Native American spirit—all parts of an animal are put to use respectfully. Students will consider paper rawhide as a surface that will be treated much like a "painter's canvas" for their pictographic expression.

2. Along with discussing the meaning of pictographs or picture writing, specifically discuss the "winter count" concept of recording people, places, and events. Buffalo robes, which were closely associated with winter count hides, and lodge murals should be explained. How will students express their ideas?

3. Although students may opt to create a lodge mural ("dream" pictographs), our focus will be an autobiographical year in the life of a student, which will include family, friends, and events. It is also possible to report an abbreviated scene in the life of the student (see Figure 8-5). Students may enjoy imagining themselves transported back in time.

4. Distribute lengths of brown butcher wrap (or grocery bags). Students will either tear the edges of the paper "hide" into an approximate buffalo robe shape or they may wish to cut edges (with this option, distribute scissors).

5. Distribute the reproducible page of patterns and designs or draw them on the board. Encourage students to develop their own personal representations. Demonstration of a "spiral" pattern on the board will help students understand the format of a winter count composition. Students may want to begin by placing a symbol of themselves in the center and spiraling out to symbolically mark people, places, and events in their "year-in-the-life" concept. Students may choose the circular spiral or may prefer a more linear representation—the two styles of the winter count hides.

6. Distribute drawing and painting materials selected for this project (see Materials). Students may begin drawing directly on the "shaped" hides, while thinking of the sequence of events as well as the selection and invention of signs and symbols. Limit the number of signs and symbols to only those necessary and remember directionality of placement.

7. Students using mixed media can certainly combine dry and wet materials for a naturalistic effect. Paint may be watered down for overall application. Edges of the paper hide may be delineated with a dark contour. Let dry.

8. Students may wish to crunch paper for an "authentic" look, particularly in the case of the hand-torn hides.

9. The framing touch, if desired, will now occur. Distribute branches or wooden dowels, lengths of twine, and the hole punch. Assemble the four wooden sticks at the corners by wrapping twine to secure the frame. Pierce holes in corner spots so that the paper hide may be attached by twine to the wooden frame.

10. Display these "winter counts" where students can respond to the symbols and stories crafted by one another. Every season is a good season to display a winter count.

NATIVE AMERICAN PATTERNS AND DESIGNS

PLAINS PICTURE WRITING

horse tracks	man	tipi
lizard	woman	
catepillar		
bear foot	life	
	person	
	parfleche	
	center	star
	thunder-bird	camp circle
	bear foot	arrow-point
tribe	morning star	
bird tracks	mountains	
	cloud	
	sun	
	lightning	
horse	constellation	
wind		interior of tipi
		tipi
	morning star	flood
	buffalo skull	lightning
		tipi
		person
		path

ANCIENT SOUTHWEST PUEBLO

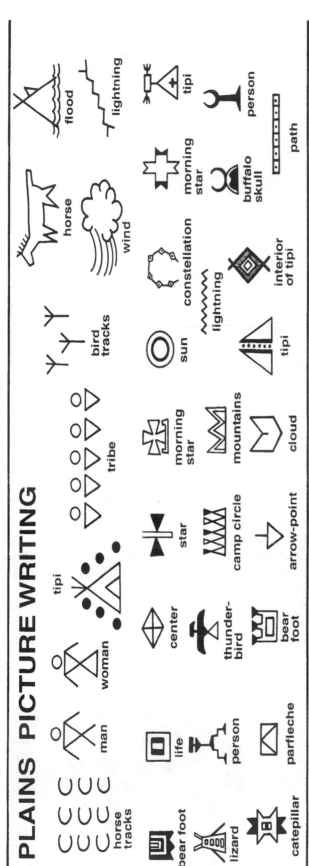

PICTOGRAPHS and their MEANINGS

four directions: north: yellow south: red east: white west: blue-green	lizard	water creature (half turtle, half fish)
	clouds and rain	butterfly
		deer
rabbit	turtle	snake
	star	lion
bear claw	eagle	sun Kachina

BONUS : TRAVEL LIGHT WITH PARFLECH LUGGAGE

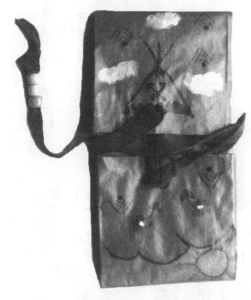

▲ Figure 8-7. This parflech luggage offers a symbolic view of everyday life. Its "rawhide" companion—the tipi—is shown surrounded by coded symbols. Overall surface design is balanced and serene.

Do you know what the word *parflech* means? Parflech is the name for rawhide that has been processed so that it may be decorated for utilitarian purposes. A parflech is, in fact, a rawhide container that became part of the basic travel items produced by the equestrian tribes of the Great Plains, along with those of the plateau and basin areas. It's surprising to note that among all the items made of rawhide—saddles, drums, sheaths, hats, and tipis—the parflech was the most common item of all. Basically, the parflech is a flat, rectangular, yet expandable case into which clothing, dried herbs and food, sacred objects, and medicine—as well as other materials for storage—are neatly placed. These handy and decorative objects were water resistant and lightweight, perfectly designed for the traveling lifestyle of the Plains people. Portable and practical, the rectangular parflech offered a perfect opportunity for applied geometric design.

To make your own portable parflech luggage, students will determine scale. Do you need a small carry-on piece? Or would an efficiently-sized travel case suit your needs? To produce individual parflech luggage, you will need proportional brown or tan craft paper (9″ × 12″ is fine; 12″ × 18″ or 18″ × 24″ may also be selected).

Note: See the directions for making a parflech envelope. Rulers, oil pastels or crayons, hole punch, and lengths of twine or "leather" ribbon (natural colors) will be required to complete this lesson. Beads may be used for parflech closure tie decoration. Students' designs may include borders, matching or reverse pictographic scenes, or simply geometric "box and border" designs favored by the women who painted buffalo robes. For additional ideas, refer to the patterns and designs reproducible. Designs should have a feeling of symmetry that continues in a "wraparound" manner from front to back.

Upon design completion, punch two central holes as indicated on the directions and loop through the holes with lengths of "leather" ribbon to be used for closure. For students to put their parflech luggage case to use, special mementos, lucky charms, and letters may be kept inside for a safe journey.

Figure 8-8. This parflech not only holds special mementos and good design elements, it also holds the viewer's artistic interest. "Box and border" design plays against a free style of picture shown in oppositional flaps. You *can* take it with you! ▶

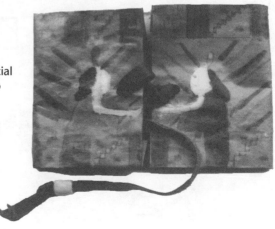

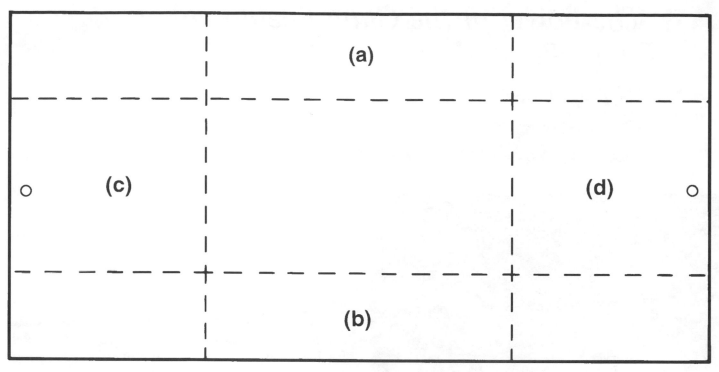

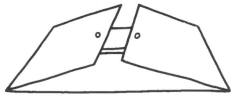

Directions for Making a Paper Parflech

First fold flaps (a) and (b) horizontally across on dotted lines. Then fold flaps (c) and (d) on their dotted lines. Design the front and back of the parflech. Upon completion, punch holes where shown on flaps (c) and (d) to insert ribbon and tie.

INCLUDES : "POSSIBLE" BAGS

With a *possible bag,* any design is possible! Young children will ε possible bag which was used by the Crow, Cheyenne, and Si leather container. Our "possible" bag model is simply a brown lu or grocery bag with fringed trim (pinking shears may be used string or yarn handle drawn through the top. The winning feature of the "possible" bag is its roomy style. Elements of nature and geometric design are suggested for "possible" bag motifs.

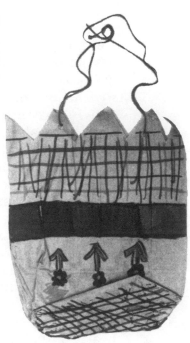

Figure 8-9. This "possible" bag made by a first-grade student could carry a favorite toy, a homework assignment, or a peanut butter and jelly sandwich, "wrapped"—without any difficulty! ▶

ACTIVITY 3

The Power of the Clay: Pueblo Pots and Spirit Bowls

Clay/Mixed Media

BONUS: SWEET DREAMCATCHER: CIRCULAR "WEB WEAVING"

INCLUDES: NAVAJO EYEDAZZLERS!

▲ Figure 8-10. People who live in the desert wish for rain. It is no surprise that the southwest pottery shows symbols fallling and designs that depict clouds, thunderbolts, mountains, and rain. Images pictured on pots are a kind of "picture prayer"; symbols such as birds and feathers are believed to carry the prayer to the heavens. Pueblo pottery does not concern itself with realistic representation; if the pot captures the spirit of the creature, life and art remain in balance. This young student artist's work was inspired by ancient Mimbre pottery and the work of contemporary Acoma potter Lucy Lewis, who uses the same sources in her powerful vessels.

Earth, fire, wind, and water combine to give the potter all the tools needed to make the pot. Earth is clay, clay is earth. Ever since the ancient days, pots were believed to contain a spirit life. When water occupied a vessel, it exchanged with the clay its own life-giving essence. The relationship among the pot, its maker, and its purpose has always held a spiritual place in the heart of Native Americans. The notion that an object exists solely for its aesthetic or utilitarian function is an alien concept to the first Americans. As we admire a clay pot for the simplicity and beauty of its design, we are being offered at the same time a view of the Native American universe.

Thankfully, early pots still exist, preserving ideology, techniques, and living history and spirituality. It is estimated that the first inhabitants of the American Southwest began to shape pottery and construct houses around 300 B.C. The *Mogollon* (moh-go-YOHN) people were ancient pueblo dwellers, living in the mountains of New Mexico and Arizona. Out of this culture emerged the *Mimbres,* from which an outstanding ceramic tradition was established. One of the most distinctive cultures of the southwest, the Mimbres are remembered for their dramatic black-and-white pottery. The Mimbres excelled in their Classic periods, which took place A.D. 1100–1300. Mimbre pots were both ceremonial and utilitarian. The two basic styles included purely *geometric design,* while the other presented *stylized animals and humans.* Southwestern people who produced memorable pottery and weaving were the *Anasazi* (on-uh-SAW-zee), meaning "the Ancient Ones," and the *Hohokam* (hoh-hoh-kahm), or "Vanished Ones." Powerful Pueblo pots are offered to us today, keeping the value given to the preservation of tradition.

The majestic and graceful tradition of Pueblo pottery has continued throughout the centuries. The sources of ideas, techniques, and basic vessel forms remain very much intact. Respect for tradition has not been compromised with the growth of new ideas. The old techniques of coiling are still used by Pueblo potters who hold a most respectful position in Native America society. It is amazing to realize that the classic clay vessel forms have been hand-built, smoothed, and polished to perfection. With a minimal use of tools and technology, the results are spectacular. An economy of color is favored—black, white, and basic earth tones—while glazing is not viewed as vital to the life of the pot. Tradition and innovation work side by side to bring individualized and artistic meaning to pots produced in the Southwest pueblos. Mother Earth and Clay Woman seem to guide the hands and protect the hearts of their creative spirit children to this very day.

MATERIALS

(for pueblo pottery)

- white pottery clay
- clay tools (see Teacher Preparation)
- oaktag (see Teacher Preparation)
- plastic bags (see Teacher Preparation)
- black glaze or black acrylic paint (see Teacher Preparation)
- small brushes
- paper towels

(for spirit bowls)

- raffia
- leather shoestrings
- pony beads
- feathers
- plastic drinking straws

TEACHER PREPARATION

This activity provides the teacher and students with two options for their pueblo pottery: *Option #1* (see Figure 8-10) is classic pueblo pottery based on Mimbre traditions, and *Option #2* (see Figure 8-11) is an ancient "spirit bowl" with a contemporary feeling. **Note:** The teacher should know that the clay method used here is traditional to pueblo pottery and is the same for both options: the coil technique. Prepare the classroom for clay work. Remember to have plastic drinking straws on hand for Option #2.

▲ Figure 8-11. It is quite natural for Native Americans to combine the elements of their environment into a majestic object. The harmonious blending of textures provides not only visual and tactile satisfaction, they also contain a way of thinking about the world. There is usually meaning associated with specific materials, especially the feather. Feathers may be considered sacred; for example, the feather of an eagle may not be acquired without special permission from a medicine man. Materials mixed together may comprise a "medicine bundle" which has various uses—yet all are considered protective. This holistic world view is captured in the "medicine" spirit bowls made by these sixth-grade students who combine materials and techniques successfully.

DIRECTIONS

1. Discuss the nature of Native American pueblo pottery. Using the pictorial references provided on reproducible page 279, discuss the meaning and interpretation of simple design symbols and the ideas behind them. Many pots use geometrics based on natural elements such as wind, rain, sun, and water. Students may want to proceed with stylized animal and human forms as well. (Surface pattern and design refer to Option #1 only.)

2. Demonstrate standard coil-making techniques for creating a pot, bowl, or other vessel. Show students how to smooth coils together in building pot by gently rubbing one coil into another to create a smooth surface. Fingers and/or tools may be used. (For Option #2, the pot will be smoothed *only on the inside*.)

3. Distribute clay to students according to proportion determined. Students will build their pueblo pots using the demonstrated standard coil method. If more than one clay period is needed for this step, wrap "working pot" with wet paper towels and plastic bags. (For Option #2, holes must be pierced with plastic straws along the rim of the pot while clay is still moist.) Let dry.

4. The smooth white clay vessels are now ready to receive black design work. Distribute black acrylic paint accordingly. Brushes and water will accompany black paint. (If glazing method is chosen, teacher will supervise the simple black glaze needed.) Paint designs on the Mimbres pot (kiln-fire if using glazing method). For Option #2, leave the bowl natural or paint one banded area with acrylic paint. Let dry.

5. For Option #2, distribute "spirit" materials—leather shoestrings, feathers, beads, raffia, and so forth. First, loop leather shoestrings through previously pierced holes to create the "woven" element of the pot. Allow for excess to extend beyond the mouth of the pot in order to attach feathers, beads, and raffia. Additional materials, textures, and objects may be further used to create "spirit bundles," a grouping of natural elements to ensure harmony, or *hojho*.

6. Native American pueblo pottery may be gathered for display. Circular placement would respect a basic idea of directionality as part of balance and order. Pots inspired by nature are bringers of joy!

BONUS : SWEET DREAMCATCHER: CIRCULAR "WEB WEAVING"

The *Ojibwa* people of the Great Lakes treasured good dreams as the source of all wisdom. To Native American societies overall, dreams are considered a powerful source for the pictorial representations that will keep the dreams alive. Dreams and visions help to connect all worlds—from the spiritual to the everyday. Dreams are so important that a person who "dreams well" would receive the respect of the community and might even be given Healer status! If one dreams of a specific animal or bird, an association is formed that will carry over into a personal protective animal companion. It is important to have good dreams!

In the beginning it is said that Spider Woman—Earth Goddess of Creation—provided the Native American people with the gift of weaving. This special attribute would take many creative forms. Inspired by the spider's web in nature, Northern and Southeastern Woodland Indians wove their ideas into a circular object, now known as a dreamcatcher. Children, in

◄ Figure 8-12. A middle-years student named Janet must have a pet spider to have learned the webbing technique so well! This tightly woven web demonstrates a confident use of artistic license—note the incorporation of the beads. Many dreamcatchers weave in other small items such as "fetish animal charms" (see Activity 4). True to tradition, Janet has left a central opening that respects the spirit of benevolent Spider Woman. Weaving and pottery—even structures, like the *kiva*—leave an entrance space for the spirits of the First People.

particular, would be protected from bad dreams when a dreamcatcher hung above them as they slept peacefully. With this guardian dreamcatcher, bad spirit dreams could not enter, for they would become hopelessly entangled in the web. Overcome by the morning sun, bad dreams dissolved and disappeared. Good dreams, on the other hand, are welcome—they move easily through the web and are stored in the magic feather that is part of the dreamcatcher. Good dreams are forever.

Dreamcatchers are right up there with nightlights and teddy bears when it comes to a good night's rest! For students to make their own dreamcatcher, or to give them as gifts, a hoop is needed. Embroidery hoops work well because they are strong and will hold the web in place.

Note: Teacher may use other rigid hoops available or may create a hoop from the bamboo sticks that are used to hold balloons (available at craft/party stores). With this method, the stick will need to be soaked in water (to soften) and then shaped and tied into a circle. String is needed for this lesson as well as scissors, glue, feathers, and beads. Please see the looping process on "How to Make a Dreamcatcher", on page 286, for construction of "dream weaving." Beads may be incorporated in the process. Notice that a central hole is shown. This honors Spider Woman! The top is established by a looped string that will enable the dreamcatcher to be hung. To attach a feather, loop a piece of string to the bottom of the hoop. Slide bead through looped string and tie a large knot. Place a "dot" of glue on feather quill slip through bead to glue feather in place. Sweet dreams!

◄ Figure 8-13. Each dreamcatcher has its own expressive technique—even its own personality! Sixth-grader Daniel creates an uplifting effect with his lighter-than-air dreamcatcher. In Native America, the feather is a treasured object that may be given as a gift to another person—or passed on in ceremony. The Apache, make dreamcatchers with the feathers of the owl, a wise creature who guards in the night.

Figure 8-14. Don't you just love this early child-hood "abstract" rendition of our dreamcatcher? A simple looping, combined with beads and feathers, still does the job. All bad dreams stop here! ►

HOW TO MAKE A DREAMCATCHER

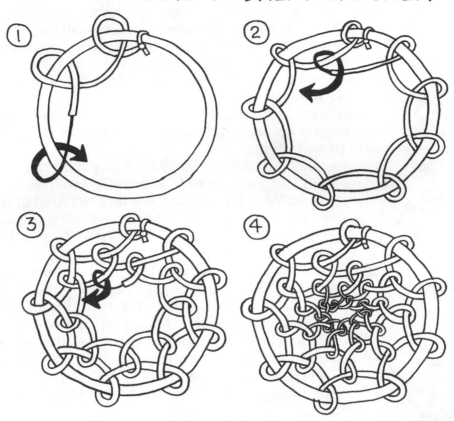

INCLUDES : NAVAJO EYEDAZZLER

The Navajo in the southwest acknowledge the spirit of Spider Woman through their magnificent weaving. It is generally agreed tha the Navajo learned weaving from the Puel culture where men set up their looms in th *kiva*—a sacred underground lodge for men However, today Navajo women may sit beneat the shade of a tree, outside the *hogan*—a dom shaped structure that means "home place" in tl Navajo language. On their upright looms, wor spin and weave old and new traditions. Before tl were rugs, there were blankets. The chief's blar denoted status in the community. The Navajo cl blanket provides a classic example of Nav; weaving in its striped-design proportion. recognition for the Navajo blanket-weaving grew, demands for woven products increased. Trading posts and new railroad systems saw the shift from Navajo blanket to Navajo rug. Many influences were woven into the Navajo rugs so prized today—the Mexican *saltillo sarape* is one major source for pictorial weaving. As the *dineh* (the people) became less isolated, ideas flowed in from Europe, the Orient, and from other Native American tribes such as the Plains, with the symbols used in buffalo hides and tipi paintings.

▲ Figure 8-15. The Navajos learned much about weaving from Pueblo artisans no more than 300 years ago. In Navajo design geometric, the diamond pattern was tops. This stunning artroom weaving displays a wonderful abstract use of the diamond element. Better yet, the animated edges of the half diamond form reminds us of the stunning Navajo eyedazzler. The weaving shown here was done through standard classroom method, yet conveys the Navajo upright loom effect. Mounted on a branch, this fringed weaving pleases the senses.

Before the pictorial rugs developed, there were geometrics. Early Navajo rug design was nonrepresentational. This geometric period existed in response to a cultural restriction against the overrepresentation of sacred beings as well as sacred crops, such as corn and squash. The "diamond" shape was highly favored. Geometric rugs conform to bands of color that are horizontal to rug length: stripes or groups of stripes are arranged in zones. A brilliant assimilation of elements occurs with the classic Navajo eyedazzler which honors past traditions while introducing new ideas. An eyedazzler is defined by a diamond-shaped motif that is made "electric" by repetitive "lightning bolt" banded patterning that becomes part of the diamond design. The dazzling effect occurs through the "electrical discharge" of the repetition of joined triangle shards both inside and outside of the diamond. Individual eyedazzlers vary in their use of this effect; there is no single formula. Considered by many to be the apex of geometric patterning achievement, eyedazzler rugs were further enhanced by the use of so-called "Germantown" yarn which provided an even more brilliant color use.

▲ Figure 8-16. This is a fine student example of the traditional geometric Navajo weaving with its horizontal bands of color. Is it just a simple weaving or a spiritual interpretation of Earth, Sea, and Sky?

Later Navajo rug weaving reveals the expansion of the culture itself—a favored theme is technology and transportation. One charming example will show a locomotive chugging along the track while sacred birds and beings fly as messengers from Earth to sky. The incorporation of sacred symbols has since stirred great controversy, particularly with the *yeis* or "holy people," because these are representations that have become available outside of their ceremonial moorings.

Yeis or *yeibichais* are sacred deities that have been traditionally used only for sand paintings—they were not permanent, nor were they woven. Sandpainting was done only by medicine men for sacred healing purposes. However, by the 1900s, conditions for woven *yeis* tapestries had been established within the cultural community and have since become a part of Navajo weaving tradition; yet it is a matter that still raises concern. One may learn about the Rainbow Guardian figure that creates a three-cornered, open border on yeis tapestry—as well as recognize a Kachina spirit as it is presented by the Navajo rug. From the Native American perspective, weaving itself is sacred art.

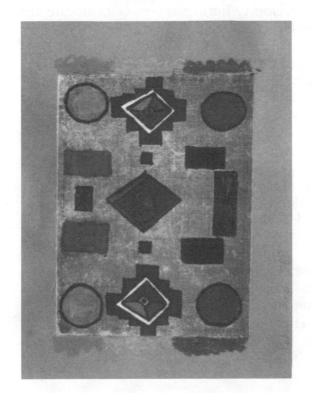

◄ Figure 8-17. Technology has entered the realm of Navajo weaving in this paper rug. The student artist built upon a computer-generated design system with other drawing materials and added yarn edge that can surely fool the eye. The basic directional cross, circles, squares, and rectangles—and, of course, diamond—definitely qualify this tricky rug as geometric.

ACTIVITY 4

Mudhead! Koshari, Clowns, and Kachinas of the Southwest

Clay Figures

INCLUDES: PAPER KACHINA DANCER

BONUS: LUCKY ANIMALS: PERSONAL CHARM ZUNI NECKLACE

▲ Figure 8-18. Two Koshari making merry. Watch out for their uncensored sense of humor when it comes to making fun of human folly. The clown on the right holds a bowl that may have contained water. Koshari find it amusing to dowse the crowd in water or—better yet—spit watermelon seeds at passersby! If you meet a Koshari holding a slice of watermelon, don't say we didn't warn you!

In the Season of the Kachina, it is the time to dance, sing, pray, laugh, play, and reunite. The Kachina culture is as much a part of the Southwest as are the ever-present peaks and mesas. While many celebrate the Season of the Kachina, the Hopi people continue to be most associated with this life-cycle ceremony. Kachinas are most commonly known outside of the Hopi world as remarkable carved figures shown in full dance costume, complete with masks and headdresses. By definition, Kachinas are ceremonial dancers; they are also dolls that teach Native American children about heritage and tradition. Kachinas are sacred intermediaries who represent natural forces central to Hopi existence. (See the "four directions" wheel for an illustration of the Kachina seasons.)

The elements of Rain, Cloud, Father Sky, Mother Earth, Animals, and the Sacred Crops are embodied by Kachinas. Hopis believe that when a person departs from this world, his or her spirit is carried up to the clouds to return as rain that will nourish the Earth. Crops will grow and life will be sustained. The Hopi life cycle is a circle of time into which the Kachina season naturally fits. It occurs between the winter and summer solstices. The Kachina dancers live in the mountains of the nearby San Francisco Peaks from late July. The ceremony honors the force of nature and the ancestors. It is a blessing to the community that has drama, belief, joy, and honor.

Kachina dancers are magnificent creatures who deserve an opening performance. Here is where the clowns come in: Before the Kachinas, they descend from the sky. Can you imagine black-and-white striped beings with big pointed horns on their heads climbing out, all at once, over the adobe rooftops? They are the *Koshari,* probably the best known of the Kachina clowns, said to be of Tewa origin. As clowns, they are The Delightmakers, who serve many roles in Kachina ceremony. A combination of jester, shaman, teacher, and priest, the Koshari behave outrageously. Yet, there is a method to their mockery, at which they are quite skilled—and that is to keep order through embarrassment and absurdity! Koshari will happily target members of the Pueblo community who may not have upheld Hopi behavioral codes. Audience members understandably fear the wit of the Koshari, who uphold the traditions and moral standards needed in society—they show how *not* to behave! When Koshari mock inappropriate action, all ages and all social positions are fair game! These ritual clowns are considered sacred while empowered to turn that which is sacred upside-down! Mudheads (*Koyemshi*) are also

▲ Figure 8-19. The laugh is on us. If we believe we've never seen this Koshari before, check the figure to the left in Figure 8-18. In perfect keeping with Hopi clown tricks, this striped fellow turns the world upside-down without missing a beat.

clowns, although they are not sacred and appear exactly as their name indicates—heads of mud! They follow in order after the Koshari in the Kachina Festival. With knob-like protrusions on top of their heads, and eyes and mouth like doughnuts, Mudheads resemble earth-colored space cadets! Their looks and their silly antics are pure comedy. Everything they do and say is *backwards*! No one can climb a ladder sideways and inside-out better than a Mudhead. They just keep getting it wrong! As much fun—and enlightenment—as the Koshari bring, they retreat from their escapades when the Kachina dancers appear. At this point, the sacred clowns transform into caring helpers who will serve and attend the Kachina dancers. The Koshari, in this role, allow the ceremony to progress—while the zany Mudheads continue to just be their own silly selves!

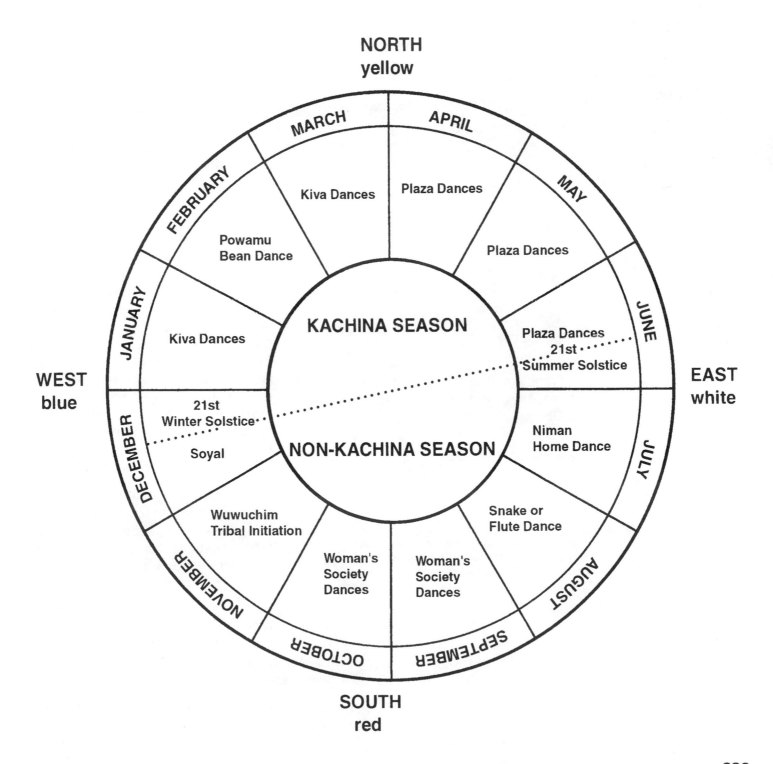

MATERIALS

- air-dry white or terra-cotta clay (see Teacher Preparation)
- clay tools
- oaktag
- small brushes
- black and brown acrylic paints (see Teacher Preparation)

TEACHER PREPARATION

There are two types of clay for two types of clowns: white clay for the **Koshari** and terra-cotta for the **Mudheads.** Air-dry clay is recommended. The teacher will use the standard procedures for setting up a clay lesson and prepare the art classroom accordingly. Black and brown acrylic paints are all that is necessary for basic Koshari and Mudhead figures; other selected colors may be added if desired.

The teacher will find that photographs of Koshari, along with Kachina, are readily available in print through good travel guidebooks. Of course, Figures 8-18 through 8-21 will provide visual examples. The teacher may want examples of figures in advance of lesson. Naturally, if the teacher or anyone else has carved Hopi figures, bring them to class!

DIRECTIONS

▲ Figure 8-20. "In this corner" . . . we have a featherweight Mudhead boxer who holds his gloved hands against his worried little face. Even with the urging of a referee, a glance at the competition in the opposite corner seems to immobilize his courage. Note the "warm-up" gesture of his worthy opponent. Referee's stripes add a witty touch.

1. Discuss the role of the clown in Hopi culture. Compare and contrast the Koshari with clowns students may have seen elsewhere. What do clowns have in common? One important feature is their exaggerated gestures. If appropriate to the class, ask students to demonstrate movement that is gestural and comic. **Note:** Silly behavior may be "frozen" by the teacher's snap of fingers. **Hint:** One student at a time works well.

2. Point out that certain movements fall into specific categories: tumbling, stretching, cowering, "overacting," and so forth. Students will consider the poses they will give their clay figure along with any small props or costume details. It may be fun to make a "career" figure: prizefighter, politician, chief, or artist.

3. Distribute supplies. Follow standard clay procedures. The posturing of the figure should be completed in one classroom period.

4. The beauty of clay is that it is malleable and forgiving, which will allow students to experiment with various comic postures in clay while developing the figure.

5. Students who are making Koshari may let these dry after the conical horns. Mudheads will require six little balls f mouth, ears, and top knot. After attachment of the "l create doughnut forms by inserting pencil point into protrusions. Let figure dry.

6. Distribute painting supplies when Mudheads and Koshar are completely dry. Koshari will need only black paint to create black and white stripes. Ring eyes with black circle. If authenticity is desired, Mudheads should probably remain terra-cotta in appearance with clothing and othe details painted on their little clay bodies. There is no rul(however, against painting the terra-cotta clay white, yellov green, or any color desired. Let dry.

7. As you can plainly see, Koshari and Mudheads do well in crowds and figure groups, or may stand or tumble alone. A showcase display of these animated and adorable "nudges"—the Hopi clowns—will guarantee to bring smiles and delight!

▲ Figure 8-21. The popularity of art from the Southwest often divides objects into commercial or ceremonial categories. Crafts made for the tourist market are no less cherished by the collector. A fine example exists in this seated Mudhead drummer. The drum beat is the pulse of all Kachina dancers. Don't you love his boots?

INCLUDES : PAPER KACHINA DANCER

It is estimated that there are some 360 Kachina spirits that represent the forces of nature that control life. The paper dancer shown here is highly stylized—a full-scale abstraction of Kachina representation with emphasis on design elements favored in the Americas. Who is he or she? Judging from the symbol in the center, this could be a rain or flower spirit. The thunderbolt and pyramid stair-stepping element used on hands and upper torso is part of art and architecture from North to South America! Note the interesting *tablita,* or headdress, that may recall the *Poli Sio* or Butterfly Kachina headdress, too. Kachina dancers have specific names, identities, and attributes. *Eototo* is the chief of all Kachinas; he controls the seasons and the ceremonies.

When students design their 3- to 4-foot tall paper Kachina, they will first need a length of paper cut from a roll. Pencils, paint, crayon, and markers will assist—along with a look at Native American symbols (see the reproducible of designs from Activity 2). Students will fold paper lengthwise and symmetrically to create in pencil *one half* of their Kachina figure. When drawing is complete, cut and open. Students now have one full-designed figure to paint and decorate. Will it be a Mother Kachina, a Sunshine, or a Rain Kachina? Or will it represent one of the Four Sacred Crops? Inspiration for student Kachinas may come from southwest references, their own imaginations, or even from illustrations found in children's books that help us learn all about our Native American brothers and sisters. The Kachina dancers may be placed along a protected exterior or interior wall (affixed with tape) to bring good health, strength, productivity, and serenity.

▲ Figure 8-22. "All Kachinas Welcome".

Bonus : LUCKY ANIMALS: PERSONAL CHARM ZUNI NECKLACE

▲ Figure 8-23. This student chose Lizard for his necklace, a creature in great favor for its agility and balance. In the curved posture, Lizard brings safety and protection.

Early mineral objects found in the Ancient Southwest were in the natural shape of animals and people . . . these small stone forms were believed to contain the spirit of the living being itself. To become known as *fetishes,* the little sculptures of land, sea, and air creatures were carved, polished, and treasured. Fetishes, which may be made from bone, mineral, stone, or other natural elements, serve as tiny animal guardians to their keepers. Sometimes the fetishes are wrapped with arrowheads or shells—perhaps combined with herbal medicine bundles—to improve well-being. Turquoise, considered a very sacred and magical stone, is used in the miniature realm of the fetish. An individual's magic animal charm is a personal article, scaled for pocket-sized portability. The chosen animal is by no means incidental: its identity may be traced to a dream source or found object. The finely carved fetish is most notably credited to the craft of the Zuni: hence, the Zuni fetish. The animal's power is culturally understood.

Animals are deeply respected for their attributes and ability to bring about well-being. Meet some of the essential creatures found in power objects and fetishes:

TURTLE

Longevity, reliability, provider of home. Turtle is the symbol for Mother Earth.

An origin story places Turtle at the center of creativity: Earth forms upon Turtle's back. Hence, our first land was Turtle Island!

EAGLE

Divine Spirit with infinite wisdom. A teacher with great integrity.

"Eagle flies the highest . . . sees everything," . . . Birds are considered Divine messengers between Heaven and Earth.

LIZARD

Balance, conservation, and agility.

Curved Lizard represents safety and protection.

COYOTE

Prankster with hidden wisdom. Ability to laugh at one's own mistakes.

Coyote is a trickster who is featured in many tales.

FROG

Rainmaker. Links water and Earth. Promotes emotional healing.

Frog, like other water creatures, is considered important in bringing water to the dry land.

BEAR

Symbol of Power, Strength, and Courage. Bear is a medicine healer with curative powers.

Bear is a favored animal, found often in carved effigies. Bear has stature throughout North America, particularly in the Great Northwest as well as Southwest Native America.

This is a *partial* list. Animals are considered sacred and are associated with The Four Directions. Wolf, for instance, is an animal of the East, the direction from which good comes. Wolf is a teacher and a Pathfinder. And . . . you should know about the ancient human figure who dates back to the Anasazi culture . . . KOKOPELLI, the round-back, flute-playing dancer—Bringer of Music, Spirit, and Joy! A joy it will be when students select an animal with attributes they would want to "carry with them" . . . in a fetish charm activity to provide personal adornment. The fetish necklace can be traced back to at least one thousand years ago. This Activity Bonus will enable students to sculpt their own good-luck animal charms. To create the necklace, use the same materials listed in Activity 3 for Spirit Bowls. Leather shoestrings may be substituted with twine or cord (eliminate plastic straws and raffia). Use an air-drying clay. **Note:** A small piece of soft wire will facilitate a good hole for necklace cord.

Students will model a simple representation of a favored animal guardian; one charm per student is fine (two will also do). Pierce holes in animal while clay is wet. When dry, holes will allow for passage of cord needed for necklace. Let dry. The finished Zuni fetish animal may now be threaded with cord. Add beads and feathers as desired. Wear with the confidence of a mountain lion!

Note: Fetishes by general definition are concealed as a sort of secret power animal companion. Students may want to create small "surplus" charms for this purpose. Another *wonderful* home for clay animal fetish figures is along the side—or inside—of a clay pueblo pot! Of course, the best time to attach a fetish animal to clay is while they are both still *wet.* Yet, there is no reason not to try to glue fetish charms in place; you will probably come up with some cleaver ideas . . . just like Coyote!

◀ Figure 8-24. Eagle soars on this pendant! The student must be a creative visionary who sees the bigger picture! The Four Cardinal Directions apply to animals—Eagle flies to the East. Eagle is very important to Southwestern culture.

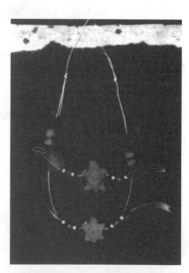

▲ Figure 8-25. Double your luck with a two-tiered Zuni animal fetish necklace. Two turtles are better than one!

ACTIVITY 5

Raven Invites You to a Potlatch Party!

Chilkat Dance Blanket

BONUS: RAVEN BOX OF DAYLIGHT!

The monumental totem pole is a tribute to the art of carving and to the visual power of Northwest Coastal art. The crest poles, which have many uses, are emblazoned with heraldic themes. The animals, mythical beings, and human transformation forms represent, foremost, clan history. In the Northwest there is a design system that is codified by three major linear representations: the *ovoid,* the *U-form,* and the *S-form*—held within a *formline.* Blanket, rattle, mask, hat, paddle, crest pole, and cedar box deliver these highly evolved, stylistic elements that express tribal as well as individual ideas. The concept of lineage is ever present: It is in the formal order of clan animals that appear on crest poles. The presence of the animals also "bears out" Northwest Coastal mythology. Totem pole Thunderbirds, Ravens, Whales, Bears, and even Sea Monsters transform from animal to human . . . from carved wood cedar to woven dance cape.

The Northwest Coastal culture is distinct in many ways. It is essentially a material culture that enjoys both the accumulation and distribution of wealth and valued possessions. Consistent with Native American belief, every part of life is connected to the whole—the totem pole stands for and is literally part of home, family, and ancestor. The designs of symbolic animals carry from pole to home interior. In order to include crest poles, a large house would have been commissioned with input from an architect, designer, and skilled craftpersons. An enormous commitment required complete cooperation—workers would be fed and sheltered by the owner during complicated construction.

After the completion of this massive project, which may have taken several years, the carved crest pole would be raised. At this point, a great celebration—known as a *potlatch*—would take place. Guests would assemble to admire the work as well as witness and validate the crests depicted in the carving that showed the owner's hereditary ancestors. The drum would beat dramatically as the pole was pulled over

▲ Figure 8-26. Chilkat blankets like this one would impress the honorable guests at a potlatch party where showing off your best wares and generous hospitality was the thing to do. Status was measured by the ability of the host to give away voluminous amounts of food along with highly valued objects. The more that was given away, the more honor and respect was returned. The great feast could go on for days with dancing, singing, game playing, gossiping, and endless storytelling! This tradition was forbidden by the non-Indian government for a while . . . it appears the tradition has been revived and the party goes on!

scaffolding to stand upright and in balance. When the colossal pole stood up, the artists and carvers danced! Among the most favored of material objects were blankets that were used not only for ceremony; they also became precious payment for a job well done!

Perhaps one of the most consistently admired articles was the Chilkat dance blanket. Women of specific tribal societies, such as *Haida, Tlingit,* and *Tsimshian,* wove beautiful, ceremonial robes known as Chilkat blankets. These masterful weavers were also resourceful, for the same great cedar that provided wood for poles and boxes helped provide the fibers for these magnificent woven robes. To wear a Chilkat blanket was a sign of wealth and status: High-ranking officials, such as chiefs and nobles, would have worn these very identifiable and stylized garments. The design system of ovoid, S-form, and U-form, and the outline of the formline, are boldly represented in Chilkat blanket formats. Colors used for the blankets are

Native America

typically black, yellow, white, and a bluish-green. Embellished with fringe, the pictorial power contained in the blanket projects a bold sense of monumentality found in the crest poles. The defining blanket shape makes reference to a distinctive architectural form: The Chilkat blanket visually recalls a rectangular, pointed-roof house when turned upside-down! Houses, after all, hold family, friends, ancestors . . . and memories and potlatch ceremonies. Chilkat blankets dance at potlatches and contain the universal spirit of Northwest Coastal art.

MATERIALS

- 18″ × 24″ yellow and black construction paper (see Teacher Preparation)
- black and blue colored markers
- white oil pastels
- pencils
- scissors
- yardsticks (optional)
- raffia/yarn
- hole punch
- glue sticks
- reproducible page: "Northwest Coastal Art and Design"

TEACHER PREPARATION

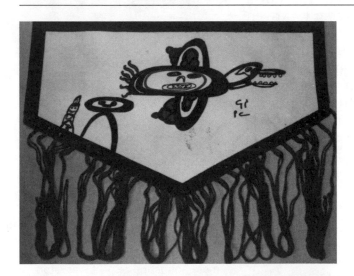

▲ Figure 8-27. Raven flies boldly on this Chilkat dance blanket—a bird with a mission. Trickster that Raven is, he seems to have acquired teeth, no doubt needed for the job at hand. A face appears within his body, a common device that indicates the human–animal transformation that is so much a part of Northwest Coastal mythology. *Formline* helps to accentuate all pictorial elements in the blanket design by defining linear expression. Formlines, like contour lines, are most moving when they vary in line weight, changing from thick to thin. Note the curious marks below raven's head—these are borrowed from the *Inuktitut* alphabet, an Arctic Inuit (Eskimo) society. (See Activity 6.) Raven also flies in the Arctic—he gets around!

The teacher will need yellow paper, a color traditionally used for Chilkat blankets. If large-size yellow paper is not available, perhaps a length may be supplied from a yellow display paper roll. Black construction paper will serve as a frame; cut one-inch strips to accommodate the yellow A-frame form of the blanket. A useful learning objective for this lesson is the opportunity for students to learn about the linear drawing vocabulary used in Northwest Coast design. The teacher will make this information available (refer to reproducible page 298). Consider whether or not Chilkat blanket formats will be precut for students before the lesson begins.

DIRECTIONS

1. Discuss totem poles and their design in relation to the Chilkat dance blankets students will make. With the aid of pictorial reference, point out the design elements that comprise Northwest Coastal art: *ovoid, U-form, S-form,* and the *formline* (the strong black outline that defines the contour). Question what parts of what animal might these design elements represent. Ask students to qualify their answers. It may help to list the favored animals of the Northwest to guide students' imagination: Raven, Whale, Thunderbird, Frog, and, of course, Bear. Don't forget to describe these creatures as clan animals. Discuss the cultural connections among these animals, Chilkat blankets, and potlatch festivals.

2. Distribute materials (withholding the raffia/yarn). Include charts you may have for Northwest Coast design elements (see the reproducible). The paper will need to be cut to scale. Fold paper in half. To conform to the "pointed house" format, simply cut downward from top of form to desired point on outside of paper (yardsticks may be used if desired). Open.

3. Glue black paper strips to the five-sided blanket. With hole punch, create a fairly regular line of holes across the "roof" of the upside-down house.

4. Students begin drawing. Note that traditional Chilkat blankets tend to avoid vacant space; the teacher should decide if this idea is one that he/she would like to enforce. Designs may be set up in a central symmetrical manner with accompanying design elements on all sides. Students may use their own sense of design or adhere to a boxy, multiple-paneled scheme. Students will interpret animals and humans in their own way, using the "language" of the Northwest Coastal visual system.

5. Apply color. Note that the waterbased markers may not be easily used over the white oil pastels. On the contrary, white oil pastels should be used to accent areas and details, respecting the marker-colored areas.

6. How do students know when they are finished? This is, of course, the great cosmic question. According to Native American belief, the answer may be: "When everything is in its place and there is balance and harmony."

7. Insert raffia/yarn into punched holes. Individual insertion may vary in thickness. Looping raffia/yarn before inserting offers another fringing method possibility (see Figure 8-27). Knot strands and bunch raffia/yarn as desired. Students may have their own ideas for fringing techniques. Adjust fringe with scissors.

8. *". . . Are we gonna dance or what?"* Many Native Americans will tell you that there is nothing like a good dance party. Students may wish to "wrap themselves up in their art" for a living display, after which Chilkat blankets may be mounted in the ceremonial lodge known as "your school." Take time for responses to student interpretations of clan animals and mythical creatures designed with Northwest Coast inspiration. Such a wealth of artistic imagery makes you wish for a good, old-fashioned Potlatch!

BONUS : RAVEN BOX OF DAYLIGHT!

. . . **T**he world was once in total darkness. Selfish *Sky Chief* kept all the light in a cedar treasure box, far above and away in his heaven lodge. Raven the Trickster, a messenger who traveled between sky and earth, planned to solve the problem. But how? Raven was a trickster with transformation power! He turned himself into a human baby who fooled the daughter of Sky Chief into believing him to be her own child. Raven was taken into the House of Sky Chief who loved his new grandson—even though he still had his little beak! Raven discovered that Sky Chief had a beautiful cedar box in which he kept the Sun—and the Moon and the Stars. Raven cried and begged his new grandfather to let him play with the box until Sky Chief gave in. Out rose the *STARS*, which Raven released through the SMOKE HOLE in the great lodge to scatter all over the night sky, twinkling brightly. Raven was scolded harshly. Yet soon he begged to play with the cedar box again. Once more, Sky Chief gave in. This time, the MOON rose . . . up, up . . .

NORTHWEST COASTAL ART AND DESIGN

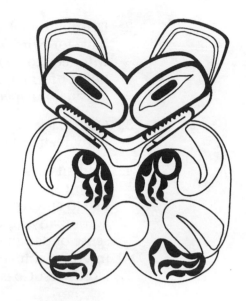

© 1999 by Prentice Hall

Ovoids	S-Forms	U-Forms

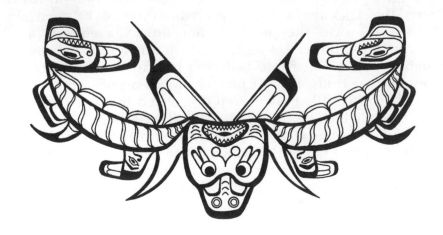

through the smoke hole and into the starry sky! Raven was scolded by Grandfather once again. Raven promised to behave, but, another request from the spoiled grandson, and the box was opened for the last time. This time, the sun rose up through the smoke hole and filled the world with light! Raven had finished his work—he let the *sun and the universe out of the Sky Chief's cedar box*! It was time for Raven to return to his bird self and fly out of the smoke hole, too. When Sky Chief realized who Raven really was, and what had been done, he was angry and sad. He had become attached to his treasures and to his tricky little grandson. The once-selfish Sky Chief had grown wiser and now understood. And that is how clever and tricky Raven brought light to the world.

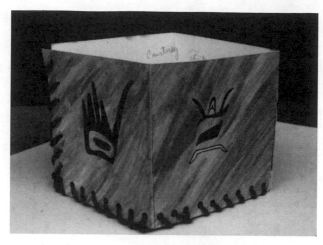

▲ Figure 8-28. A paper box that respects the wood-grain appearance of cedar displays a symbolic Northwest Coast story with a single representation on each side. A human hand appears at left clearly defined by a thumb and four fingers. Human hands have the grace and beauty associated with the hands that make art. This particular motif is a classic one in the north used as an insignia by artists in the British Columbia region. In a universal sense, this hand conveys the spirit of *all* art made by hand.

The Raven story is an essential element in Northwest Coastal mythology. Raven, as a Trickster, is a mischievous fellow who resorts to magic and trickery in order to make matters right. He is a *transformation* creature—which is not unusual in Native American art—part human, part animal, part trouble, part Good Samaritan. He is portrayed in dance with full costume: mask, hat, rattle, and blanket. Raven would regularly appear to tell variations of the origin story as part of the potlatch festival. The symbol for Raven—who is not the only mythological bird or animal that appears in Northwest myth—is ever present on objects of art. People of the region had among them wonderful carvers who represented Raven and other important mythological and clan animals on carved and painted objects. The cedar box, another product of the great red cedar, holds a special meaning. It is more than a box; it is a "cosmic container." Boxes and chests were mythical and practical—storing all sorts of material objects—including blankets. According to Raven, the cedar box held the stars, moon, and sun!

Students will honor the master carvers of the Great Northwest with boxes made of yet another product of a tree—paper! Keep in mind that the cedar wood boxes were made of planks that received three deep grooves in precisely measured places. The box itself was actually folded into the groves which resulted in four sides! This provides a way of doing paper cedar boxes for the students (refer to diagram on page 301). Imagine the expertise of the Northwest artists in both carving and joinery!

To make the paper treasure box, use the reproducible pattern provided (or use alternative box-making technique). Needed for this activity are oaktag, markers, crayon, black cord/yarn, hole punch, ruler, scissors, and pattern. Students will refer to the Northwest Coast design page to guide them in their ideas. Encourage students to feature their own symbolic ideas, yet the story of Raven must be told. Remind students that conventional Northwest box design may feature an animal with head appearing on one side, back view appearing on the other side, with the animal's sides corresponding to two box sides. Other motifs and clan animals are supported by this activity. Distribute paper and all other materials.

Students will trace the box, draw, and "carve" with color the story of choice with Northwest Coastal motifs. Bold line or *formline* will enhance the box appearance. Cut box form when figurative work is complete and the surface of the box suggests a cedar wood grain. Punch holes along areas that will be joined (see Figure 8-28). Using yarn/cord, students will "stitch" box closed. Lid is optional.

A treasure box alternative (see Figure 8-29) requires copper or aluminum repoussé with a felt or velour lining for completed box. As you can see, this is a longer project with dazzling results. The metal foil box shown here demonstrates the box lid formed to fit the body of the box, along with a true treasure—a Raven pendant. This box has captured Raven, but lets him out to be admired when worn by a student metalworker. The Northwest Coast people were knowledgeable in engraving techniques and would apply their skills when gold and silver coins were introduced. *Haida* and *Tlingit* artists produced bright and shining objects, as will the students who try the foil technique for their Raven treasure boxes.

▲ Figure 8-29. A box of daylight would shine like this splendidly crafted Raven box made by an eighth-grade student. The box tells the tale of Raven and how he tricked Sky Chief into giving light to the world. The Sun, Moon, and Stars were in the box that was jealously guarded by the Sky Chief, until Raven worked his wily ways. Student artist Matthew provides the lid with a watchful eye. Raven, who appears on the "treasure" pendant, outsmarted the Sky Chief and was able to release the glowing Sun, the shining Moon, and the dazzling Stars that scattered through the night sky. The engraved box represents Sun, Moon, Stars, and, of course, Raven. Students who try this foil repoussé box of daylight will learn how to fit the entire universe into a box and to let everything out when the time is right.

PAPER BOX PATTERNS

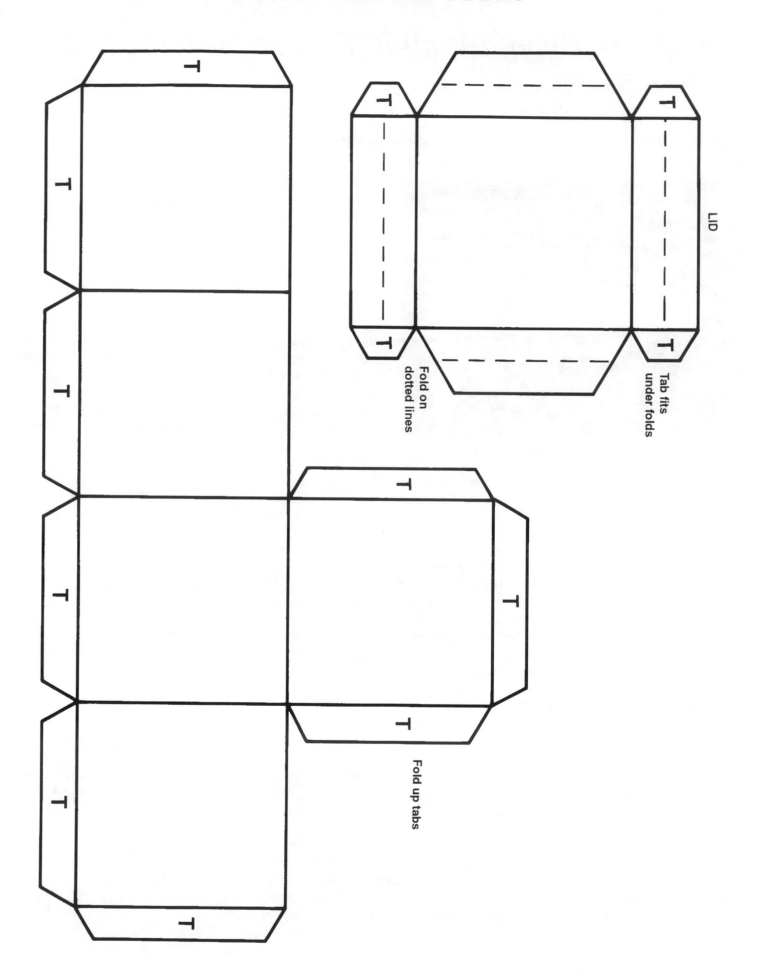

© 1999 by Prentice Hall

LID

Fold on
dotted lines

Tab fits
under folds

Fold up tabs

SLIDE 34

ACTIVITY 6

Once Upon a Walrus Tusk Scrimshaw

Arctic "Prints and Etchings"

B O N U S : BLUEBERRY WOMAN: MASKS OF THE NORTH

I N C L U D E S : PRINTS IN THE SNOW: A STAMPED "ICE-SCAPE"

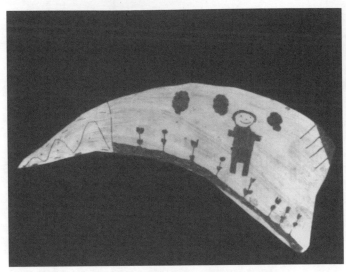

▲ Figure 8-30. "I Dream of Wildflowers in the Spring" . . . a second-grade "walrus tusk carver" portrays her view of spring coming to the tundra. An iceberg appears on the pointed end of the tusk, while on the opposite end, rays of sun break through.

The people of the North live where the weather is harsh. Although there are four seasons, it is a land of blizzards, ice storms, and snow. One might assume that the need for survival would be so demanding that the making of art would be of no great concern. Survival is certainly an issue in the Northern Territories, yet artmaking has always been a deeply rooted and profoundly important part of these remarkable cultures. The word "Eskimo" has been used to describe groups of societies that inhabit northern regions. Eskimo groups prefer the term *Inuit* to describe themselves. An individual is described by the word *Inuk*, meaning "person," in the *Inuit* language of *Inuktitut. Inuit,* the group name, translates as "the people." There are places in Alaska where the word *Eskimo* is still used. The word *Inuit* is presently accepted in place of Eskimo. Inuit, or Eskimo, live in Alaska and Canada, some in Greenland, and Siberia (Russia). It is no longer true that most (Eskimos) live in igloos and travel only by dogsled. Conventional modern housing has, for the most part, replaced the igloos. While still used as transportation across icy fields, dogsleds now have snowmobiles for companions!

The Inuit culture predates recorded history. Since the beginning, the inhabitants of the Arctic found a way to endure within the challenging environment. Animals have always been critical to survival—hunting and fishing are necessary to stay alive. Arctic peoples formed a very special relationship with the animals who clothed, fed, transported, and kept them warm. To the Arctic people, animals were life-giving and therefore to be respected. Animals were not killed for sport. Inuits offer blessings and prayers and ask for forgiveness from the animals they must hunt. The distinction between animal and human is as flexible here as it is with Native American and Canadian Indians who, along with the Inuits, were the region's first Native inhabitants. Animals almost became family members and helped give the tools, materials, and images to Inuit art. This explains why animals are a constant theme in sculpture, drawings, prints, and carved objects.

Carving into animal bone and tusk is a longstanding tradition within Inuit/Eskimo culture. The technique known as *scrimshaw* is the careful incising and decorative carving of shells, bone, and ivory. It is a craft at which the people of the North have long excelled. Scrimshaw put to use the parts of the animal that would be saved after the animal gave its spirit to the hunter or carver. A respect for beautiful craft and natural materials not only pleased the senses and recorded the skills of the people, it was also believed to keep the spirit forces content. Good art can only bring goodwill! Tools and everyday objects are things of beauty in a culture that survives endless dramatic environmental adventures. Mythology, belief, and artistic mastery were captured in a finely etched walrus tusk.

The etching and incising of bone is an ancient Northern art, while the art of printmaking in Arctic regions is a recent one. Regions that had once prospered in trade, commerce, trapping, and whaling, would suffer a decline. A love of art has helped to revive important cultures that were threatened. Thanks to a highly developed talent in carving and pictorial expression, Arctic cultures enjoyed a renaissance as their original art was recognized outside the immediate community. It wasn't until the first half of the twentieth century that the possibilities of printmaking were introduced, which allowed for a florescence of images from an etching craft long mastered. When the graphic work of lyrical carvings and etchings of Inuit artists is seen, one can almost hear the polar bears sing!

▲ Figure 8-31. Puffin listens patiently as Sea Lion repeats some local gossip. As is usually the case with gossip, another "set of whiskers" is somewhere nearby, listening in to the conversation! The eavesdropper is known to the Inuit as *puiji,* meaning "those who show their noses above water." Air-breathing sea animals fall into this definition—such as our nosy seal. This wonderful little Arctic escapade is created in the same manner as the walrus tusk scrimshaw using a lighter coverage of white paint to create a more varied surface technique. We could call this an Arctic moment!

MATERIALS

- 9" × 12" oaktag
- newspaper
- pencils
- white tempera paint
- waxy black crayon

- scissors
- large metal paper clip (see Teacher Preparation)
- masking tape

◄ Figure 8-32. Portrait of Seal, an honored animal who has provided for the Arctic peoples for centuries. People of the North feel spirit kinship with animals. They are very much aware of specific species as well as individual animals within a specific group. Is that a spirit form of Snow Owl in the upper left of the etching? *Okpik* is the Inuktitut word for Snowy Owl, in the language of the Inuit people. He is a lucky guardian spirit who watches over all of nature—Polar Bear and Geese in particular. Here he seems to be watching over Mother Seal. It is important to hunt only the proper animals which will keep life in balance in the north.

TEACHER PREPARATION

The teacher will want to provide "etching" tools for this "tusk" carving lesson. In the resourceful manner of the Inuit culture, large metal paper clips may be "opened" (pull open on end of clip). Masking tape will be used to wrap around the remaining loop which provides the handle. It is advised to prepare these simple tools in advance of lesson. **Safety Note:** Advise students to take care with sharp ends and to apply only to paper at all times. Black crayons will be used to cover the tusk surface; the thick waxy kind will work most effectively. The teacher will set up for painting procedure. White paint will be the only color used. Prepare a sample "tusk" to demonstrate the etching technique.

DIRECTIONS

1. Define the Inuit/Eskimo art, both geographically and culturally. Where do the Inuit live? What kind of weather would we expect in the northern regions—Arctic, Canada, and Alaska? Talk about the importance of animals to Inuit life and their respect for the animals they must hunt. Define tusk; use chalkboard to depict basic tusk shape for students as a reference (do not erase until end of lesson). The terms "etching," "carving," and "scrimshaw" should accompany teacher's drawing of a tusk. Circle "scrimshaw" and "etching."

2. Bring forward sample paper "tusk" (made in advance) for demonstration of "scrimshaw" technique. Show students the simple etching technique that will be used with their new "tools." The term *etching* should be explained. Put simply, an etching is both a verb and a noun. To "etch" means to "scratch out" or incise a surface that will result in the creation of a line drawing. When a professional printing process is used on an etched surface plate, the print made will be called an *etching*. **Note:** Etching is similar to carving in its subtractive process of removal; etching used for scrimshaw is an incisive, linear method.

3. Distribute pencils and paper. Students will create a walrus tusk shape, going from one end of the paper to the other horizontally, side-to-side (see Figure 8-30 for shape). Students should be reminded that this shape also looks like a horn and has to be fat on one end and skinny on the other, ending in a point. Distribute newspapers (to cover desks) along with black crayons. Students will begin to cover the tusk form with thick black crayon until no white of the paper shows.

4. Distribute painting supplies along with white tempera paint. Students will now cover the black crayon by brushing white paint over the entire surface. Let dry.

5. Distribute scissors and paper clip "etching tools." Students think about the scene that will be portrayed on the walrus tusk. A simple expression of life imagined in the Arctic or surrounding regions is fine. Other suggestions include dog sledding, playing on a snowbank, walking in showshoes (an invention of the Arctic people), or building a snow shelter (igloo). Sedna is the Mermaid of the North, responsible for creating sea life. Perhaps students would like to picture Sedna swimming on their scrimshaw tusks.

6. Students will begin to "etch" their ideas. Lines may remain as contour lines in some places, while other areas may be etched out entirely to use black to create larger areas of visual contrast. Different etching techniques may be used, such as hatching, cross-hatching, and stippling.

7. If the walrus tusk is a gift of the animal, then the scrimshaw is the gift of the carver. Would students, after responding to each other's work, be receptive to a big trade? If so, perhaps the pencil now will be used for a friendship message, to be inscribed on the back of the tusk before the exchange. In case you were wondering . . . these tusks make terrific bookmarks! Tusks help tell Arctic tales.

▲ Figure 8-33. Canadian geese fly high over the finely etched tall trees while whales swim in the icy waters. There is great animal diversity in the north on land, sea, and in the air: narwhal, walrus, seals, polar bear, whales, musk ox, lemming, ermine, Arctic rabbits, caribou, puffin, falcon, raven, moose, and the *ptarmigan*. The Willow Ptarmigan is the state bird of Alaska.

BONUS : BLUEBERRY WOMAN: MASKS OF THE NORTH

Have you ever heard the story of a legendary folk character named Blueberry Woman? In the North, a tale is told about a woman whose job was to pick enough blueberries to fill her woven basket. Blueberry Woman was said to have become distracted from her task and began to dance. She danced and danced around the Arctic land until she became an Inuit legend. This is a so-called "Lazy Woman" story, which, while charming, lacks the reality of the demanding nature of women's work. Who wove the basket? Who sewed the clothes? Who prepared the food brought in by the men from the hunt? Who hunted the small birds? Who decorated and embellished the clothing for the family? Why, it was the woman!

▲ Figure 8-34. "Blueberry Woman".

Blueberry Woman is characterized in mask form (see Figure 8-34). A student-made Blueberry Woman mask conveys an accurate description of recognizable characteristics. It is a miniature ceramic mask that conveys characteristic features. As shown, Blueberry Woman wears snow goggles—an invention of Eskimo/Inuit people, displays two red "rosy cheek" circles on either side of her nose, and is marked with a specific linear chin tattoo. In this case the goggles may have a supernatural power and the chin tattoos indicate her Arctic association. Finger masks of similar scale were very much in use by women during special occasions. The finger masks would be animated by looping two fingers through the base of the piece so that several finger masks could carry out conversations on the same hand—to the delight of children. Inuit people passed long winters with many amusing stories, games, and good-natured tricks. In spite of the severity of the environment, the Inuit were filled with poetry and humor. The spiritual realm of life—dealing primarily with animal spirits, celestial beings, and ancestors—created a need for festivals and gatherings. At these times mask dances took place. Festivals also provide a social occasion.

The extraordinary range of spirit masks express the forces of nature. Not unlike the masks of their Northwest Coastal counterparts, Inuit masks conveyed the power of transformation. Moving parts would be opened to reveal "other selves," both animal and human. The mask would move in accordance with the movement of the dancer, impersonating snapping beaks, flapping wings, and hands that function like opening doors (see Figure 8-35C). Multiple appendages appear in Inuit masks. Inuit people did not use U-forms, S-forms, or ovoids. Masks

▲ Figure 8-35a.

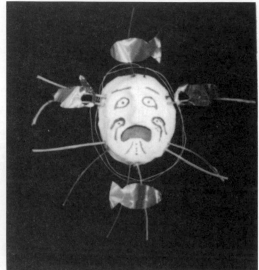

▲ Figure 8-35b.

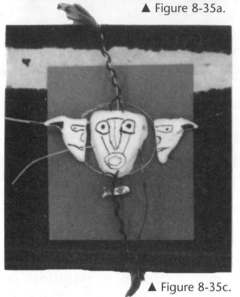

▲ Figure 8-35c.

▲ Figure 8-35d.

of the Inuit Arctic peoples have a recognizable set of bent wood hoops (see Figure 8-35b) that appear often as a three-tiered "halo." This is not a framing device: The hoops refer to the levels of the Inuit universe—lower, middle, and upper. Masks convey Inuit cosmology and belief. Styles, of course, vary. Objects such as favored animals—much like fetishes (see Activity 4)—may be added. Eskimo masks may also be regarded as a personal guardian animal spirit. Students who provided the stunning miniature Inuit masks have incorporated stylistic features traditional to these northern people. For example, the *Ingalik* of Alaska, carvers of complex wooden masks, often utilized features as shown in Figure 8-35a. One might expect to find the cousins of Blueberry Woman along with abstract interpretations of Bear Spirit and forces of nature such as Wind Spirit in the masks of the north. Perhaps, the student-made miniature mask (Figure 8-35d) represents the Spirit of the Moon which defines the months of the *Inupiat* (North Eskimo) year. Did you know that *September* is the *Moon When Birds Fly South* and that *May* is the *Moon When Rivers Flow*? Students who wish to make miniature Inuit/Eskimo masks need only to mix the elements of nature (as shown) with natural materials and their own creativity. If the results look anything like these masks, the spirits are sure to be pleased.

INCLUDES : PRINTS IN THE SNOW! A STAMPED "ICE-SCAPE"

Printmaking has become a vital art form to the people of the north. It is a means of income as well as cultural and personal expression. The Inuit and their neighbors have proved themselves, over the ages, to be wonderful carvers—one only needs to think of soapstone sculptures to remember this special skill. Surprisingly, it was not until the first half of the twentieth century that northern people became more versatile in the printmaking arts. The Hudson Bay Company, in 1948, began a program to support the arts. The legendary trailblazer James Houston, who exchanged ideas with Arctic artists, helped to innovate the printmaking movement. With the help of government support, art cooperatives, influences from outside sources such as Japan—world-reknowned for their woodblock prints—Inuit artists have proliferated in printmaking techniques and design. Stone cuts, stenciled prints, etchings, lithographs, and even drawings have expanded to the point where northern graphic arts are internationally exhibited, collected, and appreciated.

Is it possible that the first print ever discovered came from an Ice Age toddler who pressed his fur-wrapped shoe—called a *Mukluk*—into the snow? This shaky fact remains unconfirmed, but we know that the stamp print still remains a ready means of teaching the nature of printmaking. There are many commercial stamps available today—virtually an artform in its own right. For this classroom "Ice-scape," simple snowflake stamps will do just fine. Fish and other creatures may also be used. Students will create a mixed-media print by both drawing and stamp printing a scene that could occur in Canada, Alaska, Siberia, or Greenland.

▲ Figure 8-36. The young boy shown here has chosen the subject of ice fishing and seems quite happy about his catch. Dogs, who obligingly pull sleds across the tundra, are also faithful fishing companions. It's probably pretty cold. Igloo and snowfall indicate frigid temperatures that cheer on the young fisherman. In this kind of weather, we can only hope he didn't forget his *parka*!

Russia, Europe, Ireland, and the British Isles

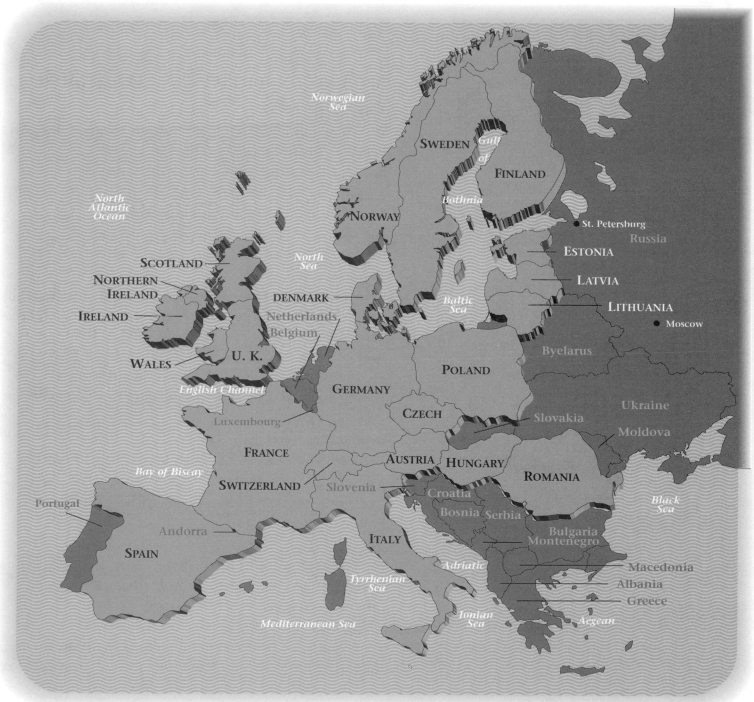

Norwegian Sea

North Atlantic Ocean

SWEDEN

Gulf of Bothnia

FINLAND

NORWAY

St. Petersburg

Russia

ESTONIA

North Sea

LATVIA

SCOTLAND

LITHUANIA

NORTHERN IRELAND

DENMARK

Baltic Sea

IRELAND

Netherlands

Moscow

Belgium

WALES

U. K.

POLAND

Byelarus

English Channel

GERMANY

Luxembourg

CZECH

Slovakia

Ukraine

Moldova

FRANCE

AUSTRIA

HUNGARY

ROMANIA

Bay of Biscay

SWITZERLAND

Slovenia

Croatia

Black Sea

Portugal

Bosnia

Serbia

Andorra

ITALY

Bulgaria

Montenegro

SPAIN

Adriatic

Macedonia

Tyrrhenian Sea

Albania

Greece

Ionian Sea

Aegean

Mediterranean Sea

Russia, Europe, Ireland, and the British Isles

The lacquer-painted wooden egg represents Ukranian *Pysanky*.

Student work inspired by the ancient Irish *Book of Kells*.

The Polish rooster is a symbol of vitality and renewal.

ART ACTIVITIES FOR BECOMING CULTURE SMART

Activity 1
Snowmaidens and Firebirds: "Russian Lacquer" Box Art
Russian "Treasure Box" Painting
BONUS: RUSSIAN TEAROOM—THE CLASSIC SAMOVAR!

Activity 2
Matrioshka: Little Mother of Russia
Family Dinner Placecards/Toymaking Arts
BONUS: EGGS, FABERGÉ OR UKRANIAN? . . . AND ICONS!

Activity 3
Sassy Lithuanian Sashes: Eastern Europe Bands Together!
Friendship Weaves Through Romania, Hungary, Czech Republic, Latvia, and Lithuania . . . in Stitches and in Words

Activity 4
Proud Polish Rooster Crows: Kuku Ryku!
Polish Wycinanki and Quilling/Standing Paper Sculpture

Activity 5
Irish Spirit, Celtic Skill: The Book of Kells
The Decorated Letter With Border Illuminations/Irish Book Design

Activity 6
Glad to Be Plaid! Wee Bonnie Scottish Castles
Pop-up Castles/Clan Tartans

Activity 7
Now Seating: Alice in British Wonderland!
Alice in Wonderland Playing "Card" Characters
BONUS: THE ABC'S OF ENGLISH CHAPBOOKS

Activity 8
The Wonder of Europe: Grand Sightseeing Postcard Tour!
Natural and Architectural Wonders/3-D Mail Art/Arts Advocacy!

To know the Art of Russia, Europe, Ireland, and the British Isles . . . . .

. . . . . *is to cover a* broad territory—both geographically and artistically. Russia today is the largest country in the world. The cultures of Russia are diverse; its borders are eastern Europe, the Middle East, Mongolia, China, and the Arctic and Pacific oceans. Siberia, in the north Arctic region, is Russian territory. At the northeast lies the Bering Strait; at the southeast, the land meets the Sea of Japan. Russia spans two continents—Europe in the west and Asia in the east, separated by the Ural Mountains. Ancient cultures that form a part of Russia's history range from Scythia on the Black Sea to Sweden. A Swedish Viking chieftain named *Rurik* gave Russia its name. Of all the influences and origins that compose the soul of the Slavic land called Russia, central to art and belief was the influence of *Byzantium,* as seen in the painted and inlaid Byzantine icons. The impact of western European culture has also been great, and has been assimilated into Russian art and society.

A summary of Russia in artistic terms includes icons, mosaics, frescoes, onion-domed architecture, popular folk art, such as hand-colored prints called *luboks,* shining lacquer box art, wooden carvings, paintings, and sculpture. Treasures of the church and the imperial courts fill out Russian art history. The palaces of Czars and Czarinas once overflowed with riches and glittering regalia such as the Fabergé eggs. As opulence and splendor gave way to a revolutionary Russia, icon painting was transformed into the more decorative themes of Russian lacquer art. Folk tales and legends hold a special place in Russian hearts. The span of arts for which Russia is renowned—drama, ballet, the theatrical stage, and certainly literature—draws freely upon folk traditions. Post-revolutionary Russia brought the growth of the graphic arts and film. Painting included social realism and modern abstraction, as seen in the work of Vasily Kandinsky, who once said, "Painting is a language . . . to speak to our soul of its daily bread."

Eastern Europe, like Russia, is the source of great folk traditions in weaving, embroidery, carving, paper crafting, ceramics, and woodworks. The grouping of countries referred to as eastern Europe embraced a wide variety of customs and religious beliefs. Ukraine, once called the breadbasket of the Soviet Union, is also known as the cradle of Russian civilization. To understand the zesty nature of European folk life is to know the pleasure of a bowl of *borscht,* introduced in the Ukraine. Borscht, a beet soup, is an eastern European and Russian delight, especially when served in a crockery bowl patterned with spring flowers. Nature and the cycles of the harvest abound in the favorite dishes; the floral, vegetable, and symbolic design motifs are an integral part of the eastern European household and culture. Most of the regions are forested, accounting for the skill in wood crafting—from puppets and furniture to architecture and sculpture. Constatin Brancusi, the sculptor, was born in rural Romania, surrounded by woods. Brancusi's "Bird in Space" launched modern sculpture and—with the refusal of customs officials to recognize the work as art—legally raised the twentieth-century question, "What is art?" The influence for "Bird" is believed to be a mythical bird, called *Maiastra,* that is seen as a repeated architectural motif on Romanian village rooftops in the form of "skylark" ridge tiles.

Seafaring was a great influence on the art of Nordic Europeans. The Vikings were skilled wood carvers and metal workers; the carved prows of Viking ships were visually dramatic—powerful sculpture afloat! Their curvilinear interlacing designs also appeared on memorial stones marked with incised letters called *runes.* In Ireland, manuscript illumination, in the hands of monks, produced such magnificent books as the *Book of Kells.* An intricate interweaving of linear forms and zoomorphic elements established the basis of Celtic design. From ships to brooches, from vellum to stone, the arts of northern Europe bear a characteristic resemblance. Along with inspiration from land and sea, religion played a central role in art development; the appearance of the cross as a foundation for design structure is prominent. The Celtic knot, a symbol used by Druids in pre-Christian Ireland, forms an endless circle to suggest endurance and eternity. *The Book of Kells* employed the Celtic knot as an ornamental motif.

European civilization grew with the rise of the great cathedrals in central Europe. Towns and trade developed in the Middle Ages, along with a social system that supported artisans and guilds. Italy and northern Europe entered the Renaissance, a period of great growth in art and science not seen since the Golden Age of the Greeks. It was a period that would lead to exploration and discovery. Dutch trade, Spanish and Portuguese sea expeditions, and French and English expansion and colonization increased commerce and positioned Europe for empire building. The changes that occurred during this time had an impact on world history that could not then have been imagined.

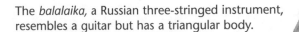

The *balalaika,* a Russian three-stringed instrument, resembles a guitar but has a triangular body.

ACTIVITY 1

Snowmaidens and Firebirds: "Russian Lacquer" Box Art

Russian "Treasure Box" Painting

B O N U S : RUSSIAN TEAROOM—THE CLASSIC SAMOVAR!

▲ Figure 9-1. Snowmaiden was the daughter of Mighty Winter and "Faerie" Spring. When lovely Snowmaiden reached the age of sixteen, her parents grew fearful for her safety in the world. Advice was sought from the Spirit of the Wood, who warned that Snowmaiden must always hide from the strong dangerous rays sent to Earth by Sun god, Yarilo. Along with this, Snowmaiden must never fall in love! Alas, when winter turned to spring, Snowmaiden lost her heart to a handsome young man. A walk in the woods, the music from a flute, and sweet promises led her outside her own little cottage. She fell in love, as predicted, and lovely Snowmaiden melted as surely as snow in the early spring sun. This is a legend of springtime and a cautionary tale of love.

Firebirds and fairy tales, the spiraling patterned onion domes cast against the snowy Moscow sky, while zesty folk dancers leap, arms crossed, against their flowing shirts . . . ballerinas, dancing bears, a three-horsed *troika* . . . are all to be found on Russian lacquer box art! Such romantic and dramatic images are offered when one envisions the great, vast land of Russia! Who can think of this geographically and politically charged nation without imagining sweeping movie themes, great novels, brilliant musicians and composers, and theatrical arts? Although Russia is difficult to define in simple terms, its rich history and heritage is delightfully captured on lacquer boxes! The mood of Russia throughout the centuries has been of great aristocratic grace, hardy survival of long Russian winters—mixed with humor, melancholy, and adventure!

Russian lacquer box art has always been exquisitely descriptive of Russian life. A primary subject of this lacquer painting was altered by the Russian Revolution, after which religious icon painting was no longer tolerated. Lacquer artists then concentrated on themes of landscapes, birds and flowers, and the architectural beauty of the towns and villages. Most important, classic Russian folktales and their specific characters came to grace vividly the shining black boxes, trays, and various objects. The scale of the painting is typically small, which is why this art is often viewed as a miniature painting. The Snowmaiden, *Snegurochka . . . Vasilisa* (a Russian Cinderella) . . . the Girl with the Golden Hair (reminiscent of Rapunzel) . . . *Baba Yaga* (a terrible witch), and many other story characters are distinctly Russian *and* universal. The decorative style of lacquer box art, encapsulated in elegant gold borders, does not ignore its past—elongated icon styles can still be seen in the proportions and compositions of this splendid folk art. Characteristic styles of Russian lacquer box art can be identified with four art-producing villages outside of Moscow: Fedoskino, Kholui, Mstera—and Palekh, where ancient Russian art is very much alive. History, fantasy, Czar and Czarina, bravery and beauty, great heroics as well as everyday scenes are the miracles of Russian lacquer box art.

MATERIALS

- pencils
- manila or white paper
- rulers
- acrylic gloss medium
- brushes (assorted sizes)

- water containers
- gold pens (nontoxic)
- boxes (see Teacher Preparation)
- reproducible page: "Russian Design Elements"

TEACHER PREPARATION

This rewarding "treasure box" lesson will require cardboard/paper boxes provided by the teacher and/or student. (Boxes shown in Activity 1 are recycled from the resource room; they could have been used for sending AV film or print matter.) Some suggestions for boxes, which are preferably sturdy, are recycled jewelry boxes with good painting surface, gift boxes, small paper boxes used for closet storage, and—in a pinch—shoe boxes. Hat boxes would be beautiful. Local arts and crafts stores carry plain boxes that students may purchase if not in the art budget. Painting will take place on the lid of the box. (Note: Authentic Russian lacquer boxes made today are typically produced in a dry-baked papier-mâché process.)

The teacher may want to have additional references on Russia available for preparatory sketches. Moscow skyline, Russian fairy tale books, images of a Moscow circus, or the Bolshoi ballet can provide alternative themes for box illustrations.

This lesson, which requires several class periods for completion, may be considered a "studio" lesson inasmuch as it requires preparation that is similar to painting acrylic canvas and directly emerges from Russian painting tradition. The teacher will want to decide if students will prepare the black gesso painting surfaces or the teacher (with assistants) will

▲ Figure 9-2. Is she The Girl With the Golden Hair or a damsel in distress? Shown here in actual size, this handpainted, miniature box is so finely detailed that a magnifying glass is needed to appreciate it! As one might expect, lacquerware is indeed highly lacquered! Many coats are required to create a high luster.

do the job. If black gesso is unavailable commercially, simply use white gesso, let dry, then coat with black acrylic paint. Use the usual painting set-up (cups, towels, etc.) when studio painting begins. "F.Y.I.":—Black Russian boxes may be expected to have bright red interiors!

◄ Figure 9-3. Student Marcus Robinson, age 13, brightly interprets onion-dome architecture with all the splendor of Samarkand! Flying over the rooftops is our Firebird. The famous Russian folk tale of the Firebird tells of a sweet and heroic young orphan girl named Maryushka who becomes a wonderful handicraft artist. She was soon known far beyond the small village where she lived—until word of her marvelous skills reached Kaschey, a terrible ogre. So jealous of her art was he that he transformed himself into an eagle and turned Maryushka into a Firebird. He did capture her, but could not capture her spirit, for she shed her beautiful magic feathers across the land so that those who appreciate the beauty of art could carry on her tradition.

DIRECTIONS

1. Discuss pictures and themes common to Russian lacquer box art: folktales and legends, Moscow city architecture (onion dome forms), mythology and, if desired, ballet, circus, and theater. Pay particular attention to costume! Point out the importance of decorative flowers in borders and designs. Look at the very Russian use of bright colors against black background trimmed in gold! The weather and the seasons will be of consideration, particularly winter and spring.

▲ Figure 9-4. An ornate treatment by Allyson gives us a snowy Russian winter amidst churches and cathedrals. Note that even in the heart of winter is the promise of another spring—tiny flowers press through newly fallen snow.

2. Distribute paper, pencils, and rulers. Use as a reference the border designs on the reproducible. Students will frame out space to be used for the decorative border with ruled lines as a guide. Sketch-paper size should conform in proportion to dimension of the box that will be painted. Point out that the proportions of figures evolved from icon painting tradition are therefore elongated. Reproducible can help as idea starters.

3. Students will want to concentrate on a single "scene" that describes a story, place, or theme. Draw the selected idea: for example, the Czar and Czarina in a sled against the backdrop of a snowy Moscow night. Specific characters or elements of Russian folk legend should either be spatially planned or included in the original sketch; the painting of the box may be done in stages, such as background or foreground formatted first.

4. After a satisfactory sketch has been made, students will draw their border and scene on a dry black box lid (see Teacher Preparation). Students may want to sketch in major shapes—details can be added later.

5. Students begin their border design on the box format. Bring forward paints in painting trays or palettes (see Teacher Preparation). Students paint their enchanted scenes!

6. Is the box lid compositionally pleasing? Be sure to include the elements that will further identify this box as Russian. Refer to the reproducible. When paint is dry, use gold pens to delineate form and details.

7. Russian painters apply numerous coats of lacquer or varnish to make their boxes shine and to protect their art. Students (or teacher) will apply acrylic gloss medium, using two or three coats, for a similar effect.

8. Student lacquer box painters must not hide their treasures! Display them where all can admire this art, which students will forever have for keepsakes, letters, jewelry, tickets to the ballet, and other treasured moments.

BONUS : RUSSIAN TEAROOM—THE CLASSIC SAMOVAR!

In Russia, where the summers are short and the winters very long, tea is a necessary comfort. The *samovar* is the quintessential Russian teapot in which many "glasses of tea" are kept hot. While there are various shapes and sizes for this tea-making urn, its identity is unmistakably associated with Russian culture. Anyone who has seen a samovar and enjoyed its brew will not soon forget its accommodating and pleasing presence. Some samovars are crafted of gleaming brass, while others wear the flowers, leaves, birds, and fruit that come to life along "Mother Volga . . . the river that is the joy of the Russian heart . . ." Designs inspired by nature and the elegance of the pot itself are often found in Russian tearooms as well as in Russian homes, surrounded by other crafts—and, of course, the Russian people themselves.

Students will enjoy an introduction to the samovar if they've not had the previous pleasure. For those whose heritage contains a samovar, this activity will be equally welcome. Using the form suggested in the full-page template, students will create their own samovar with decoration suggested through Russian motif. Much like the classic Greek vase, the samovar has a strong shape that invites design ideas. Consider the fact that the shape is three-dimensional and round and that it will need a teaspout somewhere. Students may create a "reversible" samovar or continue the design from front to back. While "simple" works well, students may be encouraged to elaborate on basic design ideas. In fact, the samovar may inspire the pictorial development of a tearoom environment. This may be accomplished by gluing the samovar onto a larger drawing paper. Using markers, crayons, and other applied materials, a complete tearoom may indeed sprout up! (If this idea is appealing, there is no need to create a two-sided samovar.) Now relax and . . . (don't try this without an experienced Russian or Ukranian on hand nearby) . . . have a nice, hot *glass* of tea!

Figure 9-5. Students cut a "potbellied" samovar shape out of paper and fold this symmetrical shape for efficient cutting, handles and all. Decorate with the flowers found on the banks of the Mother Volga River, the hearts of lovers who are reunited, and any other symbol or shape that seems to fit the vessel. The base should be distinguished from the body. If you add a spout, you may enjoy an old-fashioned glass of Russian tea!

RUSSIAN DESIGN ELEMENTS

Firebird

Snowmaiden

Stylized Firebird

Mythical Lion

SAMOVAR TEMPLATE

ACTIVITY 2

Matrioshka: Little Mother of Russia

Family Dinner Placecards/Toymaking Arts

BONUS: EGGS, FABERGÉ OR UKRANIAN? . . . AND ICONS!

▲ Figure 9-6. Family values! Matrioshka figure group belongs together. This group, which at first appears to be an extended family, can be taken to represent the diversity of Russia. Isn't it wonderful that creativity allows us to change uniform shapes into individuals!

She's a doll, the bright little **Matrioshka** (mah-tree-osh-kah), who wears a *babushka* (scarf) as she stands with a serene smile for Mother Russia! *Babushka* also means grandmother, who enjoys her kerchief, too! Matrioshka, which literally means "little mother" in Russian, is more than a darling little mother figure—she is a symbol. Bright with painted flowers and leaves, the wood-crafted Matrioshka is identified with rebirth and renewal. Her body form is egg-shaped, her expression is one of love.

Traditionally shown in patterns of yellow, red, green, and black, the Matrioshka is not alone—for she carries within her a nesting family. Children, parents, husbands, even pets are inside her friendly shape. What could be more motherly than to contain your family within? Whether mother, father, sister, or brother, all individuals may indeed be regarded as the sum total of the individual. Matrioshka can also be viewed as a "stages-of-development" doll, realizing that we all grow from egg to baby, to youth, and to maturity. Matrioshka reminds us that we are never alone, for the people and experiences of our life remain with us and help us grow.

The history of folk art in Russia is long, while the history of the Matrioshka itself is relatively short. The Matrioshka dolls that are now so popular everywhere had their start with a group of artist designers at the Children's Educational Workshop in Moscow, at the end of the 19th century. Intended to maintain a hearty tradition of wood turning and toymaking crafts, the Matrioshka toys embody direct skill, charm, and family sentiment. Commercial production of Matrioshkas soon followed and grew. Matrioshka connoisseurs will recognize how doll appearance conforms to region of production. Even though the largest doll is usually Matrioshka herself, the mother-figure doll sets have grown interpretive. One might encounter Russian nesting dolls that represent specific families—politicians, famous artists—even a mother hen, nested with all her chicks!

Figure 9-7. As seen here, with his wife and family, we have a big papa figure. Note the adorable little ones. ▶

318

MATERIALS

- 12″ × 18″ white oaktag (substitute heavy drawing paper)
- colored markers
- scissors
- "multicultural markers"(optional), also known as people colors (Binney-Smith Crayola™)

- pencils/erasers
- reproducible page: "Matrioshka Templates"

TEACHER PREPARATION

The teacher will want to consider the size and number of each student's Matrioshka family before the amount of paper needed for this lesson is determined. Additionally, students may use Matrioshka templates (see the reproducible) to outline directly onto oaktag. Older students may want to take the challenge of interpretation. If the teacher has a collection of scarves with floral motifs and, of course, actual nesting dolls, now is surely the time to bring them to class. If not, create a paper Matrioshka example. Be sure the colored markers include Russian favorites of yellow, red, green, and black. Finished "dolls" may function as special family-dinner placecards. However, these Matrioshkas can stand on their own anytime, for any occasion!

DIRECTIONS

1. *"How many boys and girls have ever seen a Matrioshka nesting doll?"*

   Provide Matrioshka sample(s). Three important words should be written on the board:

   - Matrioshka
   - Babushka
   - Russia

   Have students repeat these words along with you so that they are learned along with the lesson. Discuss the toymaking tradition as well as its identity as a family. Explain how dolls nest within one another. If dolls are available, allow students to examine them.

▲ Figure 9-8. About 400 miles outside of Moscow sits the town of Semyonov, where the popular Semyonov Matrioshka doll is produced. Her scarf, her rosy cheeks, and central floral design identify her. As in all Matrioshka nesting dolls, sets range from a very tiny "baby" piece to the large mother doll. Usually five or six other figures are nested inside a shell form, although numbers and styles can vary.

2. Distribute paper, templates, scissors, and pencils. Cut out the desired template forms. Fold paper in half. Place the top of the forms on the fold of the paper. Trace the outline of the template and remove. Cut out Matrioshka. Use pencil to draw her face in the center and a "babushka" around her face. Students will think about their own family and the people they love: baby sisters, older brothers, grandma, and so forth, using the Russian style.

▲ Figure 9-9. Matrioshkas are best when they are as individual as the dollmakers themselves. Students proudly display their own sense of self through color, shape, and design. Note that the same amount of attention given to the doll's frontal view is carried over to the reverse side. Fronts and backs are equally important.

3. Draw patterns, designs, or floral motifs on the front and back of the body form.

4. Distribute markers. Apply bright, clear color to dolls. Support students' use of multicultural markers for variety of skin tones that will allow students to recognize themselves in their creation. (Do not feel compelled to emphasize this option; let matters unfold naturally.)

5. Depending on number of family members determined, decide when Matrioshka sets are complete. Dolls may be "stored" inside each other, ranging from the largest to the smallest figure, in anticipation of their appearance at the family table. (**Note:** Matrioshka may easily be converted into decorative ornaments, for they are all-occasion paper dolls.) Did you know that the word *petrushka* is Russian for doll?

BONUS : EGGS, FABERGÉ OR UKRANIAN? . . . AND ICONS

Hatch an icon from an egg, whether or not you like your eggs Fabergé or Ukranian. Eggs are indeed important in Russian and Ukranian culture, for they represent the universal theme of rebirth in nature. Of course, an egg is not simply an egg. When in the Ukraine, decorated eggs can represent many things—waves, hearts, fruits of nature, and   ancient symbols. The **Pysanky** eggs, as they are known, are typically created through a resist technique using wax and dyes. Their appeal is the honest charm of folk art. The Fabergé eggs, on the other hand, are quite another matter. These fabulously elaborate eggs are in the category of precious jewelry and are fantastic objects for collection. These eggs do not crack easily, for they are made of precious metals and priceless jewels. These eggs originated in Russian courtly aristocracy, by Karl Fabergé, who was the Czar's jeweler. As one might imagine, no expense was spared for His Majesty. Fabergé eggs are most highly prized to this very day.

The tradition of jeweled elaboration existed in Russia since the early days of the Byzantine. From glittering mosaic to jewel-encrusted gold, the Russian icon emerged from the Byzantine icon as a specific expression of artistic value. Icons may also be as simple as Ukranian eggs when painted directly onto humble wood. Historically, the icon is a religious figure representing a saint or holy personage. Icons are products of Eastern Orthodox faith and appear in St. Basil's Cathedral in Moscow, among other locations. Icons are also found in houses.

How to recognize an icon? Along with the materials mentioned, the icon itself appears as a full-figure or portrait-style representation that has shared characteristics. Icons are not naturalistic in appearance. They are stylized, elongated forms that often appear to be staring beyond the viewer's gaze. Dark eyes and long necks often appear under a hooded garment, ornate embellishments may accompany or be part of the image. As in the development of Russian lacquer art box, icon painting may embrace themes that are not necessarily religious. For instance, the icon proportion is applied to the representation of popular folk heroes. The important icon style is very much ingrained in Russian art history.

A way for students to learn about Fabergé design, Ukranian Pysanky, and icon painting is suggested in the following Bonus Activity. Use materials listed, and add paper fasteners, gold doilies, watercolors, and crayons. "Jewels" and gold pens are optional, but highly suggested. Glitter pens and sparkle pipe cleaners will make eggs *very* Fabergé-like! The mere simplified approach of Pysansky design motif will be incorporated on the reverse side (see pages 310 and 320 for examples.)

▲ Figure 9-10. St. George the Dragon Slayer is a beloved subject for Russian icons. This authentic icon is tiny in size, painted on wood, and displays a style of painting found in both icon and Russian lacquerware art.

MATERIALS

- white oaktag
- markers
- glue
- ribbons, jewels, gold doilies, gold pens, glitter pens, sparkle pipe cleaners
- pencil
- scissors
- crayons
- pinking shears
- watercolor paints
- brushes
- paper fasteners

Figure 9-11. Art educator Bette Lawrence crafted this beautiful example of icon technique, complete with metallic and jewel overlays. Does *this* particular *icon of Western art* look familiar? ▶

HOW TO HATCH AN ICON FROM AN EGG

1. Draw egg shapes of approximately eight inches onto white oaktag and cut out. Each student will glue together an egg "pocket" to contain a portrait icon.

2. With white glue, create a seam and join the two egg blanks together. One egg will be your Fabergé; the other will be your Pysanky.

◄ Figures 9-12a &
9-12b. Student
art shows plain and
fancy eggs. Simple
and direct designs
work best for our
Pysanky egg. On
the fancy side is
the fabulous
Fabergé egg,
shown in *b*. ►

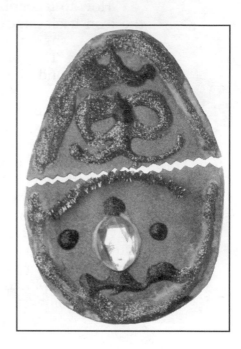

3. Create a crayon-resist Ukranian egg using simple folk motifs. Paint with watercolors and let dry. Flip egg over lightly!

4. Using decorative swirls and whirls, design a fancy egg with markers. Add trim of ribbons, jewels, and gold doilies, if desired. Plan for the egg to be cut with pinking shears at the center. Set aside.

5. Using slightly smaller proportioned paper, create an icon portrait. Suggested subjects: Czar, Czarina, and examples in the illustrations. It may also be a self-portrait or one of a leader, hero, or famous Russian dancer! Use icon principles by outlining features in black marker (similar to a face in stained glass). Cut out the icon. Use a gold doily or illustration shown on page 323 for headdress, if desired. Apply markers or crayons for skin and costume. Set aside.

6. Cut in half with pinking shears or use a zig-zag cut. Punch holes in the corner of one side of each half and place a paper fastener through the holes to create a hinge, allowing for overlap. The egg should open and close on one side.

7. Slip the icon into the egg. Close the egg. When all the icon painters and eggmakers are finished, have a "Grand Opening." **Note of interest:** Teachers may want to develop with students a simple eggstand designed to display these marvelous eggs.

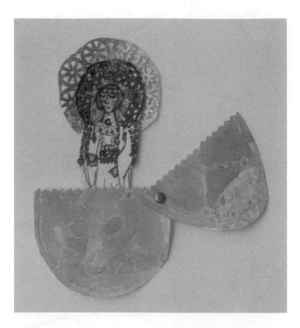

▲ Figure 9-13. Crack open this double-sided egg to hatch a beautiful and detailed icon made by Angela. The icon herself looks like she would be a perfect guardian angel.

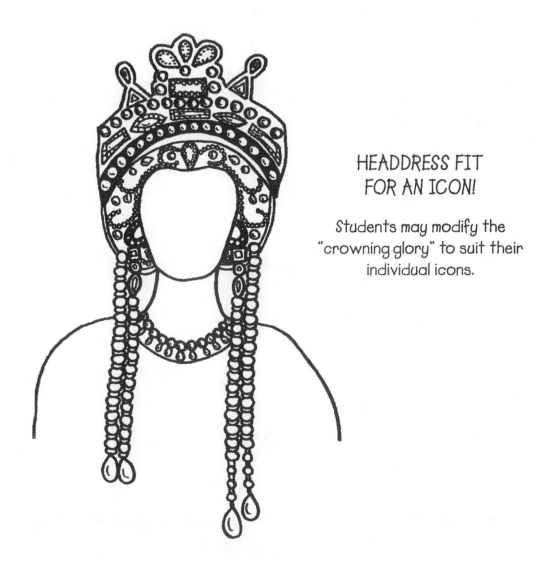

HEADDRESS FIT FOR AN ICON!

Students may modify the "crowning glory" to suit their individual icons.

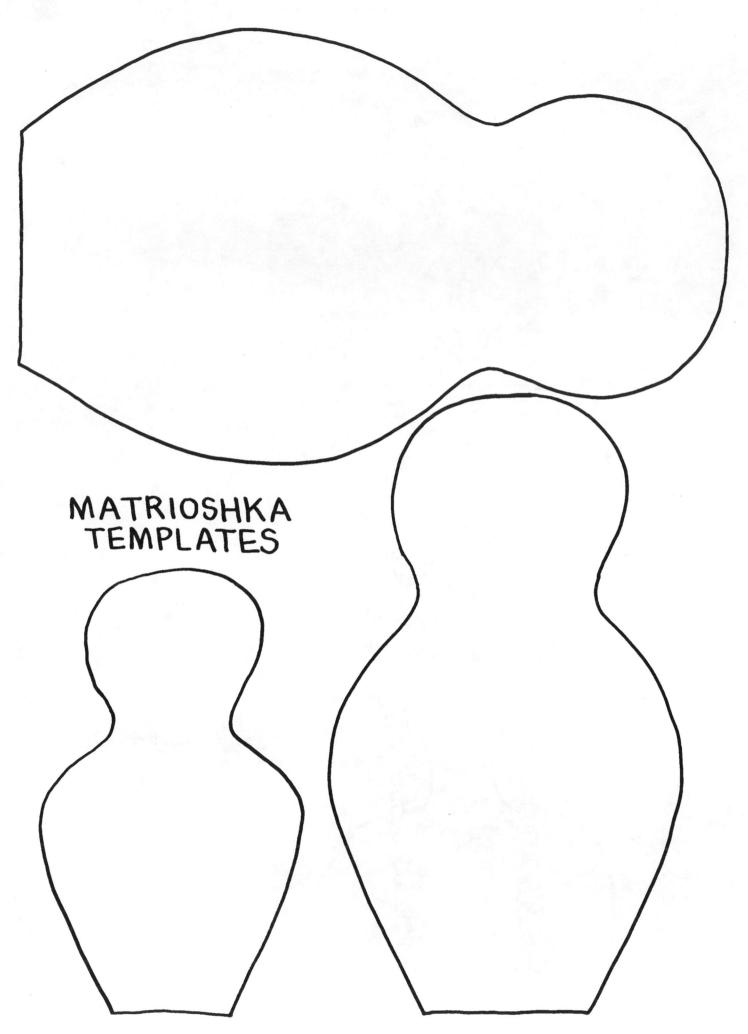

MATRIOSHKA
TEMPLATES

ACTIVITY 3

Sassy Lithuanian Sashes: Eastern Europe Bands Together!

Friendship Weaves Through Romania, Hungary, Czech Republic, Latvia, and Lithuania . . . in Stitches and in Words

In Lithuania they call them sashes, these woven ornamental bands that are rich with symbol, story, and craft. There are Lithuanian people today who smile as they remember the coded, hidden meanings of the delightful sashes, often seen as belts or neckties. Many sashes reveal affection in their specific stitched patterns. Lucky is the Lithuanian fellow who is gifted with such a sash from his sweetheart. A love given in art lasts forever; it is a woven record of the heart.

Sashes can be romantic, chatty, or ceremonial. Country folk attach little bells to sashes of cattle as they are led to pasture to celebrate early spring. Sashes are used also as decorative tapestries for the home as well as for adornments in weddings, births, and departures. The mythical Lithuanian goddess Laima . . .

▲ Figure 9-14. Like friendship itself, this woven treasure of lace, paper, burlap, and loving care create a union of sentiment and balance.

"spreads the newborn babies a lifetime sash of happiness" . . . according to ancient folklore.

Bands of beauty dazzle alongside embroidery and beadwork. These are the living arts of Eastern Europe. In the Baltic states of Latvia, Lithuania, and Estonia, people still proudly display traditional costumes on customary holidays. Estonians enjoy their Mid-Summer Day celebration with dance and song. People still love a big bonfire where sashes fly and spirits soar!

In Romania embroidery and beadwork sparkle. Age-old motifs appear in the bright colors for which the region is known. Romania's gregarious neighbor, Hungary, is alive with glorious handiwork! The crafts burst with the flowers and fruit that nature has granted this forested country. Try a steaming bowl of **goulash**—a *Magyar* (Hungarian) specialty, or absorb yourself in the rhythms of a zesty violin, or chuckle to the wisdom of old proverbs—you just might find yourself all wrapped up in the thriving folk life of Eastern Europe!

MATERIALS

- 12" × 18" white paper
- lace trim (see Teacher Preparation)
- 12" × 18" colored construction paper
- 1/4" graph paper
- burlap strips
- scissors
- glue sticks
- colored markers

- rulers
- pencils
- clear self-stick vinyl (optional, see Teacher Preparation)
- quote books (optional, see Teacher Preparation)
- reproducible page: "Lithuanian Fabric Designs"

TEACHER PREPARATION

The teacher may precut paper strips in various widths; likewise, cut flat burlap into bands. For the lacy effect, plastic lace tablecloth, which is usually sold either by roll or by package, is recommended. The plasticized effect is stiffer than cloth lace, which makes the weaving easier. Students will create their own paper looms as well as frames that will serve as a border. This lesson will teach textural weaving and terms of other fabric arts—along with the role of crafts in expressing human feeling. The utilitarian outcome of this lesson is the production of an actual placemat to be used within the students' home, if desired. For domestic use, obtain clear self-stick vinyl or clear lamination sheets and follow product directions. This will protect the paper weave and enable the placemat to be wiped and used again and again. The teacher should bring into class various examples of fabric arts, such as a woven scarf, a stitchery sampler, a lace handkerchief, and a beaded bag for students to appreciate with all their senses. Refer to the reproducible and any other visual references of stitching. Make quotation books and books of proverbs and sayings available to complete the lesson.

▲ Figure 9-15. Student Rachel Choi wove a precise and skillful design. A sweet little enamelware dish from Austria and "golden" *Khokhloma* lacquerware from Russia sit upon it. Nearby the very source of inspiration for the arts of Eastern Europe and Russia sits—bright flowers and leafy greens.

DIRECTIONS

1. Discuss the tradition of weaving as well as other handicrafts in Eastern Europe. A vocabulary list may be developed on the board to include cross-stitch, embroidery, lacemaking, and weaving. A simple diagram of a loom is provided on page 327.

2. Offer various examples of handicraft items in order for students to understand similarities and differences between stitched items. The focus will now be upon the art of cross-stitching and its ability to create words, patterns, and figures. Distribute cut paper strips, along with visual references.

3. Students will block out patterns and designs on graph paper with pencil, using the grid as their guide. Encourage students to include words, names, and their own designs. Apply colored markers to represent stitches that describe the designs drawn. Set aside.

4. Students are now ready for weaving. Distribute colored construction paper and follow the directions shown on page 327.

   a. Fold colored (not white) construction paper in half.

   b. Using a ruler, draw a line on 3 sides where the paper opens, about 1/2".

   c. Use ruler to create lines from "end line" to fold, about 1/2" apart.

   d. Cut along lines, except "end line."

   e. Open folded warp. You have a loom!

5. Distribute burlap, lace, and colored paper to begin weaving. Be sure that students understand "one under . . . one over" as the method that enables strips to band together. Demonstrate, if necessary. Students will alternate between colors and textures. **Note:** Cross-stitch paper bands work best when used as border brackets and as a central means of balance. These bands should "not" be woven; use glue to secure them in place.

6. Complete woven mat by applying lace borders using glue. Trim ends of strips and glue down ends onto edge of loom.

7. Distribute white paper and quote books. Discuss the messages that quotes and proverbs contain. Allow students to quote *themselves!* In a decorative manner, students will write a quote or friendship message on white paper using markers. Glue to the back of the weaving. Here are some student selections:

HOW TO MAKE A LOOM

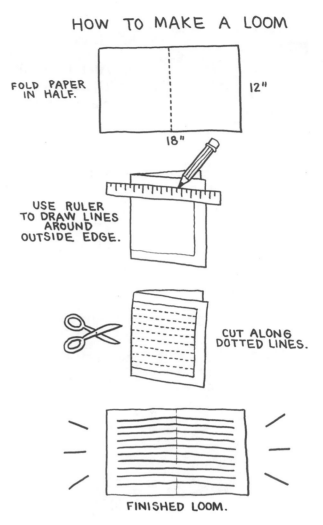

FOLD PAPER IN HALF.

12"

18"

USE RULER TO DRAW LINES AROUND OUTSIDE EDGE.

CUT ALONG DOTTED LINES.

FINISHED LOOM.

▲ Figure 9-16. It is precious to see the triumph Lauren has had in coordinating a variety of woven materials.

- *"Family and Friends are hidden treasures."*

- *"He who gives to me teaches me to give."*

- *"Every way up has its way down."*

- *"A life without love is like a year without summer."*

- *"The sun shines brighter after a shower."*

▲ Figure 9-17. The proverb on the reverse side of Deniece's placemat.

8. Please see *How to Frame a Weaving* directions below.

9. Friendship mats from Eastern Europe may be displayed in all their glory. These placemats are representative of life's continuity. May they then find a place in the homes of children and their families. In the Czech words of an Eastern European poet: *"Lâska . . . rodi lásku"* . . . "Love breeds love!"

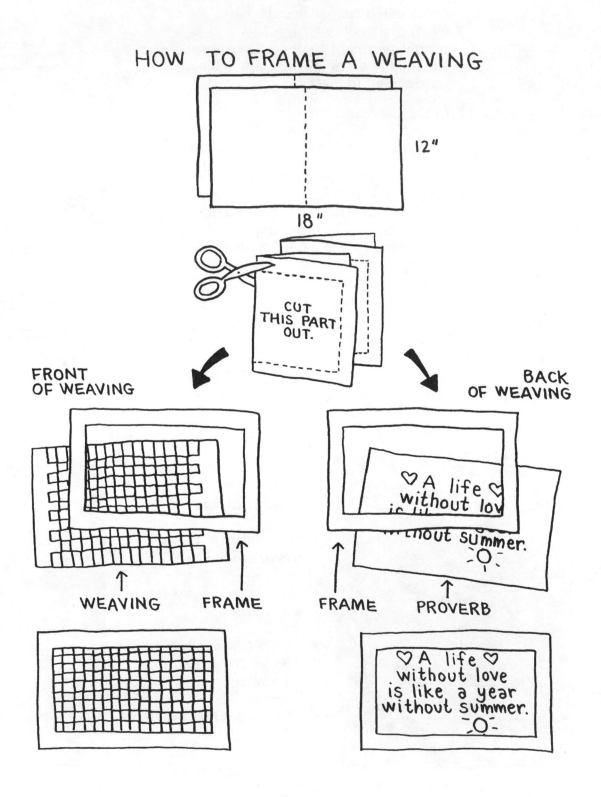

LITHUANIAN FABRIC DESIGN

ACTIVITY 4

Proud Polish Rooster Crows: Kuku Ryku!

Polish Wycinanki and Quilling/Standing Paper Sculpture

▲ Figure 9-18. What a curly tail this crowing rooster has! The cut-paper wing and surrounding symbols represent Polish *Wycinanki* while the tail is truly quilled. Note the carry-over of quilling around our rooster's wakeful eye. The student artist is Jacob Kaster.

Dzien Dobry (jen-DUB-rih)! In other words, *good day!* The spirit of Poland—where the greeting of *Dzien Dobry* resounds—is one of enthusiasm for living, respect for family traditions, and strong ethnic pride. Dance to the polka, laugh a lot, have a little *kielbasa* (a delicious Polish sausage), and enjoy! Did you know that the "polka dot" is traced to the colorful spotted patterns and designs that pepper lively Polish polka dance costumes? The flair of the Polish people is found in their daily lives as well as in their arts. One of Poland's widely known and greatest talents is the art of paper crafts.

In art as in life, certain symbols are constant. The perfect way to present the motifs that symbolize essential elements is the decorative arts. In Poland the art of cut paper—*wycinanki* (vee-chee-nahn-kee)—expresses clearly and colorfully that which is important to our universal well-being. Among the most popular of all creative symbols is that of the crowing rooster. Polish roosters do not greet the new day with *cock-a-doodle-do*—they proudly bellow *Kuku Ryku! Kuku Ryku!* The rooster is associated with vitality, productivity, and renewal. Paper Polish rooster art—appearing alone or in duplicate, symmetrical designs (depending on its regional origin)—conveys the same meaning. A healthy rooster is a blessing to the community where birds, fowl, roosters, and cockerels ensure good returns! After all, it is also the rooster who helps to beget the egg—symbol of universal rebirth, not to mention, it is the rooster who brings up the sun! Polish children know, from a dear little fairy tale they've been told, that the rooster is responsible for cheering up the wind and keeping the world in motion. It is said that the sorrowful wind once stopped blowing altogether—for seven long years—and the world grew still. Clever Rooster approached the wind with a cheery story, a joke, and a great big *Kuku Ryku!* The wind burst into laughter, rustling the trees, making rivers flow, and filling the air with the fragrant perfume of flowers that burst into bloom! The wind blew again because of merry rooster and blows to this very day. May the Earth turn forever in joy and *Sto Lat* (Stoh-lat) . . . May you live one hundred years—which is exactly what *Sto Lat* means!

MATERIALS

- 12" × 18" tagboard (for rooster template, see Teacher Preparation)
- 12" × 18" colored construction paper
- scissors
- assorted paper scraps
- toothpicks

- heavy-duty scissors
- pencils
- fadeless or origami paper
- white glue
- reproducible page: "Rooster Template"

TEACHER PREPARATION

The teacher should cut the rooster form and 8″ × 2″ crossbar paper stand templates from tagboard for students in advance of lesson. Cut as many as the number of students in the class.

The teacher will also need assorted colored construction paper on which the roosters will be traced by students. The universal paper art of quilling (also known as paper filigree) is combined in this lesson with the Polish art of *wycinanki* in a direct, interpretive form. **Quilling** is simply the art of arranging rolled and shaped paper strips to make a design. Our rooster will have a quilled tail, appropriately placed on his tail feathers. (A quill also refers to the tail feather of a bird.) In order to quill or scroll strips of paper, toothpicks are needed. The colored paper to be coiled around the toothpicks should be of lighter weight than construction paper—origami, lightweight paper, or even bright-colored photocopy paper could be used. Paper strips for quilling should be 1/4″ to 1/2″ and may be precut by either the teacher or cut by student. It is best that the teacher experiment with the simple quilling technique (see the illustration on page 332) before demonstrating the class.

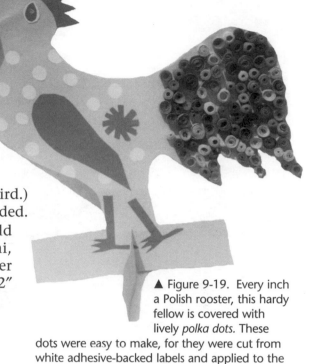

▲ Figure 9-19. Every inch a Polish rooster, this hardy fellow is covered with lively *polka dots*. These dots were easy to make, for they were cut from white adhesive-backed labels and applied to the rooster form. One rooster leg seems ready for a dancing kick. Polka, anyone? Brian Richard is the proud student who crafted this Rooster.

DIRECTIONS

1. Introduce students to the Polish rooster. A response of **dzien dobry** would be most welcome. The Polish fairy tale of the rooster and the wind (see page 330) may be told as well.

2. Distribute tagboard templates, construction paper, pencils, scissors, glue, and colored paper scraps.

3. Students will trace the rooster template onto 12″ × 18″ colored paper. Cut out the shapes (rooster and crossbar stand). Apple white glue to templates and cover entire surface. Apply cut colored construction paper form to oaktag and smooth out surface by hand.

4. Add beak, eye, crown, wing, feet, and "waddle" (that wiggly little flap that hangs below the beak) made from assorted paper scraps. Add interpretive symbols or even polka dots.

5. Distribute lighter-weight colored paper to be used in quilling, along with toothpicks. Follow the instructions for quilling. Demonstrate how to form quilled scrolls. Point out that quills look best when they are grouped closely together.

6. Quills will be rolled and applied to tail feathers by squeezing a generous dab of glue down first into which the quill will be set. Repeat until the tail appears full. **Note:** Quills become heavier than they appear. It is wise to check the "weight" of the tail feathers section as you are adding more quills. If quills begin to set the figure off balance, correct the problem by reinforcing with heavier paper or another layer of tagboard to the back. Other quills may be used to accent eyes, crown, and so forth. Let dry.

7. Cut a 2-inch slit at the center of the base. Insert the crossbar that has already been prepared (see page 333).

8. How proudly the rooster stands! He crows about Polish solidarity or brotherhood. He crows about the human spirit and maybe even sings the National Polish Anthem:

"Poland will never die
as long as we are alive."

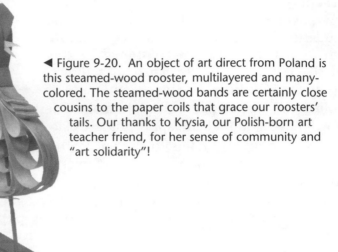

◀ Figure 9-20. An object of art direct from Poland is this steamed-wood rooster, multilayered and many-colored. The steamed-wood bands are certainly close cousins to the paper coils that grace our roosters' tails. Our thanks to Krysia, our Polish-born art teacher friend, for her sense of community and "art solidarity"!

HOW TO QUILL PAPER

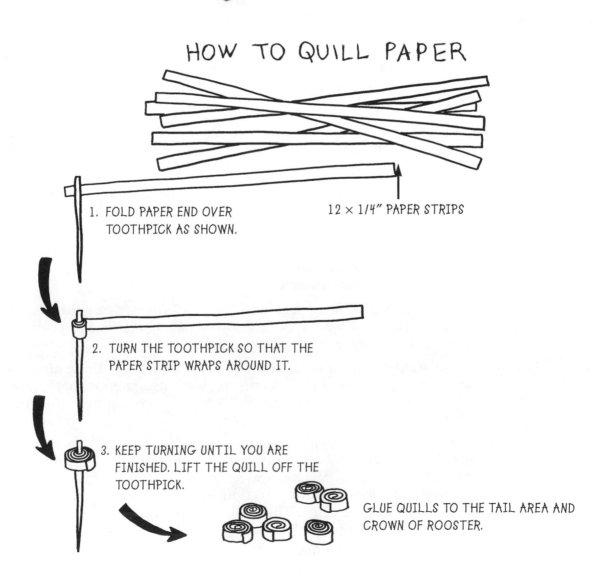

12 × 1/4" PAPER STRIPS

1. FOLD PAPER END OVER TOOTHPICK AS SHOWN.

2. TURN THE TOOTHPICK SO THAT THE PAPER STRIP WRAPS AROUND IT.

3. KEEP TURNING UNTIL YOU ARE FINISHED. LIFT THE QUILL OFF THE TOOTHPICK.

GLUE QUILLS TO THE TAIL AREA AND CROWN OF ROOSTER.

POLISH ROOSTER TEMPLATE

ACTIVITY 5

Irish Spirit, Celtic Skill: The Book of Kells

The Decorated Letter With Border Illuminations/Irish Book Design

▲ Figure 9-21.

"There once was a letter named "M"
That arrived on the back of a pen
While it seemed quite unique
To be joined at the beak
The claws at the base count to ten."

This original limerick riddle might explain the meaning of the student's art.

Neither paper nor the printing press had been introduced in Europe at the time when the stunning **Book of Kells** appeared in Ireland around 700 A.D. This renowned and distinguished Celtic manuscript, illuminated by monks in an Irish monastery over the centuries, is the single greatest source for intricate and interlocking border design. The Celts have an honored tradition in the decorative arts, particularly in enamelwork jewelry and metal, as well as in the written arts. Ireland, after all, has excelled in word, story, and poem. Great Irish writers, storytellers, and musicians have dazzled the world with their Gaelic talents. The playful, witty nature of the Irish spirit is literally illuminated in its manuscript art. The birthplace of the limerick is none other than Ireland!

It could be said that the Book of Kells arrived on . . . "the flight feather of a crow". . . whose gift to the Irish monks was the vital quill pen. The technical ability that made illuminated pages shine also fashioned the highly effective writing instrument. While the Book of Kells appears to be a quite complex design, its essential components are basic and simple. Design framework was created with compasses and rulers, which would then be filled with color and detail. Vivid illuminations of birds, angels, flowers, animals, and imaginative beasts were interlaced with ribbons of color and ink, filling borders and providing quite original human and animal forms. Here is a treasury of pictures and stories along with an extraordinary alphabet; the letter N, for example, is constructed by two men pulling at each other's beards! The Book of Kells contained the Latin words of the gospels of Matthew, Mark, Luke, and John. Originally the Book of Kells was an altar book used for worship and study, and was usually kept and protected in a shrine. For centuries it was located at the monastery of Kells near Dublin, Ireland. It was stolen in the year 1007, but it was eventually found. This precious manuscript illuminated on pages made from parchment and painted with brilliant yet unstable colors gave scholar-artists cause for alarm, for not every manuscript survives time; however, no need to worry. The Book of Kells has gracefully held sway for over 1,200 years and can still be seen today—on display at Trinity Library in Dublin, Ireland.

MATERIALS

- soft-lead pencils/erasers
- practice paper
- 12" × 18" white paper
- watercolor paint
- black permanent markers (fine-to medium-tipped)

- colored fine-tipped markers (see Teacher Preparation)
- reproducible page: "Celtic Design Elements"

TEACHER PREPARATION

The teacher may have images of the **Book of Kells** (available often as coloring books) and/or other Celtic decorated letters and designs. It is a good idea to demonstrate interlocking snake patterns on board to establish the idea of "knotting." An explanation for the nature of a decorated or illuminated letter will also be useful. Terms such as symmetry, interlacing, and illumination may be emphasized. A brief discussion about Ireland and its history will add dimension to this decorative arts lesson. **Note:** There are three approaches to the Book of Kells shown in these photos. One uses water-based color, another is a "pure line" illumination, and the third is a mix of tissue, pen, and other media. The directions explain the decorated letter. However, teachers are encouraged to continue with the page illumination.

▲ Figure 9-22. *Aye* . . . there's so much to love about Ireland! Our student artist—who has memories of a visit to Ireland—wished to feature in her interlacing illustration a field of four-leaf clovers against a very special tree that grows on the Emerald Isle. She gives us a small vignette of the Irish countryside recalled. At the center of her design are the infamous interlocking snakes. It was St. Patrick who brought Catholocism to Ireland. Did St. Patrick drive out snakes? In the old days it's said that snakes lived in books. And did you know if you boiled an Irish book you could make a potion that would cure *any* snake bite! *Sure 'n begorra!*

DIRECTIONS

1. Discuss the unique challenge of interlacing linear art, perfected by the Celts in ancient Ireland. A board demonstration will help students visualize their challenge. References to real-world elements such as snakes and ropes may help the lesson become immediately concrete. Explain to students that the border will be interlaced first, after which each student's own initial letter will be placed in the center of the page. Distribute copies of "Celtic Design Elements" to students.

2. Distribute all paper, pencils, and rulers. Students will practice interlacing and interlocking forms on practice paper.

3. Fold 12″ × 18″ white paper into quarters. Please see directions.

4. Distribute permanent markers. Line applications require varying line thicknesses.

PENCIL TRANSFER TECHNIQUE

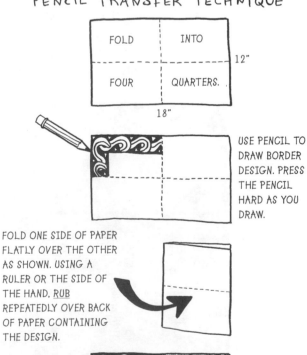

FOLD INTO FOUR QUARTERS. 12″ 18″

USE PENCIL TO DRAW BORDER DESIGN. PRESS THE PENCIL HARD AS YOU DRAW.

FOLD ONE SIDE OF PAPER FLATLY OVER THE OTHER AS SHOWN. USING A RULER OR THE SIDE OF THE HAND, RUB REPEATEDLY OVER BACK OF PAPER CONTAINING THE DESIGN.

OPEN THE PAPER TO REVEAL THE RUBBED DESIGN.

5. When borders are complete, students will draw their initials into the central space in pencil. Encourage students to transform their monogram into an imaginary or existing creature by adding "creature features" such as claws, beaks, tails, fins, scales, and wings.

6. When the creature has been developed, outline the contour of the letter with permanent markers. Use watercolor supplies and colored markers to decorate the letter. The results should be visually arresting, quizzical and curious! Let dry.

NOTE:

Students may continue with illuminations by creating an "illuminating illustration" of Irish themes. In this case, simply follow steps 1–4. Compose the central space with combinations of interlacing ribbons, simple forms, and medallions or other formats that please the eye. Here are a few suggestions suitable for Irish illuminations:

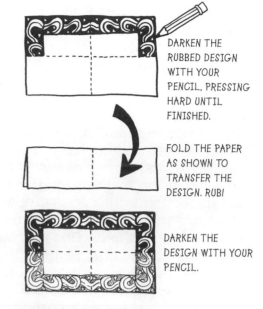

DARKEN THE RUBBED DESIGN WITH YOUR PENCIL. PRESSING HARD UNTIL FINISHED.

FOLD THE PAPER AS SHOWN TO TRANSFER THE DESIGN. RUB!

DARKEN THE DESIGN WITH YOUR PENCIL.

BORDER IS COMPLETED!

- a field of four-leaf clovers
- leaping leprechauns
- the Blarney Stone*
- Irish potatoes (spuds may grow into interlocking patterns)
- Emerald Isle
- castles/cottages
- snakes/St. Patrick
- Shillelagh stick
- beautiful, smiling Irish eyes!

May the "Luck of the Irish" be with you . . . *as the road rises to greet you* . . . on a shining Irish morn!

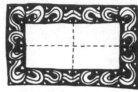

◄ Figure 9-23. Another idea for Irish book art illumination is the use of a cut paper-and-tissue overlay combination. This illumination was inspired by a children's book, *A Book of Kells,* by Deborah Lattimore. One young lad saves another in the face of an attack by a Viking ship. Interlacing border art may be simple or complex and may well contain story elements along with a variety of original and traditional motifs.

* "Blarney" is flattery, coaxing, and smooth talk. The Blarney Castle in County Cork has a stone that, it is told, will increase blarney skill. All a person has to do is kiss the Blarney Stone—upside down!

CELTIC DESIGN ELEMENTS

ACTIVITY 6

Glad to Be Plaid! Wee Bonnie Scottish Castles

Pop-Up Castles/Clan Tartans

▲ Figure 9-24. A sturdy plaid castle is not only bold . . . it looks architecturally structural, too!

There is nothing more Scottish than the tartan plaid. Specific colors and *setts* (patterns) represent families and districts—even corporate institutions! Individual plaid identities may be found in *The Register of All Publicly Known Tartans* where details of more than 2,000 plaids (and counting) demonstrate Scottish loyalty and clan pride. The first woven check known as tartan can be traced back to the 3rd century! An archaeological sample was discovered in a pot near a Roman wall at Falkirk. Clans and chiefs, bagpipes, kilts, castles, and golf—yes, *golf* is a Scottish contribution—help form a vision of Scotland yesterday and today.

It makes perfect sense that the kilt, which utilizes the woven fabric of tartan plaid, is uniquely Scottish. Why? The kilt is completely practical. Above all else the Scots, who are often described as thrifty, prefer to consider themselves as entirely practical! Did you know that kilts were originally blankets? The versatility of the garment, which requires about sixteen yards of woolen cloth, is impressive. For sleeping, it returns to its blanket form; in battle, the kilt allows freedom of movement. Walking across rough heather moors in a kilt makes sense only if one has stockings—argyle socks to protect against scratchy thistles—and, yet, thistles are the national emblem of Scotland! A good Scot is always prepared. The pouch that accompanies the kilt provides storage, protection, and a fashionable accessory.

Kilts would not be kilts without the plaids and tartans that identify each one with families and clans. The geometry of the plaid is not unlike the math used in architectural structures. Plaids and castles are steady companions in Scotland. There are three types of patterns or *setts:* symmetrical, asymmetrical, and equal check (the simplest tartan which uses only two colors). If you see a black and red check you may know a *MacGregor,* which is also known as *Rob Roy* in informal dress. Repeated colors represent clans and families. It is a thrill to recognize the plaid or tartan that represents a specific community, tribe, or family lineage. For instance, the "two white line" plaids of the *MacDonell* clan identifies the MacDonell clan of Glengarry, a plaid that can be traced to its castle or origin. Like bird watching, *"tartan-spotting"* is a source of Scottish satisfaction. Let's cheer for—and toast to the Scottish spirit with *slainte mhath* (pronounced slan-ja-va)—"good health" to all tribes, families, and clans!

▲ Figure 9-25. A meeting of clans! Scots are not only practical, they are poetic, too!

MATERIALS

- 12″ × 18″ oaktag
- 18″ × 24″ white paper
- rulers (optional)
- crayons/oil pastels
- pencils and erasers
- colored markers

- scissors
- white glue
- sponges
- reproducible pages: "Kilt Talk" and "Sample Clan Tartans"

TEACHER PREPARATION

This simple lesson will reinforce the concepts of horizontal and vertical linear placement through the formation of plaid *setts.* The other objective that will be addressed is color mixing, which will occur mainly in the "intersection" of lines within the plaid. Students will also learn the Scottish device of the "guarded line" pattern through repetition within the overall plan of their own family tartan. The application of plaid to a European castle form will speak to the structural nature of design.

The teacher will want to gather images of castles—Edinburgh Castle, Eilean Donan castle, and the infamous Balmoral Castle are all in Scotland! (**Note:** World-famous artist and architect Charles Rennie MacIntosh was quite popular in the early 1900s for his very stylized and severe design, which reveals a powerful verticality—reminiscent of Scottish fabric design.)

The teacher may want to refer to the following book on family tartans: *Identifying Guide to Clans and Tartans,* edited by Blair Urquhart (Secaucus, NJ: Chartwell, 1994). Examples of plaid and tartan should not be difficult to find for use as examples for this lesson. Fabric store remnants, wallpaper book patterns, old flannel shirts, or any other clothing items should be on hand. Students themselves may wish to wear plaid on the day of the lesson; perhaps students wear uniforms of plaid. Naturally, if the teacher has access to a kilt, bagpipe, or other regalia (argyle socks included) or reasonable facsimile, now is the time to bring it in to class. Small sponges of foam, precut to enable the pop-up effect for the castle, are also needed. Vocabulary words in "Kilt Talk" should be incorporated into the lesson at the teacher's discretion.

▲ Figure 9-26. A plaid castle floats inside a moat where the fearsome Loch Ness monster appears to be taking a dip!

DIRECTIONS

1. Discuss the brief history of tartan and plaid clan designs. Discuss clan *setts* along with the intended application of these plaids . . . *bonnie* plaid castles! Present the materials (see Teacher Preparation). Discuss and analyze the geometrical nature of plaid. (The word *bonnie* means "fair and fine" . . . handsome or lovely with a cheerful glow.)

2. Distribute 12″ × 18″ oaktag. Students will design simple castles to accommodate the clan plaid they select or originate. For family clan association, students may imbue their tartans with favorite colors. Traditional Scottish colors are red, green, black, white, blue, and yellow. Purple, brown, and orange often occur in the blending. There is no reason why students cannot create colorful tartans in brighter color schemes, if they wish. Distribute the reproducible "Sample Clan Tartans."

3. Think of the castle as your family home or "palace of origin"! Consider customary castle features—turrets, battlements, arrow loops, gatehouse, and moats. Begin the plaid plan with selected colors. Decide whether or not individual plaids or tartans will be widebanded and bold or block-like checkered, or of a multi-linear sett (note that variety is part of this choice). Using pencil, with ruler or by freehand, create the plaid grid inside the castle contour. Repetition of horizontal and vertical lines is basic to plaid design. Allow areas to have breathing room as they are placed on the page (these create the blocks). Try using the guarded line (see "Kilt Talk" and "Sample Clan Tartans"). Identify sett features such as intersections, overchecks, and guards.

▲ Figure 9-27. What's this? A giant? He is a castle guard any lad or lassie could value!

4. Develop a castle landscape along with any other details desired, such as highlander, chiefs, mythological monsters, red deer, bagpipers, or miniature golf course.

5. Distribute foam pieces and glue. Apply glue to both sides of foam pieces and mount plaid oaktag castle on the "green and purple" heather!

6. A student critique, lead by the classroom chief (teacher) will allow students to share their choices of color and design for their family clans as well as express how it feels to build a castle out of plaid!

Figure 9-28. The Highland Register, the pouch, the feather . . . and the kilt! It all adds up to one proud Scot. Courtesy of Louise Smith. ▶

Kilt Talk (A SCOTTISH VOCABULARY)

BADGE: The clan badge is the heraldic crest of the chief surrounded by a strap and buckle which may be worn by the clansman.

BLACK WATCH: Nickname applied to the Independent Companies c. 1700 who kept watch on the activities of the Jacobite clans (black meaning secret or undercover) and later (1739) the 3rd Regiment.

BROWNIES: "Little people" of Scottish folklore regarded as magical and mischievous!

CASTLE: A large, fortified building or group of buildings often used by an entire community.

CLAN: A group of people with a common ancestor; a large family forming a close group.

DRESS TARTAN: A tartan in which one of the background colors has been changed to white. Used in kilts for Highland dancing.

GUARDED LINE: A wide line that is flanked by two narrower lines.

GUARDS: A design element in tartan where black lines on either side or a narrow stripe give added definition.

HARD TARTAN: Very fine but densely woven, coarse wool tartan produced until the mid-19th century.

HORIZONTAL LINE: A line that runs parallel to the horizon.

HUNTING TARTAN: Green or subdued tartan for informal or everyday wear.

ILK: Same place, as in "of that Ilk," where a person's name is the same as the name of his or her territorial designation.

INTERSECTION: The point at which two lines cross.

KILT: A knee-length pleated skirt of tartan wool, worn as part of a Scottish Highland man's dress or by women and children.

OVERCHECK: A narrow stripe superimposed on the structure of a tartan design.

PARALLEL LINES: Lines that run alongside each other and never touch.

PATTERN: The repeating of various lines or shapes.

PHILABEG: A length of single-width tartan cloth with fixed pleats.

SETT: Another word for pattern, which is used to describe the area of the design that is repeated.

TARTAN: The distinctive pattern of a Highland clan, with colored stripes crossing at right angles.

THREAD COUNT: The number of threads of each of the sequence of colors of the sett.

SAMPLE CLAN TARTANS

MAC KINTOSH

CLARK

GOW

SINCLAIR

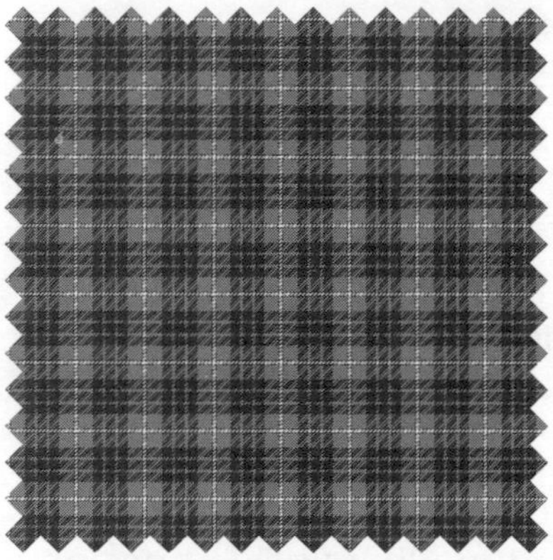

HAMILTON

MAC DUFF

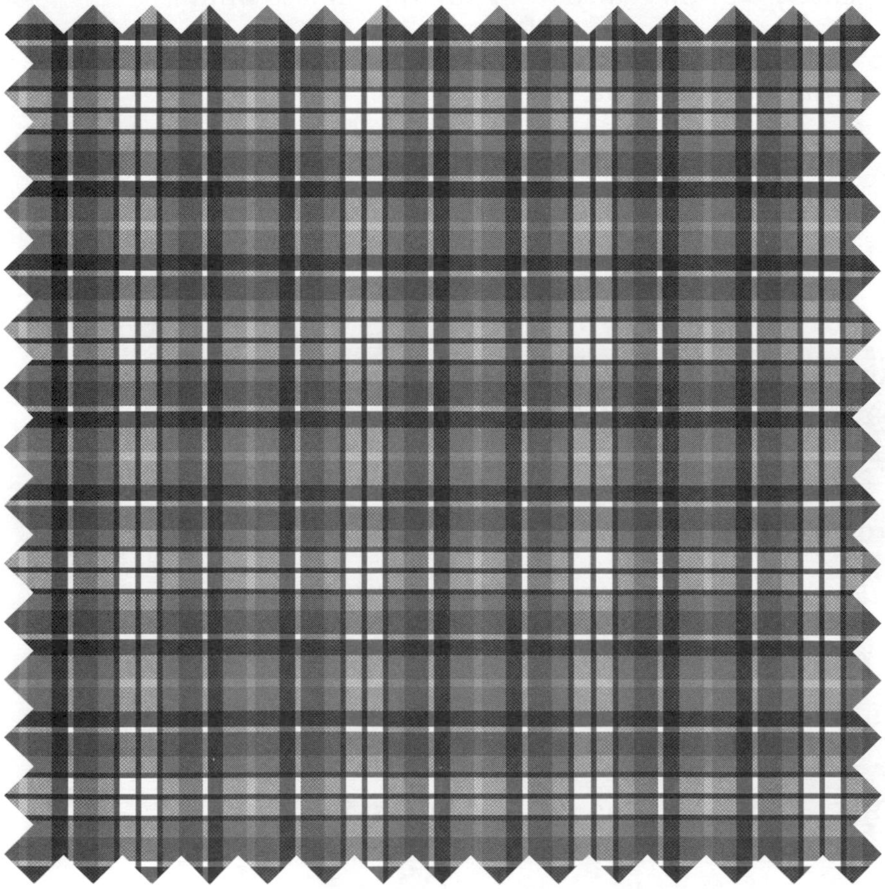

TEALL OF TEALLACH

MAC DONALD
(**Note:** A good example of the "guarded line".)

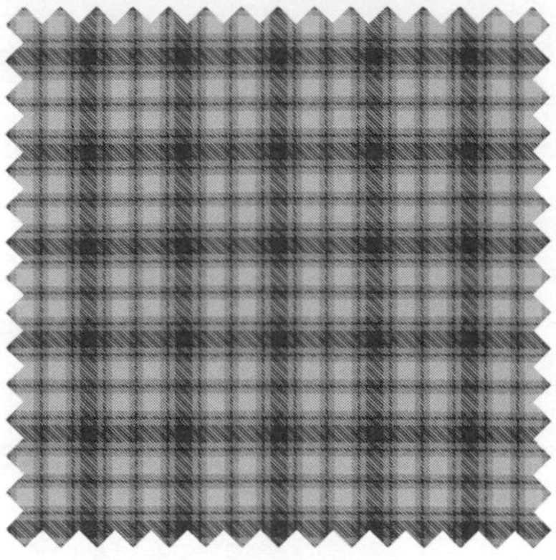

SKENE

ACTIVITY 7

Now Seating: Alice in British Wonderland!

Alice in Wonderland Playing "Card" Characters

BONUS: THE ABC'S OF ENGLISH CHAPBOOKS

Without falling through the rabbit hole, you can enter the land where kings and queens still rule and where tea parties may have extraordinary etiquette! Merry old England—as well as England today—has always held dear the tradition of the monarchy. At the same time, the British subjects are great masters of wit who also enjoy the art of satire. One only needs to acknowledge "The Bard," William Shakespeare (1564–1616), to know the extent of British contribution to drama, theater, and literature. "Shakespearean" has come to have specific meaning in Western culture. Theatrically speaking, the comic and tragic Shakespearean plays portray characters with universal emotions that are familiar to people of diverse cultures and ages. With sharp insight and wit, this English writer set a Western literary standard in motion. And what were among his favorite themes? The ups and downs of kings and queens!

Royalty has a key place in one remarkable and fantastic tale where animals have voices and little girls may shrink or stretch according to plot! A device that a latter-day writer named Lewis Carroll used in *Alice in Wonderland,* published in 1865, was to feature an absurd group of players including none other than a deck of cards! The playing cards have long been associated with the suits of the royal house, with their kings, queens, jacks, and jesters. *Alice in Wonderland* is populated with members of an upside-down monarchy. Carroll created an irresistible world of nonsense and meaning. Birds appear as barristers (wigs and all), fish and frogs as royal footmen—and there is a British mouse who wishes only to

▲ Figure 9-29. The Royal Couple! As usual, the Queen has much to say, as the King remains "poker-faced."

speak in French! Perhaps the most memorable of events is the tea party held by a Mad Hatter who makes up and changes his own rules. Carroll did not place the Queen of Hearts at this table; he saved her for another unforgettable scene where her "Equally-Irrational Majesty" boldly orders her servants—who are merely cards themselves—to **paint the roses red!** In a world such as this, one can only enjoy the poking of fun at the society. So with a little whimsy and absurdity, this tale of "Jabberwocky" makes its own kind of sense. As the fantastic story draws to a close, Alice, the main character, gains confidence in her own judgment. She stands up to the ridiculous King and ferocious Queen when accused of wrong doing. Alice objects . . . "I don't believe there's an atom of meaning in it." The King replies, "If there's no meaning, it saves the world a lot of trouble." . . . After all, Alice reminds them, *"You're nothing but a pack of cards!"* Exactly!

◀ Figure 9-30. Is he an artist, a gardener, or just a joker with a paintbrush in one hand and a pail of paint in the other? Alice wondered, too. . . . "Would you mind telling me, please, why are you painting these roses?" asked Alice, "Why the fact is . . . Miss, this here ought to have been a *red* rose tree, and we put a white one in by mistake; and if, the Queen was to find out, we should all have our heads cut off, you know." No wonder the joker is in a hurry.

MATERIALS

- 18″ × 24″ oaktag (see Teacher Preparation)
- scissors
- 18″ × 24″ newsprint
- yardsticks
- pencils/erasers
- stapler

- colored markers
- white glue
- sponges (option—see Teacher Preparation)
- paint/paper (option—see Teacher Preparation)

TEACHER PREPARATION

"You're nothing but a deck of cards!" is the basis for our "players" who may be invited to a mad classroom tea party. The teacher will want to have a deck of playing cards on hand as reference for this lesson. Standard picture playing cards should be readily available in 52-card packs. This lesson emphasizes *Alice in Wonderland* and the mad tea party; however, the cards themselves have their own history. The pack the teacher will use is English in origin and was popular from around the end of the 19th century. Playing cards may provide an opportunity for lesson development, yet it is wise to note that the cards themselves are, after all, based on the monarchy. The design commonly used today depicts the costumes worn during the reigns of Henry VII and Henry VIII.

Oaktag should be in plentiful supply, for it will form the "body" of the kings, queens, jacks, and jokers the students will create. Heads, arms, and legs—plus additional parts—will also be formed from oaktag.

Optional: If the teacher wishes to create cup and saucer, save oaktag to be cut in 3″ × 9″ strips. Design cup with Wonderland characters. Staple closed. Glue paper handle to cup. Place cup on paper plate cut to size. Apply stream of white glue around cup to affix, if desired. Again, a paper tablecloth may be executed by applying bright colors in paint with square sponge in a checkered pattern to a length of display paper, cut to tabletop size.

A copy of *Alice in Wonderland* (abridged suggested) and costume books illustrating various periods in English history should be on hand for this lesson.

DIRECTIONS

1. Briefly discuss the story of *Alice in Wonderland,* emphasizing the tea party. Discuss what a tea party is and whom one might invite! Talk about the Queen of Hearts and the other cards in the story. Explain the intent of this lesson to students. A large paper tea party is in order.

2. Distribute pencils, newsprint, and first sheet of oaktag (see Teacher Preparation). Have the students round off the corners on one 3″ × 9″ oaktag with scissors to create the card shape. Do the same to the newsprint. Using the yardstick, have the students make a border around both the oaktag and the newsprint. Fold the newsprint in half.

◄ Figure 9-31. **"Table for two! Table for two! Will His and Her Majesty please be seated."** It's time for High Tea. May we interest you in some clotted cream? (Yes, this really is one of the amenities of High Tea, a cherished English tradition that rivals the "coffee break.") Is the Queen displeased with her king or her cup of tea? Or is this simply how things are in Wonderland!?!

3. On the top half of the newsprint, students will draw a head and shoulders for their royal guest in pencil; they may choose a King, Queen, Jack, or Joker. Be sure to create a fancy hairstyle, crown, and patterns on the clothes. Select the "suit"—diamond, spade, club, or heart. It's a *pip!*

4. When the design is finished, have the student fold the paper in half so that the pencil drawing is inside and touches the other half of the paper. Rub on the back of the drawing so that the pencil marks from the original drawing are transferred onto the other half of the paper. Open up the newsprint and trace over the imprint to make the transfer darker. The student should now have a duplicate head upside-down, like a playing card.

5. Rub the design from the newsprint onto the oaktag. Trace the pencil line with black permanent marker. Color the design with colored markers. Consider the intricacy of the patterns.

6. Students will use a second piece of oaktag to create the head, arms, and legs of the card. Again, be sure to add a fancy hair style, crown, and lovely leggings and sleeves. When drawing faces, students should consider the personality of the Wonderland character they will portray. When finished, cut out the pieces and staple to the playing card.

7. Do we wish to be seated at this mad tea party? (See Teacher Preparation.) Are we standing regally, displayed on a classroom wall? Are there any mobile characters, such as the Joker, who will be "painting the roses red on wheels"? Now is the time to *reveal your cards.*

BONUS : ABC'S OF ENGLISH CHAPBOOKS

In 17th-century England, one might have found a popular ballad printed on a **broadside,** which originally was a large sheet of paper also known as a **broadsheet.** Essentially, a large sheet of paper would have been printed on one or both sides and often folded. In this category of "street literature," available inexpensively to the common "bloke," such pamphlets would be referred to as *chapbooks.* These chapbooks were sold by the "chapman," a hawker who would be sure to get your attention, in the manner of the corner newspaper vendor. Expect chapbooks to commonly contain poems, ballads, local catastrophes, common crimes, and stories of the day. Often chapbooks were inked from woodblock prints. Chapbooks were an affordable means to educate, enlighten, horrify, or intrigue the reader, enhanced by pictorial illustrations.

The class's chapbooks will honor the English language, which is among the most widespread languages used internationally. The English alphabet is learned by English and American school

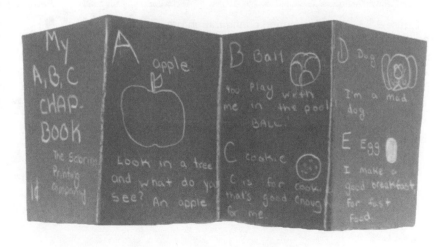

Figure 9-32. What a wonderful way to teach the ABC's, illustration, publishing, and the book arts all in one accordion-folded Chapbook! ▶

children as well as countless other classrooms around the world. The educational chapbooks the students will "publish" will teach the ABC's with words and pictures. By using black paper and white crayon, student chapbooks will approximate the printed page.

It's never too early to learn about deadlines! Deadlines are a fact of life. Both students in their homework assignments and authors in their publication dates live and die by deadlines! These ABC chapbooks will have deadlines, and students will have both the pride and pressure of authorship.

How to make a chapbook? You will need black 12" × 18" paper and a white crayon; white pencils may be used in combination with crayon. First, fold black paper lengthwise. Fold again at center, then once again in halves. Open; you should have eight distinct sections. The upper-left rectangle will serve as the cover; the next space functions as page one. Pages follow sequentially from that point. Students must decide, along with the teacher, how much of the alphabet they wish to complete. If the lesson is extended beyond the deadline, both sides of the chapbook are available for completion. Students should think about the illustration of the alphabet letter with an object that begins with the same letter. Two class periods are quite reasonable for side one. Forty-five minutes to an hour for four pages equals eight pages completed in a given time frame.

Quote: "Authors must make smart decisions without undue procrastination." Encourage students to work directly and swiftly, without sacrificing quality. Of course, offer help as needed. There is no greater feeling than to have done an honest day's work, particularly when you are both author and illustrator. We think you may have a bestseller on your hands! *Extra! Extra! Read all about it!*

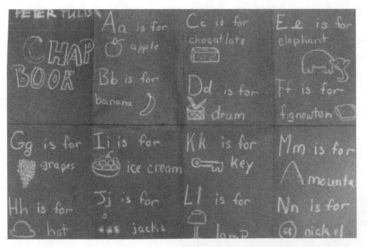

▲ Figure 9-33. A well-designed configuration presents simple, readable objects. Don't you just love the letter "F" for Fig Newton? How about the "C" for chocolate?

▲Figure 9-34. The use of the reversal of white lettering on black background is well articulated in this Chapbook. We are reminded that the pressure and sensitivity applied to drawing pays off visually. A beautiful Chapbook—a "print" in progress and a chance to share art talent. Wouldn't a first grader love to learn with an original alphabet Chapbook? Older student artists, (third grade and up recommended), may make author appearances in earlier grades!

ACTIVITY 8

The Wonder of Europe: Grand Sightseeing Postcard Tour!

Natural and Architectural Wonders/3-D Mail Art/Arts Advocacy!

Have you ever noticed that the love of travel can be contagious? Travelers will offer vivid stories of their trips—the sights, the sounds, and even the smell of places they have encountered. So descriptive are they, you almost feel as though you were there, too. Before you know it, you start looking for your passport! And, why not? Travel is exhilarating—whether you climb to the top of the Matterhorn in the Swiss Alps, run with the bulls in Pamplona, Spain (run *fast*), or stand in admiration of great artistic works, such as Michelangelo's *David* in Florence, Italy.

People do travel for many reasons, yet travel for travel's sake is a strong, vital drive: We human beings are curious creatures. We want to learn about each other and ourselves—our origins, accomplishments, cultural gifts—and the bounty of our natural world. It may be the fjords of Norway, the rocks at Stonehenge, or the Eiffel Tower in Paris that beckon . . . as any good traveler will tell you, direct, authentic travel experience is the best teacher. It is a

▲ Figure 9-35. "You know you're in Florence when . . ." a handsomely constructed dome, as pictured in this postcard, rises before the Florentine sky . . . a *trattoria* is waiting just around the corner, pleased to serve you delicious Northern Italian cuisine (remember, European dinners are customarily served late in the evening) . . . and the fleur-de-lis symbol turns up here and there. The fleur-de-lis, often seen in France, is the crest symbol of the city of Florence, where the Italian Renaissance began!

means of powerful cultural exchange. American writer Mark Twain once said . . . "Travel is fatal to prejudice . . ." If you plan to travel, bring an open mind and an open heart.

Europe is an established tourist attraction: a variety of countries form the densely populated, compact continent. In Western Europe, there are distinct, individual nations that have their own defining landmarks, scenic sites, ancient and modern structures, time-honored customs, and diverse traditions. Overall, art and artists are held in high regard in Europe. You see statues that commemorate artists as readily as any political figure—what a thrill to see a statue of Vincent van Gogh in the town square! In fact, most of the European painters who are known throughout art history have offered us favorite scenes of Europe with their memorable paintings. Cafes, theaters, bridges, churches and cathedrals, European landscape—as well as the Europeans themselves—have been brilliantly documented by many artists over the centuries. For a painted record of Europe, travel back in time, through the Renaissance, the Middle Ages . . . and find yourself in the caves of Lascaux, France, or Altimira, Spain, where early Stone Age art can also be found! There is *so* much to see, do, and appreciate in Europe. Pack your camera, your sketchbook, and call your travel agent in the morning!

MATERIALS

- 9" × 12" drawing paper
- pencils
- rulers
- fine-tip colored markers
- scissors
- ballpoint pens or fine-tip markers
- Model Magic™ (optional, see Teacher Preparation)
- gold/silver pens (optional)

347

TEACHER PREPARATION

This activity will highlight specific European countries and their identifiable features through *mail art.* Note that you have a fine opportunity to promote Arts Advocacy!! The teacher may elect to present a 2-D or 3-D (partial relief) postcard lesson: Model Magic™ is recommended for use in 3-D postcard. Along with the 3-D clay choice, the teacher will need white glue and toothpicks (for defining details). **Tip:** Rolling pins and wax paper may be used to make thin clay slabs. Place the modeling clay between two sheets of wax paper, and press flat with a rolling pin. Cut shapes—buildings, clouds, trees, and so forth—directly out of the modeling clay slab (with scissors) while within the wax paper. Peel away wax paper, and apply "3-D" parts to postcard with glue. Color may be applied to wet or dry clay; dry works best for lasting color appearance. Standard clay manipulation is effective. (Model Magic™ may be trimmed with scissors directly.)

For this lesson presentation, gather any postcards the teacher (and students) may have and will share, particularly those of European destinations. A picture atlas for reference and map will be most helpful. Additionally, travel magazines and travel sections/advertisements from the newspaper are also encouraged for "mail art" travel lesson. Books on European architectural history, geography, and, of course, travel guides and maps will assist students. To depict a location when a national holiday or festival occurs can't help but to celebrate the culture!

DIRECTIONS

1. Bring maps, books, and other references forward to provide concrete information for the opening discussion. How many students know where Europe is located? What are the countries of Europe? Let's talk about it!

2. Students may brainstorm about the landmarks and features they associate with specific countries. Assist student progress. Try this list as a starter set!

• **ITALY**

Rome—the Coliseum; the Vatican/St. Peter's Square; The Sistine Chapel

Florence—Leaning Tower of Pisa; Uffizzi Gallery, Michelangelo's *David; El Duomo* by Brunelleschi

Venice—Bridge of Sighs; gondolas; St. Mark's Square

Sicily—The Mediterranean Culture

• **GERMANY**

– Black Forest; half-timbered houses

– People wearing lederhosen

– Castles on the Rhine

– woodcarving; cuckoo clocks

▲ Figure 9-36. We arrive in Paris, France—just in time to celebrate Bastille Day, a national holiday of the French Republic held on July 14. Fireworks fill the night! The Eiffel Tower—once considered a monstrous eyesore—has become the indisputable mascot of Paris. On the evening of the Bastille *soiree,* it's easy to see why Paris is called The City of Lights! Note the *kiosks* that lure the grand boulevards.

- **SCANDINAVIA**

  Denmark—The Little Mermaid Statue in the Copenhagen Harbor, a tribute to native son Hans Christian Andersen, famous fairy tale author

  Norway—The fjords; Norwegian woven design crafts (mittens, hats, and scarves)

  Sweden—"DaLarna" model horse; Ancient Rune Stone; Winter Sports, ice and snow

  Lapland—Reindeer, wolves, and Elk

- **FRANCE**

  Paris—Eiffel Tower; Cafes, Arc de Triomphe; Artists at Montmartre; Notre Dame

  The French Riviera—Resorts and little museums along the southern coast

- **AUSTRIA**

  Salzburg—Mozart's birthplace

  - Vienna Opera House

  - Edelweiss

- **SPAIN**

  - Flamenco dancers/toreadors; The Alahambra; The Mosque at Cordoba/influence of Moors

  Madrid—The Prado Museum

  Ancient Iberia

- **SWITZERLAND**

  - The Alps; Alpine horns; yodelers and mountain climbers in feathered hats

- **NETHERLANDS/BELGIUM/LUXEMBOURG**

  - The historic city of Bruges in Belgium—Lacemaking; Dutch windmills/Dutch wooden shoes, tiles; Tulips and Delft pottery; "Venice of the North"—Amsterdam, leading port of the Netherlands

- **PORTUGAL**

  Capital of Lisbon—tiles; sailing vessels/fishing villages/exploration

- **ENGLAND**

  London—Big Ben Clock tower; double-decker buses; Buckingham Palace

  Stonehenge—Ancient stone formation

  The White Cliffs at Dover

- **ADD YOUR OWN IDEAS TO THE LIST!**

▲ Figure 9-37. Sun, sand, and sailing set in a charming fishing village atmosphere. The smell of newly-baked bread fills the air. You don't have to ask if the seafood is fresh in this place! Often visited in conjunction with its next-door neighbor Spain, Portugal has a strong history all its own. Big old *Sol* shines brightly above the Belém Tower in the capital city of Lisbon. The lovely Portuguese language is spoken here. No wonder Portugal is a traveler's delight.

3. Student attention should be given to a country of interest. Perhaps heritage, family friends, and/or pen pals may influence choice. Keep in mind the following categories for postcard pictures into which the brainstorming will fit into three categories:

- **Ancient Ruins/early structures:** England— Stonehenge; Roman coliseum

- **Feats of Engineering:** Paris—Eiffel Tower; Great Cathedrals of Europe

- **Vernacular (regional) Architecture: England**— cottages, gardens; Germany— half-timbered houses; Switzerland—chalets

- **Natural Formations and Magestic Elements:** Norway fjords; Rivers, Oceans, Mountains, Lakes specific to regions (for example, Lake Geneva in Switzerland)

4. The more focused the subject is, the more site-specific it will be! Emphasize to students that their postcard image must immediately convey a specific European place. Distribute materials.

5. Students will fold paper in half: one half for "practice," the other half for the final card. Measure a border in pencil of 1/4"–1/2". Sketch in the selected country site or scene. Use references. **Note:** Students using 3-D clay will incorporate clay materials for planning and production (see Teacher Preparation).

6. Upon completion of satisfactory sketch, cut away "practice half" (save for later). Continue to develop postcard scene. Add color to Model Magic™ after it is completely dry to assure line and color clarity. Students should also let the postcard "set" for a few days before sending it as "arts advocacy." Be sure it is in top-notch condition!

7. Are locales recognizable? Lettering may be used, yet postcard images should stand on their visual strength. Indigenous animals, regional fashion or national costume, and transportation may all help to give "a picture postcard" of the selected destination.

8. Finish 2-D (or 3-D) scenes. Create the postcard's reverse side by measuring, with ruler, a format for writing the message (design of postage stamp optional); a line down the center of card is fine. **Note:** The 3-D cards will require a separate "reverse" writing side that will be glued to their backs. (This later application of written format is less demanding than asking students to interrupt their 3-D process; second card will also provide backing.)

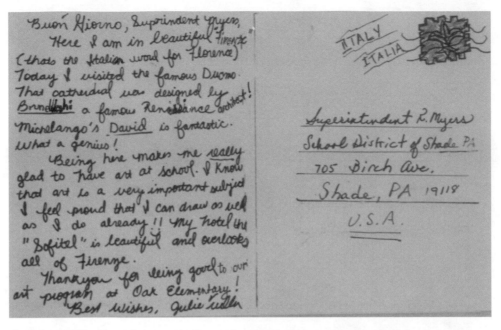

Buon Giorno, Superintendent Myers,
    Here I am in beautiful Firenze
(that's the Italian word for Florence).
Today I visited the famous Duomo.
That cathedral was designed by
Brunelleschi, a famous Renaissance architect!
Michelango's *David* is fantastic.
What a genius!
    Being here makes me really
glad to have art at school. I know
that art is a very important subject
I feel proud that I can draw as well
as I do already!! My hotel the
"Sofitel" is beautiful and overlooks
all of Firenze.
    Thank you for being good to our
art program at Oak Elementary!
    Best wishes, Julie Willa

Superintendent R. Myers
School District of Shade PA
705 Birch Ave.
Shade, PA 19118
U.S.A.

▲ Figure 9-38. Arts advocacy via the postcard! All ready to send to the school superintendent's office.

9. Compose a short message that contains "fact and feeling": write (with ballpoint pen) to give an interesting fact about the selected scene and describe a feeling about being in this specific European Country.

Note: If *Arts Advocacy* is planned, address the postcard to an administrator, superintendent, local legislator, business, or community leader. Write a compelling remark about where art can take you!

The 2-D postcards *may* be mail-worthy—check with your local post office. The 3-D postcards will need a padded envelope and any other mailing protection suggested. Package the 3-D card accordingly! Other students who prefer to send their cards to a friend, family member, principal, teacher—or to mail them to themselves!—should be supported . . . just as those who want to save, trade, or simply post their European Mail Art, should know they are free to do so.

Note: A brief language phrase borrowed from the country can be featured in the student card: "Un Bon Mot" (French for *"A Good Word"*) or "una buen viaja" (Spanish for *"Have a good trip!"*).

The United States of America

New Hampshire

Maine

NEW YORK

Vermont

MASSACHUSETTS

PENNSYLVANIA

Rhode Island

Connecticut

WEST VIRGINIA

NEW JERSEY

Delaware

Maryland

Washington

Montana

North Dakota

Minnesota

Michigan

Oregon

Idaho

Wyoming

SOUTH DAKOTA

Wisconsin

Nevada

Utah

Nebraska

Iowa

Illinois

Indiana

Ohio

CALIFORNIA

Colorado

Kansas

Missouri

Kentucky

Virginia

ARIZONA

New Mexico

Oklahoma

Tennessee

North Carolina

Arkansas

South Carolina

TEXAS

Alabama

Georgia

Mississippi

Florida

LOUISIANA

Alaska

Hawaii

The United States of America

A demi-mask graces the face of this young Mardi Gras celebrant. In New Orleans, Louisiana, feathered masks of this type are readily available. More elaborate masks may be found at the city's Mask Maker's Guild—or in the French Market in February where many American mask makers exhibit and sell their work.

"The West" has become a symbol for a brave and rugged way of life that boasts of American spunk and good old-fashioned "know-how." The cowboy is an American hero who—while mythologized in Hollywood legend—really does exist. In Europe, as elsewhere, it was so often the cowboy who stood for the American spirit. From county sheriffs to Texas Rangers, the West has captured the American imagination. This cowboy dons a scarf to honor another American hero, the Native American Indian chief.

ART ACTIVITIES FOR BECOMING CULTURE SMART

■ **Activity 1**
One Great American Lady: A Heritage Welcome to the U.S.A.
Life-size Heritage Figures/Monumental Paper Art/Statue of Liberty

Activity 2
Give My Regards to Broadway . . . America on Stage, From Coast to Coast
"Showcards"/Advertising Poster Art/Graphic Color and Design

■ **Activity 3**
The Fabulous Fraktur: Folklife Thrives in Community Art
Decorative Certificates/Calligraphy/Traditional Folk Arts
BONUS: CAN YOU SAY SCHERENSCHNITTE (SHA'R-ON-SCHNIT)?
INCLUDES: QUILT OF MANY CULTURES

■ **Activity 4**
Let the Good Times Roll: A Jazzy Portrait of Mardi Gras
Costume Portraits for Carnival/Ir"resist"ible Fancyheads!
DOUBLE BONUS: HARLEQUINS! AND MUMMERS STRUT: A PHILADELPHIA NEW YEAR'S PARADE

■ **Activity 5**
There's No Place Like Home: Celebrate the U.S.A.!
Mixed Media Collage/Montage: Architectural and Interior Design

"Take me out to the ball game" . . . is the American call to action! Baseball is the quintessential sport, along with football and basketball, in the U.S.A.: "The Great American National Pastime." This "commemorative" picture may recall a great moment in baseball—perhaps the day the student artist hit the home run to win the game!

To know the Art of The United States of America . . . . .

. . . . . one must understand the identity of the country called America. There are many ways to view American art and to measure its social history. Often, the country is defined by the time lines of expeditions, colonization, and the arrival of waves of immigrants. In the best of views, the United States of America is the "Birthplace of Liberty—the Home of the Free and the Brave." The dualities that have challenged American ideals must be acknowledged, along with pride in American achievement. Multiple "Americas" are represented in its growth; history books give information, yet the arts tell the stories. Broadway plays have not only entertained and amused, they have produced candid portrayals of social strife and political struggle in dynamic forms. In plays and musicals, the many facets of American society are revealed. The musical theater classic *Showboat* tackles the subject of racial suffering. *West Side Story* predicts a growing problem of urban gangs and youth violence. Through the arts, a mirror is held up to American past, present, and future.

Plymouth Rock marked the arrival of the *Mayflower* pilgrims in 1620. The Statue of Liberty, in New York Harbor, held her torch over the massive migrations from Europe to the United States, through Ellis Island, at the turn of the twentieth century. Unlike other immigrations, the Middle Passage of African slaves from West Africa to the United States was by no means an escape from persecution, nor was it a voluntary migration. The years that followed produced the painful Civil War, after which segregation and civil rights remained social issues. America was also home to indigenous Native Americans, who were mistreated and uprooted in great numbers. Every event, group, person, tradition, custom, and heritage is America, giving the country its direction. As a collective culture, the American people are described as straightforward and optimistic. Art is a way to accept ourselves and celebrate all ethnic, religious, and cultural contributions— it is an opportunity to dissolve boundaries. Art is the juncture where all worlds meet.

For a long time, the term *American art* was used interchangeably with *Colonial art*—or art shaped by traditional British taste. The heritage of fine furniture making, portrait and landscape painting, and a range of decorative arts is still valued. The meaning of American art has by now been expanded to include the quilting of African–American women, the visionary painting of Native American artists, the folklife and crafting skill brought to this country by the men and women of eastern Europe and Russia—and, of course, the artists and the art movements that grew up in America. The American people may rightfully boast of the originality of the African-based jazz and Delta blues. The Harlem Renaissance brought such outstanding musicians and painters as Jacob Lawrence and Romare Bearden. The growth of regional schools of art includes an intimate array of urban and rural scenes of American life. Such artists as Georgia O'Keeffe and Alexander Calder exemplify American originality and ingenuity. Architecture in America rose with the invention of the skyscraper, while architects like Frank Lloyd Wright endeavored to create simultaneously harmony with nature and the environment. While many American artists "colonized" in Paris, the opposite is sometimes true; Dadaist Marcel Duchamp came to New York to declare love and fascination for the American city. The witty, creative, and worldly Man Ray was born in a row house in Philadelphia, in a neighborhood called "South Philly"—home to the festival tradition of The Mummers. The Creole culture of New Orleans explodes with inventiveness in the annual eye-dazzling Mardi Gras—to the beat of Cajun rhythm and *zydeco*.

Arts that have sprung from the mountains of Appalachia, the cowboy and rodeo traditions of the American West, the heartlands of Middle America, the traditions of the American South, and the rocky, seafaring cultures of the Northeast are bountiful indeed! From the Pennsylvania Dutch fraktur . . . to the fanciful cowboy boots of Texas . . . to the gingerbread Victorian facades of San Francisco in California, the United States of America has no shortage of artistic diversity. Once known as a "melting pot," America has become a dazzling mosaic of color, sound, energy, and hope. The new growth of American populations from Asia, Latin America, and points east and west brings expanded meaning and spirit to America, and a greater meaning to the American sentiment: "There's no place like home."

This sweet little Pennsylvania-German pinch pot is all heart. It was crafted in an art classroom in response to the signs and symbols of regional folklife.

ACTIVITY 1

One Great American Lady: A Heritage Welcome to the U.S.A.

Life-size Heritage Figures/Monumental Paper Art/Statue of Liberty

▲ Figure 10-1a. Proud Polish-American heritage blazes in this student's life-sized self portrait. Attention has been paid to the shawl, which seems to move with the breeze. This young American citizen has the comfort of a trusty friend tucked into her arm—a Swedish teddy bear!

The Statue of Liberty in New York Harbor has greeted more than 17,000,000 immigrants from other shores, raising their hopes and dreams as highly as she holds her burning torch against the sky. She is an impressive structure and an awesome sight. One hundred two feet tall, the Statue of Liberty stands proudly on a 150-foot pedestal. The torch and flame were the first part of this statue to reach the United States from Paris, France, by way of Philadelphia, Pennsylvania. The Statue of Liberty herself is, you might say, an immigrant—she is French, a Franco-American! The Statue of Liberty was designed by the French sculptor Frederic Auguste Bartholdi. In his Parisian studio, the artist engaged a female model who helped develop the vision for the great woman that now stands against the famous New York City skyline.

Ideas for Bartholdi's methods of construction were inspired by a 17th-century statue he had seen in Italy. Many renowned hands and minds assisted in raising what is now among the tallest monuments in the world. Gustave Eiffel helped engineer the iron infrastructure (yes, the same Eiffel of the Eiffel Tower). A project of this size requires collaboration! At one point, American sculptor Gutzon Borglum, creator of Mount Rushmore, helped correct the lighting in the flame. Contributions from American newspaper giant Joseph Pulitzer also aided in financing the many-layered project. The Statue of Liberty herself, made of thin copper plates that move like a skin in response to weather and wind, stands firmly for the liberty of all nations.

The Statue of Liberty was a gift from France to the United States to mark the U.S.'s centennial celebration of its independence from Great Britain. She is truly international, for the seven spikes of her crown represent the seven continents and seas of our world. With tablet and torch in hand, she is both strong and flexible—a woman of compassion, conviction, and hope. "She has come to stand for the common hope of the old world and the new . . . the peace of mankind—all people living together in justice, mutual respect, and prosperity. This hope has come closest to being realized in America . . . by free men from many nations," stated American President Dwight D. Eisenhower. This message is as true today as always. The mighty, colossal, and classical lady in the harbor remains faithful. All are welcome, all are equal: This is the spirit that has made America the diverse and tolerant land known throughout the world for its willingness to embrace these ideals. We have our struggles, yet America is a living, growing nation that continues to strive for . . . *"liberty and justice for all."*

Figure 10-1b. Teddy bears and other precious objects have been carried to the New World. The little bear may have originated from Austria or Germany—he is wearing *lederhosen*. Perhaps Teddy spent his early years in Sweden: he is wearing knitted Norwegian mittens and socks. Note the famous Swedish *Dalarna* horses on his little legs! Teddy's expression seems to indicate that he is in need of a little reassurance himself! ▶

MATERIALS

- white kraft paper
- nontoxic black permanent markers
- tempera paint
- pencils
- colored markers
- scissors (optional)

- acrylic luster/metallic paint (optional)
- "wiggle" eyes and other notions (see Teacher Preparation)
- glue (optional)
- reproducible page: "A Wonderful Way to Display Our Proud Heritage!"

TEACHER PREPARATION

Do we have some souvenirs, replicas, and books that honor the indomitable Statue of Liberty? Teacher and students may wish to bring objects to class for this cultural heritage lesson. Students should be encouraged to interview their grandparents or "elders" for what they remember about their families' arrival in the United States. If objects are portable (with household permission secured!) they may be brought to class for storytelling and personal accounts. Objects such as a shawl, a vest, a crocheted handbag, socks, mittens, hair combs— and especially toys—will all help bring the immigrant and settlement experience closer to home. Books that show diverse national world costumes would also be helpful. Teacher may wish to share ideas shown on pages 358 and 359.

The teacher will want to precut lengths of white kraft paper to "life-size" or approximate size of students participating in the lesson. **Teacher Note:** This project may become a "buddy" project if desired. Students may wish to give the new American citizens they will create "a little" something to take with them as a special gift. Objects that may be held in the statues' hand include fans, photoalbums, cassette tapes, toys, or other ideas inspired by actual items. The emphasis is upon heritage and pride, yet not so exclusively personal that we cannot exchange our objects and ideas! Also, if the teacher wishes to use "real world" details such as toy "wiggle" eyes, trim, lace doilies, and other notions, please have on hand the white glue needed for attaching. Luster or metallic acrylic paint will recall the sterling material presence of our Lady Liberty, to whom this activity is dedicated.

DIRECTIONS

1. Discuss the amazing structure we know as The Statue of Liberty and what she represents. Ask students to bring forward any objects they may have garnered from their households. While this lesson focuses on the Ellis Island experience, no one should feel excluded here. However, realize that the matter of how people came to be Americans is sometimes a sensitive subject, so handle this with care. Also, realize that this discussion may require more than the usual introduction time allotted.

2. Before students begin, have them think about what objects would be carried to the "New World." Objects may be personal items or representational of cultural ideas. Place precious objects out of harm's way. Distribute paper, pencils, markers, paints, and any other materials to be included in the lesson. Show (or reproduce copies of) "A Wonderful Way to Display Our Proud Heritage!" in order to generate ideas for objects.

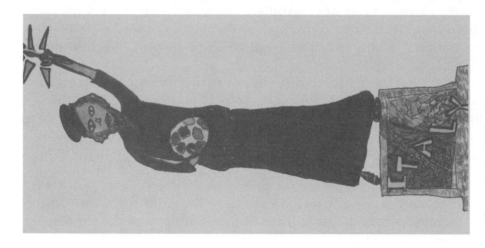

▲ Figure 10-2. This Spanish Statue of Liberty, ESPAÑA, looks as though she might burst into a fiery Flamenco dance at any moment! She stands for Spain, Puerto Rico, the Dominican Republic, Cuba, Mexico, Central and South America . . . and all other places where "Spanish spoken here" holds true. The Spanish and Asian cultures are among the fastest-growing numbers of new Americans today. Of course, Puerto Rico is a United States commonwealth.

▲ Figure 10-3. Michael Anastasio, a young student, proudly upholds an Italian Renaissance tradition: painting. With palette in hand—one that resembles the planet Earth—Michael reaches for the star. He is grounded on another superior Italian art form: marble and stone masonry.

▲ Figure 10-4. America would not be at all American without its strong African heritage. Not all groups arrived in America through the New York Harbor—there are many migrations. "The Middle Passage" is often used to describe the arrival of Africans to America, and there is much to reflect upon collectively. Ours is a complex, powerful history. This youthful girl stands with pride and dignity. In her right hand she holds an Akuaba doll, which also resembles the sign of the *ankh*, an Egyptian symbol for life. In her other hand is a candelabrum that represents Kwanza. This African-American holiday, founded in the United States in 1966, celebrates African values with seven candles to honor: Faith, Creativity, Purpose, Self-determination, Cooperative economics, Collective work . . . and Unity.

3. Students will sketch an outline of the Statue of Liberty posture—one arm raised, the other hand holding a tablet or tablet-sized object. Base may be included in the page design. Reinforce what is meant by life-size and give meaning of colossal or monument-sized structure.

4. Students' pencil drawing should reflect understanding of proportion, scale, and balance. Garments selected to reflect students' heritage(s) should convey a sense of national origin (Old World). Drawings will include a precious object clutched in one hand, supplied by exchange with classmate or by students' own personal design. (See the photos on page 358.)

▲ Figure 10-5. Miniature horse and wooden cart from Sicily.

▲ Figure 10-6. Bumblebee crochet with satin closure. Handcrafted purse from England.

◄ Figure 10-7. Male and female dolls in traditional garments from Greece.

5. Apply color either before or after black permanent marker line has been drawn to define the statue of heritage. Add accents or novelty details.

6. To complete the picture, students may paint the background to represent sky behind the colossal figure (lustrous paint is very effective here) or cut figure away from roll paper for direct mounting.

7. How many Statues of Liberty can you fit into a display? The more the merrier and the more multicultural . . . just like America!

ACTIVITY 2

Give My Regards to Broadway . . . America on Stage, From Coast to Coast

"Showcards"/Advertising Poster Art/Graphic Color and Design

▲ Figure 10-8. *West Side Story* is an enduring tale that is both tragic and full of life. The musical score is an absolute classic! This student, Gillian, created a Broadway "window card" that says just enough visually to suggest the energy and longing of an unforgettable play. She has captured a moment in time.

The houselights dim, the theater grows dark. As the curtains part, a magical world opens. What appears on the stage is larger than life—a spectrum of lights and costumes, a spectacle set to music! Such an extraordinary thrill! And what are we actually seeing? A corner of the ordinary world made grand through the brilliance of Broadway. As Americans, we are in fact seeing ourselves.

American musical theater is surely "made in America." It is a unique, indigenous art form that blends dance, song, drama, tragedy, comedy . . . and "the sound of music." Musicals are among the most popular theatrical productions and deal with a full array of subjects and human conditions. America's more serious social problems were spotlighted when musical theater came of age. It was in the 1920s that the production of *Show Boat* received rave reviews. In it, the song "Ol' Man River" expressed the deep pain of racial injustice in America. Musicals faced social issues as they grew to become a beloved form of entertainment. Broadway is the story of America on stage. Each decade has brought several top shows that express the American experience. *Porgy and Bess*, the first folk opera, gave us the song "Summertime" and presented a stylized drama of black life in the 1930s. In the years that followed came the unforgettable *Peter Pan*, representing a dominant Broadway feature—fantasy! Literature infused musical engagement in shows like *My Fair Lady*, based on Bernard Shaw's *Pygmalion*, portraying a myth of transformation. Later, the enormously popular *West Side Story* with musical score by Leonard Bernstein depicted the tragic, bittersweet tale of love set against the rivalry of two urban gangs. The story was based on none other than Shakespeare's *Romeo and Juliet*! It is both classic and current—American, universal, and ageless.

When the Father in *The Fiddler on the Roof* bellows "Tradition!" the singer is striving to find balance between the Old World and the New World. The contemporary play *Rent* asks us to understand the meaning of living with AIDS in an often indifferent society. Yes, America is democratic, a land where opinions and ideas can be expressed without fear of government oppression—yet we recognize that we are not without fault. Broadway gives America a chance to laugh at itself, to cry with shame and rise with hope, to marvel at dazzling creativity and to perhaps better understand the identity of the young country known collectively as the United States of America.

MATERIALS

- white tagboard (see Teacher Preparation)
- 12" × 18" manila
- pencils/erasers
- colored markers
- tempera paint (see Teacher Preparation)
- brushes

TEACHER PREPARATION

This lesson offers many learning opportunities, which include visual and graphic arts, musical performance, dance, literature, social commentary, and, of course, the performing arts. The focus of this activity is primarily graphic design within the production of a showcard. However, the teacher should consider thematic development of the lesson with costume design, theater history, puppet design, mask making, stage design, and other theater arts. These are, after all, all the elements that make a Broadway show.

The teacher will precut white tagboard (or reasonable substitute) to 14″ × 22″ dimension. This graphic specialty, according to size, is known as a **showcard.** The dimensions fit into the window display on the outside of the theater and box office to advertise the play "Now Showing." Unlike posters, these announcements are intended as window cards and must conform to the dimensions of the display window. The image used for a showcard is generally the same as the image that appears on the cover of the songbook. This image has been determined to represent a particular production.

The teacher will want to gather playbills, songsheets, and, if available, examples of showcards. Theater posters are fine to use as well and often do appear as window cards; yet they should be identified as posters rather than showcards. If Broadway theater posters are not available, other good examples of poster design, ones that advertise events, will substitute, such as the work of French artist Toulouse-Lautrec. It is *strongly* recommended that teachers have Broadway show tunes playing during the production of the showcard lesson; *Annie!* is a sure thing . . . *West Side Story* and *Cats* are wonderful, too—you choose!

Although tempera paint is suggested, acrylic paint will also work well. Have you ever heard of showcard paint? How do you think it came by that name?

If you are doing Broadway, then props such as top hats and canes (borrowed from the music department) cannot hurt your ratings!

DIRECTIONS

1. Ask students if they would like to take a trip to Broadway. Develop a meaning for musical theater in a class discussion. Use the chalkboard to list favorite plays and musicals with which students may be familiar. Note that many plays have gone to the film media. Students may know musicals through the cinematic media (sometimes even the reverse is true). Discuss examples of poster art. What makes them visually effective? Do they convey their message clearly and quickly? Pay attention to use of space—plan to leave visual breathing room.

Figure 10-9. John, age 13, acquired his showcard idea from a hit that went from Hollywood to Broadway. The California connection to New York's Broadway is a strong one—many stage productions become popular films, and vice versa. Hollywood has, indeed, shaped public perceptions about America. Broadway, however, is still highly regarded by actors for its immediacy and vitality; it is, after all, *live and on Stage*! ▶

2. Distribute pencils and manila paper for practice. ***Hold paper vertically!*** Think about lettering with its relationship to accompanying visuals.

3. When ready, distribute all other painting supplies. Students transfer practice ideas onto showcard-sized tagboard. Begin graphic illustration of the showcard "as the band plays on."

4. When almost completed, stop for a classroom critique. Is the headline bold enough? Does the type style of the headline fit the theme of the show? Does the illustration "say" everything that is needed about the show? Is the color used effectively in the overall design? If so, complete the showcards.

5. As they say on Broadway . . . "Let's go on with the show!" Display your window cards with great pride and remember, "There's no business like showcard business!"

▲ Figure 10-10. Students may create original showcard ideas based on existing ones. Did you ever hear of a Broadway show called *Jazz*? It's coming soon . . . *sure* to play to *S.R.O.* (Standing Room Only)! Order your tickets now!

ACTIVITY 3

The Fabulous Fraktur: Folklife Thrives in Community Art

Decorative Certificates/Calligraphy/Traditional Folk Arts

BONUS: CAN YOU SAY SCHERENSCHNITTE (SHA'R-ON-SCHNIT)?

INCLUDES: QUILT OF MANY CULTURES

The most dynamic feature of art made in the community spirit is that it offers a living, breathing record of daily life. The Central European tradition of the Fraktur links the present with the past by documenting life's events. In the 17th century, Pennsylvania-German people developed an expressive way to register important events such as births and weddings. Unlike the standard certificates we routinely use today, these Pennsylvanians embellished surfaces with signs and symbols of meaning; thus, the Fraktur was born. The term *Fraktur* itself comes from the word "fracture"; this refers to the style of writing they used in which the letters had spaces or breaks between them, much like the German printing tradition. Birds, tulips, hearts, and angels decorated areas that framed the writing. Frakturs are a form of graphic art founded in both houses of worship and in schools. The elements of religious symbolism can be found along with "baroque" calligraphy. As one might expect, expressive styles will vary with individuals and communities.

▲ Figure 10-11. The American eagle flies above this sweet birth announcement. This is a patriotic Fraktur for sure!

A group of Americans known today as "the Plain People" are the Mennonites. Included in this group are the Amish, who reside primarily in Pennsylvania but who may also live in other communities, such as Northern Indiana and upper New York State. The Amish are a

unique society who generally live peacefully in the modern world in the same manner in which they lived hundreds of years ago—without modern conveniences, and still using horse and buggy for most of their travel. Goodwill and brotherhood are common values. Most Mennonites arrived in America from Switzerland, Germany, and Austria. While other groups produced Fraktur, it is said that the greatest output was from the Mennonite community. Some hold

◄ Figure 10-12. It was a bright, sunny afternoon in October when a baby girl was born to a family that would give her a heartfelt welcome.

that Fraktur is a graphic art: two-thirds calligraphy, one-third symbol! The first public exhibit of Fraktur was held in 1902 in Lancaster County, Pennsylvania. It is a folk art consistent with other genres such as quilt, barn signs, stove plates, and tombstones. Clearly, each of these folk art forms suggests the elements of daily life. Frakturs were not usually hung on the wall but were commonly glued inside the cover of the family bible or under the lid of a hope chest. Folk artists working today are often recognized for their individual style of art.

The work of community artisans infused the crafting of common objects with cultural history, personal stories, beliefs, powerful metaphors, and universal values. We are reminded that art, like learning itself, comes in many inspired forms. The vitality of folklife was well understood by the great educator John Dewey, who knew that we may often learn as much from a well-crafted farm tool as we might from a work of Elgin marble. He reminds us . . . "Education is not preparation for life, education is life itself." Art, life, and community are present, for instance, in an Italian wedding cake made from an old treasured family recipe, in a log cabin quilt patch, and in the stitchery of a simple sampler. All these precious objects, like the Fraktur, spell folk life art.

MATERIALS

- parchment paper (see Teacher Preparation)
- felt-tipped calligraphy pens
- photocopy or manila paper
- rulers
- fine-tipped black permanent markers
- pencils/erasers

- watercolors
- gold/silver pens (optional)
- brushes (assorted, include fine-tipped)
- glue sticks
- construction paper or tagboard
- reproducible page: "Pennsylvania-German Designs"

TEACHER PREPARATION

Materials listed are ideal for this lesson, yet "reasonable facsimile" substitutes are acceptable. Precut parchment paper to "certificate" size; prepare construction paper or tagboard for mount, leaving at least a one-inch border as indicated. Samples of Gothic or German-style calligraphy may be available in computer fonts that can then be generated along with other certificate-style lettering for classroom reference. Books and charts that illustrate calligraphy styles, such as Chancery Italic, will also help, along with book art references.

This lesson has artistic, personal, cultural, and community values: There are many possibilities for parchment certificates. The *vorschiften* (German word that refers to Frakturs) may highlight any number of events. The original use was to recognize outstanding students for work well done. House blessing certificates for home or school would certainly be welcome additions for this activity. However, students will be asked to design a Fraktur to announce the wonderful day they were born. **Note:** Some students might enjoy producing wedding certificates for parents—even birth certificates for beloved pets.

Figure 10-13. Artist-educator Margaret Hill Alcala uses a Fraktur to reflect on the events of her life as they evolved through her name and its changes. Using a traditional Pennsylvania-German format, Margaret infuses the document with the vitality of her own creativity. The experience of name changes, which may begin early in life, do tell an insightful story about our own lives—particularly the lives of women. ▶

DIRECTIONS

1. Begin the lesson by asking students if they know the month, day, hour, and the year of their birth. Ask for student definitions of these vital statistics along with any other more poetic meanings, such as a description of the weather or season during which they were born. Using the board, frame out a format for the Fraktur birth certificates, placing in the center the following:

    _____ (your name) was born on this day _____ (your birthday).

    (Students may add parents' names if desired. **Note:** Teacher will want to respect the sensitivity of the student population as well as consider the appropriateness of making this personal information public.)

    or

    On this day _____ (date of wedding),
    _____ (mother's name) and _____ (father's name)
    were joined in marriage.

2. Distribute practice paper (photocopy paper or manila) and pencils. Students will began to plan their decorated page using all references on hand—flowers, birds, hearts (Pennsylvania-German style), vines, stars, and angels (see the reproducible page of these design symbols). Encourage students to use their ideas of symbols in designing the Fraktur. Effusive decoration is optional—simplicity works well.

◀ Figure 10-14. The format for this "highly rare Fraktur" is that of the *roundel:* The formula is one hundred percent visual. Is there any doubt to its meaning? It seems to speak of the cycle of life through the love of two people joined in marriage.

3. When students are ready, distribute other materials listed, along with rulers. It's a good idea to *lightly* insert guide lines for the calligraphy that will illuminate the Fraktur. Color should be applied with a fine brush. Lines should be made thoughtfully.

4. Students will try their hand at a calligraphy style when writing their words in a "certified" fashion using calligraphy pen. Add finishing touches with gold and silver pens, if desired. Erase the pencil guide lines carefully.

5. When a visually well-balanced and nicely stated certificate is complete, a Fraktur is born. Mount on tag or construction paper with glue sticks and display. Birds fly and hearts soar when a joyful spirit like you enters this world!

BONUS : CAN YOU SAY *SCHERENSCHNITTE* (SHA'R-ON-SCHNIT)?

The art of **scherenschnitte** came to America from Central and Eastern Europe. Swiss, Polish, Austrian, and German papercutters were geniuses with the scissors. After all, the word *scherenschnitte* literally translates as "scissors cutting"! Scherenschnitte

may be used to make greeting cards, valentines (called *liebesbreit*), documents, and countless other items. The design motif for scherenschnitte is similar to the Fraktur; in fact, scherenschnitte was often used during the Middle Ages to decorate the borders of certificates. While scherenschnitte is a European art, it has been influenced by exchange of many cultures. Early designs are quite reminiscent of Eastern motifs, particularly those of the Islamic culture. Chinese paper cuts are also among the most exquisitely crafted paper arts in the world. In addition, it should be noted that scherenschnitte enjoyed great popularity in France, particularly under Louis XV whose frugality was remembered in the paper silhouette, an inexpensive means for a portrait. It is true that with scherenschnitte, thrifty people can readily recycle every scrap of paper in the household! In earlier times, children found scherenschnitte a fine rainy-day activity. To find out how students may do their scherenschnitte, see the diagram at the

Meet the Distelfink! The universal bird symbol appears in Pennsylvania-German Distelfink design as both a spiritual greeting and a good luck *welcome sign*!

right. Be sure to include paper backing—for all one really needs to do scherenschnitte is bright construction paper and scissors that are not dull and in good working order. What a wonderful way to say "Happy Birthday" now that we know from your Fraktur when that special day occurs!

1. Trace a symmetrical design on a folded piece of paper.

2. Carefully cut along the lines of your design.

3. When cutting has been completed, open your design carefully. Color may be added to the design.

4. Mount your design on construction paper for all to see!

▲ Figure 10-15. What a personality this tree has! It seems to grow in meaning the longer one contemplates its animated form. Eastern Europeans, Russians, and Celts before Christianity believed in "spirits of the woods." Here is an artistic interpretation that captures our curiosity. What else can one expect from the scherenschnitte tree?

"Paper Cutting" Vocabulary

German/Swiss	scherenschnitte (sha'r-on-schnit)
Polish	wycinanki (vee-chee-non'-kee)
Chinese	chien-chih (jian'-jeh)
Dutch	knippen (knip'-pen)
Japanese	monkiri (mon-kee-ree)

The Jewish people are also known for imaginative and skillful paper arts. The Jewish paper cuts are pictorial, symbolic, and even humorous. Along with this is the extraordinary art of the ***kettubah***—a Hebrew marriage certificate. The kettubah marks the occasion of the marriage ceremony and may include Hebrew calligraphy along with decorative elements. The kettubah sometimes incorporates paper-cut designs. The kettubah is used and treasured by many Jews upon the occasion of the wedding. It is believed that Portuguese Jews brought the art of paper cutting to Holland in the 1600s.

▲ Figure 10-16. Teacher demonstrates a Valentine, scherenschnitte style.

INCLUDES: QUILT OF MANY CULTURES

The quilt has come to symbolize the fabric of America. In each culture, quilts have specific meaning. Quilts have served as maps that helped African–Americans find their way north during times of slavery. From the Appalachian mountains to the windy New England coast, and west to the brisk and even frigid Rocky Mountains, quilts have kept Americans warm. At the same time, Hawaiian quilt makers were evolving on the islands with bold, highly contrasted motifs of nature, including

◄ Figure 10-17. Edith Lilly is a West Virginian quilter who has gifted the author with her delightful quilts over the years. Crib covers with ABC building blocks and baby shoes commemorated children's births—as was her habit for those she considered "family." The personal story behind this simple yet exquisitely crafted quilt is that Mrs. Lilly regarded the close friends of her artistic son to be stitched into her own life. Stan Lilly was a wonderful art teacher and illustrator who passed from this world and is very much missed by his friends. The quilt serves as a great comfort and a reminder of gentle Stan and his lovely West Virginia family ways.

the welcoming pineapple! Quilts were brought on the Mayflower by practical Pilgrims who used them to soften their hard beds. Quilts soon became an American tradition as fabric became more available. Regional styles developed; an Amish quilt would appear in an orderly and symmetrical format while a powerful African–American tradition developed in the south based on dynamic African design that would infuse energy into traditional European motifs. Quilts play a particularly important role in the lives of African-American women, who introduced a narrative style. (See Section 2 for African design origins.)

The meanings of quilts are as multi-layered as the quilt itself. Beyond fulfilling the basic needs of clothing and shelter, quilts have come to represent family histories, portrait albums, personal stories, friendship, life's occasions, and memories. The quilt that is patched or pieced together combines fragments of many lives—a living archaeology of the American people. The transformation from sad remnant of a worn garment to a bright and useful new quilt is as remarkable as the human spirit.

If your students combine their ideas to make a quilt such as the one seen here, what amulets might they bring or make (Model Magic™ is good) for attachment in places such as the central squares? Keep in mind that poetry, thought, quotes, and "vital" information may become part of the quilt. What a wonderful way to celebrate our collective heritage!

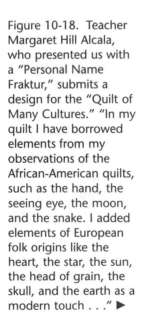

Figure 10-18. Teacher Margaret Hill Alcala, who presented us with a "Personal Name Fraktur," submits a design for the "Quilt of Many Cultures." "In my quilt I have borrowed elements from my observations of the African-American quilts, such as the hand, the seeing eye, the moon, and the snake. I added elements of European folk origins like the heart, the star, the sun, the head of grain, the skull, and the earth as a modern touch . . ." ▶

ACTIVITY 4

Let the Good Times Roll: A Jazzy Portrait of Mardi Gras

Costume Portraits for Carnival/Ir"resist"ible Fancyheads!

DOUBLE BONUS: HARLEQUINS! AND MUMMERS STRUT: A PHILADELPHIA NEW YEAR'S PARADE

▲ Figure 10-19. If the King is the star of Carnival . . . then the Sun King Rex is the center of the Mardi Gras universe! The circular, radiating design of this harlequin-style portrait dazzles like a comet in the night sky.

In New Orleans it is said that winter lasts about ten minutes, making "The Big Easy" the perfect city in which to throw a great party! The ingredients of the New Orleans Mardi Gras are as spicy and delightful as its world-renowned cuisine. In this city, traditions spring from French, African, Caribbean, Canadian, Spanish, Native American, Philippine, and other groups of diverse origin. Take these roots, add the birthplace of jazz plus a most distinctive Creole culture and you have the only place in America where a carnival, such as Mardi Gras, can endure with exuberance!

In 1837, New Orleans held its first street parade for Mardi Gras. The carnival season occurs yearly on January 6, which is twelve days after Christmas; this is called The Twelfth Night and marks the beginning of masked balls and street parades. In fact, the presence of Mardi Gras is felt all yearlong in the city that hugs the banks of the Mississippi River. Masks, ball gowns, tiaras, and scepters can be found in shops along the French Quarter as elsewhere. Who can really separate Mardi Gras from New Orleans!

The season of Mardi Gras actually begins February 4 and ends on "Fat Tuesday" (***Mardi*** is French for ***Tuesday: Gras*** for ***Fat***). Like other carnivals held around the world—Trinidad, Tobago; Nice, France; Cologne, Germany; and Rio de Janeiro in Brazil—Mardi Gras is a pre-Lenten celebration with strong pagan and Christian elements. Everybody cuts loose—after preparing all year for this grand spectacle. To describe the Mardi Gras parade is to ask that we allow our imaginations to conjure crowds, dazzle, noise, aromas, and more than a little bit of madness, while Louisiana *zydeco* and *Cajun* music play. There are huge colorful floats, elaborate costumes, glittering pageantry, and dancing in the street. ***Allons dans*** is French for "let's dance" and that tells you that it's time for Mardi Gras! The stars of the parade, who are part of the floats, are called *krewe* members, a carnival club that selects a king, queen, and court! "Second lines" are the revelers who extend the parade as it marches. Parade goers, usually wearing costumes in purple (*justice*), green (*faith*), and gold (*power*) may shout at krewe members *"throw me something, mistah!"* The doubloons and beads go flying to the people on the street.

Colors, sights, and sounds transform "the Crescent City" during the Mardi Gras exhibition. In New Orleans, the oldest city in the South, Mardi Gras means many things to many people. With America's largest Creole population, the mixture of cultures explodes into a galaxy of cultural and individual expressions. Mardi Gras characters such as Wild Man, Flagboy, Queen, and Big Chief are able to present feathers, sequins, rhinestones, and beads that celebrate their own proud ethnic origins. Costumes express ideas as original as the Mardi Gras performers themselves. In this atmosphere of fantasy and illusion comes creativity on parade!

Mardi Gras is the pride of New Orleans, Louisiana, and home to the unique American musical form we know as **jazz**. The music is foremost a mixture of rhythms from West Africa, harmony from European classical music, gospel song, spirituals dating back to slavery days, and Southern Blues. A gift of the African–American spirit, jazz is a true American original. New Orleans cannot be imagined without jazz accompaniment. As they say in New Orleans, *"Let the good times roll!"* (in French, *les bon temps rouler!*)

Figure 10-20. Could this be The Queen? All feathers and finery, her portrait is framed in gold (foil, that is). The Mardi Gras was fashioned after the Parisian carnival. New Orleans was founded by the French in 1718. Long live the Queen! ▶

▲ Figure 10-21. Zig-zagging line gives an electrical charge to this Mardi Gras portrait. The student artist has captured the feeling of the vibrant Carnival atmosphere—bells, streamers, and jazzy!

MATERIALS

- 18″ × 24″ white paper
- glitter (in pens and/or shaker containers)
- crayons or oil pastels (fluorescent optional)
- metal kraft foil (optional)
- black tempera
- brushes (large and small)
- bright feathers (optional)
- white glue
- scissors
- black nontoxic permanent markers
- pencils
- larger construction paper for mounting
- mirrors trimmings (see Teacher Preparation)

TEACHER PREPARATION

This lesson is about the power of fantasy and imagination, both are necessary ingredients for art and for carnival costume design. It is also a means to teach portraiture in a most eye-catching manner. Most important, this activity honors the key ingredient of jazz—improvisation! To this end, the teacher will want to stimulate students' imagination by providing an array of masks, props, or costumes—perhaps available through thrift stores or Halloweens past and present. Images of Mardi Gras from travel guides and other pictorial references are good. Try to acquire decorative notion mirrors for student use. This is a multisensory experience that will result in a portrait head with an elaborate, carnival headdress—thus, the Fancyhead! Jazz tapes or CDs—even old records (LPs) should be played during this activity. Great jazz and blues artists such as Billie Holiday, Miles Davis, and Mississippi John Hurt (Master of Delta Blues) can be introduced, along with other great musical artists of this genre. Cajun and zydeco are mighty lively—just like Louisiana hot sauce—so play accordingly. It can't hurt to offer a little Rhythm and Blues!

Nice little extras for this flashy portrait can be beads, notion mirrors, trimmings, even some holiday trim—Mardi Gras artists are brilliant at recycling after Fat Tuesday ends. For the teacher who wants a "sweet authenticity," no respectable Mardi Gras party is complete without serving a baked specialty called "King's Cake," which is made of cinnamon-filled dough in the shape of a hollow circle. For most busy teachers this spells cinnamon donuts. The King Cake is topped with a yummy glaze and sprinkled with colored sugar. Three colors of the sugar toppings are green, gold (yellow), and purple. King Cakes today are baked with a wide variety of fillings: They are the favored Mardi Gras snack and dessert. Ask around for the King Cake for we are told that the carnival treat is shipped throughout the U.S.A.

◀ Figure 10-22. An authentic Mardi Gras mask, this feathered original may be purchased in New Orleans for a small investment. The *demi-mask* idea may be incorporated into our Mardi Gras portrait. The Harlequin and other *Commedia dell'Arte* characters wore demi-masks. An accessory worn at European costume balls, stunning demi-masks are still the fashion in Venice, Italy, for Carnival.

DIRECTIONS

1. Discuss the spectacle known as Mardi Gras. Props and other costume references may be presented for imagination "tickling." The wearing of these costumes as a means of preparation is discretionary; however, do at least discuss how it feels to wear something really outrageous. Explain to students that a portrait head will be painted wearing a costume and headdress, too. Self-portraits are encouraged—imaginary portraits accepted: here come the Fancyheads!

2. Distribute pencils and paper. Draw the basic portrait to include neck and shoulders.

3. Once basic portrait format is established, elaborate with headdress of choice (see the photos for ideas). Here is a place where carnival costume design will be considered. Basic ideas, such as the sun, bird plumage, and electrifying geometrics that make for "Fancyheads" are suggested. Sketch in ideas.

4. When ready, distribute color materials. Define costume parts, face colors, background, and so forth. When compositional unity is achieved, distribute black tempera with painting supplies. (Thin the tempera paint with water for overlay purposes.) Apply to areas selected. Let dry.

5. Distribute glue, feather, glitter, and any other decorative notions. Apply glitter first—use thoughtfully to accent specific areas or contours. Add feathers along with other costume effects. Black permanent marker may be used to delineate areas that appear in pencil.

6. Foil and mounting paper may be distributed for a "big finish."

7. Portraits—like jazz—should have a rhythm, style, surprise, and a life of their own. Now is the time to create your own Mardi Gras parade of glittering, glowing, Fancyhead portraits! . . . "Les bon temps rouler!"

BONUS : HARLEQUINS

The marvelous Mardi Gras is a form of street theater that includes characters representing many worlds. In 16th-century Italy, a traveling troupe of actors and actresses took their talents all over Europe. The ***Commedia dell'Arte*** delighted audiences for centuries with their lovable melodrama and exaggerated pranks. Perhaps the strongest feature of the *Commedia dell'Arte* was its use of improvisation. This allowed characters to develop great elements of surprise within the storyline. Male and female performers usually played the same role throughout their careers. *Commedia dell'Arte* has specific "stock" characters that could immediately be recognized by their appearance, personality, and behavior. ***Harlequin,*** a bold, crafty fellow is a ***trickster.*** Consistent with trickster traits, Harlequin was clever, playful, charming, self-centered, and usually scheming to make matters right. Harlequin is easy to spot because his diamond-patterned outfit has a strong visual punch! Harlequin may be a jester, but he's no fool. Did you know that the term ***slapstick*** is traced back to the theatrical prop—a wooden stick—carried by our Harlequin?

◄ Figure 10-23. Springy Harlequin has been fitted for his coffee-filter collar, completing his stunning appearance!

Figure 10-24. A Harlequin with a sequined belt, striped tights, jester hat, and mischievous smile fits the description of a playful Trickster. ▶

Don't be surprised if a Harlequin jumps off a float on Bourbon Street during Mardi Gras. The attachment that Europeans who settled in Louisiana have for this unstoppable character has helped to keep Harlequin alive to this day. Full of mischief and ***lazzi***—a *Commedia dell'Arte* word—is Italian for the gestures, puns, and slapstick gags used to distract the audience when sets are changed. Harlequin has vast appeal. Artists have remembered Harlequin in their work, from the serious Cézanne, whose son Paul posed for him in a Harlequin outfit, to the enigmatic Picasso. In fact, Picasso strongly identified with the Harlequin character. Proof of this can be found in Picasso paintings throughout his long life. Some even say the Harlequin was used by Picasso as his alter ego; think of *The Three Musicians.* Art images of Harlequin are plentiful for introducing this activity.

Students will create a jumpy little version of their own Harlequin. Teachers will want to emphasize the diamond pattern, known as ***lozenge,*** for its unmistakable identification with the Harlequin. Use 12" × 18" oaktag for the Harlequin body parts (see the photos). Head and torso will be one element (don't forget to include the cap); arms and legs will be cut in pairs. Paper fasteners are necessary, as are scissors, markers, and other drawing media—pompoms and trim will not be refused. And, oh! that *ruffled collar* may be fashioned so nicely from a *white coffee filter* (the kind called "baskets" for their shape and ruffled edges). Preparatory sketches may be used to improvise the figure. Decorate the Harlequin with theatrical wardrobe—tights, jacket, hat, and other details. Draw in the mask. Top it off by fitting the ruffled collar (coffee filter cut to size) around Harlequin's neck and glue in place. Join parts of Harlequin with paper fasteners. The completed Harlequin character should bring a sense of fun and merriment. Remember the spirit of "lazzi" when Harlequins and their moveable gestures are displayed!

BONUS : MUMMERS STRUT: A PHILADELPHIA NEW YEAR'S PARADE

We dance on . . . from New Orleans, Louisiana, to Philadelphia, Pennsylvania, the "Cradle of Liberty." It was in Philadelphia in 1776 that the Declaration of Independence was signed, officially declaring the United States a free nation. Along with its history, Philadelphia is a City of Art—with the first art institution in the nation, the Pennsylvania Academy of Fine Arts, holding sway on Broad Street, the city's wide main street. Mary Cassatt, Henry O. Tanner, and Thomas Eakins are among its illustrious alumni. Creativity on Broad Street—which also boasts of the "Avenue of the Arts"—is not hard to find! Every New Year's, Broad Street bursts forth with floats, feathers and finery, string bands, and great revelry. The history of the *Mummers Parade* has all the diversity one expects of a large Northeastern American city. In its early days, Swedish, English, German, and Irish settlers living in South Philadelphia combined to form the Mummers Parade. The word "mummers" has English and Germanic roots. The German noun *mumme* means "disguise" or "masquerader." Mummers, as a word, became the way to define the masked and costumed figures who would bring in the New Year as a regional tradition. In the 1860s, southern African–Americans arrived north with innovations for the parade. Minstrel elements were incorporated and banjos played. The *cakewalk,* a white interpretation of a black plantation dance, preceded the famous Mummers' "Strut." Black composer James Bland wrote "Oh! Dem Golden Slippers" in 1879; it was later adopted as the Mummers' theme song. The three-tiered umbrella, which bobs up and down in Comic division, was yet another contribution to the Mummers Parade.

In a once chiefly Italian-American community, known affectionately as South Philly, the Mummers Parade came of age. The famous South Street . . . "The Hippest Street in Town" . . . marks the beginning of a neighborhood where musical legends were made. World-renowned opera great Mario Lanza—as well as many stars of Rock n' Roll—are natives to South Philly. It was also in this neighborhood that the stars and legends of the Philadelphia Mummers Parade sprung forward too, mostly after the end of World War II. The tradition expanded across the city, with many neighborhoods involved. Today, South Philly has grown into a richly blended community with Cambodian residents, as well as African–Americans—and a mix of other groups and individuals.

◀ Figure 10-25. Student art—a paper plate Mummer!

Just like the Mardi Gras, clubs or divisions of Mummers prepare all year for their "strut down Broad Street." Mummering is literally a family tradition handed down from one generation to the next. Costumes and other "mummerabilia" are traditionally hand-crafted. Tailoring skills, brought to America from the Old World, advanced this Philadelphia performance art. The parade is built on a complex of divisions, clubs, and social organizations. Basically, the performers are divided into the following groups: The Comic Division, The Fancies, Fancy Brigades, and the String Bands. Costumes and floats are elaborate affairs that require strong engineering and construction skills. It is no coincidence that many Mummers are indeed strong in these building trades. On New Year's Day, all the work and practice gloriously come to life as the Mummers begin their strut south on Broad Street. The parade reaches City Hall, where a statue of Founding Father William (Billy) Penn tops the tower, a work done by Alexander Calder's grandfather! Judging takes place on the street below Billy Penn for the award that will be given to various divisions: any of the Comics, Fancies, Fancy Brigades, and String Bands may capture the prizes. *"Ota This World,"* for instance, led by Bill McIntyre's Shooting Stars, won in 1994 for its galactic routine. The parade ends with awards each year—and the Mummer cycle begins once again.

Now that you know about the dazzling Philadelphia Mummers Parade and the Mardi Gras, the Harlequin lessons may be further enhanced by a Mummer's snazzy backpiece! The Harlequin may be used for this development—or simply add a new character to the list. Like the Harlequin's coffee filter collar, the Mummer backpiece is another modest, disposable kitchen product—the paper plate. A Mummer with feathered backpiece would probably be a member of a string band, where this costume form is most likely to occur. Students may expand upon the carnival figure idea by adding a musical instrument to their design; banjos are perfect. Attach the festive figure to a paper plate. Decorate the colorful backpiece with feathers, applied in a circular pattern. Add sequins, trimmings, glitter, plastic beads, and "gemstone" as needed.

These little Mummers may be thematic— as are real Mummers—or simply colorful and flashy for the merriment of it all. Remember, in the world of the Mummers, glitzy is good. Mummers, above all else, must sparkle. As it's said in Philly, *"Yo! Enjoy yourself!"*

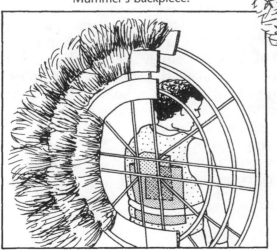

Construction of a professional Mummer's backpiece.

A Mummer in all his plumage and finery.

ACTIVITY 5

There's No Place Like Home: Celebrate the U.S.A.!

Mixed Media Collage/Montage: Architectural and Interior Design

▲ Figure 10-26. Welcome to a place of comfort, serenity, and balance. Beautiful Victorian homes can be seen throughout the cities of America in their many variations, including the fanciful Gingerbread style. San Francisco, California, cares lovingly for its sweet Victorians. Then again, so does the seaside resort town of Cape May, New Jersey, where the winter snow falls and the summer sun shines on street after street of charming Victorian homes.

▲ Figure 10-27. Christine Sullivan tidies up a corner of a house filled with holiday cheer. The trim defines the well-appointed Victorian structure—everything seems to be in order. Pay attention to detail—it certainly pays! Note the botanical print next to an heirloom grandfather clock.

The most unforgettable tale ever told in America grew to mythical status when it burst upon the silver screen in 1939. *The Wizard of Oz,* written by Frank Baum, was transformed by Hollywood into a great Technicolor epic. There is something about *The Wizard of Oz* that touches upon the American heart. A wonderful story, gloriously crafted, filled with characters so charming—and others so villainous—they are recognized and cherished from one generation to the next. "Somewhere Over the Rainbow" has almost become a national anthem for American optimism. Phrases as well as objects—the Ruby Slippers, for example—are now emblems of the American culture. From the tornado journey that lifts Dorothy away from her Kansas homestead to the mythical Land of Oz, there is, in the end, the one magic chant that will bring her back to the people she loves. Dorothy repeats . . . *"there's no place like home, there's no place like home"* . . . and there she is, safe and sound, back with Auntie Em in Kansas.

What *does* home mean to the American people? For a country that began as a safe haven for people from many lands, Americans are known for great attachment to places of dwelling. Pioneers fought hardship to settle the west, where they built their homes with their own hands. In New England, where the Mayflower landed from England at Plymouth Rock, a family house may still bear an early colonial presence. Of course, there are countless sorts of homes throughout each region of the country. Yet specific styles are selected for the diverse geography and climates of the U.S.A. and its fifty states. Home can be a beachfront bungalow on California's Pacific Coast, a wooden "Cape Cod" style house in a New England seaport town, a houseboat on the Louisiana Bayou, or a big, breezy plantation-style home in the old American South. Pueblo, town, city, valley, lake, mountain—homes are so much more than their bricks and architecture. There is no single definition for the personal meaning of home which is as emotional and spiritual as it is concrete. The place where one resides—which changes many times during a lifetime—is associated with comfort, love, community of spirit, and a sense of well-being. Friends and family are a lasting part of the picture. Perhaps there is no time when the presence of home is more deeply felt than during times that mark special occasions.

Holidays and feasts stem from the universal need to gather, enjoy, give thanks, and share stories, feelings, and memories. Universal cycles of nature—changing of seasons, harvest, birth, new moons, religious events, national victories, memorials—all seem to be an important part of being human. Customs from around the world have been brought to the United States by its inhabitants, who are diverse yet united as Americans. Once called "The Melting Pot," America today celebrates the San Genaro festival on the streets of Little Italy in New York City while neighbors in Chinatown may have recently honored the Buddha's birth. Festivals are enjoyed both inside and outside of neighborhoods and homes.

Today in America, the "Melting Pot" concept moves more easily into the metaphor of "The Mosaic"—each particle forming a sparkling complete whole, while offsetting one another's brilliance. To sing, dance, laugh, and cry as brothers and sisters who share the Earth and to live harmoniously, with both sameness and difference, is a joyous blessing. We are a human family. Together—and as one, on our precious planet—there is indeed no place like home.

MATERIALS

- 18" × 24" white paper
- newsprint or manila paper
- pencils
- color markers (assorted sizes)
- fine-tip permanent black marker (nontoxic)
- watercolors (see Teacher Preparation)
- pastel chalk (see Teacher Preparation)
- scissors

- gift catalogs/wallpaper sample books (see Teacher Preparation)
- glue sticks
- instant camera (see Teacher Preparation)
- holiday trim (option—see Teacher Preparation)
- masking tape (option—see Teacher Preparation)
- posterboards or roll display paper (see Teacher Preparation)

TEACHER PREPARATION

This activity helps us to define home in several ways:

- the architectural style(s) of the home
- the neighborhood or region of the home
- the "outside-inside" features and details
- student's perceived sense of place in association with his or her immediate world

Within these considerations, students may be asked to picture a time of holiday or special occasion. It is up to the teacher to determine where to focus the lesson (several options are shown in the photos). The use of a camera in the classroom helps to provide not only personalization, but also a means to develop the concept of *scale* (size of figure in proportion to environment). An instant camera can aid in encouraging students to pose in a posture they might assume for work or comfort (see Figure 10-27). **Hint:** Save film by posing more than one student in each shot. To use other (flash) cameras in the classroom, plan for film development turnaround time to pace out this lesson.

▲ Figure 10-28. It is a city street of stores, a laundromat, and a cafe restaurant. Who lives in that corner building? Perhaps it is a recently converted property, zoned for residential living. There, in the far left window, is our home dweller, looking quite content. Might we have an artist in a studio? Eastern American cities, such as New York and Baltimore, are the most heavily populated in the U.S.A.—although this street could be in any downtown area. As it so happens, this is a particularly clean street—the "Coin-Op Laundry" is bubbling over! Often, people live above commercial street-level properties. The author herself was born over a dress shop. To hear the story, take me to the Café Paradiso!

The teacher will find discontinued wallpaper sample books helpful for "interior design." The many mail order catalogs routinely received on house and garden accessories may come in handy, too! If your students are "planning a holiday," tree trim, press-on stars, and other small decorative touches may be appropriated.

Figure 10-29. Home on the range. Roam the vast plains of Wyoming . . . Montana . . . and south to the great state of Texas! Wherever "Bob's Happy Haven" may be, Bob has big sky, mountains, open space, and his own slice of heaven. Don't fence Bob in! ▶

Visual references for this activity should include a variety of regional house styles found in books and magazines. Students may be asked to bring in photos of their own home and family. **Note:** Students come from all circumstances; you know your own students best. Be aware that this topic may be a sensitive one, particularly to students whose families and homes are in crisis or transition. For this reason, ". . . a home I'd like to live in . . . a home remembered or imagined . . . or my dream house . . ." should be a natural part of the lesson introduction. This offers all students a way to participate comfortably in the activity.

At the completion of "There's No Place Like Home," you may want a "neighborhood-style" display. In that instance, mount houses together on display roll paper. The other recommendation for display is to mount the homes on posterboard; panoramic fanfolds are very effective. Simply join the desired number of boards together horizontally with masking tape (3–4 boards to form each fanfold). Homes will "show" beautifully on the wall, mounted, with strong, double-sided foam tape, or standing on a long table surface; try a combination of both. This activity will make a great exhibit for any number of events, holidays, and special occasions.

Figure 10-30. We know we're in a rural community, with this spacious farmhouse to greet us (peek behind the barn door). The student (in the photo at the right corner) is a good worker—and a fantastic artist/architect! Judging by the Hex Signs—intended to bring good luck—it looks like we're once again near Lancaster, Pennsylvania. Should we stop by for some shoofly pie? ▶

DIRECTIONS

1. Bring visual reference materials forward. A good "brainstorming" starter: Ask students to select images they find pleasing. Using the board, list students' elicited responses to their choices. Descriptive terms that express size, style, and building materials should be noted. Teacher may ask, "How does being there (*either inside or outside* of this *home/place*) make you feel? Safe? Comfy? Free?"

2. Now is the time to review any photographs students may have brought to class from family photo albums. Allow students enough "talk time" for their feelings to be conveyed. **Teacher note:** If you enjoy *The Wizard of Oz* story, you may incorporate a "Dorothy–tornado–Oz–Kansas" verbal scenario, with emphasis on the return to a place of safety.

3. Distribute practice paper (newsprint/manila) and pencils. Students may try several versions or ideas for homes. Determine individual homes of choice borrowed from books, drawn from direct memory, or imagination.

4. Give students the appropriate drawing materials, along with drawing paper. Wallpaper samples, gift catalogs, and so on may be made available for student use.

5. As pictorial images develop, teachers who will be using a camera may ask students to decide where they might actually be in their own picture. "What would you be doing?" is a fair question. Invite two or three students at a time to assume these poses for the camera and take the photos.

The United States of America

6. Students will soon learn that drawing a house is not unlike building one! Structures must be solidly organized. Try to keep the inside–outside look going, while paying close attention to detail. Is the house constructed of bricks, stone, wood clapboards, or other? Pictures should tell. Keep dimensional effects, such as bay windows, swinging doors, and overhanging roof elements, in mind.

7. Cut, clip, snip, color, and assemble. **Note:** Teachers who have student photos to distribute, stay tuned (others proceed to step #8). Precut the student group shots before distributing. *Instant snapshots may have a caustic binding agent! Do not peel photos apart! Wash hands after handling.* Processed photos do not have this problem. Students may cut themselves out of a photo and place themselves with a glue stick into their own picture.

8. Students may be both architect and interior designer at this stage. If a holiday is approaching, trim that house!

9. We should be in "move-in" condition by now! Using display of choice (refer to Teacher Preparation), showcase your homes!

▲ Figure 10-31. The Deissroths pose for a New Year's photo outside of their South Philadelphia row home. A multigenerational Mummers Family, Comic or Clown division, carries on a great deal of tradition. The umbrellas and attire are handcrafted. Joey "Dees" (second from top left) holds an umbrella over the head of Al, Senior. In the artroom, Joey is known as Mr. Deissroth (no clowning!) and is an excellent teacher. How proud the little house on "Two Street" (otherwise called Second Street beyond the neighborhood) must be! Creativity, love, togetherness, good times and hard times, courage, and hope flow from its doors. It's another bright day on Two Street, a new year, a new millennium . . . no question about it . . . *there's no place like home.*

Slide Credits

1. Chinese Tomb sculpture of a Dancer. Courtesy of the Freer Gallery of Art, Smithsonian Institution, Washington, D.C.

2. Tao-chi (Shih-t'ao) (1642–1707), Hanging scroll: "Bamboo in Wind and Rain." Ink on paper. H. 87 3/8" W. 27 1/2" (22 × 70 cm). Photograph © 1983 The Metropolitan Museum of Art, Edward Elliott Family Collection, Gift of Douglas Dillon, 1984. (1984.475.2)

3. Chinese Emperor Portrait. Courtesy of the Arthur M. Sackler Gallery, Smithsonian Institution, Washington, D.C.

4. Gohon Tachizuru (Standing Crane) Type Hagi Ware Glazed stoneware, 1603–1868; Early Edo period, Japan. Copyright © 1992 Asian Art Museum of San Francisco. All Rights Reserved.

5. Japan—Kimono, wedding 20th century. © The Textile Musuem. Photo by F. Khoung.

6. Queen Mother Head, Bronze, Benin. British Museum, London, Great Britain. Art Resource, NY.

7. Fon applique cloth makers in Abmoney, Republic of Benin Fon peoples, Republic of Benin. Eliot Elisofon Photographic Archives. National Museum of African Art. © Smithsonian Institution.

8. Paramount chief Nana Akyanfuo Akowuah Dateh II and his court Kumasi, Ghana. Asante peoples, Ghana. Eliot Elisofon Photographic Archives. National Museum of African Art. © Smithsonian Institution.

9. Guardian figures, called *mbulungulu,* are attached to bark boxes or bundles containing bones and other relics of clan or village ancestors, serving to protect them and as a focus for prayers and sacrifices. Werner Forman Archive, Friede Collection, New York, Art Resource, NY.

10. The Persian Illuminated manuscript, The "Nightmare of Zahhak," 28 verso from the Shahnemah. Malcolm Varon Photography.

11. Mosque Sharjah, U.A.E. The Stock Market, 171-ME-127-A2005. Photo by Scott Gog.

12. Jewish spice boxes, from the collection of The Jewish Museum, NYC. Malcolm Varon Photography.

13. Jean-Leon Gerome, French, 1824–1904, "The Carpet Merchant," 1887. The William Hood Dunwoody Fund. The Minneapolis Institute of Arts.

14. Bull-leaping (Toreador fresco), from the palace at Knossos. Minoan, ca. 1450–1400 BCE. Archaeological Museum, Heraklion, Crete, Greece, Scala/Art Resource, NY.

15. Madhya Tradesh or Uttar Pradesh, Indian, "Image of Ganesha Dancing," 10th century, sandstone. Philadelphia Museum of Art. Purchased: New Members Fund. Accession # '71-154-1.

16. Natagarh (Hudur) school, India, "The Monkey King Sugriva Sends Emissaries Led by Hanuman to Find Sita," c. 1820. 10 3/8" × 12-3/4", opaque watercolor with gold on paper. Philadelphia Museum of Art: Gift of the Board of Trustees in honor of William P. Wood, President from 1976 to 1981. Accession #1981-3-1.

17. India, Agra, Taj Mahal at sunset, pond with reflection in foreground. Leo de Wys, Inc., 138150.08. Photo by Bill Bachman.

18. Bichitr. Emperor Shah Jahan. Mughal dynasty, 1630. Gouache on paper. 22.2 × 13.4 cm. Victoria & Albert Museum, London, Great Britain, Art Resource, NY.

19. "Paradise of Green Tara," Tibetan Tanka, 19th century. Colors and gold on cotton, h. 28", silk mounts. Collection of The Newark Museum, 20.269. Art Resource, NY.

20. Hindu Festival (Bali) Asian Art. Private Collection/Bridgeman Art Library, London/ Superstock.

21. Aboriginal bark paintings, depicting kangaroos and a fork-tongued lizard. These images are made with a mixture of ochre and natural pigments. Private Collection, Prague, Czech Republic. Werner Forman Archive, Art Resource, NY.

22. Gateway of Pukeroa Pa *(Detail). Te Maori. © New Zealand Government.

23. Caribbean Market "Bananas and Bluebirds" by Catherine Gallian Saint-Clair. Source: Andre Exbrayat.

24. CFA 5 Jonkonnu Festival, Pitchy Patchy, Jamaica, 1987. The Saint Louis Art Museum.

25. Grenadines, Mustique Island, Gingerbread houses and palms. Tony Stone Images, G941D-EA4135-001Q. Photo by William J. Hebert.

26. Diego Rivera (1866–1957), "Day of the Dead—City Fiesta (Dia de muertos, La fiesta en la calle)", 1923–24. Mural, 4.17 × 3.75 m. Court of Fiestas, Level 1, South Wall. Secretaria de Education Publica, Mexico City, D.F., Mexico. Schalkwijk/Art Resource, NY.

27. Mixtec Codex, Oaxaca, Mexico, c. 1400, detail. British Museum, London, UK/Bridgeman Art Library, London/New York.

28. Three figures of Teotihuacan; ceramic; from La Ventilla, Teotihuacan; A.D. 350–650; average height: 7.5 cm; M.N.A.H. Laurie Platt Winfrey, Inc.

29. Frida Kahlo. Musee National d'Art Moderne.

30. Angel/"Angel de la Guarda." Mola, by the Kuna people, San Blas Islands, Panama. Appliqued, embroidered cotton, 15-3/4" × 19-1/2", c. 1960. Girard Foundation Collection at the Museum of International Folk Art, a unit of the Museum of New Mexico, Santa Fe. Photo by Michel Monteaux.

31. Helen Cordero, "Storyteller," circa. 1970, 9 1/2" tall, 11 children. Courtesy of Adobe Gallery, Albuquerque, New Mexico.

32. Jar, Acoma Pueblo, New Mexico. Slipped and painted earthware, 14-1/2 diameter, c. 1920. Girard Foundation Collection at the Museum of International Folk Art, a unit of the Museum of New Mexico, Santa Fe. Photo by Michel Monteaux.

33. Interior of Patlatch Lodge including ceremonial objects. Winter & Pond Collection, Photo No. PCA 87-10, Alaska State Library.

34. "My Daughter's First Steps," by Napachie Pootoogook 1990, lithograph. Reproduced with the permission of the West Baffin Eskimo Co-operative Ltd., Cape Dorset, NWT. Dorset Fine Art.

35. Russian lacquer box of Vasilisa. By Permission of Corners of the World Inc.

36. Book of Kells Initial "L" Manscripts. Trinity College, Dublin/A.K.G., Berlin/Superstock, Inc.

37. Statue of Liberty N.Y. The Image Bank. Photo by Harold Sund.

38. Taufschein for Maria Anna Transu. Hand-drawn, lettered and colored on laid paper by an anonymous artist. Northampton County, ca. 1825, (FLP 403). Rare Book Department, The Free Library of Philadelphia (FLP 403).

39. Mardi Gras Mask. The Stock Market. Photo by Kunio Owaki.

40. Doris Lee, American, 1905-1983, "Thanksgiving", oil on canvas, 1935, 71.4 × 101.6 cm. Mr. And Mrs. Frank G. Logan Prize Fund, 1935.313. Photograph © 1998, The Art Institute of Chicago. All Rights Reserved.